# Lecture Notes in Computer Science 4959

Commenced Publication in 1973
Founding and Former Series Editors:
Gerhard Goos, Juris Hartmanis, and Jan van Leeuwen

## Editorial Board

David Hutchison
*Lancaster University, UK*

Takeo Kanade
*Carnegie Mellon University, Pittsburgh, PA, USA*

Josef Kittler
*University of Surrey, Guildford, UK*

Jon M. Kleinberg
*Cornell University, Ithaca, NY, USA*

Alfred Kobsa
*University of California, Irvine, CA, USA*

Friedemann Mattern
*ETH Zurich, Switzerland*

John C. Mitchell
*Stanford University, CA, USA*

Moni Naor
*Weizmann Institute of Science, Rehovot, Israel*

Oscar Nierstrasz
*University of Bern, Switzerland*

C. Pandu Rangan
*Indian Institute of Technology, Madras, India*

Bernhard Steffen
*University of Dortmund, Germany*

Madhu Sudan
*Massachusetts Institute of Technology, MA, USA*

Demetri Terzopoulos
*University of California, Los Angeles, CA, USA*

Doug Tygar
*University of California, Berkeley, CA, USA*

Gerhard Weikum
*Max-Planck Institute of Computer Science, Saarbruecken, Germany*

Laurie Hendren (Ed.)

# Compiler Construction

17th International Conference, CC 2008
Held as Part of the Joint European Conferences
on Theory and Practice of Software, ETAPS 2008
Budapest, Hungary, March 29 – April 6, 2008
Proceedings

 Springer

Volume Editor

Laurie Hendren
McGill University, School of Computer Science
McConnell Engineering Building, Room 318
3480 University Street, Montreal, Quebec H3A 2A7, Canada
E-mail: hendren@cs.mcgill.ca

Library of Congress Control Number: 2008923179

CR Subject Classification (1998): D.3.4, D.3.1, F.4.2, D.2.6, F.3, I.2.2

LNCS Sublibrary: SL 1 – Theoretical Computer Science and General Issues

| ISSN | 0302-9743 |
|------|-----------|
| ISBN-10 | 3-540-78790-9 Springer Berlin Heidelberg New York |
| ISBN-13 | 978-3-540-78790-7 Springer Berlin Heidelberg New York |

This work is subject to copyright. All rights are reserved, whether the whole or part of the material is concerned, specifically the rights of translation, reprinting, re-use of illustrations, recitation, broadcasting, reproduction on microfilms or in any other way, and storage in data banks. Duplication of this publication or parts thereof is permitted only under the provisions of the German Copyright Law of September 9, 1965, in its current version, and permission for use must always be obtained from Springer. Violations are liable to prosecution under the German Copyright Law.

Springer is a part of Springer Science+Business Media

springer.com

© Springer-Verlag Berlin Heidelberg 2008
Printed in Germany

Typesetting: Camera-ready by author, data conversion by Scientific Publishing Services, Chennai, India
Printed on acid-free paper      SPIN: 12244546      06/3180      5 4 3 2 1 0

# Foreword

ETAPS 2008 was the 11th instance of the European Joint Conferences on Theory and Practice of Software. ETAPS is an annual federated conference that was established in 1998 by combining a number of existing and new conferences. This year it comprised five conferences (CC, ESOP, FASE, FOSSACS, TACAS), 22 satellite workshops (ACCAT, AVIS, Bytecode, CMCS, COCV, DCC, FESCA, FIT, FORMED, GaLoP, GT-VMT, LDTA, MBT, MOMPES, PDMC, QAPL, RV, SafeCert, SC, SLA++P, WGT, and WRLA), nine tutorials, and seven invited lectures (excluding those that were specific to the satellite events). The five main conferences received 571 submissions, 147 of which were accepted, giving an overall acceptance rate of less than 26%, with each conference below 27%. Congratulations therefore to all the authors who made it to the final programme! I hope that most of the other authors will still have found a way of participating in this exciting event, and that you will all continue submitting to ETAPS and contributing to make of it the best conference in the area.

The events that comprise ETAPS address various aspects of the system development process, including specification, design, implementation, analysis and improvement. The languages, methodologies and tools which support these activities are all well within its scope. Different blends of theory and practice are represented, with an inclination towards theory with a practical motivation on the one hand and soundly based practice on the other. Many of the issues involved in software design apply to systems in general, including hardware systems, and the emphasis on software is not intended to be exclusive.

ETAPS is a confederation in which each event retains its own identity, with a separate Programme Committee and proceedings. Its format is open-ended, allowing it to grow and evolve as time goes by. Contributed talks and system demonstrations are in synchronized parallel sessions, with invited lectures in plenary sessions. Two of the invited lectures are reserved for 'unifying' talks on topics of interest to the whole range of ETAPS attendees. The aim of cramming all this activity into a single one-week meeting is to create a strong magnet for academic and industrial researchers working on topics within its scope, giving them the opportunity to learn about research in related areas, and thereby to foster new and existing links between work in areas that were formerly addressed in separate meetings.

ETAPS 2008 was organized by the John von Neumann Computer Society jointly with the Budapest University of Technology and the Eötvös University, in cooperation with:

▷ European Association for Theoretical Computer Science (EATCS)
▷ European Association for Programming Languages and Systems (EAPLS)
▷ European Association of Software Science and Technology (EASST)

and with support from Microsoft Research and Danubius Hotels.

The organizing team comprised:

| | |
|---|---|
| Chair | Dániel Varró |
| Director of Organization | István Alföldi |
| Main Organizers | Andrea Tósoky, Gabriella Aranyos |
| Publicity | Joost-Pieter Katoen |
| Advisors | András Pataricza, Joaõ Saraiva |
| Satellite Events | Zoltán Horváth, Tihamér Levendovszky, Viktória Zsók |
| Tutorials | László Lengyel |
| Web Site | Ákos Horváth |
| Registration System | Victor Francisco Fonte, Zsolt Berényi, Róbert Kereskényi, Zoltán Fodor |
| Computer Support | Áron Sisak |
| Local Arrangements | László Gönczy, Gábor Huszerl, Melinda Magyar, several student volunteers. |

Overall planning for ETAPS conferences is the responsibility of its Steering Committee, whose current membership is:

Vladimiro Sassone (Southampton, Chair), Luca de Alfaro (Santa Cruz), Roberto Amadio (Paris), Giuseppe Castagna (Paris), Marsha Chechik (Toronto), Sophia Drossopoulou (London), Matt Dwyer (Nebraska), Hartmut Ehrig (Berlin), Chris Hankin (London), Laurie Hendren (McGill), Mike Hinchey (NASA Goddard), Paola Inverardi (L'Aquila), Joost-Pieter Katoen (Aachen), Paul Klint (Amsterdam), Kim Larsen (Aalborg), Gerald Luettgen (York) Tiziana Margaria (Göttingen), Ugo Montanari (Pisa), Martin Odersky (Lausanne), Catuscia Palamidessi (Paris), Anna Philippou (Cyprus), CR Ramakrishnan (Stony Brook), Don Sannella (Edinburgh), João Saraiva (Minho), Michael Schwartzbach (Aarhus), Helmut Seidl (Munich), Perdita Stevens (Edinburgh), and Dániel Varró (Budapest).

I would like to express my sincere gratitude to all of these people and organizations, the Programme Committee Chairs and members of the ETAPS conferences, the organizers of the satellite events, the speakers themselves, the many reviewers, and Springer for agreeing to publish the ETAPS proceedings. Finally, I would like to thank the Organizing Chair of ETAPS 2008, Dániel Varró, for arranging for us to have ETAPS in the most beautiful city of Budapest

January 2008                                                              Vladimiro Sassone

# Preface

The CC 2008 Programme Committee is pleased to present the proceedings of the 17th International Conference on Compiler Construction (CC 2008), which was held on April 3rd and 4th in Budapest, Hungary, as part of the Joint European Conference on Theory and Practice of Software (ETAPS 2008). As in the last few years, papers were solicited on a wide range of areas including traditional compiler construction, compiler analyses, runtime systems and tools, programming tools, techniques for specific domains, and the design and implementation of novel language constructs. We received submissions from a wide variety of areas and the papers in this volume reflect that variety.

The Programme Committee received 71 submissions. From these, 17 research papers and 1 tool demonstration paper were selected, giving an overall acceptance rate of 25%. The Programme Committee did the reviewing and paper selection completely electronically this year, in two rounds. In the first round at least three Programme Committee members reviewed the papers. After the first round we identified those papers which were definitely accepts and those which needed further discussion (about 20 papers). Our second round concentrated on the papers needing further discussion, and we added one or two more reviews to help us decide which papers to finally accept.

Many people contributed to the success of this conference. First of all, we would like to thank the authors for all the care they put into their submissions. Our gratitude also goes to the Programme Committee members and external reviewers for their substantive and insightful reviews. Also, thanks go to the developers and supporters of the EasyChair conference management system for providing a reliable, sophisticated and free service.

CC 2008 was made possible by the ETAPS Steering Committee and the local organizing committee. Finally, we are grateful to Michael Schwartzbach for giving the CC 2008 invited talk entitled *Design Choices in a Compiler Course - or - How to Make Undergraduates Love Formal Notation.*

January 2008                                                                 Laurie Hendren

# Conference Organization

## Programme Chair

Laurie Hendren, McGill University, Canada

## Programme Committee

José Nelson Amaral, University of Alberta, Canada
Eduard Ayguade, Technical University of Catalunya (UPC), Spain
Albert Cohen, INRIA Futurs, Orsay, France
Alain Darte, CNRS, École normale supérieure de Lyon, France
Martin Elsman, IT University of Copenhagen, Denmark
M. Anton Ertl, TU Wien, Austria
David Gregg, Trinity College Dublin, Ireland
Sumit Gulwani, Microsoft Research, USA
Görel Hedin, Lund University, Sweden
Richard Jones, University of Kent, Canterbury, UK
Mira Mezini, Darmstadt University of Technology, Germany
Ana Milanova , Rensselaer Polytechnic Institute, USA
Antoine Miné, Ecole Normale Supérieure, Paris, France
Anders Møller, BRICS, University of Aarhus, Denmark
Michael O'Boyle, University of Edinburgh, UK
Peter O'Hearn, Queen Mary, University of London, UK
Jens Palsberg, UCLA, USA
Simon Peyton Jones, Microsoft Research Ltd, UK
Jan Vitek, IBM T.J. Watson, USA and Purdue University, USA
Andreas Zeller, Saarland University, Germany

## Reviewers

Many thanks to the following researchers who provided official external reviews
for the Programme Committee, and to others who helped in the review process.

Christophe Alias
Christopher Barton
Richard Bennett
Josh Berdine
Paul Berube
Paul Biggar
Neil Birkbeck

Eric Bodden
Robert Bunyan
Paul Callaghan
Paul Carpenter
Adrian Cristal
Antonio Cunei
Alcino Cunha

Stephen Curial
Benoît Dupont de Dinechin
Torbjörn Ekman
Paul Feautrier
Mohammed Fellahi
François de Ferrière
Rahul Garg
John Gilbert
Alexey Gotsman
Ramaswamy Govindarajan
Daniel Grund
Sebastian Hack
Timothy Harris
Christoph Herrmann
Martin Hirzel
Timothy Jones
Andreas Krall
Akash Lal
Patrick Lam
Piotr Lesnicki
Ondřej Lhoták
Ben Lippmeier
Josep Llosa
Florian Loitsch
Simon Marlow
Xavier Martorell

Laurent Mauborgne
Bill McCloskey
Walid Najjar
Emma Nilsson-Nyman
Nate Nystrom
Prakash Panangaden
Jinpyo Park
Fernando Pereira
Cristian Perfumo
Filip Pizlo
Adrian Prantl
Fabrice Rastello
Xavier Rival
Amr Sabry
Markus Schordan
Rob Schreiber
Jorge Sousa Pinto
Jesper Honig Spring
Adam Szalkowski
Christian Thalinger
Osman Unsal
Viktor Vafeiadis
Peng Wu
Hongwei Xi
Hongseok Yang
Lukasz Ziarek

# Table of Contents

# Runtime Techniques and Tools

# Analyses

# Atomicity and Transactions

# Design Choices in a Compiler Course
## or
# How to Make Undergraduates Love Formal Notation

Michael I. Schwartzbach

Department of Computer Science
University of Aarhus, Denmark
`mis@brics.dk`

**Abstract.** The undergraduate compiler course offers a unique opportunity to combine many aspects of the Computer Science curriculum. We discuss the many design choices that are available for the instructor and present the current compiler course at the University of Aarhus, the design of which displays at least some decisions that are unusual, novel, or just plain fun.

## 1   Introduction

The compiler course is an important component in the undergraduate Computer Science curriculum. Ideally, it ties together several aspects of the education, such as formal languages (regular and context-free languages, syntax-directed translation), programming languages (features and constructs), algorithms and data structures (ASTs, symbol tables, code selection, optimization), logic (type systems, static analysis), machine architecture (target platforms), and software engineering (phase slicing, versioning, testing). At the same time, the compiler project may involve the largest and most complex piece of software that the students so far have been required to handle.

Even though most compiler courses obviously have a common basic structure, a lecturer faces a host of design choices that must be made explicitly or implicitly. In the following such choices will be presented and discussed, both in general terms (based on an unscientific study of around 50 courses) and as they apply to the current compiler course at the University of Aarhus, the design of which displays at least some decisions that are unusual, novel, or just plain fun.

## 2   Design Choices

A compiler course must teach the students how compilers work. Beyond this obvious statement hides a multitude of different choices that influence the contents of the lectures, the style of the teaching, and the experiences of the students. Compiler courses may fill different roles in the curriculum, recruit students with

L. Hendren (Ed.): CC 2008, LNCS 4959, pp. 1–15, 2008.
© Springer-Verlag Berlin Heidelberg 2008

different backgrounds, and focus on different aspects. Thus, the purpose of this section is not to describe an optimal point in the design space, but instead to make the many design choices explicit and to discuss their consequences.

## Projects

Many compiler courses are focused on a compiler project where the students implement a working compiler of parts thereof. It is possible to keep the course purely theoretical, but it seems to be the consensus that learning-by-doing is eminently suited for this topic, and that implementing a compiler is a uniquely rewarding and empowering experience for students.

A project may be monolithic, meaning that the students build a complete compiler from scratch. While initially appealing, this approach is often too demanding and may strand students that get a bumpy start. At the other end of the scale, the course may be segmented into a series of unrelated minor projects or assignments that each are concerned with different aspects of the compilation process.

In between these extremes, many courses seek to provide a phase slicing where the students hand in different parts of the compiler at various deadlines. The phases may be implicit, or they can be made explicit by specifying strict APIs for their interfaces or by introducing a string of intermediate languages. This is more manageable, but fixed interfaces tend to limit the possible software designs while many intermediate languages tend to be confusing.

The compiler project is often large, time-consuming, and viewed as a rite of passage. Its solution is typically the largest and most complex piece of software that the students have written. Correspondingly, it is also a challenge for the teacher, since the project must be planned and tested in detail.

## Source Language

The source language of a compiler is rarely a complete programming language, such as Java, C#, or Haskell. The many subtle details of such languages and their specifications are seen as distractions from the essential topics. Also, such languages typically contain many redundant features that increase the amount of grunt work in the project. Thus, most source languages are scaled-down versions of existing languages or invented for the occasion. There is a surprising fecundity, as a quick look through the hits in Google reveals the following source languages for compiler projects: Tiny, Cool, UnCool, MinC, MicroGCL, Tiger, Iota, PCAT, Tiny-C, SampleC, Lake, B-flat, DL07, Simple, Ada/CS, ice9, ALL-COT, F05, Z#, MiniCaml, MiniPascal, Pascalito, MiniOberon, SOOP, SIMP, CSX, Tigris, Minila, C--, $\mu$OCCAM, MLPolyR, Dejlisp, and (Java seems to spawn the most imitators) Decaf, Irish Coffee, Espresso, TinyJava, MiniJava (several versions), MicroJava, Fjava, Javelet, StaticJava, CSX, j--, Jack, and Joos. Most of these languages include essentially the same features, but there is of course a fundamental distinction between functional and imperative languages. The huge variety may be viewed as an instance of the *Not-Invented-Here* syndrome, but it probably just reflects that most compiler teachers are having fun with their course and cannot resist the urge to tinker. Quite often the source languages exist in two or more versions, and the students may earn extra credit by implementing versions with extra features.

An entirely different approach is to use domain-specific source languages, which is probably how most students will potentially apply their compiler skills. In this case the students may even be allowed to design their own languages in response to challenges from various application domains. The advantage is that the project then includes a component of language design, but the main disadvantage is that the resulting languages may omit many important features (and that the teacher faces a Babylonic confusion).

## Target Language

The choice of target language is less varied. Languages in the Java or C# families generally translate into the corresponding virtual machines (since JVM and .NET are quite accessible) and Pascal derivatives translate into a P-machine. Many courses choose assembly code as the target, generally x86, SPARC, or MIPS, sometimes in simplified forms such as SPIM. A third choice is to generate C-code, which seems to be a good match for domain-specific source languages. The choice of target language is also related to the discussion of frontends vs. backends in Section 5.

## Implementation Language

The implementation language is generally one with which the students are already familiar, typically Java, C#, ML, or C++. The many Java-based source languages are almost always linked with Java as implementation language, which yields a certain elegance. Other courses explicitly use distinct source and implementation languages to increase the exposure to different languages.

## That Extra Thing

Apart from the basics of compiler construction, a compiler course seems to have room for something extra. For example, the students may also acquire a detailed knowledge of functional programming if the source and implementation languages are both functional. Also, if the source language is domain-specific, then the students may leave the course with significant knowledge of the given application domain. As a final example, the compiler may be specified completely in logic programming or using an attribute grammar evaluation system, in which case knowledge of the chosen formalism is added to the outcome of the course. This also relates to the discussion in Section 5.

This ability to use a compiler course as a vehicle for *That Extra Thing* is an important design choice of which teachers should be aware.

## Specifications and Formalization

Compiler courses display a large difference in the level of formalization that is used in the specifications of languages, semantics, machines, and translations.

To a large extent this reflects the pre-qualifications of the students and the preferences of the teacher. Most aspects of compiler technology may in fact be completely formalized, but this is rarely the style used, and it is certainly possible to be precise without being formal. As discussed in Section 6, selling the idea of useful formalizations may become a main purpose in the course.

The various components of the project are typically specified rather informally, using examples or prose. If the source language is a subset of a known language, then it may be specified as the original (often huge) language specification mentally projected onto the subset of the syntax that is allowed. This is actually a brittle technique, since programs in the subsyntax for subtle reasons are not always legal in the full language (as a stupid example, imagine allowing excluded keywords as identifiers). Reading full specifications of languages or target platforms is often a both harrowing and healthy experience for students.

### Tools and Technology

Most phases of a compiler may be supported by specialized tools and, of course, entire compilers may be specified in compiler-generating frameworks. Apart from the occasional use of attribute grammar systems, compiler courses generally only automate scanning and parsing. There seems to be a certain air of conservatism in this respect, with Lex/Flex and Yacc/Bison still reigning supremely. Java and C# has specific and improved versions of such tools, as does in fact any major programming language with respect for itself. Generally, the more modern tools will offer better support, such as integrated scanners and parsers, automatic generation of AST code, and perhaps expressive power beyond LALR(1).

An alternative approach uses one-pass compilers, in the style of the classical Pascal compilers, with handwritten scanners and recursive-descent parsers. While this possesses some old-school charm, it misses out on important aspects (such as ASTs, phases, analysis, and optimizations) and it does not generalize to handle the complexities of modern languages.

### Software Engineering

The compiler project is an excellent opportunity for gaining experience with software engineering techniques. The code is large enough to show how IDEs may help the programming task, and tools for code sharing and versioning are relevant, particularly if the students work in groups. The architecture of the compiler may also be used to showcase advanced programming patterns as discussed in Section 7.

### Skeleton Code

Most courses provide the students with a starting point in the form of a skeleton of the complete compiler. This helps the students structure the code and it makes their resulting compilers more uniform and thus easier to evaluate. The skeleton may be more or less detailed, which is a useful parameter for adjusting the work load.

An alternative strategy is to provide the students with a complete compiler for a different and often simpler source language, sometimes a subset of the source language for their project. This helps in providing a complete overview and enables the students to proceed by analogy.

## Testing

Testing an incomplete compiler is a challenge. The generally recommended strategy is to output a version of the annotated AST after each phase and then manually inspect its contents. If the compiler is structured with explicit phases, a more ambitious testing harness may be possible, see Section 8. For the complete compiler it is useful to provide a test suite for diagnosing its correctness, and perhaps also for grading the project. In any case, it is important that students acquire techniques beyond black box testing of the completed compiler.

## Documentation

A compiler course is certainly not a writing class. A program as large as the constructed compiler seems to call for extensive documentation, but most courses focus instead on writing code. Almost universally, the students are asked to comment their code (often using something like Javadoc) and to write two pages for each hand-in describing the structure of their code and the algorithms the employ.

## Group Work

While a small or segmented project is suitable for an individual student, the larger projects typically allow or require project groups. The ideal size of a group seems to be three people, which corresponds well with other programming experiences. There a several benefits from project groups, including the direct training in collaboration, planning, and communication. The danger is of course that the learning outcomes may differ for the group members, in particular there is a danger of leaving a weaker member in charge of fetching sodas.

## Exams and Grading

The project is generally the dominating activity on a compiler course, but this is not always reflected with a equal weight in the examinations. The final grade is typically a weighted sum of the individual project hand-ins, a number of midterms, and a final exam. The midterms and the final exam are of course individual, while the project hand-ins are often made in groups. For group projects the weight of the compiler code varies between 25% and 50% (with 40% being the median), and for individual projects it varies between 70% and 90% (with 70% being the median). In a few cases the weight of the project is zero, which seems to provide poor alignment as discussed in Section 11. The final exam is almost invariably a standard written test, focusing on the underlying theory.

The compiler code is evaluated by a combination of code inspection and functional testing. It is a huge advantage to enable automatic evaluation of test suites, which must of course be able to handle both positive and negative test cases, as discussed in Section 8.

Quite a few courses supplement the exam with an additional possibility for winning awards for such feats as "Best Compiler" or "Fastest Runtime". Contests like these are a surprisingly effective way of spurring on the better students. A winner's cap or t-shirt (or merely a mention on a Web page) is apparently ample payment for those extra 100 hours of work.

## 3   The dOvs Course

The Department of Computer Science at the University of Aarhus has an undergraduate compiler course (called *dOvs*) in the final year of the B.Sc. program. It has the unique advantage of being a mandatory course, meaning that it is attended by around 80 students every year. Following an earlier run in 1997-2001, the course was redesigned in 2005 based on the past experiences and with explicit attention to the many design choices presented above.

## 4   A Case for Large Languages

As mentioned earlier, most source languages for compiler projects are smallish. The motivation is that the students have a limited time for their project and that a small language allows them to focus on the important concepts.

In contrast, the source language for the dOvs compiler project is huge chunk of Java. The largest language we consider is called Joos2, and it corresponds to Java 1.3 with the omission of package private declarations, some control structures, and various odds and ends. Conceptually, it is every bit as complicated as the full language. The Joos2 language is the target for students going for extra credit. The basic requirement is the Joos1 language, which further omits instance and static initializers, multi-dimensional arrays, interfaces, and simplifies local initializers and method overloading.

The benefits of using a large language is clearly that the students obtain a realistic insight in to the workings of a full compiler that they have been using for their entire previous studies. Their sense of achievement and empowerment clearly grows with the street credibility of the source language. Also, by considering a full modern programming language, the students will encounter many concepts and challenges that are absent in smaller projects, as discussed in Section 5 and in Section 6.

The challenge of a large language is of course to make the projects succeed in the given time frame. Clearly, this requires that the starting point is a large skeleton compiler. Our model implementation of the Joos2 compiler is 12,207 lines of code (hand-written that is—SableCC generates a further 64,290 lines). The skeleton that is provided is 8,466 lines of code. The remaining 3,741 lines of code must then be written by the project groups (but generally they require between 5,000 and 10,000 lines to fulfill this task). The skeleton code includes 3,000 lines of code for defining Java bytecodes and the peephole optimizer discussed in

Section 10. This leaves around 5,000 lines of real compiler code that the students are given for free. Clearly, the danger is that they could miss important points by not fully understanding this code. However, it seems impossible to complete the skeleton without having a detailed understanding of its inner workings.

The students are provided with a complete compiler for the Joos0 language, which is a tiny static subset of Joos1 that corresponds to many of the source languages used for other compiler courses. For completeness, a lecture is used on the implementation of a narrow, one-pass compiler for a subset of C that is compiled into the IJVM architecture (in 841 lines of code).

## 5   Frontend, Backend, or Middle-End?

Compiler courses can roughly be divided into two categories: those that are *frontend-heavy* and those that are *backend-heavy* (with only a few large courses managing to be both at the same time).

The first category spends a large part of the course on formal languages, in particular on finite automata and context-free parsing. The construction and correctness of LALR(1) parsing tables is still a cornerstone of many courses, sometimes consuming half the available time. Of course, LALR(1) parser generators are still the most common choice, even if many other alternatives are available, including general parsers that can handle all unambiguous languages. These compiler courses often double as formal languages courses, but even in this setting LALR(1) parsing theory is probably not the most vital topic.

The second category spends a large part of the course on code generation, register allocation, and optimization for a realistic processor architecture. In this setting, the project source language is often a simple static subset of Java or C that allows the frontend to be dealt with as painlessly as possible.

Wedged between the traditional frontend and backend is the *middle-end* which deals with the semantic analysis, including symbol tables and type checking, which the majority of compiler courses dispenses with in a single week. This actually seems paradoxical, since e.g. the vast majority of the Java and C# language specifications deal with exactly this topic. The dOvs course has been designed to be middle-end-heavy.

For the frontend, dOvs has the advantage of following a mandatory course on formal languages, so little time needs to be spent on the basic definitions. The students learn how LALR(1) tables work, but not how they are constructed. This provides a sufficient basis for understanding LALR(1) conflicts and reading error messages from SableCC. The students are provided with a SableCC specification for the Joos1 language, but with a dozen missing features that must then be added (an the resulting LALR(1) conflicts must be resolved).

The backend is naturally light, since our compiler generates Java bytecode and the JVM has a simple architecture. Even so, optimization does play a major role in the course, as discussed in Section 10.

But the majority of the course deals with the voluminous middle-end of a Java compiler: weeding of ASTs for non-LALR(1) syntactic restrictions, building the global class library, building environments, linking identifiers to declarations, resolving import declarations, checking well-formedness of the global class hierarchy, disambiguating compound names, type checking, making implicit coercions manifest, constant folding, and performing static analyses for reachability and definite assignments. Such tasks are the main challenges of modern compilers and, consequently, it seems reasonable to give them a proportional amount of attention.

## 6  Learning to Love Formal Notation

The dOvs course is designed with the clear goal that the students should learn to love formal notation. This is not a trivial task, since many students start out with the exact opposite attitude. But it is generally the case that a tool is best appreciated when it is desperately needed.

The Joos languages are formally defined by a combination of its syntax, the Java Language Specification (JSL), and a list of excluded features. As mentioned earlier, it is actually a subtle task to ensure that every Joos1 program is also a legal Joos2 program, and that every Joos2 program is also a legal Java 1.3 program.

The JLS is a formidable document that is heavy reading for anyone, in particular for undergraduate students. Thus, the lectures present compact formalized explanations of the difficult aspects of the Joos (and Java) semantics. The lectures (and the accompanying 600 slides) use appropriate formal notation to explain the sometimes convoluted semantics of Java. This happens at a time when the students are highly motivated, since they are trying to implement that semantics at the same time, and they quickly notice that the formal notation is often a direct guide to the code that must be written.

Various formalisms are in play here. The well-formedness of a class hierarchy is defined by sets and relations (DECLARE, INHERIT, and REPLACE) that are populated through inductive rules and subjected to constraints phrased in first-order logic. Static type checking is defined through ordinary inference rules, with inductively defined relations as side conditions. The static analyses for reachability and definite assignment are defined using least solutions for set constraints. Code generation is specified as a syntax-directed translation based on templates. Finally, peephole optimization is presented as the fixed-point closure of a transition relation.

As an illustration why the practicality of formal notation becomes clear, consider the rules for definite assignments. In the JSL these are defined in 474 lines of prose of the following poetic form:

The definite unassignment analysis of loop statements raises a special problem. Consider the statement while (e) S. In order to determine whether V is definitely unassigned within some subexpression of e, we need to determine whether V is definitely unassigned before e. One might argue, by analogy with the rule for definite assignment, that V is definitely unassigned before e iff it is definitely unassigned before the while statement. However, such a rule is inadequate for our purposes. If e evaluates to true, the statement S will be executed. Later, if V is assigned by S, then in the following iteration(s) V will have already been assigned when e is evaluated. Under the rule suggested above, it would be possible to assign V multiple times, which is exactly what we have sought to avoid by introducing these rules. A revised rule would be: V is definitely unassigned before e iff it is definitely unassigned before the while statement and definitely unassigned after S. However, when we formulate the rule for S, we find: V is definitely unassigned before S iff it is definitely unassigned before e when true. This leads to a circularity. In effect, V is definitely unassigned before the loop condition e only if it is unassigned after the loop as a whole! We break this vicious circle using a hypothetical analysis of the loop condition and body. For example, if we assume that V is definitely unassigned before e (regardless of whether V really is definitely unassigned before e), and can then prove that V was definitely unassigned after e then we know that e does not assign V.

In the formal notation, the definite assignment analysis is phrased in 7 slides with set constraints of the following form (that directly translates into code using a `DepthFirstAdapter` visitor pattern from SableCC):

$$\{\sigma \ \ x = E; \ S\} :$$
$$B[\![E]\!] = B[\![\{\sigma \ \ x = E; \ S\}]\!]$$
$$B[\![S]\!] = A[\![E]\!] \cup \{x\}$$
$$A[\![\{\sigma \ \ x = E; \ S\}]\!] = A[\![S]\!]$$
$$\texttt{while} \ (E)S :$$
$$B[\![E]\!] = B[\![\texttt{while} \ (E)S]\!]$$
$$B[\![S]\!] = A_t[\![E]\!]$$
$$A[\![\texttt{while} \ (E)S]\!] = A_f[\![E]\!]$$

Thus, the students experience that the formal notation is their friend that enables them to meet their deadlines. Hopefully, this will change many skeptical attitudes.

# 7 Explicit Phases through SableCC and AspectJ

As mentioned, there are countless tools for generating scanners and parsers, and still many even if they are required to be compatible with Java. We have chosen to use SableCC, which is of course to some degree a matter of taste, though it does provide most modern conveniences: integrated scanner and parser, automatic parse tree construction, and visitor patterns for tree traversals (in fact, we use a souped-up version of SableCC with more powerful features for tree navigation). However, there are more objective reasons why we feel SableCC is uniquely suited for a compiler course.

SableCC allows the specification of ASTs in a separate grammar that is really just a recursive datatype. It is then possible to specify syntax-directed translations from concrete to abstract syntax trees. Apart from being convenient, this teaches the students about inductive translations in a practical setting. This feature is also used to illustrate desugaring, by translating `for`-loops into `while`-loops during parsing.

Phase slicing can be taken to an extreme length by combining the ASTs of SableCC with simple features of AspectJ (which is the real implementation language, though the students hardly notice this). A compiler phase needs to perform one or more traversals of the AST but also to decorate the AST nodes with additional information, such as symbol environments and types. Generally this means that the class definitions for AST nodes must be extended with phase-specific fields, which poses several problems. First, the actual AST node classes are autogenerated by SableCC, so it is inconvenient and dangerous manually to extend them. Second, if the phases are considered one at a time, then it requires an awkward prescience to declare these extra AST node fields in advance. Third, the specification of a given phase will be scattered over several files, which is an inconvenient software architecture.

Using AspectJ, extra fields can be injected into the AST nodes using inter-type declarations. For example, the skeleton code for the type checking phase starts as follows:

```
public aspect TypeChecking extends DepthFirstAdapter {
    /** The static type of the expression */
    public PType PExp.type;

    /** The static type of the lvalue */
    public PType PLvalue.type;

    /** The declaration of the field referenced in this lvalue */
    public AFieldDecl AStaticFieldLvalue.field_decl;

    /** The declaration of the field referenced in this lvalue */
    public AFieldDecl ANonstaticFieldLvalue.field_decl;

    /** The declaration of the method invoked by this expression */
    public AMethodDecl AStaticInvokeExp.method_decl;

    /** The declaration of the method invoked by this expression */
    public AMethodDecl ANonstaticInvokeExp.method_decl;

    /** The declaration of the constructor invoked by this expression */
    public AConstructorDecl ANewExp.constructor_decl;

    /** The declaration of the constructor invoked by this statement */
    public AConstructorDecl ASuperStm.constructor_decl;

    /** The declaration of the constructor invoked by this statement */
    public AConstructorDecl AThisStm.constructor_decl;

    ...

}
```

Here, several autogenerated AST node classes are extended with extra fields for information synthesized by the type checker. Using this technique, all concerns of the type checker is collected in a single file, and the autogenerated code can safely be extended.

## 8   Unit Testing through Phase Mixing

Testing a compiler during development is a difficult challenge, since only a complete compiler has a functional behavior. The students are encouraged to program an AST pretty-printer that after each new phase is extended to also print the newly added AST decorations. This simple technique goes a long way, but we can do better.

The use of AspectJ means that each phase resides in a single file. The use of SableCC with syntax-directed construction of ASTs mean that the interface between phases is fixed. This combination means that the phases of two Joos compilers may literally be mixed to produce a new hybrid compiler. We exploit this property by providing a complete and correct model implementation with which the students may build and test hybrid compilers.

Assume that a group is working on the type checker. To perform a functional test of this phase, they may build a hybrid compiler consisting of the model compiler with only the type checking phase substituted by their own. To check the allround progress, they may build a hybrid compiler consisting of their own phases up to an including the type checking phase mixed with the remaining phases from the model compiler. The students must of course not be allowed access to even the class files of the model compiler (since Java is vulnerable to decompilation), so the building and testing of a model compiler is performed by submitting phases to a Web service.

The testing of a compiler is quite extensive. In a full test the compiler is exposed to a test suite of 1,149 Java programs that each test a tiny specific property. This collection has been constructed over the three years this course have run, with new test programs being added whenever another potential kind of error is discovered. A simple positive test looks as follows:

```
// TYPE_CHECKING
public class J1_constructoroverloading {
  public int x = 0;
  public J1_constructoroverloading() {
    this.x = 23;
  }
  public J1_constructoroverloading(int x) {
    this.x = x;
  }
  public static int test() {
    J1_constructoroverloading obj1 = new J1_constructoroverloading();
    J1_constructoroverloading obj2 = new J1_constructoroverloading(100);
    return obj1.x + obj2.x;
  }
}
```

By convention, correct runs will always return the value 123. A typical negative test looks like:

```
// JOOS1: PARSER_WEEDER,JOOS1_THIS_CALL,PARSER_EXCEPTION
// JOOS2: TYPE_CHECKING,CIRCULAR_CONSTRUCTOR_INVOCATION
public class Je_16_Circularity_4_Rhoshaped {
  public Je_16_Circularity_4_Rhoshaped() {
    this(1);
  }
  public Je_16_Circularity_4_Rhoshaped(int x) {
    this(1,2);
  }
  public Je_16_Circularity_4_Rhoshaped(int x, int y) {
    this(1);
  }
  public static int test() {
    return 123;
  }
}
```

It must generate the kind of error that is mentioned in the comments for respectively Joos1 and Joos2.

In general a test program may produce many different status values, depending on the success or failure of the compilation, the assembling, the class loading, the runtime, and the output. A snippet of the output from the test driver looks as follows:

| J1 A ComplementSideEffect | >| [OKAY] | stdout stderr | [SUCCESS] | [SUCCESS] | [CORRECT] |
| J1 A ConcatInSimpleInvoke | >| [OKAY] | stdout stderr | [SUCCESS] | [SUCCESS] | [CORRECT] |
| J1 A ConcatInStaticInvoke | >| [OKAY] | stdout stderr | [SUCCESS] | [SUCCESS] | [CORRECT] |
| J1 A Conditionals NoInstructionAfterIfKiss | >| [OKAY] | stdout stderr | [SUCCESS] | [SUCCESS] | [CORRECT] |
| J1 A FieldInitialization Before | >| [OKAY] | stdout stderr | [SUCCESS] | [SUCCESS] | [CORRECT] |
| J1 A FieldInitialization NonConstant Before | >| [FAIL] | stdout stderr | [SUCCESS] | [SUCCESS] | [INCORRECT] |
| J1 A GreaterOrEqual | >| [OKAY] | stdout stderr | [SUCCESS] | [SUCCESS] | [CORRECT] |
| J1 A LazyEagerAndOr | >| [OKAY] | stdout stderr | [SUCCESS] | [SUCCESS] | [CORRECT] |
| J1 A LazyEval | >| [OKAY] | stdout stderr | [SUCCESS] | [SUCCESS] | [CORRECT] |
| J1 A String ByteShortCharInt | >| [OKAY] | stdout stderr | [SUCCESS] | [SUCCESS] | [CORRECT] |
| J1 A StringConstAKO ANE | >| [OKAY] | stdout stderr | [SUCCESS] | [SUCCESS] | [CORRECT] |
| J1 arithmeticoperations | | [OKAY] | stdout stderr | [SUCCESS] | [SUCCESS] | [CORRECT] |

The entries in the table are links that display all further details. In the first year, the test driver ran directly on a web server which was run to the ground as it quickly turned out that the students became addicted to using it. Subsequently we have implemented automatic filtering so only those tests relevant to the submitted phases are used, and the test driver now uses a farm of 17 dedicated test servers.

Another advantage of phase mixing is that students failing to complete a given phase may still continue the project by relying on the corresponding phase from the model compiler.

## 9   Incremental Feedback

The students receive extensive feedback during the course. The online test driver provides a continual evaluation of their code. We have a webboard staffed by teaching assistants, where 12% of the questions receive replies within 5 minutes, 42% within 1 hour, and 94% within 12 hours. Also, each group has a 30 minute weekly consultation with a teaching assistant. Finally, the groups must maintain a documentation blog, where they also receive feedback.

We also monitor the students closely. All activity in the system is logged and used for various statistics. A primary one is the activity curve, which shows how hard the students are working as a function of time (measured as a weighted sum of the logged activities). Each year has shown exactly the same pattern, which looks as follows:

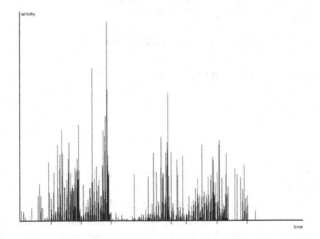

There are of course some marked spikes for each deadline, but overall the work load has a reasonable distribution.

The project is evaluated through points that are awarded for each phase. These are broken down into tiny individual components in the range between 0 and 2 points, which ensures a uniform evaluation. The students can see these points on a group homepage as soon as they have been awarded. Chasing points becomes something of an obsession.

We also maintain a visual presentation of how close the groups are to completing the next hand-in:

There is one horizontal line for each group showing the proportion between test programs passed (green) and failed (red), sorted by success rate for effect and anonymity. The collected pictures are also stored in 10-minute snapshots as a fascinating movie, showing the struggle between red and green as the groups work towards the next deadline.

The extensive logging is also useful to prevent cheating. In the few cases we have experienced, suspicions of code similarity were easily confirmed by observing anomalous behaviors in the log files.

## 10   The Peephole Contest

One hand-in deals with peephole optimization of Java bytecode. The syntax-directed code generation often produces naive code that is ripe for optimization. We have developed a domain-specific language for specifying such peephole patterns, one of which may look as follows:

```
pattern p25 x: //comparison_in_ifcmp2
     x ~ ifcmp (e0, 10)
         ldc_int (i0)
         goto (l1)
         label (l2)
         ldc_int (i1)
         label (l3)
         if (e1, l4)
    && i0 == 0
    && i1 != 0
    && l0 == l2
    && l1 == l3
    && e1 == eq
    && degree l2 == 1
 -> 4 ifcmp (negate e0, l4)
         ldc_int (i1)
```

The compiler then contains a peephole engine that will apply all such patterns on the generated code until no pattern is applicable.

The students are invited to compete in creating the most effective collection of peephole patterns, measured in the total size of the bytecode generated for a benchmark suite. The winners receive a highly coveted t-shirt:

The bar is set fairly high, as the winning group generally produces hundreds of sophisticated patterns to secure their position. Without the competition, it is unlikely that this extra effort could be mobilized (at the last stage of the project).

## 11   Exams and Grading

The projects are evaluated on a scale between 0% and 110% (including extra credit). The highest ever score so far is 107%. The project is weighted with 70% in the final grade, which is large considering that the project is done in a group. However, the principle of *alignment* dictates that the exam should reward the activity which best promotes learning, and this is clearly the project work.

To ensure individual grades, the course concludes with a 75 minute multiple-choice test (allowing partial knowledge) that covers the basic theory and details about the project. Multiple-choice tests are unfairly viewed as being superficial, but the questions may in fact be quite deep:

---

Consider the method invocation `A.B(1,2,3)`. To which category can `A` *not* belong?

| | | |
|---|---|---|
| a | ☐ | A class name. |
| b | ☐ | A static field name. |
| c | ☐ | A non-static field name. |
| d | ☐ | A local name. |
| e | ☐ | A package name. |
| f | ☐ | A formal name. |

---

Clearly, superficial knowledge is not enough to answer such questions. The multiple choice test often yields a final difference of one to two grades among group members, and it invariably rewards those students that the teaching assistants predict to be the best.

The students generally do well, and many receive their highest grade in their degree program in this course:

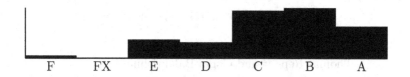

F     FX     E     D     C     B     A

## 12   Conclusion and Acknowledgements

Compiler courses are important and have been taught for a long time. We have identified many design choices that are available to teachers and have discussed some of their consequences.

The dOvs course has been designed with explicit consideration of these choices and with the goal of being novel and fun. The main characteristic of the course is that the project is huge and complicated, forcing the students to appreciate software engineering techniques and to grow to depend on formal notation as a guide to express the semantics of the source language in the implementation.

The course and its extensive infrastructure has been developed and implemented in close collaboration with Aske Simon Christensen, Janus Dam Nielsen, and Johnni Winther.

# Improved Memory-Access Analysis
# for x86 Executables[*]

Thomas Reps[1,2] and Gogul Balakrishnan[3,**]

[1] University of Wisconsin
[2] GrammaTech, Inc.
[3] NEC Laboratories America, Inc.
reps@cs.wisc.edu, bgogul@nec-labs.com

**Abstract.** Over the last seven years, we have developed static-analysis methods to recover a good approximation to the variables and dynamically allocated memory objects of a stripped executable, and to track the flow of values through them. It is relatively easy to track the effects of an instruction operand that refers to a global address (i.e., an access to a global variable) or that uses a stack-frame offset (i.e., an access to a local scalar variable via the frame pointer or stack pointer). In our work, our algorithms are able to provide useful information for close to 100% of such "direct" uses and defs.

It is much harder for a static-analysis algorithm to track the effects of an instruction operand that uses a non-stack-frame register. These "indirect" uses and defs correspond to accesses to an array or a dynamically allocated memory object. In one study, our approach recovered useful information for only 29% of indirect uses and 33% of indirect defs. However, using the technique described in this paper, the algorithm recovered useful information for 81% of indirect uses and 90% of indirect defs.

## 1 Introduction

Research carried out during the last decade by our research group [64,65,6,56,55, 7,8,36,4,49,9] as well as by others [48,22,33,14,2,31,13,44,32,3,54,37,21,46,28, 19,16,34,66] has developed the foundations for performing static analysis at the machine-code level. The machine-code-analysis problem comes in two versions: (i) with symbol-table/debugging information (unstripped executables), and (ii) without symbol-table/debugging information (stripped executables). Many tools address both versions of the problem, but are severely hampered when symbol-table/debugging information is absent.

In 2004, we supplied a key missing piece, particularly for analysis of stripped executables [6]. Previous to that work, static-analysis tools for machine code had rather limited abilities: it was known how to (i) track values in registers and,

---

[*] Supported by NSF under grants CCF-0540955 and CCF-0524051 and by AFRL under contract FA8750-06-C-0249.

[**] Work performed while at the University of Wisconsin.

L. Hendren (Ed.): CC 2008, LNCS 4959, pp. 16–35, 2008.
© Springer-Verlag Berlin Heidelberg 2008

in some cases, the stack frame [48], and (ii) analyze control flow (sometimes by applying local heuristics to try to resolve indirect calls and indirect jumps, but otherwise ignoring them).

The work presented in [6] provided a way to apply the tools of abstract interpretation [27] to the problem of analyzing stripped executables, and we followed this up with other techniques to complement and enhance the approach [56, 47, 55, 7, 8, 4, 9]. This body of work has resulted in a method to recover a good approximation to an executable's variables and dynamically allocated memory objects, and to track the flow of values through them. These methods are incorporated in a tool called CodeSurfer/x86 [5].

It is relatively easy to track the effects of an instruction operand that refers to a global address (i.e., an access to a global variable) or that uses a stack-frame offset (i.e., an access to a local scalar variable via the frame pointer or stack pointer). In our work, our algorithms are able to provide useful information for close to 100% of such "direct" uses and defs.

It is much harder for a static-analysis algorithm to track the effects of an instruction operand that uses a non-stack-frame register. These "indirect" uses and defs correspond to accesses to an array or a dynamically allocated memory object. This paper describes a technique that had an important impact on the precision obtained for indirect uses and defs in CodeSurfer/x86. As we describe in §5, in one validation study on a collection of stripped device-driver executables, the algorithm reported in [8] recovered useful information for only 29% of indirect uses and 33% of indirect defs. However, using the improved technique described in this paper, the algorithm recovered useful information for 81% of indirect uses and 90% of indirect defs.

The remainder of the paper is organized as follows: §2 motivates the work by describing some of the advantages of analyzing machine code. §3 explains some of the ideas used in CodeSurfer/x86 for recovering intermediate representations (IRs). §4 describes an extension that we made to CodeSurfer/x86's IR-recovery algorithm, which had an important impact on precision. §5 presents experimental results that measure the gain in precision. §6 discusses related work.

## 2   The Case for Analyzing Machine Code

Recent research in programming languages, software engineering, and computer security has led to new kinds of tools for analyzing programs for bugs and security vulnerabilities [38,60,35,26,17,12,20,39,30]. In these tools, static analysis is used to determine a conservative answer to the question "Can the program reach a bad state?" [1] Some of this work has already been transitioned to commercial products for source-code analysis [17, 11, 29, 23].

---

[1] Static analysis provides a way to obtain information about the possible states that a program reaches during execution, but without actually running the program on specific inputs. Static-analysis techniques explore the program's behavior for *all* possible inputs and *all* possible states that the program can reach. To make this feasible, the program is "run in the aggregate"—i.e., on descriptors that represent *collections* of memory configurations [27].

However, these tools all focus on analyzing *source code* written in a high-level language. Unfortunately, most programs that an individual user will install on his computer, and many commercial off-the-shelf (COTS) programs that a company will purchase, are delivered as stripped machine code (i.e., neither source code nor symbol-table/debugging information is available). If an individual or company wishes to vet such programs for bugs, security vulnerabilities, or malicious code (e.g., back doors, time bombs, or logic bombs) the availability of good source-code-analysis products is irrelevant.

Less widely recognized is that even when source code is available, source-code analysis has certain drawbacks [40, 62]. The reason is that computers do not execute source code; they execute *machine-code* programs that are generated from source code. The transformation that takes place between high-level source code and low-level machine code can cause there to be subtle but important differences between what a programmer intended and what is actually executed by the processor. Consequently, analyses that are performed on source code can fail to detect certain bugs and vulnerabilities.

For instance, during the Windows security push in 2002, the Microsoft C++ .NET compiler was found to introduce a vulnerability in the machine code for the following code fragment [40]:

```
memset(password, '\0', len);
free(password);
```

Assume that the program has temporarily stored the user's password—in clear text—in a dynamically allocated buffer pointed to by the pointer variable password. To minimize the lifetime of the password, which is sensitive information, the code fragment shown above zeroes-out the buffer pointed to by password before returning it to the freelist. Unfortunately, the compiler's useless-code-elimination algorithm reasoned that the program never uses the values written by the call on memset, and therefore the call on memset could be removed—thereby leaving sensitive information exposed in the freelist.

Such a vulnerability is invisible in the source code; it can only be detected by examining the low-level code emitted by the optimizing compiler. Elsewhere [56, 10, 4], we have called this the WYSINWYX phenomenon (**W**hat **Y**ou **S**ee **I**s **N**ot **W**hat **Y**ou e**X**ecute).

WYSINWYX is not restricted to the presence or absence of procedure calls; on the contrary, it is pervasive. Some of the reasons why analyses based on source code can provide the wrong level of detail include

- Many security exploits depend on platform-specific details that exist because of features and idiosyncrasies of compilers and optimizers. These include memory-layout details (such as the positions—i.e., offsets—of variables in the runtime stack's activation records and the padding between structure fields), register usage, execution order (e.g., of actual parameters at a call), optimizations performed, and artifacts of compiler bugs. Bugs and security vulnerabilities can escape notice when a tool is unable to take into account such fine-grained details.

- Analyses based on source code[2] typically make (unchecked) assumptions, e.g., that the program is ANSI C compliant. This often means that an analysis does not account for behaviors that are allowed by the compiler and that can lead to bugs or security vulnerabilities (e.g., arithmetic is performed on pointers that are subsequently used for indirect function calls; pointers move off the ends of arrays and are subsequently dereferenced; etc.)
- Programs are sometimes modified subsequent to compilation, e.g., to perform optimizations or insert instrumentation code [61]. They may also be modified to insert malicious code. Such modifications are not visible to tools that analyze source code.

In short, even when source code is available, a substantial amount of information is hidden from source-code-analysis tools, which can cause bugs, security vulnerabilities, and malicious behavior to be invisible to such tools.

The alternative is to perform static analysis at the machine-code level. The advantage of this approach is that the machine code contains the actual instructions that will be executed; this addresses the WYSINWYX phenomenon because it provides information that reveals the actual behavior that arises during program execution. Although having to perform static analysis on machine code represents a daunting challenge, there is also a possible silver lining: by analyzing an artifact that is closer to what is actually executed, a static-analysis tool may be able to obtain a *more accurate* picture of a program's properties!

The reason is that—to varying degrees—the semantic definition of every programming language leaves certain details unspecified. Consequently, for a source-code analyzer to be sound, it must account for *all* possible implementations, whereas a machine-code analyzer only has to deal with *one* possible implementation—namely, the one for the code sequence chosen by the compiler.

For instance, in C and C++ the order in which actual parameters are evaluated is not specified: actuals may be evaluated left-to-right, right-to-left, or in some other order; a compiler could even use different evaluation orders for different functions. Different evaluation orders can give rise to different behaviors when actual parameters are expressions that contain side effects. For a source-level analysis to be sound, at each call site it must take the join ($\sqcup$) of the results from analyzing each permutation of the actuals.[3] In contrast, an analysis of an executable only needs to analyze the particular sequence of instructions that lead up to the call.

Static-analysis tools are always fighting imprecision introduced by the join operation. One of the dangers of static-analysis tools is that loss of precision by the analyzer can lead to the user being swamped with a huge number of reports of potential errors, most of which are false positives. As illustrated in Fig. 1,

---

[2] Terms like "analyses based on source code" and "source-code analyses" are used as a shorthand for "analyses that work on IRs built from source code."

[3] We follow the conventions of abstract interpretation [27], where the lattice of properties is oriented so that the confluence operation used where paths come together is join ($\sqcup$). In dataflow analysis, the lattice is often oriented so that the confluence operation is meet ($\sqcap$). The two formulations are duals of one another.

because a source-code-analysis tool summarizes more behaviors than a tool that analyzes machine code, the join performed at $q$ must cover more abstract states. This can lead to less-precise information than that obtained from machine-code analysis. Because more-precise answers mean a lower false-positive rate, machine-code-analysis tools have the potential to report fewer false positives.

There are other trade-offs between performing analysis at source level versus the machine-code level: with source-code analysis one can hope to learn about bugs and vulnerabilities that exist on multiple platforms, whereas analysis of the machine code only provides information about vulnerabilities on the specific platform on which the executable runs.

Although it is possible to create source-code tools that strive to have greater fidelity to the program that is actually executed—examples include [18, 51]—in the limit, the tool would have to incorporate all the platform-specific decisions that would be made by the compiler. Because such decisions depend on the level of optimization chosen, to build these choices into a tool that works on a representation that is close to the source level would require simulating much of the compiler and optimizer inside the analysis tool. Such an approach is impractical.

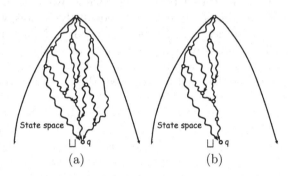
(a)    (b)

**Fig. 1.** Source-code analysis, which must account for all possible choices made by the compiler, must summarize more paths (see (a)) than machine-code analysis (see (b)). Because the latter can focus on fewer paths, it can yield more precise results.

In addition to addressing the WYSINWYX issue, performing analysis at the machine-code level provides a number of other benefits:

- Programs typically make extensive use of libraries, including dynamically linked libraries (DLLs), which may not be available as source code. Typically, source-code analyses are performed using code stubs that model the effects of library calls. Because these are created by hand, they may contain errors, which can cause an analysis to return incorrect results. In contrast, a machine-code-analysis tool can analyze the library code directly [36].
- The source code may have been written in more than one language. This complicates the life of designers of tools that analyze source code because multiple languages must be supported, each with its own quirks.
- Even if the source code is primarily written in one high-level language, it may contain inlined assembly code in selected places. Source-code-analysis tools typically either skip over inlined assembly [24] or do not push the analysis beyond sites of inlined assembly [52]. To a machine-code-analysis tool, inlined assembly just amounts to additional instructions to analyze.

– Source-code-analysis tools are only applicable when source is available, which limits their usefulness in security applications (e.g., to analyzing code from open-source projects).

## 3  CodeSurfer/x86: A Platform for Recovering IRs from Stripped Executables

Given a stripped executable as input, CodeSurfer/x86 [5] recovers IRs that are similar to those that would be available had one started from source code. This section explains some of the ideas used in the IR-recovery algorithms of CodeSurfer/x86 [4, 6, 8].

The recovered IRs include control-flow graphs (CFGs), with indirect jumps resolved; a call graph, with indirect calls resolved; information about the program's variables; possible values for scalar, array, and pointer variables; sets of used, killed, and possibly-killed variables for each CFG node; and data dependences. The techniques employed by CodeSurfer/x86 do not rely on debugging information being present, but can use available debugging information (e.g., Windows .pdb files) if directed to do so.

The analyses used in CodeSurfer/x86 are a great deal more ambitious than even relatively sophisticated disassemblers, such as IDAPro [41]. At the technical level, they address the following problem: *Given a (possibly stripped) executable E, identify the procedures, data objects, types, and libraries that it uses, and, for each instruction I in E and its libraries, for each interprocedural calling context of I, and for each machine register and variable V in scope at I, statically compute an accurate over-approximation to the set of values that V may contain when I executes.*

It is useful to contrast this approach against the approach used in much of the other work that now exists on analyzing executables. Many research projects have focused on *specialized* analyses to identify aliasing relationships [33], data dependences [2,22], targets of indirect calls [31], values of strings [21], bounds on stack height [54], and values of parameters and return values [66]. In contrast, CodeSurfer/x86 addresses all of these problems by means of a set of analyses that focuses on the problem stated above. In particular, CodeSurfer/x86 discovers an over-approximation of the set of states that can be reached at each point in the executable—where a *state* means *all* of the state: values of registers, flags, and the contents of memory—and thereby provides information about aliasing relationships, targets of indirect calls, etc.

One of the goals of CodeSurfer/x86 is to be able to detect whether an executable conforms to a standard compilation model. By "standard compilation model" we mean that the executable has procedures, activation records (ARs), a global data region, and a free-storage pool; might use virtual functions and DLLs; maintains a runtime stack; each global variable resides at a fixed offset in memory; each local variable of a procedure $f$ resides at a fixed offset in the ARs for $f$; actual parameters of $f$ are pushed onto the stack by the caller so that the corresponding formal parameters reside at fixed offsets in the ARs for $f$; the program's instructions occupy a fixed area of memory, and are not self-modifying.

During the analysis performed by CodeSurfer/x86, these aspects of the program are checked. When violations are detected, an error report is issued, and the analysis proceeds. In doing so, however, we generally choose to have the analyzer only explore behaviors that stay within those of the desired execution model. For instance, if the analysis finds that the return address might be modified within a procedure, it reports the potential violation, but proceeds without modifying the control flow of the program. Consequently, if the executable conforms to the standard compilation model, CodeSurfer/x86 creates a valid IR for it; if the executable does not conform to the model, then one or more violations will be discovered, and corresponding error reports will be issued; if the (human) analyst can determine that the error report is indeed a false positive, then the IR is valid. The advantages of this approach are (i) it provides the ability to analyze some aspects of programs that may deviate from the desired execution model; (ii) it generates reports of possible deviations from the desired execution model; (iii) it does not force the analyzer to explore all of the consequences of each (apparent) deviation, which may be a false positive due to loss of precision that occurs during static analysis.

**Variable and Type Discovery.** One of the major stumbling blocks in analyzing executables is the difficulty of recovering information about variables and types, especially for aggregates (i.e., structures and arrays). When performing source-code analysis, the programmer-defined variables provide us with the compartments for tracking data manipulations. When debugging information is absent, an executable's data objects are not easily identifiable. Consider, for instance, an access on a source-code variable x in some source-code statement. At the machine-code level, an access on x is performed either directly—by specifying an absolute address—or indirectly—through an address expression of the form "[$base + index \times scale + offset$]", where $base$ and $index$ are registers and $scale$ and $offset$ are integer constants. The variable and type-discovery phase of CodeSurfer/x86 [8, 4] recovers information about variables that are allocated globally, locally (i.e., on the stack), and dynamically (i.e., from the freelist). The recovered variables, called $a\text{-}locs$ (for "abstract locations") are the basic variables used in CodeSurfer/x86's value-set-analysis (VSA) algorithm [6, 8, 4].

To accomplish this task, CodeSurfer/x86 makes use of a number of analyses, and the sequence of analyses performed is itself iterated [4, 8]. On each round, CodeSurfer/x86 uses VSA to identify an over-approximation of the memory accesses performed at each instruction. Subsequently, the results of VSA are used to perform aggregate structure identification (ASI) [53], which identifies commonalities among accesses to an aggregate data value, to refine the current set of a-locs. The new set of a-locs are used to perform another round of VSA. If the over-approximation of memory accesses computed by VSA improves from the previous round, the a-locs computed by the subsequent round of ASI may also improve. This process is repeated as long as desired, or until the process converges. By this means, CodeSurfer/x86 bootstraps its way to a set of a-locs that serve as proxies for the program's original variables.

```
 1: decl worklist: set of ⟨CallStringₖ, Node⟩
 2:
 3: proc ContextSensitiveVSA()
 4:     worklist := {⟨∅, enter⟩}
 5:     absEnv_enter := Initial values of global a-locs and esp
 6:     while (worklist ≠ ∅) do
 7:         while (worklist ≠ ∅) do
 8:             Remove a pair ⟨cs, n⟩ from worklist
 9:             m := Number of successors of node n
10:             for i = 1 to m do
11:                 succ := GetSuccessor(n, i)
12:                 edge_ae := AbstractTransformer(n → succ, absMemConfigₙ[cs])
13:                 cs_set := GetCSSuccs(cs, n, succ)
14:                 for (each succ_cs ∈ cs_set) do
15:                     Propagate(succ_cs, succ, edge_ae)
16:                 end for
17:             end for
18:         end while
19:         GMOD' := ComputeGMOD()
20:         if (GMOD' ≠ GMOD) then
21:             for each call-site c ∈ CallSites and cs ∈ CallStringₖ do
22:                 if inc[cs] ≠ ⊥ then worklist := worklist ∪ {⟨cs, c⟩}
23:             end for
24:             GMOD := GMOD'
25:         end if
26:     end while
27: end proc
28:
29: proc GetCSSuccs(pred_cs: CallStringₖ, pred: Node, succ: Node): set of CallStringₖ
30:     result := ∅
31:     if (pred is an exit node and succ is an end-call node) then
32:         Let c be the call node associated with succ
33:         for each succ_cs in absMemConfig_c do
34:             if (pred_cs ⤳^cs succ_cs) then
35:                 result := result ∪ {succ_cs}
36:             end if
37:         end for
38:     else if (succ is a call node) then
39:         result := {(pred_cs ≪^cs c)}
40:     else
41:         result := {pred_cs}
42:     end if
43:     return result
44: end proc
45:
46: proc Propagate(cs: CallStringₖ, n: Node, edge_ae: AbsEnv)
47:     old := absMemConfigₙ[cs]
48:     if n is an end-call node and round > 0 then
49:         Let c be the call node associated with n
50:         edge_ae := GMODMergeAtEndCall(edge_ae, absMemConfig_c[cs])
51:     end if
52:     new := old ⊔^ae edge_ae
53:     if (old ≠ new) then
54:         absMemConfigₙ[cs] := new
55:         worklist := worklist ∪ {⟨cs, n⟩}
56:     end if
57: end proc
```

**Fig. 2.** Context-sensitive VSA algorithm with GMOD-based merge function

## 4   GMOD-Based Merge Function

This section describes one of the extensions that we made to our IR-recovery algorithm that had an important impact on precision. The context-sensitive VSA algorithm associates each program point with an AbsMemConfig:

$$\mathsf{AbsMemConfig} = (\mathsf{CallString_k} \rightarrow \mathsf{AbsEnv_\perp})$$

where an AbsEnv value [4,8] maps each a-loc and register to an over-approximation of its set of possible values (referred to as a *value-set*), and a CallString$_k$ value is an abstraction of the structure of the run-time stack.[4] The context-sensitive VSA algorithm characterizes a set of concrete states by a set of calling contexts in which those states can arise.

Fig. 2 shows the context-sensitive VSA algorithm, which is based on a work-list. For the time being, consider the statements that are underlined as being absent. The entries in the worklist are ⟨CallString$_k$, Node⟩ pairs, and each entry represents the calling contexts of the corresponding node that have not yet been explored. The algorithm selects an entry from the worklist, executes the abstract transformer for each edge out of the node, and propagates the information to all the successors of the node.

For all nodes, including an end-call[5] node, the algorithm combines the result of the abstract transformer with the old abstract state at the successor. Although *Propagate* computes a sound AbsEnv value

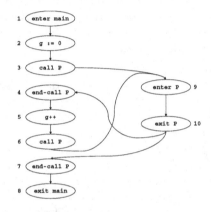

**Fig. 3.** Example showing the need for a GMOD-based merge function

for an end-call node, it may not always be precise. Consider the interprocedural CFG (ICFG) shown in Fig. 3. In any concrete execution, the only possible value for g at node 4 is 0. However, context-insensitive VSA (i.e., VSA with call-strings of length 0) computes the range $[-2^{31}, 2^{31} - 1]$ for g at node 4. In context-insensitive VSA, the call-return structure of the ICFG is ignored (i.e.,

---

[4] Let CallSites denote the set of call-sites in an executable. The executable's *call graph* is a labeled multi-graph in which each node represents a procedure, and each edge (labeled with a call-site in the calling procedure) represents a call. A call-string in the call graph is a finite-length path $(c_1 \ldots c_n)$ such that $c_1$ is a call-site in the entry procedure. CallString is the set of all call-strings.

A call-string suffix of length $k$ [59] is either $(c_1 \ldots c_k) \in$ CallString, or $(*c_1 \ldots c_k)$, where $c_1, \ldots, c_k \in$ CallSites; the latter, referred to as a *saturated* call-string, represents the set of call-strings $\{cs \mid cs \in \mathsf{CallString}, cs = \pi c_1 \ldots c_k, \text{ and } |\pi| \geq 1\}$. CallString$_k$ is the set of saturated call-strings of length $k$, plus non-saturated call-strings of length $\leq k$.

[5] An end-call node represents the return site for a call node.

the ICFG is considered to be an ordinary graph). Note that $6 \rightarrow 9$ is a back-edge, and hence is a suitable location for widening to be performed [15]. Consider the path $\pi = (6, 9, 10, 4)$. Although $\pi$ is an invalid execution path, context-insensitive VSA explores $\pi$. The effects of statement g++ at node 5 and the results of widening at $6 \rightarrow 9$ are propagated to node 4, and consequently, the range computed for g at node 4 by context-insensitive VSA is $[-2^{31}, 2^{31} - 1]$ (due to widening and wrap-around in 32-bit arithmetic). One possible solution to the problem is to increase the length of call-strings. However, it is impractical to increase the length of call-strings beyond a small value. Therefore, increasing the call-string length is not a complete solution to the problem.

```
1: proc GMODMergeAtEndCall(in_c: AbsEnv, in_x: AbsEnv): AbsEnv
2:    in'_c := SetAlocsToTop(in_c, GMOD[X])
3:    in'_x := SetAlocsToTop(in_x, U − GMOD[X])
4:    out := in'_c ⊓^ae in'_x
5:    return out
6: end proc
```

**Fig. 4.** GMOD-based merge function. GMOD[X] represents the set of a-locs modified (directly or transitively) by procedure X, and $U$ is the universal set of a-locs)

Suppose that we modify *Propagate* in Fig. 4 by adding line [50], which invokes procedure *GMODMergeAtEndCall*. *GMODMergeAtEndCall* takes two AbsEnv values: (1) $in_c$, the AbsEnv value at the corresponding call node, and (2) $in_x$, the AbsEnv value at the corresponding exit node. Let C and X be the procedures containing the call and exit nodes, respectively. *SetAlocsToTop(ae, AlocSet)* returns the AbsEnv value $ae[a \mapsto \top^{vs} \mid a \in AlocSet]$. Operation $ae_1 \sqcap^{ae} ae_2$ yields a new AbsEnv value in which the set of values for each a-loc (register) is the meet of the value-sets for the corresponding a-loc (register) in $ae_1$ and $ae_2$.

In the earlier implementation of *Propagate* (i.e., when *Propagate* does not call *GMODMergeAtEndCall* on line [50]), the value-sets of all a-locs in $in_x$ are propagated to the end-call node. In contrast, when *Propagate* does call *GMODMergeAtEndCall*, only the value-sets of a-locs that are modified (directly or transitively) in procedure X are propagated from $in_x$ to the AbsEnv value at the end-call node. The value-sets for other a-locs are obtained from $in_c$. Because procedure P does not modify global variable g, using *GMODMergeAtEndCall* during context-insensitive VSA results in better information at nodes 4 and 7; at node 4 the range for g is $[0, 0]$, and at node 7 the range for g is $[1, 1]$.

The actual implementation [4, Ch. 7] of *GMODMergeAtEndCall* is slightly more complicated. In addition to combining the information from the call-site and the exit node, it performs the following operations:

- At the exit node, the stack pointer esp points to the activation record of callee X. The value of esp in the AbsEnv value returned by *GMODMergeAt-EndCall* is adjusted to point to the activation record of caller C .
- The value of the frame pointer ebp is set to the value of ebp in $in_c$. This change corresponds to the common situation in which the value of ebp at the exit node of a procedure is usually restored to the value of ebp at the call-site. (This is

one of the aspects of the executable that VSA checks; a report is issued to the user if the behavior does not conform to what is expected.)
– The values of those a-locs that go out of scope, such as the local variables of callee X, are set to a special invalid abstract address.

The procedure shown in Fig. 4 uses GMOD information [25]; i.e., for each procedure $P$ in the executable, information is required about the set of a-locs that $P$ could possibly modify (directly or transitively). To perform GMOD analysis, information is required for each instruction about the set of a-locs that the instruction could possibly modify (i.e., IMOD information [25]). However, complete information about the a-locs accessed by each instruction is not available until the end of VSA. As discussed in §3, CodeSurfer/x86 makes use of a number of analyses, and the sequence of analyses performed is itself iterated. At the end of each round of VSA, GMOD information is computed for use during the next round of VSA (see lines [19]–[25] in Fig. 2); i.e., the GMOD sets for use during VSA round $i$ are computed using the VSA results from round $i-1$. For the initial round of VSA ($i = 0$), *GMODMergeAtEndCall* is not used.[6] For each subsequent round, procedure *GMODMergeAtEndCall* is used as the merge function.

The process mentioned above may not be sound in the presence of indirect jump and indirect calls. In addition to determining an over-approximation of the set of states at each program point, VSA also determines the targets of indirect jumps and indirect calls. For pragmatic reasons, if VSA determines that the target address of an indirect jump or indirect call is $\top^{vs}$, it does not add any new edges.[7] Consequently, in the presence of indirect jumps and indirect calls, the ICFG used during round $i - 1$ of VSA can be different from the ICFG used during round $i$. Therefore, for round $i$ of VSA, it may not be sound to use the GMOD sets computed using the VSA results from round $i - 1$. To ensure that the VSA results computed by round $i$ are sound with respect to the current ICFG, the context-sensitive VSA algorithm of Fig. 2 does not terminate until the GMOD sets are consistent with the VSA results (see lines [19]–[25] in Fig. 2): when VSA reaches a fix-point in round $i$, the GMOD sets are recomputed using the current VSA results (GMOD′ on line [19] in Fig. 2) and compared against the current GMOD sets; if they are equal, then the VSA results are sound, and VSA terminates; otherwise, all call-sites $c \in$ CallSites are added to the worklist (line [22]) and VSA is resumed with the new worklist (line [5]). (For each call-site $c$, only those call-strings that have a non-$\bot$ AbsEnv at $c$ are added to the worklist (line [22] in Fig. 2).) Even though VSA is restarted from a non-$\bot$ state by *reinitializing* the worklist (line [22]), VSA is guaranteed to converge because *Propagate accumulates* values at each program point using join ($\sqcup$); see line [52].

## 5   Experiments

This section describes a study that we carried out to measure the gain in precision that was obtained via the technique presented in §4. The study measured

---

[6] Alternatively, *GMODMergeAtEndCall* could be called with GMOD[X] $= U$.

[7] A report is issued so that the user will be aware of the situation.

**Table 1.** Running times for VSA with and without the GMOD-based merge function. (For the drivers listed above in **boldface**, round-by-round details of the percentages of strongly-trackable indirect operands are given in Fig. 7.)

| Driver | Procedures | Instructions | Running time (seconds) No GMOD | With GMOD |
|---|---|---|---|---|
| **src/vdd/dosioctl/krnldrvr** | 70 | 284 | 34 | 25 |
| src/general/ioctl/sys | 76 | 2824 | 63 | 58 |
| src/general/tracedrv/tracedrv | 84 | 3719 | 122 | 45 |
| **src/general/cancel/startio** | 96 | 3861 | 44 | 32 |
| src/general/cancel/sys | 102 | 4045 | 43 | 33 |
| **src/input/moufiltr** | 93 | 4175 | 369 | 427 |
| src/general/event/sys | 99 | 4215 | 53 | 61 |
| src/input/kbfiltr | 94 | 4228 | 370 | 404 |
| src/general/toaster/toastmon | 123 | 6261 | 576 | 871 |
| **src/storage/filters/diskperf** | 121 | 6584 | 647 | 809 |
| src/network/modem/fakemodem | 142 | 8747 | 1410 | 2149 |
| **src/storage/fdc/flpydisk** | 171 | 12752 | 2883 | 5336 |
| src/input/mouclass | 192 | 13380 | 10484 | 13380 |
| src/input/mouser | 188 | 13989 | 4031 | 8917 |
| src/kernel/serenum | 184 | 14123 | 3777 | 9126 |
| **src/wdm/1394/driver/1394diag** | 171 | 23430 | 3149 | 12161 |
| src/wdm/1394/driver/1394vdev | 173 | 23456 | 2461 | 10912 |

certain characteristics of the variables and values discovered by IR-recovery. The characteristics that we measured provide information about how good the recovered information would be as a starting point for some client tool that needs to perform additional static analysis on the executable. In particular, because resolution of indirect operands is a fundamental primitive that essentially any subsequent analysis would need, we were particularly interested in how well our techniques could resolve indirect memory operands that use a non-stack-frame register (e.g., accesses to arrays and heap-allocated data objects).

To evaluate the effect of using the GMOD-based merge function on the precision of value-set analysis, we selected seventeen device drivers from the Windows Driver Development Kit [63] release 3790.1830; see Tab. 1. The executable for each device driver was obtained by compiling the driver source code along with the harness and OS environment model used in the SDV toolkit [11] (see [9] for more details). The resulting executable was then stripped; i.e., symbol-table and debugging information was removed.

We analyzed each executable using two versions of VSA: (1) VSA without the GMOD-based merge function (as sketched at the beginning of §4), and (2) VSA with the GMOD-based merge function shown in Fig. 4. For the experiments, we used a Dell Precision 490 Desktop, equipped with a 64-bit Intel Xeon 5160 3.0 GHz dual core processor and 16GB of physical memory, running Windows XP. (Although the machine has 16GB of physical memory, the size of the per-process virtual user-address space for a 32-bit application is limited to 4GB.)

Except for the difference in the merge function, all other parameters, such as the lengths of call-strings, the number of rounds of VSA-ASI iteration, etc., were the same for both versions. We ran VSA-ASI iteration until convergence, and then, based on the results of the final round of each run, we classified the memory operands in the executable into *strongly-trackable*, *weakly-trackable*, and *untrackable* operands:

- A memory operand is *strongly-trackable* (see Fig. 5) if
    - the lvalue evaluation of the operand does not yield $\top^{vs}$, and
    - each lvalue obtained refers to a 4-, 2-, or 1-byte (inferred) variable.
- A memory operand is *weakly-trackable* if
    - the lvalue evaluation of the operand does not yield $\top^{vs}$, and
    - at least one of the lvalues obtained refers to a 4-, 2-, or 1-byte (inferred) variable.
- Otherwise, the memory operand is *untrackable*; i.e., either
    - the lvalue evaluation of the operand yields $\top^{vs}$, or
    - all of the lvalues obtained refer to an (inferred) variable whose size is greater than 4 bytes.

VSA tracks value-sets for a-locs whose size is less than or equal to 4 bytes, but treats a-locs greater than 4 bytes as having the value-set $\top^{vs}$ [6, 55, 4]. Therefore, untrackable memory operands are ones for which VSA provides no useful information at all, and strongly-trackable memory operands are ones for which VSA can provide useful information.

We refer to a memory operand that is used to read the contents of memory as a *use-operand*, and a memory operand that is used to update the contents of memory as a *kill-operand*. VSA can provide some useful information for a weakly-trackable kill-operand,

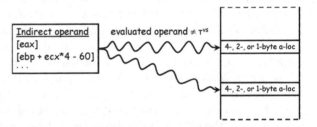

**Fig. 5.** Properties of a strongly-trackable memory operand

but provides no useful information for a weakly-trackable use-operand. To understand why, first consider the kill-operand [eax] in "mov [eax], 10". If [eax] is weakly-trackable, then VSA may be able to update the value-set—to a value other than $\top^{vs}$—of those a-locs that are (i) accessed by [eax] and (ii) of size less than or equal to 4 bytes. (The value-sets for a-locs accessed by [eax] that are of size greater than 4 bytes already hold the value $\top^{vs}$.) In contrast, consider the use-operand [eax] in "mov ebx, [eax]"; if [eax] is weakly-trackable, then at least one of the a-locs accessed by [eax] holds the value $\top^{vs}$. In a mov instruction, the value-set of the destination operand (ebx in our example) is set to the join ($\sqcup^{vs}$) of the value-sets of the a-locs accessed by the source operand ([eax] in our example);

**Table 2.** Percentages of trackable memory operands in the final round

| Category | Geometric Mean (for the final round) | | |
|---|---|---|---|
| | Strongly-trackable indirect uses | Strongly-trackable indirect kills | Weakly-trackable indirect kills |
| Without GMOD-based merge function | 29% | 30% | 33% |
| With GMOD-based merge function | 81% | 85% | 90% |

consequently, the value-set of `ebx` would be set to $\top^{vs}$—which is the same as what happens when `[eax]` is untrackable.

We classified memory operands as either *direct* or *indirect*. A *direct* memory operand is a memory operand that uses a global address or stack-frame offset. An *indirect* memory operand is a memory operand that uses a non-stack-frame register (e.g., a memory operand that accesses an array or a heap-allocated data object).

**Direct Memory Operands.** For direct use-operands and direct kill-operands, both versions perform equally well: the percentages of strongly-trackable direct use-operands and both strongly-trackable and weakly-trackable direct kill-operands are 100% for almost all of the drivers [4, §7.5.1].

**Indirect Memory Operands.** Tab. 2 summarizes the results for indirect operands. As shown in Tab. 2, when the technique described in §4 is used, the percentages of trackable indirect memory operands in the final round improve dramatically. (Note that the "Weakly-trackable indirect kills" are a superset of the "Strongly-trackable indirect kills".)

Fig. 6 shows the effects, on a per-application basis, of using the GMOD-based merge function on the percentages of strongly-trackable indirect use-operands, strongly-trackable indirect kill-operands, and weakly-trackable indirect kill-operands.

For the six Windows device drivers listed in **boldface** in Tab. 1, the graphs in Fig. 7 show the percentages of strongly-trackable indirect operands in different rounds for the two versions. The graphs show the positive interaction that exists between VSA and ASI: the percentages of strongly-trackable indirect operands increase with each round for both versions. However, for the VSA algorithm without the GMOD-based merge function, the improvements in the percentages of strongly-trackable indirect operands peter out after the third round because the value-sets computed for the a-locs are not as precise as the value-sets computed by the VSA algorithm with the GMOD-based merge function.

Columns 4 and 5 of Tab. 1 show the times taken for the two versions of VSA. The running times are comparable for smaller programs. However, for larger programs, the VSA algorithm with the GMOD-based merge function runs slower by a factor of 2 to 5. We believe that the slowdown is due to the increased precision during VSA obtained using the GMOD-based merge function. We use applicative AVL trees [50] to represent abstract stores. In our representation, if the value-set of a-loc $a$ is $\top^{vs}$, meaning that $a$ could hold any possible address or value, the AVL tree for the abstract store has no entry for $a$ (and abstract

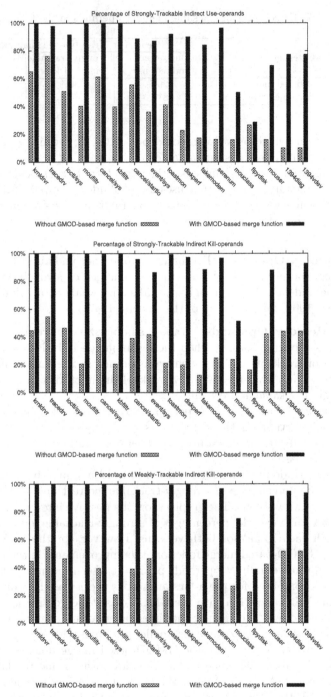

**Fig. 6.** Effects of using the GMOD-based merge function on the percentages of strongly-trackable indirect use-operands, strongly-trackable indirect kill-operands, and weakly-trackable indirect kill-operands

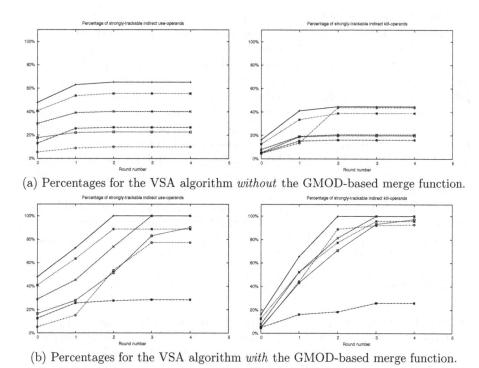

(a) Percentages for the VSA algorithm *without* the GMOD-based merge function.

(b) Percentages for the VSA algorithm *with* the GMOD-based merge function.

**Fig. 7.** Percentage of strongly-trackable indirect operands in different rounds (for the six device drivers listed in **boldface** in Tab. 1)

operations on such values are performed quickly). When a technique improves the precision of VSA, there will be more a-locs whose value-set is not $\top^{vs}$; consequently, there will be more entries in the AVL trees for the abstract stores, and each abstract operation on the abstract store takes more time.

## 6    Related Work

A large amount of related work has already been mentioned in the body of the paper. This section discusses a few additional issues.

Knoop and Steffen [45] introduced the use of merge functions in interprocedural dataflow analysis as a way to handle local variables at procedure returns. At a call site at which procedure $P$ calls procedure $Q$, the local variables of $P$ are modeled as if the current incarnations of $P$'s locals are stored in locations that are inaccessible to $Q$ and to procedures transitively called by $Q$—consequently, the contents of $P$'s locals cannot be affected by the call to $Q$. To create the abstract state at the end-call node in $P$, the merge function integrates the stored abstract values for $P$'s locals into the abstract state returned by $Q$. This idea is used in many other papers on interprocedural dataflow analysis, including [58,42,47,1], as well as several systems (e.g., [57,43]).

Note that this model agrees with programming languages like Java, where it is not possible to have pointers to local variables (i.e., pointers into the stack). For machine-code programs, as well as programs written in languages such as C and C++ (where the address-of operator (&) allows the address of a local variable to be obtained), if $P$ passes the address of a local to $Q$, it is possible for $Q$ (or a procedure transitively called from $Q$) to affect a local of $P$ by making an indirect assignment through the address. Conventional interprocedural dataflow-analysis algorithms address this issue by (i) performing several preliminary analyses (e.g., first points-to analysis, which is used to determine IMOD information [25] for individual statements, and then GMOD analysis [25]), and (ii) using the GMOD-analysis results to create sound transformers for the primary interprocedural dataflow analysis of interest.

The approach taken in the algorithm from §4 is similar, except that because VSA is not only the primary interprocedural dataflow analysis of interest but is also used to obtain points-to information, VSA and GMOD analysis are iterated.

# References

1. Alur, R., Madhusudan, P.: Adding Nesting Structure to Words. In: Ibarra, O.H., Dang, Z. (eds.) DLT 2006. LNCS, vol. 4036, pp. 1–13. Springer, Heidelberg (2006)
2. Amme, W., Braun, P., Zehendner, E., Thomasset, F.: Data dependence analysis of assembly code. In: IJPP 2000 (2000)
3. Backes, W.: Programmanalyse des XRTL Zwischencodes. PhD thesis, Universitaet des Saarlandes (In German) (2004)
4. Balakrishnan, G.: WYSINWYX: What You See Is Not What You eXecute. PhD thesis, C.S.Dept., Univ.of Wisconsin, Madison, WI, TR-1603 (August 2007)
5. Balakrishnan, G., Gruian, R., Reps, T., Teitelbaum, T.: CodeSurfer/x86—A Platform for Analyzing x86 Executables. In: Bodik, R. (ed.) CC 2005. LNCS, vol. 3443, pp. 250–254. Springer, Heidelberg (2005)
6. Reps, T., Balakrishnan, G.: Analyzing Memory Accesses in x86 Executables. In: Duesterwald, E. (ed.) CC 2004. LNCS, vol. 2985, pp. 5–23. Springer, Heidelberg (2004)
7. Reps, T., Balakrishnan, G.: Recency-Abstraction for Heap-Allocated Storage. In: Yi, K. (ed.) SAS 2006. LNCS, vol. 4134, pp. 221–239. Springer, Heidelberg (2006)
8. Reps, T., Balakrishnan, G.: DIVINE: DIscovering Variables IN Executables. In: Cook, B., Podelski, A. (eds.) VMCAI 2007. LNCS, vol. 4349, pp. 1–28. Springer, Heidelberg (2007)
9. Balakrishnan, G., Reps, T.: Analyzing stripped device-driver executables. In: Ramakrishnan, C.R., Rehof, J. (eds.) TACAS 2008. LNCS, vol. 4963, pp. 124–140. Springer, Heidelberg (2008)
10. Balakrishnan, G., Reps, T., Melski, D., Teitelbaum, T.: WYSINWYX: What You See Is Not What You eXecute. In: VSTTE 2007 (2007)
11. Ball, T., Bounimova, E., Cook, B., Levin, V., Lichtenberg, J., McGarvey, C., Ondrusek, B., Rajamani, S.K., Ustuner, A.: Thorough static analysis of device drivers. In: EuroSys 2006 (2006)
12. Ball, T., Rajamani, S.K.: The SLAM Toolkit. In: Berry, G., Comon, H., Finkel, A. (eds.) CAV 2001. LNCS, vol. 2102, Springer, Heidelberg (2001)

13. Bergeron, J., Debbabi, M., Desharnais, J., Erhioui, M.M., Lavoie, Y., Tawbi, N.: Static detection of malicious code in executable programs. IJRE 2001 (2001)
14. Bergeron, J., Debbabi, M., Erhioui, M.M., Ktari, B.: Static analysis of binary code to isolate malicious behaviors. In: WETICE 1999 (1999)
15. Bourdoncle, F.: Efficient chaotic iteration strategies with widenings. In: Int. Conf. on Formal Methods in Prog. and their Appl. 1993 (1993)
16. Brumley, D., Newsome, J.: Alias analysis for assembly. CMU-CS-06-180, School of Comp.Sci., Carnegie Mellon University, Pittsburgh, PA (December 2006)
17. Bush, W.R., Pincus, J.D., Sielaff, D.J.: A static analyzer for finding dynamic programming errors. Software: Practice and Experience 30, 775–802 (2000)
18. Chandra, S., Reps, T.: Physical type checking for C. In: PASTE 1999(1999)
19. Chang, B.-Y., Harren, M., Necula, G.C.: Analysis of low-level code using cooperating decompilers. In: Yi, K. (ed.) SAS 2006. LNCS, vol. 4134, pp. 318–335. Springer, Heidelberg (2006)
20. Chen, H., Wagner, D.: MOPS: An infrastructure for examining security properties of software. In: CCCS 2002 (2002)
21. Christodorescu, M., Goh, W.-H., Kidd, N.: String analysis for x86 binaries. In: PASTE 2005 (2005)
22. Cifuentes, C., Fraboulet, A.: Intraprocedural static slicing of binary executables. In: ICSM 1997 (1997)
23. CodeSonar, GrammaTech, Inc., http://www.grammatech.com/products/codesonar
24. CodeSurfer, GrammaTech, Inc., http://www.grammatech.com/products/codesurfer
25. Cooper, K.D., Kennedy, K.: Interprocedural side-effect analysis in linear time. In: PLDI 1988 (1988)
26. Corbett, J.C., Dwyer, M.B., Hatcliff, J., Laubach, S., Pasareanu, C.S., Robby, Zheng, H.: Bandera: Extracting finite-state models from Java source code. In: ICSE 2000 (2000)
27. Cousot, P., Cousot, R.: Abstract interpretation: A unified lattice model for static analysis of programs by construction of approximation of fixed points. In: POPL 1977 (1977)
28. Cova, M., Felmetsger, V., Banks, G., Vigna, G.: Static detection of vulnerabilities in x86 executables. In: ACSAC 2006 (2006)
29. Coverity Prevent, http://www.coverity.com/products/prevent_analysis_engine.html
30. Das, M., Lerner, S., Seigle, M.: ESP: Path-sensitive program verification in polynomial time. In: PLDI 2002 (2002)
31. De Sutter, B., De Bus, B., De Bosschere, K., Keyngnaert, P., Demoen, B.: On the static analysis of indirect control transfers in binaries. In: PDPTA 2000 (2000)
32. Debray, S.K., Linn, C., Andrews, G.R., Schwarz, B.: Stack analysis of x86 executables (2004), www.cs.arizona.edu/~debray/Publications/stack-analysis.pdf
33. Debray, S.K., Muth, R., Weippert, M.: Alias analysis of executable code. In: POPL 1998 (1998)
34. Van Emmerik, M.J.: Static Single Assignment for Decompilation. PhD thesis, School of Inf.Tech.and Elec.Eng., Univ.of Queensland, Brisbane, AU (May 2007)
35. Engler, D.R., Chelf, B., Chou, A., Hallem, S.: Checking system rules using system-specific, programmer-written compiler extensions. In: OSDI 2000 (2000)

36. Gopan, D., Reps, T.: Low-Level Library Analysis and Summarization. In: Damm, W., Hermanns, H. (eds.) CAV 2007. LNCS, vol. 4590, pp. 68–81. Springer, Heidelberg (2007)

37. Guo, B., Bridges, M.J., Triantafyllis, S., Ottoni, G., Raman, E., August, D.I.: Practical and accurate low-level pointer analysis. In: CGO 2005 (2005)

38. Havelund, K., Pressburger, T.: Model checking Java programs using Java PathFinder. STTT 2(4) (2000)

39. Henzinger, T.A., Jhala, R., Majumdar, R., Sutre, G.: Lazy abstraction. In: POPL 2002 (2002)

40. Howard, M.: Some bad news and some good news, MSDN, Microsoft Corp. (October 2002), http://msdn2.microsoft.com/en-us/library/ms972826.aspx

41. IDAPro disassembler, http://www.datarescue.com/idabase/

42. Jeannet, B., Loginov, A., Reps, T., Sagiv, M.: A Relational Approach to Interprocedural Shape Analysis. In: Giacobazzi, R. (ed.) SAS 2004. LNCS, vol. 3148, pp. 246–264. Springer, Heidelberg (2004)

43. Kidd, N., Reps, T., Melski, D., Lal, A.: WPDS++: A C++ library for weighted pushdown systems (2004), http://www.cs.wisc.edu/wpis/wpds++/

44. Kiss, Á., Lehotai, G., Jász, J., Gyimóthy, T.: Interprocedural static slicing of binary executables. In: SCAM 2003 (2003)

45. Knoop, J., Steffen, B.: The interprocedural coincidence theorem. In: Pfahler, P., Kastens, U. (eds.) CC 1992. LNCS, vol. 641, pp. 125–140. Springer, Heidelberg (1992)

46. Kruegel, C., Kirda, E., Mutz, D., Robertson, W., Vigna, G.: Automating mimicry attacks using static binary analysis. In: USENIX Sec. Symp. 2005 (2005)

47. Lal, A., Reps, T., Balakrishnan, G.: Extended Weighted Pushdown Systems. In: Etessami, K., Rajamani, S.K. (eds.) CAV 2005. LNCS, vol. 3576, pp. 434–448. Springer, Heidelberg (2005)

48. Larus, J.R., Schnarr, E.: EEL: Machine-independent executable editing. In: PLDI 1995 (1995)

49. Lim, J., Reps, T.: A system for generating static analyzers for machine instructions. In: Hendren, L. (ed.) CC 2008. LNCS, vol. 4959, pp. 36–52. Springer, Heidelberg (2008)

50. Myers, E.W.: Efficient applicative data types. In: POPL 1984 (1984)

51. Nita, M., Grossman, D., Chambers, C.: A theory of platform-dependent low-level software. In: POPL 2008 (2008)

52. PREfast with driver-specific rules, WHDC, Microsoft Corp. (October 2004), http://www.microsoft.com/whdc/devtools/tools/PREfast-drv.mspx

53. Ramalingam, G., Field, J., Tip, F.: Aggregate structure identification and its application to program analysis. In: POPL 1999 (1999)

54. Regehr, J., Reid, A., Webb, K.: Eliminating stack overflow by abstract interpretation. In: Trans. on Embedded Comp. Systs. 2005 (2005)

55. Reps, T., Balakrishnan, G., Lim, J.: Intermediate-representation recovery from low-level code. In: PEPM 2006 (2006)

56. Reps, T., Balakrishnan, G., Lim, J., Teitelbaum, T.: A Next-Generation Platform for Analyzing Executables. In: Yi, K. (ed.) APLAS 2005. LNCS, vol. 3780, pp. 212–229. Springer, Heidelberg (2005)

57. Schwoon, S.: Moped system, http://www.fmi.uni-stuttgart.de/szs/tools/moped/

58. Seidl, H., Fecht, C.: Interprocedural analyses: A comparison. In: JLP 2000 (2000)

59. Sharir, M., Pnueli, A.: Two approaches to interprocedural data flow analysis. In: Program Flow Analysis: Theory and Applications, Prentice-Hall, Englewood Cliffs (1981)
60. Wagner, D., Foster, J., Brewer, E., Aiken, A.: A first step towards automated detection of buffer overrun vulnerabilities. In: NDSS (February 2000)
61. Wall, D.W.: Systems for late code modification. In: Giegerich, R., Graham, S.L. (eds.) Code Generation – Concepts, Tools, Techniques. Springer, Heidelberg (1992)
62. C++ for kernel mode drivers: Pros and cons, WHDC web site (February 2007), http://www.microsoft.com/whdc/driver/kernel/KMcode.mspx
63. http://www.microsoft.com/whdc/devtools/ddk/default.mspx
64. Xu, Z., Miller, B., Reps, T.: Safety checking of machine code. In: PLDI 2000 (2000)
65. Xu, Z., Miller, B., Reps, T.: Typestate Checking of Machine Code. In: Sands, D. (ed.) ESOP 2001. LNCS, vol. 2028, Springer, Heidelberg (2001)
66. Zhang, J., Zhao, R., Pang, J.: Parameter and return-value analysis of binary executables. In: COMPSAC 2007 (2007)

# A System for Generating
# Static Analyzers for Machine Instructions[*]

Junghee Lim[1] and Thomas Reps[1,2]

[1] Comp. Sci. Dept.; Univ. of Wisconsin-Madison, WI; USA
[2] GrammaTech, Inc.; Ithaca, NY; USA
{junghee,reps}@cs.wisc.edu

**Abstract.** This paper describes the design and implementation of a language for specifying the semantics of an instruction set, along with a run-time system to support the static analysis of executables written in that instruction set. The work advances the state of the art by creating multiple analysis phases from a specification of the concrete operational semantics of the language to be analyzed.

## 1  Introduction

The problem of analyzing executables to recover information about their execution properties, especially for finding bugs, security vulnerabilities, or malicious code (e.g., back doors, time bombs, or logic bombs), has been receiving increased attention. However, much of this work has focused on *specialized* analyses to identify aliasing relationships [13], data dependences [2,8], targets of indirect calls [12], values of strings [7], bounds on stack height [20], and values of parameters and return values [24]. In contrast, Balakrishnan and Reps [3,5] developed ways to address all of these problems by means of an analysis that discovers an overapproximation of the set of states that can be reached at each point in the executable—where a *state* means *all* of the state: values of registers, flags, and the contents of memory. Moreover, their approach can be applied to stripped executables (i.e., neither source code nor symbol-table/debugging information is available).

Although their techniques, in principle, are language-independent, they were instantiated only for the Intel IA32 instruction set. Our motivation is to provide a systematic way of retargeting those analyses—and others yet to be created—to instruction sets other than IA32.

The situation that we face is actually typical of much work on program analysis: although the techniques described in the literature are, in principle, language-independent, implementations are often tied to a specific language or intermediate representation (IR). For high-level languages, the situation has been addressed by developing common intermediate languages, e.g., GCC's RTL, Microsoft's MSIL, etc. The situation is more serious for low-level instruction sets,

---

[*] Supported by ONR under grant N00014-01-1-0796 and by NSF under grants CCF-0540955 and CCF-0524051.

L. Hendren (Ed.): CC 2008, LNCS 4959, pp. 36–52, 2008.
© Springer-Verlag Berlin Heidelberg 2008

because of (i) instruction-set evolution over time (and the desire to have backward compatibility as word size increased from 8 bits to 64 bits), which has led to instruction sets with several hundred instructions, and (ii) a variety of architecture-specific features that are incompatible with other architectures.

To address these issues, we developed a language for describing the semantics of an instruction set, along with a run-time system to support the static analysis of executables written in that instruction set. Our work advances the state of the art by creating a system for automatically generating analysis components from a specification of the language to be analyzed. The system, called TSL (for "**T**ransformer **S**pecification **L**anguage"), has two classes of users: (1) instruction-set-specification (ISS) developers and (2) analysis developers. The former are involved in specifying the semantics of different instruction sets; the latter are involved in extending the analysis framework. In designing TSL, we were guided by the following principles:

 - There should be a formal language for specifying the semantics of the language to be analyzed. Moreover, ISS developers should specify only the abstract syntax and a concrete operational semantics of the language to be analyzed—each analyzer should be generated automatically from this specification.
 - Concrete syntactic issues—including (i) decoding (machine code to abstract syntax), (ii) encoding (abstract syntax to machine code), (iii) parsing assembly (assembly code to abstract syntax), and (iv) assembly pretty-printing (abstract syntax to assembly code)—should be handled separately from the abstract syntax and concrete semantics.[1]
 - There should be a clean interface for analysis developers to specify the abstract semantics for each analysis. An abstract semantics consists of an *interpretation*: an abstract domain and a set of abstract operators (i.e., for the operations of TSL).
 - The abstract semantics for each analysis should be separated from the languages to be analyzed so that one does not need to specify multiple versions of an abstract semantics for multiple languages.

Each of these objectives has been achieved in the TSL system: The TSL system translates the TSL specification of each instruction set to a common intermediate representation (CIR) that can be used to create multiple analyzers (§2). Each analyzer is specified at the level of the meta-language (i.e., by reinterpreting the operations of TSL), which—by extension to TSL expressions and functions—provides the desired reinterpretation of the instructions of an instruction set (§3).

Other notable aspects of our work include

**1. Support for Multiple Analysis Types.**
 - Classical worklist-based value-propagation analyses.
 - Transformer-composition analyses [11,22], which are particularly useful for context-sensitive interprocedural analysis, and for relational analyses.

---

[1] The translation of the concrete syntaxes to and from abstract syntax is handled by a generator tool that is separate from TSL, and will not be discussed in this paper.

– Unification-based analyses for flow-insensitive interprocedural analysis.

In addition, an emulator (for the concrete semantics) is also supported.

**2. *Implemented Analyses.*** These mechanisms have been instantiated for a number of specific analyses that are useful for analyzing low-level code, including value-set analysis [3,5] (§3.1), def-use analysis (for memory, registers, and flags) (§3.2), aggregate structure identification [6] (§3.3), and generation of symbolic expressions for an instruction's semantics (§3.4).

**3. *Established Applicability.*** The capabilities of our approach have been demonstrated by writing specifications for IA32 and PowerPC32. These are nearly complete specifications of the languages, and include such features as (1) aliasing among 8-, 16-, and 32-bit registers, e.g., al, ah, ax, and eax (for IA32), (2) endianness, (3) issues arising due to bounded-word-size arithmetic (overflow/underflow, carry/borrow, shifting, rotation, etc.), and (4) setting of condition codes (and their subsequent interpretation at jump instructions).

The abstract transformers for these analyses that are created from the IA32 TSL specifications have been put together to create a system that essentially duplicates CodeSurfer/x86 [4]. A similar system for PowerPC32 is under construction. (The TSL-generated components are in place; only a few mundane infrastructure components are lacking.) We have also experimented with sufficiently complex features of other low-level languages (e.g., register windows for Sun SPARC and conditional execution of instructions for ARM) to know that they fit our specification and implementation models.

There are many specification languages for instruction sets and many purposes for which they have been used. In our work, we needed a mechanism to create abstract interpreters of instruction-set specifications. There are (at least) four issues that arise: during the abstract interpretation of each transformer, the abstract interpreter must be able to (i) execute over abstract states, (ii) execute both branches of a conditional expression, (iii) compare abstract states and terminate abstract execution when a fixed point is reached, and (iv) apply widening operators, if necessary, to ensure termination. As far as we know, TSL is the first system with an instruction-set-specification language and support for such mechanisms.

Although this paper only discusses the application of TSL to low-level instruction sets, we believe that only small extensions would be needed to be able to apply TSL to source-code languages (i.e., to create language-independent analyzers for source-level IRs), as well as bytecode. The main obstacle is that the concrete semantics of a source-code language generally uses an execution state based on a stack of variable-to-value (or variable-to-location, location-to-value) maps. For a low-level language, the state incorporates an address-based memory model, for which the TSL language provides appropriate primitives.

The remainder of the paper is organized as follows: §2 introduces TSL and the capabilities of the system. §3 explains how CIR is instantiated to create an analyzer for a specific analysis component. §4 describes quirky features of several instruction sets, and discusses how those features are handled in TSL. §5 discusses related work.

## 2   Overview of the TSL System

This section provides an overview of the TSL system. We discuss how three analysis components are created automatically from a TSL specification, using a fragment of the IA32 instruction set to illustrate the process.

### 2.1   TSL from an ISS Developer's Standpoint

Fig. 1 shows part of a specification of the IA32 instruction set taken from the manual [1]. The specification is only semi-formal: it uses a mixture of English and pseudo-code.

| | |
|---|---|
| General Purpose Registers: | ADD   r/m32,r32; Add r32 to r/m32 |
| EAX,EBX,ECX,EDX,ESP,EBP,ESI,EDI,EIP | ADD   r/m16,r16; Add r16 to r/m16 . . . |
| Each of these registers also has 16- or 8-bit subset names. | Operation: DEST ← DEST + SRC; |
| Addressing Modes: [sreg:][offset][([base][,index][,scale])] | Flags Affected: The OF,SF,ZF,AF,CF, and |
| EFLAGS register: ZF,SF,OF,CF,AF,PF, . . . | PF flags are set according to the result. |

**Fig. 1.** A part of the Intel manual's specification of IA32's ADD instruction

Our work is based on completely formal specifications, which are written in a language that we designed (TSL). TSL is a strongly typed, first-order functional language with a datatype-definition mechanism for defining recursive datatypes, plus deconstruction by means of pattern matching. Fig. 2 shows the part of the TSL specification that corresponds to Fig. 1. Much of what an ISS developer writes is similar to writing an interpreter for an instruction set in first-order ML [14]. An ISS developer specifies the abstract syntax grammar by defining the constructors for a language of instructions (lines 2–10), a concrete-state type (lines 13–15), and the concrete semantics of each instruction (lines 23–33).

TSL provides 5 basetypes: INT8, INT16, INT32, INT64, and BOOL. TSL supports arithmetic/logical operators $(+, -, *, /, !, \&\&, ||, \text{xor})$, bit-manipulation operators $(\sim, \&, |, \hat{}, \ll, \gg, \text{right-rotate, left-rotate})$, relational operators $(<, <=, >, >=, ==, !=)$, and a conditional-expression operator (? :).

TSL also provides several map-basetypes: MEMMAP32_8_LE, MEMMAP32_16_LE, VAR32MAP, VAR16MAP, VAR8MAP, VARBOOLMAP, etc. MEMMAP32_8_LE maps from 32-bit values (addresses) to 8-bit values, VAR32MAP from var32 to 32-bit values, VARBOOLMAP from var_bool to Boolean values, and so forth. Tab. 1 shows the list of some of the TSL *access/update* functions. Each *access* function takes a map (e.g., MEMMAP32_8_LE, VAR32MAP, VARBOOLMAP, etc.) and an appropriate key (e.g., INT32, var32, var_bool, etc.), and returns the value that corresponds to the key. Each *update* function takes a map, a key, and a value, and returns the updated map. The *access/update* functions for MEMMAP32_8_LE implement the little-endian storage convention.

Each specification must define several reserved (but user-defined) types: var64, var32, var16, var8, and var_bool, which represent storage components of 64-bit, 32-bit, 16-bit, 8-bit, and Boolean types, respectively; instruction; state; as well as the

```
[1]  // User-defined abstract syntax
[2]  reg32: EAX() | EBX() | . . . ;
[3]  flag: ZF() | SF() | . . . ;
[4]  operand32: Indirect32(reg32 reg32 INT8 INT32)
[5]    | DirectReg32(reg32)| Immediate32(INT32) |...;
[6]  operand16: . . . ;
[7]   . . .
[8]  instruction
[9]    : ADD32_32(operand32 operand32)
[10]   | ADD16_16(operand16 operand16) | . . . ;
[11] var32: Reg32(reg32);
[12] var_bool: Flag(flag);
[13] state: State(MEMMAP32_8_LE  // memory-map
[14]              VAR32MAP        // register-map
[15]              VARBOOLMAP);    // flag-map
[16] // User-defined functions
[17] INT32 interpOp(state S, operand32 I) { . . . }
[18] state updateFlag(state S, . . . ) { . . . }
[19] state updateState(state S, . . . ) {
[20]   with(S) (
[21]     State(mem,regs,flags): . . .
[22] }
[23] state interpInstr(instruction I, state S) {
[24]   with(I) (
[25]     ADD32_32(dstOp, srcOp):
[26]     let dstVal = interpOp(S, dstOp);
[27]         srcVal = interpOp(S, srcOp);
[28]         res = dstVal + srcVal;
[29]         S2 = updateFlag(S, dstVal, srcVal, res);
[30]     in ( updateState( S2, dstOp, res ) ),
[31]       . . .
[32]   )
[33] }
```

```
[1]  template <typename INTERP>
[2]  class CIR {
[3]    class reg32 { . . . };
[4]    class EAX: public reg32 { . . . };
[5]    . . .
[6]    class operand32 { . . . };
[7]    class Indirect32: public operand32 { . . . };
[8]    . . .
[9]    class instruction { . . . };
[10]   class ADD32_32: public instruction { . . .
[11]     enum  TSL_ID id;
[12]     operand32 op1;
[13]     operand32 op2;
[14]   };
[15]   . . .
[16]   class state { . . . };
[17]   class State: public state { . . .
[18]     INTERP::MEMMAP32_8_LE  mapMap;
[19]     INTERP::VAR32MAP        var32Map;
[20]     INTERP::VARBOOLMAP      varBoolMap;
[21]   };
[22]   . . .
[23]   static state interpInstr(instruction I, state S) {
[24]     state ans;
[25]     switch(I.id) {
[26]       case ID_ADD32_32: {
[27]         operand32 dstOp = I.op1;
[28]         operand32 srcOp = I.op2;
[29]         INTERP::INT32 dstVal = interpOp(S, dstOp);
[30]         INTERP::INT32 srcVal = interpOp(S, srcOp);
[31]         INTERP::INT32 res = INTERP::Add(dstVal,srcVal);
[32]         state S2 = updateFlag(S, dstVal, srcVal, res);
[33]         ans = updateState(S2, dstOp, res);
[34]       } break;
[35]       . . .
[36]     }
[37]     return ans;
[38]   }
[39]]};
```

**Fig. 2.** A part of the TSL specification of IA32 concrete semantics, which corresponds to the specification of ADD from the IA32 manual. Reserved types and function names are underlined.

**Fig. 3.** A part of the CIR generated from Fig. 2

reserved function interpInstr. (These are underlined in Fig. 2.) These form part of the API available to *analysis engines* that use the TSL-generated transformers (see §3). The reserved types are used as an interface between the CIR and analysis-domain implementations.

The definition of types and constructors on lines 2–10 of Fig. 2 is an abstract-syntax grammar for IA32. The definitions for var32 and var_bool wrap the user-defined types reg32 and flag, respectively. Type reg32 consists of nullary constructors for IA32 registers, such as EAX() and EBX(); flag consists of nullary constructors for the IA32 condition codes, such as ZF() and SF(). Lines 4–7 define types and constructors to represent the various kinds of operands that IA32 supports, i.e., various sizes of immediate, direct register, and indirect memory operands. The reserved (but user-defined) type instruction consists of user-defined constructors for each instruction, such as ADD32_32 and ADD16_16, which represent instructions with different operand sizes.

**Table 1.** *Access/Update* functions

| |
|---|
| MEMMAP32_8_LE MemUpdate_32_8_LE_32(MEMMAP32_8_LE *memmap*, INT32 *key*, INT32 *v*); |
| INT32 MemAccess_32_8_LE_32(VAR32MAP *mapmap*, INT32 *key*); |
| VAR32MAP Var32Update(VAR32MAP *var32Map*, var32 *key*, INT32 *v*); |
| INT32 Var32Access(VAR32MAP *var32Map*, var32 *key*); |
| VARBOOLMAP VarBoolUpdate(VARBOOLMAP *varBoolMap*, var_bool *key*, BOOL *v*); |
| BOOL VarBoolAccess(VARBOOLMAP *varBoolMap*, var_bool *key*); |

The type state specifies the structure of the execution state. The state for IA32 is defined on lines 13–15 of Fig. 2 to consist of a memory-map, a register-map, and a flag-map. The *concrete semantics* is specified by writing a function named interpInstr (see lines 23–33 of Fig. 2), which maps an instruction and a state to a state.

## 2.2 Common Intermediate Representation (CIR)

Fig. 3 shows part of the TSL CIR automatically generated from Fig. 2. Each generated CIR is *specific* to a given instruction-set specification, but *common* (whence the name CIR) across generated analyses. Each generated CIR is a template class that takes as input INTERP, an abstract domain for an analysis (lines 1–2). The user-defined abstract syntax (lines 2–10 of Fig. 2) is translated to a set of C++ abstract-syntax classes (lines 3–15 of Fig. 3). The user-defined types, such as reg32, operand32, and instruction, are translated to abstract C++ classes, and the constructors, such as EAX(), Indirect32(_,_,_,_), and ADD32_32(_,_), are subclasses of the appropriate parent abstract C++ class. Each user-defined function is translated to a static CIR function.

Each TSL basetype and basetype-operator is prepended with the template parameter name INTERP; INTERP is supplied for each analysis by an analysis designer. The with expression and the pattern matching on lines 24–25 of Fig. 2 are translated to switch statements in C++[2] (lines 25–36 in Fig. 3). The function calls for obtaining the values of the two operands (lines 26–27 in Fig. 2) correspond to the C++ code on lines 29–30 in Fig. 3. The TSL basetype-operator + on line 28 in Fig. 2 is translated to the CIR member function INTERP::Add, as shown on line 31 in Fig. 3. The function calls for updating the state (lines 29–30 in Fig. 2) are translated into C++ code (lines 32–33 in Fig. 3).

## 2.3 TSL from an Analysis Developer's Standpoint

The generated CIR is instantiated for an analysis by defining (in C++) an *interpretation*: a representation class for each TSL basetype, and implementations of each TSL basetype-operator and built-in function. Tab. 2 shows the implementations of primitives for three selected analyses: value-set analysis (VSA, see §3.1), def-use analysis (DUA, see §3.2), and quantifier-free bit-vector semantics (QFBV, see §3.4).

---

[2] The TSL front end performs *with-normalization*, which transforms all multi-level with expressions to use only one-level patterns, via the pattern-compilation algorithm from [18,23].

**Table 2.** Parts of the declarations of the basetypes, basetype-operators, and map-access/update functions for three analyses

| VSA | DUA | QFBV |
|---|---|---|
| [1] class VSA_INTERP { | [1] class DUA_INTERP { | [1] class QFBV_INTERP { |
| [2]   // basetype | [2]   // basetype | [2]   // basetype |
| [3]   typedef ValueSet32 INT32; | [3]   typedef UseSet INT32; | [3]   typedef QFBVTerm32 INT32; |
| [4]   . . . | [4]   . . . | [4]   . . . |
| [5]   // basetype-operators | [5]   // basetype-operators | [5]   // basetype-operators |
| [6]   INT32 Add(INT32 a, INT32 b) { | [6]   INT32 Add(INT32 a, INT32 b) { | [6]   INT32 Add(INT32 a, INT32 b) { |
| [7]     return a.addValueSet(b); | [7]     return a.Union(b); | [7]     return QFBVPlus32(a, b); |
| [8]   } | [8]   } | [8]   } |
| [9]   . . . | [9]   . . . | [9]   . . . |
| [10]   // map-basetypes | [10]   // map-basetypes | [10]   // map-basetypes |
| [11]   typedef Dict<var32,INT32> | [11]   typedef Dict<var32,INT32> | [11]   typedef Dict<var32,INT32> |
| [12]       VAR32MAP; | [12]       VAR32MAP; | [12]       VAR32MAP; |
| [13]   . . . | [13]   . . . | [13]   . . . |
| [14]   // map-access/update functions | [14]   // map-access/update functions | [14]   // map-access/update functions |
| [15]   INT32 Var32Access( | [15]   INT32 Var32Access( | [15]   INT32 Var32Access( |
| [16]     VAR32MAP m, var32 k) { | [16]     VAR32MAP m, var32 k) { | [16]     VAR32MAP m, var32 k) { |
| [17]       return m.Lookup(k); | [17]       return m.Lookup(k); | [17]       return m.Lookup(k); |
| [18]   } | [18]   } | [18]   } |
| [19]   VAR32MAP | [19]   VAR32MAP | [19]   VAR32MAP |
| [20]   Var32Update( VAR32MAP m, | [20]   Var32Update( VAR32MAP m, | [20]   Var32Update( VAR32MAP m, |
| [21]     var32 k, INT32 v) { | [21]     var32 k, INT32 v) { | [21]     var32 k, INT32 v) { |
| [22]       return m.Insert(k, v); | [22]       return m.Insert(k,v); | [22]       return m.Insert(k, v); |
| [23]   } | [23]   } | [23]   } |
| [24]   . . . | [24]   . . . | [24]   . . . |
| [25] }; | [25] }; | [25] }; |

Each interpretation defines an abstract domain. For example, line 3 of each column defines the abstract-domain class for INT32: ValueSet32, UseSet, and QFB-VTerm32. To define an interpretation, one needs to define 42 basetype operators, most of which have four variants, for 8-, 16-, 32-, and 64-bit integers, as well as 12 map *access/update* operations. Each abstract domain is also required to contain a set of reserved functions, such as *join*, *meet*, and *widen*, which forms an additional part of the API available to analysis engines that use TSL-generated transformers (see §3).

## 2.4   Generated Transformers

The TSL system provides considerable leverage for implementing static-analysis tools and experimenting with new ones. New static-analyses are easily implemented: each static-analysis component is created via abstract interpretation of the TSL code that defines the concrete semantics of the instruction set. In particular, all abstract interpretation is performed at the *meta-level*: an analysis designer adds a new analysis component to the TSL system by (i) redefining the TSL basetypes, and (ii) providing a set of alternative interpretations for the primitive operations on basetypes. This implicitly defines an alternative interpretation of each expression and function in an instruction-set's concrete operational semantics, and thereby yields an abstract semantics for an instruction set from its concrete operational semantics.

**Table 3.** Transformers generated by the TSL system

| Analysis | Generated Transformers for "add ebx,eax" |
|---|---|
| 1.VSA | $\lambda S.S[\text{ebx} \mapsto S(\text{ebx}) +^{vsa} S(\text{eax})]\ [\text{ZF} \mapsto (S(\text{ebx}) +^{vsa} S(\text{eax}) = 0)]\ [\textit{more flag updates}]$ |
| 2.DUA | $[\ \text{ebx} \mapsto \{\text{eax, ebx}\},\ \text{ZF} \mapsto \{\text{eax, ebx}\},\ \dots\ ]$ |
| 3.QFBV | $(\text{ebx}' = \text{ebx} +^{32} \text{eax}) \wedge (\text{ZF}' \Leftrightarrow (\text{ebx} +^{32}\text{eax} = 0)) \wedge (\text{SF}' \Leftrightarrow (\text{ebx} +^{32}\text{eax} < 0)) \wedge \dots$ |

Consider the instruction "add ebx,eax", which causes the sum of the values of the 32-bit registers ebx and eax to be assigned into ebx. When Fig. 3 is instantiated with the three interpretations from Tab. 2, lines 23–33 of Fig. 2 implement the three transformers presented (using mathematical notation) in Tab. 3.

## 2.5   Measures of Success

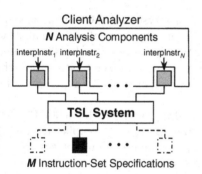

**Fig. 4.** The interaction between the TSL system and a client analyzer. The grey boxes represent TSL-generated analysis components.

The TSL system provides two dimensions of parameterizability: different instruction sets and different analyses. Each ISS developer specifies an instruction-set semantics, and each analysis developer defines an abstract domain for a desired analysis by giving an interpretation (i.e., the implementations of TSL basetypes, basetype-operators, and *access/update* functions). Given the inputs from these two classes of users, the TSL system automatically generates an analysis component. Note that the work that an analysis developer performs is TSL-specific but *independent* of each language to be analyzed; from the interpretation that defines an analysis, the abstract transformers for that analysis can be generated automatically for *every* instruction set for which one has a TSL specification. Thus, to create $M \times N$ analysis components, the TSL system only requires $M$ specifications of the concrete semantics of instruction sets, and $N$ analysis implementations (Fig. 4), i.e., $M + N$ inputs to obtain $M \times N$ analysis-component implementations.

One measure of success is demonstrated by our effort to use TSL to recreate the analysis components used in CodeSurfer/x86 [4]. We estimate that the task of writing transformers (for eight analysis phases used in CodeSurfer/x86) consumed about 20 man-months; in contrast, we have invested a total of about 1 man-month to write the C++ code for the set of TSL interpretations that are used to generate the replacement components. To this, one should add 10–20 man-days to write the TSL specification for IA32: the current specification for IA32 consists of 2,834 (non-comment, non-blank) lines of TSL.

Because each analysis is defined at the meta-level (i.e., by providing an interpretation for the collection of TSL primitives), abstract transformers for a given analysis can be created automatically for *each* instruction set that is specified in TSL. For instance, from the PowerPC32 specification (1,370 non-comment, non-blank lines, which took approximately 4 days to write), we were immediately able to generate PowerPC32-specific versions of *all* of the analysis components that had been developed for the IA32 instruction set.

It is natural to ask how the TSL-generated analyses perform compared to their hand-coded counterparts. Due to the nature of the transformers used in one of the analyses that we implemented (affine-relation analysis (ARA) [17]), it was possible to write an algorithm to compare the TSL-generated ARA transformers with the hand-coded ARA transformers that were incorporated in CodeSurfer/x86. On a corpus of 542 instruction instances that covered various opcodes, addressing modes, and operand sizes, we found that the TSL-generated transformers were equivalent in 324 cases and *more precise* than the hand-coded transformers in the remaining 218 cases.[3]

In addition to leverage and thoroughness, for a system like CodeSurfer/x86—which uses multiple analysis phases—automating the process of creating abstract transformers ensures *semantic consistency*; that is, because analysis implementations are generated from a *single* specification of the concrete semantics, this guarantees that a *consistent* view of the concrete semantics is adopted by all of the analyses used in the system.

It takes approximately 8 seconds (on an Intel Pentium 4 with a 3.00GHz CPU and 2GB of memory, running Centos 4) for the TSL (cross-)compiler to compile the IA32 specification to C++, followed by approximately 20 minutes wall-clock time (on an Intel Pentium 4 with a 1.73GHz CPU and 1.5GB of memory, running Windows XP) to compile the generated C++.

## 3    Generation of Static Analyzers

In this section, we explain how various analyses are created using our system, and illustrate this process with some specific analysis examples.

---

[3] For 87 cases, this was because in rethinking how the ARA abstraction could be encoded using TSL mechanisms, we discovered an easy way to extend [17] to retain some information for 8-, 16-, and 64-bit operations. (In principle, these could have been incorporated into the hand-coded version, too.)

The other 131 cases of improvement can be ascribed to "fatigue factor" on the part of the human programmer: the hand-coded versions adopted a pessimistic view and just treated certain instructions as always assigning an unknown value to the registers that they affected, regardless of the values of the arguments. Because the TSL-generated transformers are based on the ARA interpretation's definitions of the TSL basetype-operators, the TSL-generated transformers were more thorough: a basetype-operator's definition in an interpretation is used in *all* places that the operator arises in the specification of the instruction set's concrete semantics.

As illustrated in Fig. 4, a version of the interface function interpInstr is created for each analysis. Each analysis engine calls interpInstr at appropriate moments to obtain a transformer for an instruction being processed. Analysis engines can be categorized as follows:

- *Worklist-Based Value Propagation (or Transformer Application)* [TA]. These perform classical worklist-based value propagation in which generated transformers are applied, and changes are propagated to successors/predecessors (depending on propagation direction). Context-sensitivity in such analyses is supported by means of the call-string approach [22]. VSA uses this kind of analysis engine (§3.1).
- *Transformer Composition* [TC]. These generally perform flow-sensitive, context-sensitive interprocedural analysis. DUA (§3.2) uses this kind of analysis engine.
- *Unification-Based Analyses* [UB]. These perform flow-insensitive interprocedural analysis. ASI (§3.3) uses this kind of analysis engine.

For each analysis, the CIR is instantiated with an interpretation by an analysis developer. This mechanism provides wide flexibility in how one can couple the system to an external package. One approach, used with VSA, is that the analysis engine (written in C++) calls interpInstr directly. In this case, the instantiated CIR serves as a *transformer evaluator*: interpInstr is prepared to receive an instruction and an abstract state, and return an abstract state. Another approach, used in DUA, is employed when interfacing to an analysis component that has its own input language for specifying abstract transformers. In this case, the instantiated CIR serves as a *transformer generator*: interpInstr is prepared to receive an instruction and a default abstract state[4] and return a transformer specification in the analysis component's input language.

The following subsections discuss how the CIR is instantiated for various analyses.

### 3.1  Creation of a TA Transformer Evaluator for VSA

VSA is a combined numeric-analysis and pointer-analysis algorithm that determines a safe approximation of the set of numeric values and addresses that each register and memory location holds at each program point [5]. A *memory-region* is an abstract quantity that represents all runtime activation records of a procedure. To represent a set of numeric values and addresses, VSA uses *value-sets*, where a value-set is a map from memory regions to strided intervals. A strided interval consists of a lower bound $lb$, a stride $s$, and an upper bound $lb + ks$, and represents the set of numbers $\{lb, \ lb + s, \ lb + 2s, \ ..., \ lb + ks\}$ [21].

***The Interpretation of Basetypes and Basetype-Operators.*** The abstract domain for the integer basetypes is a value-set. The abstract domain for BOOL

---

[4] In the case of transformer generation for a TC analyzer, the default state is the identity function.

is Bool3 ({FALSE, MAYBE, TRUE}), where MAYBE means "may be FALSE or may be TRUE". The operators on these domains are described in detail in [21].

***The Interpretation of Map-Basetypes and Access/Update Functions.***
The abstract domain for memory maps (MEMMAP32_8_LE, MEMMAP32_16_LE, etc.) is a dictionary that maps each abstract memory-location (i.e., the abstraction of INT32) to a value-set. The abstract domain for register maps (VAR32MAP, VAR16MAP, etc.) is a dictionary that maps each variable (var32, var16, etc.) to a value-set. The abstract domain for flag maps (VARBOOLMAP) is a dictionary that maps a var_bool to a Bool3. The *access/update* functions access or update these dictionaries.

VSA uses this transformer evaluator to create an output abstract state, given an instruction and an input abstract state. For example, row 1 of Tab. 3 shows the generated VSA transformer for the instruction "add ebx, eax". The VSA evaluator returns a new abstract state in which ebx is updated with the sum of the values of ebx and eax from the input abstract state and the flags are updated appropriately.

## 3.2   Def-Use Analysis (DUA)

*Def-Use* analysis finds the relationships between *definitions* (*defs*) and *uses* of state components (registers, flags, and memory-locations) for each instruction.

***The Interpretation of Basetypes and Basetype-Operators.*** The abstract domain for the basetypes is a set of *uses* (i.e., abstractions of the map-keys in states, such as registers, flags, and abstract memory locations), and the operators on this domain perform a set union of their arguments' sets.

***The Interpretation of Map-Basetypes and Access/Update Functions.***
The abstract domains of the maps for DUA are dictionaries that map each *def* to a set of *uses*. Each *access* function returns the set of *uses* associated with the key parameter. Each *update* function $update(D, k, S)$, where $D$ is a dictionary, $k$ is one of the state components, and $S$ is a set of *uses*, returns an updated dictionary $D[k \mapsto (D(k) \cup S)]$ (or $D[k \mapsto S]$ if a strong update is sound).

The DUA results (e.g., row 2 of Tab. 3) are used to create transformers for several additional analyses, such as GMOD analysis [10], which is an analysis to find modified variables for each function $f$ (including variables modified by functions transitively called from $f$) and live-flag analysis, which is used in our version of VSA to perform trace-splitting/collapsing (see §3.4).

## 3.3   Creation of a UB Transformer Generator for ASI

ASI is a unification-based, flow-insensitive algorithm to identify the structure of aggregates in a program [6]. For each instruction, the transformer generator generates a set of ASI commands, each of which is either a command to *split* a memory region or a command to *unify* some portions of memory (and/or some registers). At analysis time, a client analyzer typically applies the transformer generator to each of the instructions in the program, and then feeds the resulting set of ASI commands to an ASI solver to refine the memory regions.

***The Interpretation of Basetypes and Basetype-Operators.*** The abstract domain for the basetypes is a set of *dataref*s, where a *dataref* is an access on specific bytes of a register or memory. The arithmetic, logical, and bit-vector operations tag *dataref*s as *non-unifiable dataref*s, which means that they will only be used to generate *splits*.

***The Interpretation of Map-Basetypes and Access/Update Functions.*** The abstract domain of the maps for ASI is a set of *splits* and *unifications*. The *access* functions generate a set of *dataref*s associated with a memory location or register. The *update* functions create a set of *unifications* or *splits* according to the *dataref*s of the data argument.

For example, for the instruction "mov [ebx],eax", when ebx holds the abstract address $AR\_foo-12$, where $AR\_foo$ is the memory-region for the activation records of procedure *foo*, the ASI transformer generator emits one ASI *unification* command "$AR\_foo[-12{:}-9] :={:} eax[0{:}3]$".

## 3.4   Quantifier-Free Bit-Vector (QFBV) Semantics

QFBV semantics provides a way to obtain a symbolic representation—as a formula in first-order quantifier-free bit-vector logic—of an instruction's semantics.

***The Interpretation of Basetypes and Basetype-Operators.*** The abstract domain for the integer basetypes is a term, and each operator on it constructs a term that represents the operation. The abstract domain for BOOL is a formula, and each operator on it constructs a formula that represents the operation.

***The Interpretation of Map-Basetypes and Access/Update Functions.*** The abstract domain for the state components is a dictionary that maps a storage component to a term (or a formula in the case of VARBOOLMAP). The *access/update* functions retrieve from and update the dictionaries, respectively.

QFBV semantics is useful for a variety of purposes. One use is as auxiliary information in an abstract interpreter, such as the VSA analysis engine, to provide more precise abstract interpretation of branches in low-level code. The issue is that many instruction sets provide separate instructions for (i) setting flags (based on some condition that is tested) and (ii) branching according to the values held by flags.

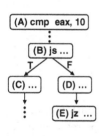

To address this problem, we use a *trace-splitting/collapsing* scheme [16]. The VSA analysis engine partitions the state at each flag-setting instruction based on live-flag information (which is obtained from an analysis that uses the DUA transformers); a semantic reduction [11] is performed on the split VSA states with respect to a formula obtained from the transformer generated by the QFBV semantics. The set of VSA states that result are propagated to appropriate successors at the branch instruction that uses the flags.

The cmp instruction shown above (A), which is a flag-setting instruction, has SF and ZF as live flags because those flags are used at the branch instructions js (B) and jz (E): js and jz jump according to SF and ZF, respectively. After interpretation of (A), the state S is split into four states, $S_1$, $S_2$, $S_3$, and $S_4$,

which are reduced with respect to the formulas $\varphi_1$: (eax $- 10 < 0$) associated
with SF, and $\varphi_2$: (eax $- 10 == 0$) associated with ZF.

$$S_1 := S[SF\mapsto T] [ZF \mapsto T] [eax \mapsto reduce(S(eax), \varphi_1 \wedge \varphi_2)]$$
$$S_2 := S[SF\mapsto T] [ZF \mapsto F] [eax \mapsto reduce(S(eax), \varphi_1 \wedge \neg\varphi_2)]$$
$$S_3 := S[SF\mapsto F] [ZF \mapsto T] [eax \mapsto reduce(S(eax), \neg\varphi_1 \wedge \varphi_2)]$$
$$S_4 := S[SF\mapsto F] [ZF \mapsto F] [eax \mapsto reduce(S(eax), \neg\varphi_1 \wedge \neg\varphi_2)]$$

Because $\varphi_1 \wedge \varphi_2$ is not satisfiable, $S_1$ becomes $\bot$. State $S_2$ is propagated to the
true branch of js (i.e., just before (C)), and $S_3$ and $S_4$ to the false branch (i.e., just
before (D)). Because no flags are live just before (C), the splitting mechanism
maintains just a single state, and thus all states propagated to (C)—here there
is just one—are collapsed to a single abstract state. Because ZF is still live until
(E), the states $S_3$ and $S_4$ are maintained as separate abstract states at (D).

## 3.5   Paired Semantics

Our system allows easy instantiations of *reduced products* [11] by means of *paired
semantics*. The TSL system provides a template for paired semantics as shown
in Fig. 5(a).

```
     [1]  template <typename INTERP1, typename INTERP2>
     [2]  class PairedSemantics {
     [3]    typedef PairedBaseType<INTERP1::INT32, INTERP2::INT32> INT32;
     [4]    . . .
(a)  [5]    INT32 MemAccess_32_8_LE_32(MEMMAP32_8_LE mem, INT32 addr) {
     [6]      return INT32(INTERP1::MemAccess_32_8_LE_32(mem.GetFirst(), addr.GetFirst()),
     [7]                   INTERP2::MemAccess_32_8_LE_32(mem.GetSecond(), addr.GetSecond()));
     [8]    }
     [9]  };
     [1]  typedef PairedSemantics<VSA_INTERP, DUA_INTERP> DUA;
     [2]  template<> DUA::INT32 DUA::MemAccess_32_8_LE_32(
     [3]                          DUA::MEMMAP32_8_LE mem, DUA::INT32 addr) {
     [4]    DUA::INTERP1::MEMMAP32_8_LE memory1 = mem.GetFirst();
     [5]    DUA::INTERP2::MEMMAP32_8_LE memory2 = mem.GetSecond();
(b)  [6]    DUA::INTERP1::INT32 addr1 = addr.GetFirst();
     [7]    DUA::INTERP2::INT32 addr2 = addr.GetSecond();
     [8]    DUA::INT32 answer = interact(mem1, mem2, addr1, addr2);
     [9]    return answer;
     [10]}
```

**Fig. 5.** (a) A part of the template class for paired semantics; (b) an example of C++
explicit template specialization to create a reduced product

The CIR is instantiated with a *paired* semantic domain defined with two interpretations, INTERP1 and INTERP2 (each of which may itself be a paired semantic
domain), as shown on line 1 of Fig. 5(b). The communication between interpretations may take place in basetype-operators or *access/update* functions; Fig. 5(b)
is an example of the latter. The two components of the paired-semantics values
are deconstructed on lines 4–7 of Fig. 5(b), and the individual INTERP1 and

INTERP2 components from *both* inputs can be used (as illustrated by the call to *interact* on line 8 of Fig. 5(b)) to create the paired-semantics return value, answer. Such overridings of basetype-operators and *access/update* functions are done by C++ explicit specialization of members of class templates (this is specified in C++ by "template<>"; see line 2 of Fig. 5(b)).

We also found this method of CIR instantiation to be useful to perform a form of reduced product when analyses are split into multiple phases, as in a tool like CodeSurfer/x86. CodeSurfer/x86 carries out many analysis phases, and the application of its sequence of basic analysis phases is itself iterated. On each round, CodeSurfer/x86 applies a sequence of analyses: VSA, DUA, and several others. VSA is the primary workhorse, and it is often desirable for the information acquired by VSA to influence the outcomes of other analysis phases by pairing the VSA interpretation with another interpretation.

# 4   Instruction Sets

In this section, we discuss the quirky characteristics of some instruction sets, and various ways these can be handled in TSL.

## 4.1   IA32

To provide compatibility with 16-bit and 8-bit versions of the instruction set, IA32 provides overlapping register names, such as AX (the lower 16-bits of EAX), AL (the lower 8-bits of AX), and AH (the upper 8-bits of AX). There are two possible ways to specify this feature in TSL. One is to keep three separate maps for 32-bit registers, 16-bit registers, and 8-bit registers, and specify that updates to any one of the maps affect the other two maps. Another is to keep one 32-bit map for registers, and obtain the value of a 16-bit or 8-bit register by masking the value of the 32-bit register. (The former can yield more precise VSA results.)

Another characteristic to note is that IA32 keeps condition codes in a special register, called EFLAGS.[5] One way to specify this feature is to declare "reg32: Eflags();", and make every flag manipulation fetch the bit value from an appropriate bit position of the value associated with Eflags in the register-map. Another way is to have symbolic flags, as in our examples, and have every manipulation of EFLAGS affect the individual flags.

## 4.2   ARM

Almost all ARM instructions contain a condition field that allows an instruction to be executed conditionally, depending on condition-code flags. This feature reduces branch overhead and compensates for the lack of a branch predictor. However, it may worsen the precision of an abstract analysis because in most instructions' specifications, the abstract values from two arms of a TSL conditional expression would be joined.

---

[5] Many other instruction sets, such as SPARC, PowerPC32, and ARM, also use a special register to store condition codes.

For example, MOVEQ is one of ARM's conditional instructions; if the flag EQ is true when the instruction starts executing, it executes normally; otherwise, the instruction does nothing. Fig. 6 shows the specification of the instruction in TSL. In many abstract semantics, the conditional expression "*cond* ? *a* : *b*" will be interpreted as a join of the original register map *b* and the updated map *a*, i.e., *join(a,b)*. Consequently,

```
[1]  MOVEQ(destReg, srcOprnd):
[2]    let cond = VarBoolAccess(
[3]               flagMap, EQ());
[4]      src = interpOperand(
[5]               curState, srcOprnd);
[6]      a = Var32Update(
[7]             regMap, destReg, src);
[8]      b = regMap;
[9]      answer = cond ? a : b;
[10]   in ( answer )
```

**Fig. 6.** An example of the specification of an ARM conditional-move instruction in TSL

*destReg* would receive the join of its original value and *src*, even when *cond* is known to have a definite value (TRUE or FALSE) in VSA semantics. The paired-semantics mechanism presented in §3.5 can help with improving the precision of analyzers by avoiding joins. When the CIR is instantiated with a paired semantics of VSA_INTERP and DUA_INTERP, and the VSA value of *cond* is FALSE, the DUA_INTERP value for *answer* gets empty *def*- and *use*-sets because the true branch *a* is known to be unreachable according to the VSA_INTERP value of *cond* (instead of non-empty sets for *def*s and *use*s that contain all the definitions and uses in *destReg* and *srcOprnd*).

### 4.3  SPARC

```
[1]  var32 : Reg(INT8) | CWP() | ...;
[2]  reg32 : OutReg(INT8) | InReg(INT8) | ...;
[3]  state: State( ..., VAR32MAP, ... );
[4]  INT32 RegAccess(VAR32MAP regmap, reg32 r) {
[5]    let cwp = Var32Access(regmap, CWP());
[6]      key = with(r) (
[7]        OutReg(i):
[8]          Reg(8+i+(16+cwp*16)%(NWINDOWS*16),
[9]        InReg(i): Reg(8+i+cwp*16),
[10]       ... );
[11]   in ( Var32Access(regmap, key) )
[12]}
```

**Fig. 7.** A method to handle the SPARC register window in TSL

SPARC uses register windows to reduce the overhead associated with saving registers to the stack during a conventional function call. Each window has 8 in, 8 out, 8 local, and 8 global registers. Outs become ins on a context switch, and the new context gets a new set of out and local registers. A specific platform will have some total number of registers, which are organized as a circular buffer; when the buffer becames full, registers are spilled to the stack to free up a sufficient number for the called procedure. Fig. 7 shows a way to accomodate this feature. The syntactic register (OutReg(n) or InReg(n), defined on line 2) in an instruction is used to obtain a semantic register (Reg(m), defined on line 1, where $m$ represents the register's global index), which is the key used for accesses on and updates to the register map. The desired index of the semantic register is computed from the index of the syntactic register, the value of CWP (the current window pointer) from the current state, and the platform-specific value NWINDOWS (lines 8–9).

## 5   Related Work

There are many specification languages for instruction sets and many purposes for which they have been used, including emulation (hardware simulation) for cycle simulation, pipeline simulation, and compiler-optimization testing; retargeting of back-end phases, such as instruction scheduling, register assignment, and functional-unit binding; and concrete syntactic issues, such as instruction encoding and decoding. While some of the existing *languages* would have been satisfactory for our purposes, their *runtime components* were not satisfactory, which necessitated creating our own implementation. In particular, as mentioned in §1, we needed the runtime to (i) execute over abstract states, (ii) possibly propagate abstract states to more than one successor at a branch node, (iii) be able to compare abstract states and terminate abstract execution when a fixed point is reached, and (iv) apply widening operators, if necessary, to ensure termination.

Harcourt et al. [14] used ML to specify the semantics of instruction sets. LISAS [9] is a specification language that was developed based on their experience with ML. Their work particularly influenced the design of the TSL language.

TSL shares some of the same goals as λ-RTL [19] (i.e., the ability to specify the semantics of an instruction set and to support multiple clients that make use of a single specification). The two languages were both influenced by ML, but different choices were made about what aspects of ML to retain: λ-RTL is higher-order, but without datatype constructors and recursion; TSL is first-order, but supports both datatype constructors and recursion.[6] The choices made in the design and implementation of TSL were driven by the goal of being able to define multiple abstract interpretations of an instruction-set's semantics.

Discussion of additional work related to TSL can be found in [15].

**Acknowledgements.** We would like to thank Gogul Balakrishnan, Denis Gopan, and Susan Horwitz for their comments on drafts of this paper, and the anonymous referees for the helpful suggestions contained in their reviews.

## References

1. IA-32 Intel Architecture Software Developer's Manual,
   `http://developer.intel.com/design/pentiumii/manuals/243191.htm`
2. Amme, W., Braun, P., Zehendner, E., Thomasset, F.: Data dependence analysis of assembly code. In: IFPP 2000 (2000)

---

[6] Recursion is not often used in specifications, but is needed for handling some loop-iteration instructions, such as the IA32 string-manipulation instructions and the PowerPC32 multiple-word load/store instructions.

3. Balakrishnan, G.: WYSINWYX: What You See Is Not What You eXecute. PhD thesis, Univ. of Wisc. (2007)
4. Balakrishnan, G., Gruian, R., Reps, T., Teitelbaum, T.: CodeSurfer/x86—A Platform for Analyzing x86 Executables. In: Bodik, R. (ed.) CC 2005. LNCS, vol. 3443, pp. 250–254. Springer, Heidelberg (2005)
5. Balakrishnan, G., Reps, T.: Analyzing Memory Accesses in x86 Executables. In: Duesterwald, E. (ed.) CC 2004. LNCS, vol. 2985, pp. 5–23. Springer, Heidelberg (2004)
6. Balakrishnan, G., Reps, T.: DIVINE: DIscovering Variables IN Executables. In: Cook, B., Podelski, A. (eds.) VMCAI 2007. LNCS, vol. 4349, pp. 1–28. Springer, Heidelberg (2007)
7. Christodorescu, M., Goh, W., Kidd, N.: String analysis for x86 binaries. In: PASTE 2005 (2005)
8. Cifuentes, C., Fraboulet, A.: Intraprocedural static slicing of binary executables. In: ICSM 1997 (1997)
9. Cook, T.A., Franzon, P.D., Harcourt, E.A., Miller, T.K.: System-level specification of instruction sets. In: DAC 1993 (1993)
10. Cooper, K., Kennedy, K.: Interprocedural side-effect analysis in linear time. In: PLDI 1988 (1988)
11. Cousot, P., Cousot, R.: Systematic design of program analysis frameworks. In: POPL 1979 (1979)
12. De Sutter, B., De Bus, B., De Bosschere, K., Keyngnaert, P., Demoen, B.: On the static analysis of indirect control transfers in binaries. In: PDPTA 2000 (2000)
13. Debray, S., Muth, R., Weippert, M.: Alias analysis of executable code. In: POPL 1998(1998)
14. Harcourt, E., Mauney, J., Cook, T.: Functional specification and simulation of instruction set architectures. In: PLC 1994 (1994)
15. Lim, J., Reps, T.: A system for generating static analyzers for machine instructions. TR-1622, C.S.Dept., Univ. of Wisconsin, Madison, WI (October 2007)
16. Mauborgne, L., Rival, X.: Trace Partitioning in Abstract Interpretation Based Static Analyzers. In: Sagiv, M. (ed.) ESOP 2005. LNCS, vol. 3444, pp. 5–20. Springer, Heidelberg (2005)
17. Müller-Olm, M., Seidl, H.: Analysis of Modular Arithmetic. In: Sagiv, M. (ed.) ESOP 2005. LNCS, vol. 3444, pp. 46–60. Springer, Heidelberg (2005)
18. Pettersson, M.: A term pattern-match compiler inspired by finite automata theory. In: Pfahler, P., Kastens, U. (eds.) CC 1992. LNCS, vol. 641, pp. 258–270. Springer, Heidelberg (1992)
19. Ramsey, N., Davidson, J.: Specifying instructions' semantics using λ-RTL (unpublished manuscript, 1999)
20. Regehr, J., Reid, A., Webb, K.: Eliminating stack overflow by abstract interpretation. In: TECS 2005 (2005)
21. Reps, T., Balakrishnan, G., Lim, J.: Intermediate-representation recovery from low-level code. In: PEPM 2006 (2006)
22. Sharir, M., Pnueli, A.: Two approaches to interprocedural data flow analysis. In: Program Flow Analysis: Theory and Applications, Prentice-Hall, Englewood Cliffs (1981)
23. Wadler, P.: Efficient compilation of pattern-matching. The Impl. of Func. Prog. Lang. (1987)
24. Zhang, J., Zhao, R., Pang, J.: Parameter and return-value analysis of binary executables. In: COMPSAC 2007 (2007)

# IDE Dataflow Analysis in the Presence of Large Object-Oriented Libraries*

Atanas Rountev, Mariana Sharp, and Guoqing Xu

Ohio State University, USA

**Abstract.** A key scalability challenge for interprocedural dataflow analysis comes from large libraries. Our work addresses this challenge for the general category of interprocedural distributive environment (IDE) dataflow problems. Using pre-computed library summary information, the proposed approach reduces significantly the cost of whole-program IDE analyses without any loss of precision. We define an approach for library summary generation by using a graph representation of dataflow summary functions, and by abstracting away redundant dataflow facts that are internal to the library. Our approach also handles object-oriented features, by employing an IDE type analysis as well as special handling of polymorphic library call sites whose target methods depend on the future (unknown) client code. Experimental results show that dramatic cost savings can be achieved with the help of these techniques.

## 1 Introduction

*Interprocedural dataflow analysis* plays an important role in compilers and various software tools. A key scalability challenge for analysis algorithms comes from large libraries. Systems are inevitably built with standard libraries (e.g., Java J2SE or C++ STL), domain-specific libraries (e.g., graphics, linear algebra, etc.), and middleware (e.g., EJB). The size of the client code is often a small fraction of the size of the library code being used by that client code.

In this paper we focus on whole-program interprocedural dataflow analysis for Java. However, the proposed approach should also be applicable to other object-oriented languages. Our target is a general category of dataflow problems referred to as *interprocedural distributive environment* (IDE) problems [1]. The goal is to reduce the cost of whole-program IDE analyses by using pre-computed *library summary information*. Library code is analyzed independently of any client code, in oder to produce a library summary stored on disk; this summary is reusable for subsequent analysis of any client code. The summary-generation analysis produces a *precise* summary: the solution for the client code, computed using the summary, is as precise as the solution what would have been computed if we were to use a whole-program analysis of client+library code.

Existing work by Sagiv et al. [1] already provides a solution for one key problem: the representation and manipulation of dataflow functions. Based on their

---

* This material is based upon work supported by NSF under grant CCF-0546040.

L. Hendren (Ed.): CC 2008, LNCS 4959, pp. 53–68, 2008.
© Springer-Verlag Berlin Heidelberg 2008

techniques, we define a general approach for library summary generation. One important problem is that the summary may contain redundant dataflow facts that do not affect the analysis of the client code. We solve this problem through *abstracted* versions of summary functions, in order to filter out callee-local details. Another key problem are polymorphic library call sites whose target methods depend on the future (unknown) client code. We propose the use of IDE type analysis to identify a subset of these sites that are client-*in*dependent and can be processed precisely. The client-dependent call sites are left unresolved in the summary, until client code becomes available. This approach also handles library callback sites that may invoke callback methods defined in future clients.

**Contributions.** This work makes the following specific contributions:

- *Whole-program analysis.* A general framework for whole-program IDE analyses for object-oriented programs, which extends the classical approach for procedural languages [2,3,4,1] through an IDE type analysis (Section 2).
- *Summary-generation analyses.* A general algorithm for summary generation with abstracted summary functions, capturing the dataflow effects of sets of control-flow paths, with special treatment of polymorphic calls.
- *Dependence analysis and type analysis.* Two instances of the general approach: an IDE data dependence analysis that plays an important role in the construction of system dependence graphs, and an IDE type analysis.
- *Experimental evaluation.* A study using the 10238 classes of the Java libraries, and 20 client programs. The experimental results show that dramatic cost savings can be achieved with the help of these techniques

## 2   Whole-Program IDE Dataflow Problems

In *interprocedural distributive environment* (IDE) dataflow problems [1], the dataflow facts are maps ("environments") from some set of symbols $D$ to lattice elements from a semi-lattice $L$. The IDE class is a general category of dataflow problems, examples of which are copy-constant propagation and linear-constant propagation [1], object naming analysis [5], 0-CFA type analysis [6,7,8], and all IFDS (interprocedural, finite, distributive, subset) problems [3] such as reaching definitions, available expressions, live variables, truly-live variables, possibly-uninitialized variables, flow-sensitive side-effects [9], some forms of may-alias and must-alias analysis [4], and interprocedural slicing [10].

A program is represented by an interprocedural control-flow graph (ICFG). Each call expression is represented by two nodes: a *call-site* node and a *return-site* node. Interprocedural edges connect a call-site node with the start node of the invoked procedure $p$, and the exit node of $p$ with the return-site node (assuming a single exit node per procedure.) An intraprocedural edge may also be added from the call-site to the return-site [1]. A *valid* ICFG path has (call-site, start) and (exit, return-site) edges that are properly matched [2,3,1].

An *environment* is a map $D \rightarrow L$ where $D$ is a finite set of symbols and $L$ is a finite-height meet semi-lattice with a top element $\top$ and a meet operator $\wedge$. Let $Env(D, L)$ be the set of all environments for a given pair $(D, L)$. The meet operator $\wedge$ extended to environments is $env_1 \wedge env_2 = \lambda d.(env_1(d) \wedge env_2(d))$. The top element in $Env(D, L)$, denoted by $\Omega$, is $\lambda d.\top$. For any $env \in Env(D, L)$, $d \in D$, and $l \in L$, $env[d \mapsto l]$ denotes an environment in which each symbol $d'$ is mapped to $env(d')$, except for $d$ which is mapped to $l$.

Functions $t : Env(D, L) \rightarrow Env(D, L)$ are *environment transformers*. A distributive transformer $t$ distributes over $\wedge$. An instance of an IDE problem is $(G, D, L, M)$ where $G$ is the ICFG and $M$ is a map that associates distributive transformers with the edges of $G$. A safe analysis for an IDE problem computes an over-approximation of the meet-over-all-valid-paths solution for any node $n$: the solution at $n$ is $\leq$ the meet of $f_q(\Omega)$ for all valid paths $q$ from the start node of the program to $n$, where $f_q$ is the composition of the transformers of $q$'s edges.

Some problems are naturally defined with the approximation that any ordering of statements in a procedure is possible; these are intraprocedurally *flow-insensitive* problems. They can be encoded by conceptually modifying each procedure's CFG to represent arbitrary compositions and meets of transformers, using a switch-in-a-loop structure [11]. In this case all nodes in the same procedure have the same solution. A *context-insensitive* problem does not distinguish the different calling contexts of a procedure. A flow- and context-insensitive problem can be modeled by a single conceptual switch-in-a-loop graph for the entire program; in this case all program statements have the same solution.

***Solving IDE Problems.*** Sagiv et al. [1] define a technique for precise computation of the meet-over-all-valid-paths solution, based on the "functional" approach by Sharir and Pnueli [2]. The first phase on the functional approach computes a *summary function* $\phi_n$ for each ICFG node $n$, representing the solution at $n$ as a function of the solution at the start node of the procedure $p$ containing $n$. If $n$ is the exit node of $p$, $\phi_n$ is a summary function for the entire procedure $p$. During a bottom-up traversal of the SCC-DAG of the call graph, the functions for $p$'s callees are used to model the effects of calls made by $p$. In the second phase, the actual solution is determined at each ICFG node through top-down propagation based on the summary functions. It is possible to merge these two phases, resulting in a single top-down algorithm which computes $\phi_n$ incrementally only for lattice elements that reach $p$'s entry. The work in [1] applies this technique to IDE problems (where $\phi_n$ are environment transformers) by using a *compact graph representation* for transformers; as a result, a summary function can be modeled by a (small) graph. The composition, meet, and application of transformers can be implemented as inexpensive graph operations, and the analysis algorithms can be designed based on a generalized form of graph reachability (essentially, graph summarization along valid paths).

## 2.1 Interprocedural Dependence Analysis

To illustrate the general approach for solving IDE problems, we will use a particular form of interprocedural dependence analysis for Java.[1] For each method $m$

---

[1] Without loss of generality, the subsequent discussion assumes a certain simplified program representation (based on Jimple in the Soot analysis framework [12]). For brevity, details of this representation are provided elsewhere [13].

with a non-void return type, the analysis computes the set of formal parameters of $m$ on which the return value of $m$ may depend directly or transitively. This output is essentially a set of *transitive-dependence summary edges* [10] which play a key role in a variety of analyses for interprocedural slicing, program refactoring, change impact analysis, etc. For simplicity, we restrict the discussion to data dependencies (control dependencies are easy to add to the formulation, and are handled by our implementation), non-exceptional flow of control, and stack memory locations (i.e., dependencies through the heap are not modeled; they could be added using a conservative approach which maps each expression `x.fld` to a single abstract location `fld`). Even with these restrictions, the analysis exhibits the essential features of flow- and context-sensitive IDE analyses.

We propose an IDE formulation[2] in which $D$ is the set of all local variables and formal parameters, and the $L$ is the powerset of the set $F$ of formal parameters, with partial order $\supseteq$ and meet $\cup$. For any $env \in Env(D, L)$, the value of $env(d)$ for local/formal $d$ in method $m$ is the set of formal parameters $f$ of $m$ such that the current value of $d$ may directly or transitively depend on the value that $f$ had at the start of $m$. The final solutions at statements *return x* in a method $m$ are used to find all formals of $m$ on which its return value may depend.[3] Each such formal parameter defines an interprocedural transitive dependence which is a key component for the construction of the *system dependence graph* [10].

For an assignment $d := expr\{d_1, \ldots, d_k\}$, where the side-effect-free non-call expression $expr$ uses $d_i \in D$, and the input environment is $env$, the transformed environment is $env[d \mapsto \bigcup_i env(d_i)]$. Here $d$ becomes dependent on every formal $f$ on which some $d_i$ is dependent. If $expr$ does not use any $d_i \in D$ (e.g., it is a constant expression), the transformed environment is $env[d \mapsto \emptyset]$. For all other non-call statements, as well as for calls without return values, the transformer is the identity function. A call $d := m(d_1, \ldots, d_k)$, can be treated as a sequence of actual-to-formal assignments, followed by the summary function for the callee method $m$, followed by an assignment of $m$'s return value to $d$ (with filtering due to scope changes). It is easy to prove that these transformers are distributive.

In general, an environment transformer can be represented by a bipartite directed graph with $2(|D|+1)$ nodes [1]. In each partition, $|D|$ nodes are labeled with $d \in D$, and one node is labeled with a special symbol $\Lambda$. The edges in the graph are labeled with functions $L \to L$. For the dependence analysis from above, there are only two kinds of edge labels: the identity function $\lambda l.l$ and the constant function $\lambda l.\emptyset$. Examples of these graphs are shown in Figure 1. The key property of this representation is that it is closed under transformer composition and meet. In essence, transformer meet corresponds to graph union, and composition is similar to graph transitive closure (with edge label composition).

---

[2] While inspired by [4], our formulation differs significantly from this previous work.

[3] In this case, a solution captures the effects of same-level valid paths [4] — that is, paths with the same number of calls and returns, starting at method entry. The solution at method entry is $\Omega[f_i \mapsto \{f_i\}]$: each formal $f_i$ of the method depends on itself, and every other $d \in D$ is mapped to $\emptyset$ (i.e., $d$ does not yet have dependencies).

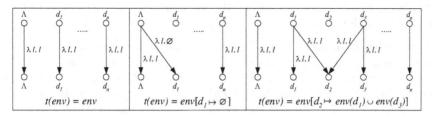

**Fig. 1.** Graph representation of environment transformers $t$

## 2.2   Type Analysis

The standard IDE formulation is applicable to procedural languages. For object-oriented languages, polymorphic calls require resolution of target methods, which can be done by any call graph construction analysis. We propose the use of one such approach: *0-CFA type analysis* [7,6,8]. This analysis has been investigated extensively, and has been shown to be a good compromise between cost and precision [14]. We we have restated 0-CFA as an IDE problem, which makes it a natural choice for use in a general IDE framework. Consider any IDE analysis $A$ which requires a call graph in order to construct its ICFG. One option is to run 0-CFA as a pre-processing step before $A$. Alternatively, 0-CFA can be embedded in $A$ by using the product of 0-CFA's environment set and $A$'s environment set, resulting in a generalized type-aware version of $A$.

***Intraprocedural IDE type analysis.*** First, we briefly outline the formulation of *intra*procedural 0-CFA analysis for Java as an IDE problem. Let $D$ be the set of all local variables, formal parameters (including `this`), and fields. Also, let $T$ be the set of all types that correspond to objects created at run time. An environment is a map $D \to 2^T$. The powerset $2^T$ is a lattice with partial order $\supseteq$ and meet $\cup$. For any environment $env$ and local/formal/field $d \in D$, the value of $env(d)$ is a set of types for the run-time objects that may be referred to by $d$.

For brevity, we discuss only the following two categories of statements; our implementation handles the general case. First, in $d := alloc(X)$, an object of type $X$ is created and a reference to it is assigned to $d \in D$. The environment transformer in this case is $\lambda env.env[d \mapsto env(d) \cup \{X\}]$; that is, type $X$ is added to the set of types for $d$. Second, for an assignment $d_1 := d_2$ where $d_1, d_2 \in D$, the transformer is $\lambda env.env[d_1 \mapsto env(d_1) \cup env(d_2)]$: the set of types for $d_2$ is added to the set of types for $d_1$. These transformers are distributive, and therefore this is an IDE problem. Since 0-CFA is a flow-insensitive analysis, the transformers do not perform "kills" — i.e., $(t(env))(d) \supseteq env(d)$ for any transformer $t$.

In our formulation, the intraprocedural aspects of 0-CFA are equivalent to combining all transformers for a method's body through transformer composition and meet. The resulting transformer is the intraprocedural solution for a method. If transformers are represented by graphs (as defined in [1]), intraprocedural 0-CFA computes a fixed point under the corresponding graph operations. The resulting graph is a "one-hop" representation of all intraprocedural 0-CFA effects of a method: given some input environment which represents the state immediately before the execution of the method, only one application of the fixed-point graph to this input is enough to produce all necessary state updates.

***Interprocedural aspects.*** Consider non-polymorphic calls (e.g., calls to static methods or constructors). Parameter passing and return values can be modeled as assignments, with the corresponding transformers. These transformers can be combined with the ones from the method bodies (with closure under composition and meet) to obtain one single transformer $t^*$ for the entire program. The value of $t^*(\Omega)$ is the type analysis solution; here $\Omega$ is the environment that assigns to each $d \in D$ an empty set of types. Since 0-CFA is flow- and context-insensitive, there is only one solution for the entire program. A polymorphic call x.m() can be represented as a switch statement, with one branch per possible target method. The set of possible targets can be determined by examining the class hierarchy. Since we are interested in *on-the-fly* call graph construction, each target is considered infeasible until evidence to the contrary is seen. To achieve this, special transformers are introduced for the outgoing edges of the multi-way branch, in order to prune the receiver types. These transformers are of the form $\lambda env.env[\, x \mapsto env(x) \cap ReceiverTypes\,]$ for a call through x. Here *ReceiverTypes* is the set of receiver types for which virtual dispatch would invoke the target method for this branch. If the pruned type set is empty, the call is ignored.

# 3    Summary Generation for Object-Oriented Libraries

Consider a large library *Lib* which is to be used by many (unknown) clients. Furthermore, suppose we already have some existing whole-program IDE dataflow analysis. Clearly, it is desirable to perform some of the analysis work for *Lib* in advance, independently of any library clients. The library summary information generated by this *summary generation analysis* can be stored on disk, and later used by a *summary-based analysis* of any client component *Main*. Our focus is on precision-preserving summary generation: for any ICFG node in *Main*, the solution computed by the summary-based analysis should be the same as the solution that would have been computed by the original whole-program analysis.

The proposed summary-generation approach performs as many transformer meets and compositions as possible in the library, and uses the result as summary information. Two key problems arise when applying this idea. First, the targets of call sites in the library may depend on the unknown code in client components. Some of these targets may be library methods that are feasible only for some (but not all) clients. Some call sites may even invoke callback methods defined in client code. Second, the library summary may contain redundant information that is internal to the library and does not affect the analysis of clients. For example, while locals in the library play an important role *during* the computation of summary functions, they may be irrelevant *after* the functions are computed.

## 3.1    Stage 1: Intraprocedural Summary Generation

For a library method that does not make any calls, the summary information can be computed as follows. The transformers for nodes in the method are

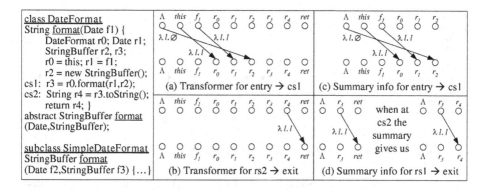

**Fig. 2.** Summary information for dependence analysis (only non-trivial edges)

combined using composition and meet: for each node $n$, the summary function is $\phi_n = \bigwedge f_q$, where the meet is over all paths $q$ from the start node to $n$, and $f_q$ is the composition of the transformers of $q$'s edges. The summary function for the exit node (represented as a graph) serves as the summary function for the method.[4] If type analysis is performed as a pre-processing step (as opposed to being embedded in the main IDE analysis), the summary information also contains the graph representation of the fixed-point transformer for type analysis.

Suppose the analyzed method contains a set of call-site nodes $cs_1, cs_2, \ldots, cs_k$ with the corresponding return-site nodes $rs_i$. In this case, the summary generation produces *a set of summary functions* $\psi_m^n$, where $n$ is the entry node or some $rs_i$, and $m$ is the exit node or some $cs_i$. Transformer $\psi_m^n$ is the meet of $f_q$ for all intra-method paths $q$ from $n$ to $m$ such that $q$ contains no calls other than $n$ and $m$. This set of summary functions captures all intraprocedural effects of the method, and leaves unresolved the effects of all calls. In addition to the set of $\psi_m^n$ (represented as graphs), the summary information for the method also contains descriptions of all call sites (e.g., compile-time target methods, actual parameters, etc.). If the type analysis is a separate pre-processing step, the summary also contains a single transformer which is the fixed-point meet and composition of all type-analysis transformers for non-call statements in the method.

▶ *Examples.* Figure 2 shows an example based on class `DateFormat` and its subclass `SimpleDateFormat` from `java.text` in the Java 1.4.2 libraries. Consider the dependence analysis from Section 2.1. Part (a) illustrates transformer $\psi_{cs_1}^{entry}$, which corresponds to a single path along which `r0`, `r1`, and `r2` are assigned (for brevity, the constructor call for `StringBuffer` is not discussed). Part (b) shows $\psi_{exit}^{rs_2}$, using an artificial variable `ret` to represent the method's return value.

---

[4] Strictly speaking, since summary generation is independent of any client code, the whole-program $D$ and $L$ are not fully known, and the summary function is not a single transformer but rather an infinite set of transformers, one per possible client.

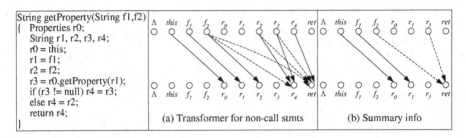

**Fig. 3.** Summary information for type analysis (only non-trivial edges)

Figure 3 shows another example, based on `java.util.Properties`, to illustrate the type analysis. The transformers for all non-call statements are combined through composition and meet. The resulting fixed-point transformer is shown in part (a) of the figure. Unlike the multiple $\psi_m^n$ needed for the flow-sensitive dependence analysis, only one $\psi$ is needed for the flow-insensitive type analysis. All edges are labeled with $\lambda l.l$. Dashed edges represent transitive relationships due to transformer composition. ◀

***Abstracted summary functions.*** The functions from Figure 2(a)/(b) and Figure 3(a) contain redundant information. Consider $\psi_{cs_1}^{entry}$ which represents the flow from the formals of the method to the actual parameters of the call at $cs_1$ (including local r0 which refers to the receiver object). Here the only relevant elements of $D$ are this, f1, r0, r1, and r2. Thus, the summary information can store an *abstracted summary function* $\widehat{\psi}_{cs_1}^{entry}$ instead of the original summary function $\psi_{cs_1}^{entry}$. Figure 2(c) shows the graph representation of $\widehat{\psi}_{cs_1}^{entry}$. Similar considerations apply to the type analysis. The only elements of $D$ that are relevant outside of the method are formals this, f1, and f2, the return variable ret, the actuals r0 and r1 at the call site, and the local r3 to which the return value of the call is assigned. Both r2 and r4 can be eliminated from transformer $\psi$; the resulting abstracted transformer $\widehat{\psi}$ is shown in Figure 3(b).

In general, for any IDE analysis, only a subset of $D$ is relevant with respect to a particular $\psi_m^n$. Depending on the specific analysis and on $n$ and $m$, this subset would typically be related to formal parameters, return statements, actuals at calls, and return values at calls. Thus, it should be possible to define a corresponding abstracted transformer $\widehat{\psi}_m^n$ that can be used instead of $\psi_m^n$ without any loss of precision. Obtaining the graph representation of $\widehat{\psi}_m^n$ should be trivial, given the already-computed representation of $\psi_m^n$. For the dependence analysis discussed earlier, $\widehat{\psi}_m^n$ can be defined as follows: (1) if $n$ is an entry node, the formals should be preserved; (2) if $m$ is an exit node, the return variable ret should be preserved; (3) if $n$ is a return-site node, the local variable to which the return value is assigned should be preserved; and (4) if $m$ is a call-site node, the actual parameters should be preserved, including the reference to the receiver object. The abstracted transformer $\widehat{\psi}$ for the type analysis can be defined similarly.

## 3.2   Stage 2: Interprocedural Summary Generation

In the standard IDE formulation, each call has a single target which is known at analysis time. For a library method that makes calls, its summary information can be computed by "inlining" the summary functions for callee methods, and then performing the intraprocedural propagation outlined above. As a result, a single summary function $\psi_{exit}^{entry}$ would be computed for the entire method.

This approach is possible only in the absence of callbacks from *Lib* to client code. If a library method $m$ contains a callback site, the complete behavior of $m$ is not known at summary-generation time, and it is not possible to create a complete summary function. This is a realistic problem, because callbacks occur often in object-oriented libraries (e.g., due to polymorphic calls in C++, Java, and C#). Consider the abstract method `format` in class `DateFormat` from Figure 2. If a client component creates a subclass with a corresponding non-abstract method `format`, call site $cs_1$ in Figure 2 could be a callback site. This situation is common for extensible object-oriented libraries. Note that $cs_1$ is not necessarily a callback site: if the client code simply uses library subclass `SimpleDateFormat`, the target of $cs_1$ would be the corresponding library method.

Even in the absence of callbacks, it may still be impossible to create precise summary functions. Consider the following Java example: library method $m$ has a virtual call `a.n()` and the compile-time type of `a` is `A`. Suppose library classes `B` and `C` extend `A`, and method `A.n` is overridden by `B.n` and `C.n`. A conservative analysis has to assume that `a.n()` could invoke any of these three methods, and thus the summary function for $m$ will depend on all three callees. But, for example, if a client instantiates only `C`, the summary would be too conservative.

***Exit calls.*** A call site is an *exit call* if it can invoke some method that "exits" the scope of the analysis and therefore the effects of the call cannot be modeled. An exit call is a virtual call `x.m()` for which (1) the declared type of `x` has possible unknown subtypes, and (2) the compile-time target method of the call can be overridden by unknown methods. A library type $T$ (class or interface type) is considered to have potential unknown subtypes in clients when $T$ or some library subtype of $T$ is public and not final.[5] The compile-time target method $m$ of the call site can have unknown overriding methods if (1) $m$ is not private and is not final, and (2) at least one of $m$'s overriding methods in the library (or $m$ itself) is non-final and is visible to clients (i.e., public or protected).

***Fixed calls.*** A *fixed call site* in the library has exactly one possible run-time target method, regardless of what the client code may be. This target is a library method and can be determined at summary generation time. Obviously, an exit call is not a fixed call. A non-exit call is fixed if any of the following cases holds. In case 1, the call invokes a static method or a constructor, and thus the run-time target is the same as the compile-time target. In case 2, the call is a virtual invocation, and conservative analysis of the type hierarchy for the entire library determines that the call has exactly one possible run-time target method

---

[5] This definition assumes that library packages are sealed, and clients cannot add new classes to them (thus, non-public types cannot be accessed directly by client code).

regardless of client code. For example, for $cs_2$ in Figure 2, r3 is of compile-time type StringBuffer which is a final class; thus, the only possible target is the corresponding method in this class. In case 3, the call is a virtual invocation, and conservative intraprocedural 0-CFA type analysis determines that the call has exactly one possible run-time target method regardless of client code. Consider a call site x.m(). In the graph representation of the transformer $\widehat{\psi}$ computed by the intraprocedural type analysis, the only edges reaching $x$ should be of the form $\Lambda \to x$; in other words, the only values of x should come from inside the method. The label on the $\Lambda \to x$ edge is exactly the set of possible types for x.

**Fixed methods.** Consider a fixed call site $cs$ and suppose that its unique target method $m$ contains only fixed calls (or no calls at all), and this property transitively holds for all methods reachable from $m$. We will refer to such $m$ as *fixed methods*. Here the effects of $m$ are fully known at summary-generation time, and can be represented by a summary function $\widehat{\psi}_{exit}^{entry}$ for $m$, computed through a bottom-up traversal of the SCC-DAG of the "fixed" library call graph (i.e., the call graph in which nodes are fixed methods and edges are fixed calls).

In the method $m'$ containing $cs$, $m$'s summary function can be instantiated as follows. Consider any pair of summary functions $\widehat{\psi}_{cs}^{n_1}$ and $\widehat{\psi}_{n_2}^{rs}$ computed in $m'$; here $rs$ is the return site corresponding to $cs$. The composition of these functions with the summary function for $m$, followed by the appropriate abstraction operations, produces a summary function $\widehat{\psi}_{n_2}^{n_1}$. If the pair $(n_1, n_2)$ already has a corresponding function (i.e., because there is some call-free-path from $n_1$ to $n_2$), the new function is merged with the old one through transformer meet.

▶ **Example.** Figure 2(b) shows $\widehat{\psi}_{exit}^{rs_2}$. Consider call site $cs_2$, which is fixed. Suppose that its target method StringBuffer.toString is also fixed, and its summary function, instantiated at the call site, results in a transformer $f_{cs_2}$ which shows a dependence from r3 to r4. The right part of Figure 2(d) shows the graph representation of $f_{cs_2}$. The composition of $f_{cs_2}$ and $\widehat{\psi}_{exit}^{rs_2}$ can be used to compute $\widehat{\psi}_{exit}^{rs_1}$. In addition to transformer composition, this computation can also abstract away r4 because this variable is neither assigned the return value at $rs_1$, nor used at method exit. In general, after a summary function is instantiated as $f_{cs}$ at a fixed call site $cs$, any pair of $\widehat{\psi}_{cs}^{n_1}$ and $\widehat{\psi}_{n_2}^{rs}$ can be used to create $\widehat{\psi}_{n_2}^{n_1}$ as an abstracted version of $\widehat{\psi}_{n_2}^{rs} \circ f_{cs} \circ \widehat{\psi}_{cs}^{n_1}$, based on the elements of $D$ that need to be preserved for $n_1$ and $n_2$. The left part of Figure 2(d) shows the graph representation of $\widehat{\psi}_{exit}^{rs_1}$ after this abstraction. This summary function together with $\widehat{\psi}_{cs_1}^{entry}$, shown in Figure 2(c), defines the final summary information. ◀

If the summary function for a fixed method $m$ is instantiated at all fixed call sites that invoke it, and if we can conservatively prove that no other call sites can directly invoke $m$ (from the library or from client code), the summary $\widehat{\psi}_{exit}^{entry}$ for $m$ does not need to be stored in the library summary at all. Due to space constraints, additional details on this optimization are presented elsewhere [13].

**Table 1.** Library summary information

| (a) Library | | | (b) Dependence Analysis | | | | (c) Type Analysis | | |
|---|---|---|---|---|---|---|---|---|---|
| *Pkg* | *Cls* | *Mthd* | *Stmt* | 1 | 2 | 3 | 4 | 1 | 2 | 3 |
| java | 1802 | 15676 | 245605 | 389024 | 584174 | 243005 | 151424 | 77940 | 111801 | 53215 |
| javax | 2265 | 17618 | 254542 | 390351 | 582970 | 278622 | 209549 | 88822 | 117102 | 65272 |
| org | 1289 | 8688 | 136945 | 180258 | 260013 | 134934 | 90893 | 55426 | 78490 | 32153 |
| com | 2373 | 18235 | 349957 | 517577 | 685128 | 323522 | 227939 | 125492 | 184347 | 84665 |
| sun | 2509 | 16973 | 508954 | 676324 | 820889 | 383865 | 246579 | 151060 | 207184 | 78291 |
| Total | 10238 | 77190 | 1496003 | 2153534 | 2933174 | 1363948 | 926384 | 498740 | 698924 | 313596 |

## 4   Experimental Evaluation

***Study 1: Summary generation.*** Our experiments used the entire standard
Java libraries from Java 2 SDK SE 1.4.2. Some characteristics of the packages
in these libraries are summarized in part (a) of Table 1: number of classes *Cls*,
number of methods *Mthd*, and number of statements *Stmt* in the intermediate
representation (IR) provided by the Soot analysis framework [12].[6] The entire set
of 10238 library classes was used as input to the summary-generation analysis.
The running time of the analysis was 5491.6 seconds (about 90 minutes), on
a single Intel Xeon 2.8GHz CPU in a Dell PowerEdge 1950 server. This time
includes all Soot-related costs, the actual analysis time, and the disk I/O. The
memory consumption was 1230.3 MB. The summary was written to disk in a
straightforward binary format, with all necessary information for dependence
analysis and type analysis. The total size of the summary file was 17.9 MB.

Part (b) of Table 1 provides relevant measurements for the dependence analysis. Our implementation generalizes the one outlined in Section 2.1 as follows.
First, as an optimization, we compute def-use chains and perform transitive dependence propagation using these chains. Second, our implementation computes
control dependencies (in addition to the data dependencies) and uses them when
computing transitive dependencies. The IDE formulation from Section 2.1 can
be easily extended to capture this generalization. Finally, we use a sparse graph
representation of transformers: trivial edges $d \to d$ are not represented.

Column 1 in part (b) of Table 1 shows the total number of edges in the graph
representation of all transformers before any transformer composition or meet is
performed. Column 2 shows the total number of such edges after intraprocedural
propagation, which starts at each node $n$ that is an entry node or a return site,
and computes summary functions $\psi_m^n$ for all $m$ reachable from $n$ along call-
free paths. Column 3 shows the total number of edges in the representation
of the abstracted transformers $\widehat{\psi}_m^n$. The reduction from column 2 to column 3
eliminates all method-local information that does not directly affect callers or
callees of a method. The overall reduction in the number of edges is 53.5%. Part
(c) shows similar measurements for the type analysis; here each method has a
single summary function. The reduction in the number of edges from column 2

---

[6] Row com includes packages com and COM; row sun includes packages sun and sunw.

**Table 2.** Whole-program vs. summary-based analysis: time (sec) and memory (MB)

| (a) Program | | (b) All Analyses | | | | (c) Dependence Analysis | | | | | |
|---|---|---|---|---|---|---|---|---|---|---|---|
| Name | $Stmts$ | $T_{wp}$ | $\Delta_T$ | $M_{wp}$ | $\Delta_M$ | $T_{wp}$ | $\Delta_T$ | $\Delta_T^{ub}$ | $M_{wp}$ | $\Delta_M$ | $\Delta_M^{ub}$ |
| compress | 71729 | 89.6 | 52.4% | 256.8 | 30.7% | 21.5 | 86.2% | 88.3% | 58.1 | 95.1% | 98.2% |
| db | 71940 | 89.8 | 51.2% | 257.2 | 30.7% | 20.7 | 78.6% | 83.2% | 58.2 | 95.0% | 98.3% |
| jb | 72713 | 87.9 | 50.0% | 259.3 | 30.6% | 20.6 | 75.8% | 80.6% | 59.3 | 93.8% | 96.9% |
| raytrace | 74738 | 92.9 | 56.6% | 262.3 | 30.3% | 21.4 | 76.6% | 79.5% | 61.0 | 91.5% | 94.7% |
| proxy | 75962 | 91.4 | 56.1% | 263.5 | 31.5% | 21.4 | 74.6% | 83.9% | 61.4 | 94.9% | 98.1% |
| jlex | 77134 | 94.4 | 43.9% | 264.2 | 30.2% | 25.3 | 60.0% | 63.2% | 62.2 | 90.7% | 93.8% |
| javacup | 78798 | 97.6 | 46.0% | 269.3 | 29.6% | 24.3 | 73.7% | 75.7% | 64.4 | 88.0% | 90.9% |
| jess | 79131 | 96.4 | 46.6% | 271.8 | 29.4% | 23.3 | 70.3% | 70.6% | 64.7 | 87.2% | 90.2% |
| jack | 81139 | 103.0 | 45.4% | 270.9 | 29.5% | 25.9 | 70.3% | 73.7% | 65.3 | 86.8% | 90.1% |
| mpegaudio | 83023 | 135.8 | 26.0% | 271.3 | 29.3% | 57.9 | 13.1% | 16.6% | 65.3 | 86.4% | 90.0% |
| rabbit | 90964 | 100.8 | 59.7% | 287.3 | 34.0% | 23.6 | 80.3% | 82.0% | 73.6 | 94.2% | 97.0% |
| sablecc | 92171 | 114.6 | 44.7% | 298.7 | 27.3% | 34.6 | 61.3% | 61.5% | 75.9 | 77.2% | 80.3% |
| javac | 95498 | 108.0 | 43.2% | 302.2 | 27.6% | 26.4 | 63.3% | 71.7% | 78.8 | 75.3% | 78.3% |
| fractal | 106433 | 110.8 | 55.0% | 315.0 | 37.1% | 25.3 | 80.3% | 84.7% | 86.6 | 94.5% | 97.3% |
| echo | 110458 | 117.0 | 64.2% | 321.5 | 37.7% | 30.4 | 85.3% | 85.8% | 90.0 | 94.6% | 97.2% |
| jtar | 113244 | 116.4 | 61.3% | 326.8 | 37.4% | 28.8 | 83.7% | 87.6% | 92.4 | 93.0% | 95.5% |
| jflex | 116938 | 144.8 | 50.9% | 334.5 | 35.3% | 50.1 | 61.3% | 61.6% | 96.1 | 86.9% | 89.5% |
| mindterm | 126362 | 144.9 | 43.2% | 345.9 | 36.1% | 49.7 | 41.5% | 41.6% | 102.2 | 86.4% | 89.0% |
| muffin | 138140 | 138.0 | 51.1% | 370.9 | 38.3% | 35.5 | 56.2% | 57.3% | 113.4 | 88.3% | 90.6% |
| violet | 153895 | 148.3 | 66.5% | 398.8 | 43.0% | 39.3 | 83.5% | 87.9% | 126.8 | 95.3% | 97.6% |

(size of $\psi$, after fixed-point transformer composition and meet) to column 3 (size of $\widehat{\psi}$, after abstracting method-local information) is 55.1%.

Out of all library methods, 25490 (33.0%) are fixed. While fixed methods tend to be smaller and simpler than non-fixed ones, the complete knowledge of their summary functions still has positive effects on the library summary. The instantiation of fixed-method summary functions at calls can be done for 63229 (20.5%) of all library call sites. This instantiation, followed by additional intraprocedural propagation and abstraction, further reduces the number of edges in the representation of summary functions: overall, from column 3 to column 4 of Table 1 part (b), there is 32.1% reduction. Since the type analysis is context-insensitive, instantiation of summary functions at call sites (an inherently context-sensitive operation) is not meaningful for it and was not performed.

***Study 2: Summary-based client analysis.*** The goal of our second study was to measure the cost benefits of summary-based analysis compared to traditional whole-program analysis. Table 2 presents the results of this study on 20 Java programs. Column *Stmts* shows the number of IR statements for all methods reported by whole-program 0-CFA as reachable. Typically, more than 90% of these methods are library methods [13].

We ran two sets of experiments. The first set, shown in part (b) of Table 2, considered the entire set of analyses employed by a Soot user: the IR building, the 0-CFA type analysis interleaved with on-the-fly call graph construction in the Spark module [14], and the dependence analysis (which uses this call graph). This is the complete start-to-finish cost that would have to be paid to obtain dependence information. The second set of experiments, shown in part (c) of Table 2, considered only the dependence analysis, without any Soot-related costs. For each experiment we measured the running time $T_{wp}$ and the peak memory consumption $M_{wp}$ of the whole-program analysis, as well as the corresponding cost reduction $\Delta_T$ and $\Delta_M$ when using summary-based analyses.

Considering dependence analysis, type analysis, and IR building together, as shown in part (b), the time savings $\Delta_T$ are 50.7% and the memory savings $\Delta_M$ are 32.8% (average across all 20 programs). A large proportion of these savings is due to Soot-related costs; such savings will be observed for any interprocedural dataflow analysis which uses 0-CFA as a preprocessing step to obtain a program call graph. When considering only the dependence analysis, in part (c), the savings are, on average, 68.8% for $\Delta_T$ and 89.8% for $\Delta_M$.

Columns $\Delta_T^{ub}$ and $\Delta_M^{ub}$ in part (c) show conservative upper bounds on the savings of the summary-based dependence analysis. These measurements were obtained using an artificial summary which contained only summary functions for type analysis, but not for dependence analysis. Thus, the only dependence analysis work was done inside the client code (of course, the resulting solution is unsound). It is impossible to achieve reductions higher than the ones observed with this artificial summary. Comparing columns $\Delta_T^{ub}$ and $\Delta_T$, as well as $\Delta_M^{ub}$ and $\Delta_M$, it is clear that the savings are very close to this upper bound.

## 5   Related Work

Various techniques have been used to achieve modularity in static analysis; some of the most relevant approaches are outlined below. A more complete discussion is available in [15], presented from an abstract-interpretation point of view.

Summary functions for interprocedural analysis date back to the functional approach [2], with refinements in [3] for IFDS problems and in [1] for IDE problems. This body of work assumes a procedural language without polymorphic calls; furthermore, there is no separation between client code and library code. A recent generalization [16], which subsumes IFDS and IDE problems, uses conditional micro-transformers to represent and manipulate dataflow functions; it would be interesting to generalize our approach to take advantage of this work.

Our summary-based analyses can be viewed as instances of the theoretical approach presented in [17]. However, this earlier work does not consider (1) type analysis and on-the-fly call graph construction, (2) abstracting away of library-local dataflow facts, or (3) compact graph representation of dataflow functions.

Most analyses that employ summaries perform bottom-up traversal of the call graph, and compute summary functions using the functions computed for the visited callees; examples include [18,19,20,21,22,23,24,25,26]. In [27], libraries are pre-analyzed but the computation of summary functions cannot be performed in the presence of callbacks. Some techniques compute summary information for a software component independently of the callers and callees of that component. One particular technique is a modular approach which computes partial analysis results for each component, combines the results for all components in the program, and then performs the rest of the analysis; examples include [28,29,30,31,32,33]. There have also been proposals for employing summary information provided by the analysis user, as in [34,35,36]. Finally, certain approaches analyze a software component when there is no available information about the surrounding environment, using conservative assumptions about unknown external code (e.g., [37,38,27,39,40,41,42,43,44,45]).

## 6   Conclusions and Future Work

Summary-based analysis shows promising potential for improving the scalability of interprocedural analysis in the presence of large object-oriented libraries. Our results indicate that summary generation can have practical cost and can produce a small summary file, and most importantly, the analysis of client code becomes substantially cheaper. Future work will investigate other IDE analyses, as well as a standardized API for storing and retrieving summary information.

## References

1. Sagiv, M., Reps, T., Horwitz, S.: Precise interprocedural dataflow analysis with applications to constant propagation. Theoretical Comp. Sci. 167, 131–170 (1996)
2. Sharir, M., Pnueli, A.: Two approaches to interprocedural data flow analysis. In: Program Flow Analysis: Theory and Applications, pp. 189–234 (1981)
3. Reps, T., Horwitz, S., Sagiv, M.: Precise interprocedural dataflow analysis via graph reachability. In: POPL, pp. 49–61 (1995)
4. Reps, T., Sagiv, M., Horwitz, S.: Interprocedural dataflow analysis via graph reachability. Technical Report DIKU-TR94-14, U. Copenhagen (1994)
5. Rountev, A., Connell, B.H.: Object naming analysis for reverse-engineered sequence diagrams. In: ICSE, pp. 254–263 (2005)
6. Grove, D., Chambers, C.: A framework for call graph construction algorithms. TOPLAS 23(6), 685–746 (2001)
7. Tip, F., Palsberg, J.: Scalable propagation-based call graph construction algorithms. In: OOPSLA, pp. 281–293 (2000)
8. Heintze, N.: Set Based Program Analysis. PhD thesis, CMU (1992)
9. Callahan, D.: The program summary graph and flow-sensitive interprocedural data flow analysis. In: PLDI, pp. 47–56 (1988)
10. Horwitz, S., Reps, T., Binkley, D.: Interprocedural slicing using dependence graphs. TOPLAS 12(1), 26–60 (1990)
11. Rountev, A., Kagan, S., Marlowe, T.: Interprocedural dataflow analysis in the presence of large libraries. Technical Report CISRC-TR01, Ohio State U (2006)
12. Vallée-Rai, R., Gagnon, E., Hendren, L., Lam, P., Pominville, P., Sundaresan, V.: Optimizing Java Bytecode Using the Soot Framework: Is It Feasible? In: Watt, D.A. (ed.) CC 2000. LNCS, vol. 1781, Springer, Heidelberg (2000)
13. Sharp, M.: Static Analyses for Java in the Presence of Distributed Components and Large Libraries. PhD thesis, Ohio State University (2007)
14. Lhoták, O., Hendren, L.: Scaling Java points-to analysis using Spark. In: Hedin, G. (ed.) CC 2003. LNCS, vol. 2622, pp. 153–169. Springer, Heidelberg (2003)

15. Cousot, P., Cousot, R.: Modular static program analysis. In: Horspool, R.N. (ed.) CC 2002. LNCS, vol. 2304, pp. 159–178. Springer, Heidelberg (2002)
16. Yorsh, G., Yahav, E., Chandra, S.: Generating precise and concise procedure summaries. In: POPL (2008)
17. Rountev, A., Kagan, S., Marlowe, T.: Interprocedural dataflow analysis in the presence of large libraries. In: Mycroft, A., Zeller, A. (eds.) CC 2006. LNCS, vol. 3923, pp. 2–16. Springer, Heidelberg (2006)
18. Chatterjee, R., Ryder, B.G., Landi, W.: Relevant context inference. In: POPL, pp. 133–146 (1999)
19. Choi, J., Gupta, M., Serrano, M., Sreedhar, V., Midkiff, S.: Escape analysis for Java. In: OOPSLA, pp. 1–19 (1999)
20. Whaley, J., Rinard, M.: Compositional pointer and escape analysis for Java programs. In: OOPSLA, pp. 187–206 (1999)
21. Cheng, B., Hwu, W.: Modular interprocedural pointer analysis using access paths. In: PLDI, pp. 57–69 (2000)
22. Ruf, E.: Effective synchronization removal for Java. In: PLDI, pp. 208–218 (2000)
23. Foster, J., Fähndrich, M., Aiken, A.: Polymorphic versus monomorphic flow-insensitive points-to analysis for C. In: Palsberg, J. (ed.) SAS 2000. LNCS, vol. 1824, pp. 175–198. Springer, Heidelberg (2000)
24. Liang, D., Harrold, M.J.: Efficient computation of parameterized pointer information for interprocedural analyses. In: Cousot, P. (ed.) SAS 2001. LNCS, vol. 2126, pp. 279–298. Springer, Heidelberg (2001)
25. Triantafyllis, S., Bridges, M., Raman, E., Ottoni, G., August, D.: A framework for unrestricted whole-program optimization. In: PLDI, pp. 61–71 (2006)
26. Cherem, S., Rugina, R.: A practical effect and escape analysis for building lightweight method summaries. In: Krishnamurthi, S., Odersky, M. (eds.) CC 2007. LNCS, vol. 4420, pp. 172–186. Springer, Heidelberg (2007)
27. Chatterjee, R., Ryder, B.G.: Data-flow-based testing of object-oriented libraries. Technical Report DCS-TR-433, Rutgers University (2001)
28. Oxhøj, N., Palsberg, J., Schwartzbach, M.: Making Type Inference Practical. In: Lehrmann Madsen, O. (ed.) ECOOP 1992. LNCS, vol. 615, pp. 329–349. Springer, Heidelberg (1992)
29. Codish, M., Debray, S., Giacobazzi, R.: Compositional analysis of modular logic programs. In: POPL, pp. 451–464 (1993)
30. Flanagan, C., Felleisen, M.: Componential set-based analysis. TOPLAS 21(2), 370–416 (1999)
31. Das, M.: Unification-based pointer analysis with directional assignments. In: PLDI, pp. 35–46 (2000)
32. Heintze, N., Tardieu, O.: Ultra-fast aliasing analysis using CLA. In: PLDI, pp. 254–263 (2001)
33. Rountev, A., Ryder, B.G.: Points-to and side-effect analyses for programs built with precompiled libraries. In: Wilhelm, R. (ed.) CC 2001. LNCS, vol. 2027, pp. 20–36. Springer, Heidelberg (2001)
34. Dwyer, M.: Modular flow analysis of concurrent software. In: ASE, pp. 264–273 (1997)
35. Guyer, S., Lin, C.: Optimizing the use of high performance software libraries. In: Midkiff, S.P., Moreira, J.E., Gupta, M., Chatterjee, S., Ferrante, J., Prins, J.F., Pugh, B., Tseng, C.-W. (eds.) LCPC 2000. LNCS, vol. 2017, pp. 227–243. Springer, Heidelberg (2001)
36. Rugina, R., Rinard, M.: Design-driven compilation. In: Wilhelm, R. (ed.) CC 2001. LNCS, vol. 2027, pp. 150–164. Springer, Heidelberg (2001)

37. Harrold, M.J., Rothermel, G.: Separate computation of alias information for reuse. TSE 22(7), 442–460 (1996)
38. Rountev, A., Ryder, B.G., Landi, W.: Data-flow analysis of program fragments. In: Nierstrasz, O., Lemoine, M. (eds.) ESEC 1999 and ESEC-FSE 1999. LNCS, vol. 1687, pp. 235–252. Springer, Heidelberg (1999)
39. Sreedhar, V., Burke, M., Choi, J.: A framework for interprocedural optimization in the presence of dynamic class loading. In: PLDI, pp. 196–207 (2000)
40. Ghemawat, S., Randall, K., Scales, D.: Field analysis: Getting useful and low-cost interprocedural information. In: PLDI, pp. 334–344 (2000)
41. Vivien, F., Rinard, M.: Incrementalized pointer and escape analysis. In: PLDI, pp. 35–46 (2001)
42. Tip, F., Sweeney, P., Laffra, C., Eisma, A., Streeter, D.: Practical extraction techniques for Java. TOPLAS 24(6), 625–666 (2002)
43. Rountev, A., Milanova, A., Ryder, B.G.: Fragment class analysis for testing of polymorphism in Java software. TSE 30(6), 372–387 (2004)
44. Rountev, A.: Precise identification of side-effect-free methods in Java. In: ICSM, pp. 82–91 (2004)
45. Xue, J., Nguyen, P.H.: Completeness analysis for incomplete object-oriented programs. In: Bodik, R. (ed.) CC 2005. LNCS, vol. 3443, pp. 271–286. Springer, Heidelberg (2005)

# An Adaptive Strategy for Inline Substitution

Keith D. Cooper[1], Timothy J. Harvey[1], and Todd Waterman[2]

[1]Rice University Houston,
Texas, USA
cooper,harv@rice.edu
[2]Texas Instruments, Inc. Stafford,
Texas, USA
twaterman@ti.com

**Abstract.** *Inline substitution* is an optimization that replaces a procedure call with the body of the procedure that it calls. Inlining has the immediate benefit of reducing the overhead associated with the call, including register saves and restores, parameter evaluation, and activation record setup and teardown. It has secondary benefits that arise from providing greater context for global optimizations. These benefits can be offset by the effects of increased code size, and by deleterious interactions with other optimizations, such as register allocation.

The difficult aspect of inline substitution is choosing which calls to inline. Previous work has focused on static, one-size-fits-all heuristics. This paper presents a feedback-driven adaptive scheme that derives a program-specific inlining heuristic. The key contributions of this work are: (1) a novel parameterization scheme for the inliner that makes it susceptible to fine-grained external control, (2) a scheme for discretizing large integer parameter spaces, and (3) effective search techniques for the resulting search space. This work provides a proof of concept that can provide insight into the design of adaptive controllers for other optimizations with complex decision heuristics. Our goal in this work is *not* to exhibit the world's best inliner. Instead, we present evidence to suggest that a program-specific, adaptive scheme is needed to achieve the best results.

## 1 Introduction

Inline substitution is a simple transformation. It replaces a procedure call with a copy of the callee's body. The complex aspect of inline substitution is the decision process–the method by which the compiler decides which call sites to inline. The goal for inlining is to decrease the running time of the complete application. Unfortunately, the decision made at one call site affects the decisions at other call sites in subtle ways that can be hard to predict.

Naively, we would expect that inline substitution is always profitable. It eliminates operations to save and restore registers, to manipulate and manage activation records, and to evaluate parameters. On the other hand, studies have shown that inlining can increase application running time, due to effects that range from increased code size to decreased effectiveness of global optimization [7]. The impact at any single call site is multiplied by its execution frequency. Modern

L. Hendren (Ed.): CC 2008, LNCS 4959, pp. 69–84, 2008.
© Springer-Verlag Berlin Heidelberg 2008

programming practices encourage many calls to small procedures. An effective decision procedure must balance many competing effects.

Existing compilers typically attack this problem with a set of static heuristics. They aim to improve performance and avoid foreseeable pitfalls, such as excessive code growth. While these heuristics usually improve the speed of the compiled code, they leave a significant amount of improvement unrealized (See § 4).

The problem with static sets of heuristics is precisely that they are static; this paper shows evidence that different input programs need different strategies. For example, inlining small routines may produce radical improvement in one program but miss opportunities in another. The difference between a good inlining decision and a bad one often lies in low-level, idiosyncratic detail that is not obvious early in compilation—properties such the demand for registers at the call site and in the callee, the execution frequency of the call, and the improved optimization that might accrue from knowledge about the actual parameters.

To address this problem, we designed and built an adaptive inliner. Many recent papers have explored aspects of adaptive optimization [25,28,3,21,15]. This work focuses on *program-specific optimization inside a single transformation*. That transformation has a huge and complex decision space; each decision changes the remainder of the problem. Our system includes a source-to-source inliner that runs quickly. It takes, as a command-line parameter, a closed-form description of an inlining heuristic and applies that heuristic to each call site in a predictable order. The design of that parameter scheme is critical to the system's success. An adaptive controller manipulates the heuristic and measures the results to discover a good heuristic for the input program.

The next section explores the decision problem for inline substitution and introduces our inliner's parameter scheme. Section 3 presents exploratory experiments that we performed to help us understand the decision spaces and to develop effective search techniques. The experimental results in Section 4 show that the adaptive inliner consistently produces faster executables than gcc's inliner. Empirical evidence from our searches suggests why no set of static heuristics will work as well as the adaptive system across a broad range of input codes.

## 2     Designing a Parameter Scheme for Inlining

Inlining decisions are made with two levels of granularity. The compiler might decide to inline all calls to a particular procedure—for example, one whose body required fewer operations than the call would. On the other hand, the compiler might only inline a call if certain of the actual parameters have known constant values that permit optimization of the inlined body. Call-site specific decisions allow greater control, but make it harder to reason about the decision procedure.

To reason about the problem, assume that we have built a simplified call graph, $CG(N, E)$, with a distinct edge $\langle a, b \rangle$ for each call in $a$ that invokes $b$ and a map from each edge to a specific call site. To simplify matters, we will elide any backedges from the graph because the recursive cycles that they represent would add another layer of complication to the inliner.

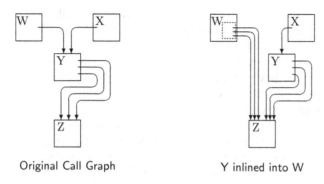

Original Call Graph                Y inlined into W

**Fig. 1.** An example call-graph

The problem of deciding which call sites to inline is hard, for several reasons. First, the impact of any particular inlining decision depends on the optimizer's effectiveness on the resulting code, which is hard to predict. Second, each decision to inline changes the call graph for subsequent decisions. To see this, consider the call graph in Figure 1.

The left side shows a call graph, where both $W$ and $X$ call $Y$, and $Y$ calls $Z$ from three distinct locations. Inlining $Y$ into $W$ produces the call graph on the right. Notice that the number of edges entering $Z$ grows from three to six and the total edge count grows from five to seven. If the compiler, instead, inlines the calls from $Y$ to $Z$, the total edge count shrinks from five to two.

If we view the decision problem as assigning a value, `inline` or `intact`, to each edge, the compiler initially faces a set of $E$ decisions, one per edge and $2^E$ possible programs that it could consider and evaluate. Each time the system inlines an edge, it changes the graph. The decision can add edges; it can remove edges; it changes the program metrics for nodes and edges. Thus, the decision problem is solved in a complex and changing environment.

Finally, the decisions are interrelated and the order of decisions can affect the results. Consider, for example, a heuristic that inlines $A$ into $B$ if neither procedure has more than ten instructions. In Figure 1, if $W$ and $Y$ each have six instructions and $Z$ has two, then inlining $Y$ into $W$ would prevent a subsequent decision to inline $Z$. On the other hand, inlining $Z$ into $Y$ first would not preclude inlining $Y$ into $W$. Order has a direct effect on outcome; similar effects arise from the order of application of multiple heuristics.

The goal of this work was to construct a system that discovers good program-specific inlining heuristics. These program-specific heuristics are expressed in terms of concrete properties of the input program. The system measures those properties and then uses them in a feedback-driven tuning phase to construct a program-specific heuristic. The current set of program metrics are:

*Statement count* - `sc`: the number of C statements contained within a procedure. It approximates procedure size. Many inlining heuristics try to mitigate object code growth by bounding the size of procedures that can be inlined.

*Loop nesting depth* - `lnd`: the number of loops in the caller that surround the call site. `lnd` proxies for execution frequency; calls in loops usually execute more often than calls outside of loops.

*Static call count* - `scc`: the number of distinct call sites that invoke the procedure in the original code. If `scc` is one, the call can be inlined with little or no code growth. If `scc` is small, the compiler might inline all of the calls and eliminate the original procedure.

*Parameter count* - `pc`: the number of formal parameters at the call. Because each parameter requires setup code, `pc` proxies for invocation cost. For small procedures, parameter setup costs can exceed the cost of inline execution [23].

*Constant-parameter count* - `cpc`: the number of constant-valued actual parameters at the call site. Constant-valued parameters may predict the benefits of optimizing the inlined code [4].

*Calls in procedure* - `clc`: the number of call sites inside the procedure that is a candidate for inlining. If `clc` is zero, the candidate is a leaf procedure. Such procedures are often small. Additionally, leaf procedures often account for a majority of total runtime.

*Dynamic call count* - `dcc`: the number of times that a call site executes during a profiling run of the program. Even minor savings at a site with with high `dcc` can produce measurable improvement. Dcc captures profiling results and gives more accurate data on which to base inlining decisions [18,6].

These metrics were chosen to enable comparison with previous studies of inlining. *The set is neither complete nor definitive*, but it is broad enough to demonstrate the power of the parameter scheme. Adding or replacing metrics is easy.

The power of our design lies not in the specific metrics that it uses, but, rather, in the parameter scheme built on top of the metrics. The inliner takes a command-line parameter, the *condition string*, that specifies a complete heuristic. The condition string is a list of clauses in disjunctive normal form. Each clause is an inequality over the program metrics, literal constants, and arithmetic operators. For example, the clause `sc - clc < 10` specifies that any procedure comprised mostly of calls should be inlined. (To be precise, the expression evaluates to true if the number of statements that are not calls is fewer than ten.) Similarly, the condition string `lnd > 0 & sc < 100 | sc < 25` returns true for any call site in a loop where the callee has fewer than 100 statements and any call that lies outside loops where the callee has fewer than 25 statements.

To apply a condition string, the inliner evaluates the expression at every call site. It inlines each call site where the string evaluates to true. Call sites are considered in a postorder walk over the call graph, starting with leaves and working toward the root. When the system inlines a call site, it updates the program metrics to reflect the transformation.[1]

The source-to-source inliner was built from Davidson and Holler's INLINER tool [10] modified to accept ANSI C. It first builds the call graph and annotates

---

[1] The current metrics cannot express heuristics that rely on the inliner's internal state: e.g., *"inline a call only if no other calls have been inlined into the caller."* Adding a metric to account for this kind of data would be straightforward.

it with the various metrics described above. It reads the condition string from the command line. Next, it evaluates the condition string at each call, in a postorder walk of the call graph that ignores backedges. If the condition string is true, the tool inlines the call and updates both the graph and its annotations. The result is a transformed source program. In our tests, we compiled the programs with gcc; individual runs of the inliner took a small fraction of the time required to compile the code with gcc.[2]

## 3   Adaptive Search of the Parameter Space

The condition string model is critical to the success of our adaptive inliner. It is not, however, sufficient to guarantee success. For that, we need an adaptive framework that can efficiently find good condition strings for each input program.[3] To guide our design efforts, we performed a series of preliminary experiments that improved our understanding of the search spaces encountered by the adaptive inliner. The experiments also provided insight into the relative importance of different program properties.

Our expressive parameter scheme creates immense search spaces. Thus, we could not exhaustively explore the spaces to improve our understanding. Instead, we conducted a series of one-, two-, and three-dimensional parameter sweeps to learn about the search space. Space constraints only permit us to discuss a small fraction of our preliminary experiments; Waterman's dissertation contains the full set of results [26].

Figure 2 shows examples of the kinds of parameter sweeps that we performed. While the individual sweeps for different programs varied in detail, several general trends emerged. Specifically, the difference between best and worst performance was significant, and it required manipulation of several parameters to achieve the best performance.

The preliminary experiments provided two kinds of insights. First, they gave us an idea of which program properties measured by the inliner had the most impact on performance. Second, they gave us an idea of the shape of the search spaces. While the search spaces contain a variety of local minima and maxima, they appear significantly smoother than the search spaces seem in the phase-ordering problem [3]. The relative smoothness of the spaces for inlining makes them appear amenable to the use of hillclimbers.

*Pruning the Search Space.* From the parameter sweeps, we learned that many parameter settings would achieve good results. Unfortunately, unrestricted

---

[2] We also experimented with Borland's C compiler for the PowerPC; both compile times and runtimes were longer than with gcc.

[3] All experiments in this paper were run on a 1GHz, dual-processor G4 Macintosh running OS X Server. Each processor has a 256kB L2 cache and 2MB L3 cache. Benchmarks were inlined with the condition string being evaluated; the resulting code was then compiled using gcc 3.3 with -O3 enabled. Each experiment ran on an unloaded machine using just one processor. When needed, we disabled inlining in gcc with -fno-inline-functions.

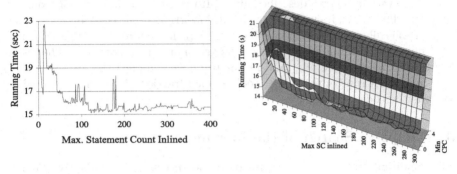

**1D Sweep of Statement Count**

**2D Sweep of Statement Count and Constant Parameter Count**

**Fig. 2.** Parameter Sweeps with `vortex`

condition strings admit huge search spaces that are impractical to search. To limit the size of those search spaces, we adopted limits on the values of parameters and on the form of the condition string. These restrictions statically prune the search space. For example, the clause $sc > k$ illustrates both problems. First, it admits an open-ended search for the unbounded parameter $k$. Second, the form of the clause limits the wrong aspect of the code; it places a lower-bound on the size of the inlined body rather than an upper bound. This clause will likely lead to large executables and little improvement. In contrast, the related clause $sc < k$ has been used productively in several systems.

We first simplified the space of possible decisions by adopting a canonical form for condition strings. The canonical string is based on our own preliminary experiments and on insights from other studies. The current system limits conditions to the form:

$$sc < A \ \mid \ sc < B \ \& \ lnd > 0 \ \mid \ sc < C \ \& \ scc = 1$$
$$\mid \ clc < D \ \mid \ cpc > E \ \& \ sc < F \ \mid \ dcc > G$$

where $A, B, C, D, E, F$, and $G$ are parameters chosen by the adaptive controller.

The first three clauses have been long been used as inlining heuristics. The first, $sc < A$, inlines any callee with fewer than $A$ statements. Small procedures cause minimal code growth when inlined; each inlined call uses roughly the same calling sequence. Thus, the strategy of inlining tiny procedures seeks maximal benefit for minimal growth. The second, $sc < B \ \& \ lnd > 0$, gives the controller a separate (presumably larger) bound for call sites inside loops because those call sites should execute more often. The third, $sc < C \ \& \ scc = 1$, sets an independent bound for procedures called from just one site, since inlining these procedures causes no code growth. (The original copy of the callee can be discarded.)

The fourth clause, $clc < D$, inlines callees that contain fewer than $D$ calls. For example, $D = 1$ inlines all leaves in the call graph. Raising the limit on `clc` produced strong results in our experiments, but has the potential to increase code size rapidly. The fifth clause, $cpc > E$ & $sc < F$, tries to capture the potential benefits from inlining a call with constant-valued parameters. The importance of constant-valued parameters to inlining has long been recognized and studied [4]. We pair the constant-parameter count with an independent limit on callee statement count to limit code growth.[4]

The final clause, $dcc > G$, captures frequently executed call sites based on data from a profiling run [6,18]. Because the benefits of inlining are multiplied by execution frequency, inlining frequent calls is often a good strategy. This clause shows, again, the importance of a strategy to limit integer parameter values. The range of values for $G$ can run from one to very large.

*Bounding Integer Parameter Values.* All of the parameter variables in the canonical string take on integer values. To limit further the search space, we must set reasonable bounds on the values for each variable—bounds that both delimit the search and avoid nonsensical values. These bounds must be program specific; for example, the upper limit on $dcc$ should be small enough to admit some inlining of hot call sites and no larger than the maximum number of executions of any call site. Our system uses a variety of measures to establish bounds on the parameters. The goal is to limit the search without eliminating good solutions.

To bound the statement-count parameters, the adaptive controller performs a fast parameter sweep. It evaluates condition strings of the form "$sc < X$", with $X = 10$ initially. The sweep doubles $X$ and reapplies the inliner until one of three conditions arises: memory constraints prevent compilation of the program; object code size has grown by a factor of ten; or the increase in $X$ produces no change from the previous value. When one of these conditions occurs, the system uses the previous value of $X$ as the maximum value for the statement-count parameter, with zero as the minimum. Other statement-count parameters are set to a multiple of this value, since they are constrained in other ways.

Bounds for the call count and constant-parameter-count variables are constants chosen from experience in our initial experiments. Call count shows good results with bounds up to three; however, $clc < 4$ produced exponential code growth in several of our benchmarks. Thus, the system limits $clc$ to the range from one to three. With the constant-parameter variable, our tests have shown no significant benefit beyond a lower-bound of three. Thus, the system limits the lower bound on $cpc$ to the range from zero to three.

The upper bound for $dcc$ is set to its largest value observed in the profile run. To set a lower bound for $dcc$, the system uses a fast parameter sweep similar to the one used to select an upper bound for $sc$. The minimum dynamic call-count required for inlining is repeatedly reduced until one of the three conditions specified earlier occurs. Table 1 summarizes these procedures.

*Discretizing Integer Parameter Ranges.* While bounding the ranges of the integer parameters does reduce the search space, it still leaves impractically many points

---

[4] While code size does not relate directly to speed, it does slow down compilation and, thus, the whole adaptive cycle. We found some huge executables that performed well, but the compile-time costs were large enough to call into question their practicality.

**Table 1.** Bounds for condition string parameters

| Parameter | Limits | Lower Bound | Upper Bound |
|:---:|:---:|:---:|:---:|
| A | sc | 0 | *fast sweep on* sc |
| B | sc | 0 | $10 * fast\ sweep\ on$ sc |
| C | sc | 0 | $10 * fast\ sweep\ on$ sc |
| D | clc | 0 | 3 |
| E | cpc | 1 | 3 |
| F | sc | 0 | *fast sweep on* c |
| G | dcc | *fast sweep on* dcc | $max(dcc)$ |

to examine. Some of the variables, such as dcc, can have extremely large bounds. For example, profiling the vortex benchmark on our training data set produces a range for dcc that runs from 57 to more than 80 million. Obviously, 80 million discrete points is too many to search. To address this problem, we discretize each large range into a set of 21 points. With this crude discretization, the condition string still generates a search space of up to 49 million points.

For our strategy to be effective, the adaptive controller must establish a good distribution of the twenty-one search points throughout the range of each discretized variable. Our first experiments divided the search points linearly across the range. We quickly realized that many parameters have extremely large ranges, but that the interesting values tend to be grouped together at lower values. We experimented with a quadratic distribution, but it succumbs to the opposite problem: points are grouped too closely together at the low end, and too sparsely at the high end. Our best results came with a hybrid of these two, a quadratic distribution with a linear coefficient: $value = c_1 x^2 + c_2 x$. Currently, the system sets $c_2$ to five, a value chosen after some tuning. The quadratic coefficient $c_1$ is program and parameter specific; it is chosen to generate the desired minimum and maximum values. Table 2 shows how these different approaches divide the parameter space for sc in vortex.

The system uses a different scheme to distribute the search points for dcc. Because the controller has a dcc value for each procedure in the program, it can distribute dcc values based on actual data. Thus, it uses a formula based

**Table 2.** Division of the sc parameter for bzip2 using different distributions

| Ordinal | 0 | 1 | 2 | 3 | 4 | 5 | 6 | 7 | 8 | 9 | 10 |
|:---:|:---:|:---:|:---:|:---:|:---:|:---:|:---:|:---:|:---:|:---:|:---:|
| Linear | 0 | 256 | 512 | 768 | 1024 | 1280 | 1536 | 1792 | 2048 | 2304 | 2560 |
| Quadratic | 0 | 13 | 51 | 115 | 205 | 320 | 461 | 627 | 819 | 1037 | 1280 |
| Hybrid | 0 | 17 | 58 | 123 | 212 | 325 | 462 | 623 | 808 | 1017 | 1250 |

| Ordinal | 11 | 12 | 13 | 14 | 15 | 16 | 17 | 18 | 19 | 20 |
|:---:|:---:|:---:|:---:|:---:|:---:|:---:|:---:|:---:|:---:|:---:|
| Linear | 2816 | 3072 | 3328 | 3584 | 3840 | 4096 | 4352 | 4608 | 4864 | 5120 |
| Quadratic | 1549 | 1843 | 2163 | 2509 | 2880 | 3277 | 3699 | 4147 | 4621 | 5120 |
| Hybrid | 1507 | 1788 | 2093 | 2422 | 2775 | 3152 | 3553 | 3978 | 4427 | 4900 |

on percentiles in the measured range. If the program has 1000 call sites with an execution frequency between the previously determined maximum and minimum, the first search point would be the dcc of the most executed call site. The second search point would be the dynamic call count of the $50^{th}$ most executed call site ($\frac{1000 \text{ points}}{20 \text{ intervals}} = 50\frac{\text{points}}{\text{interval}}$). In our experience, this distribution works well for dcc. We cannot use this approach with sc because the statement counts of a procedure change during the process of inlining. (The bottom-up order of inlining decisions means that dcc cannot change until after it has been used.)

*Searching the Spaces.* Given the canonical condition string and a set of bounds on the parameters, the question remains: how should we search this space? We elected to use a hill-climbing algorithm. As its first step, the hillclimber selects a point in the search space at random and evaluates it. Next, it evaluates the current point's neighbors, in random order. If it finds a neighbor with better results, it shifts the current focus to that point and explores that point's neighbors. This process continues until no better neighbor can be found, indicating a local minimum. Our experimental results suggest an approach that makes several descents from distinct, randomly-chosen starting points.

To implement the hillclimber, we need a concrete notion of "neighbor." The canonical condition string has seven variables that the controller can vary. We define the immediate neighbors of a point to be those arrived at by increasing or decreasing a single parameter. Thus, each point in the space defined by the canonical string has 14 potential neighbors.

The hillclimber takes the first downward step that it finds, rather than evaluating all of the current neighbors and taking the best step. Thus, it makes a *random descent* rather than a *steepest descent*. Random descent takes, on average, fewer evaluations per step. In the relatively smooth spaces that we have observed, it is more cost effective to make additional random descents than to perform fewer of the more expensive steepest descents.

*Constraining the Start Point.* The pruned search space till contains points that make poor starting points for the hillclimber. Some points produce such large transformed programs that they either fail to compile or compile so slowly that as to make the search impractical. (The hillclimber regards failure to compile as producing an infinite execution time.) Unfortunately, such points often have neighbors with the same problem. Thus, starting the search at such a point often produces no progress or painfully slow progress.

To avoid starting a search at such a point, we added a further constraint for start points. A start point must satisfy the condition: $A^2 + B^2 + C^2 + D^2 + E^2 + F^2 + G^2 \leq 400$, for the variables $A$ through $G$ in the canonical string. This constraint allows a single parameter at its maximum value, or several parameters with large values, but eliminates the unsuitable start points where too many parameters all have large initial values. The restriction only applies to a start point; the subsequent search can move outside these bounds.

**Table 3.** Improvements From Adaptive Inlining

| Method | vortex | | | bzip2 | | | mcf | | | parser | | |
|---|---|---|---|---|---|---|---|---|---|---|---|---|
| | Time | % | Dev | Time | % | Dev | Time | % | Dev | Time | % | Dev |
| gcc no inl'g | 20.95 | 100 | | 73.45 | 100 | | 48.46 | 100 | | 15.81 | 100 | |
| gcc inl'g | 17.97 | 86 | | 71.89 | 98 | | 46.94 | 97 | | 13.30 | 84 | |
| 1 descent | 15.21 | 72 | 0.51 | 71.40 | 97 | 1.84 | 47.09 | 97 | 0.42 | 12.41 | 79 | 0.13 |
| Best of 5 | 14.68 | 72 | 0.29 | 68.91 | 97 | 1.69 | 46.62 | 97 | 0.37 | 12.29 | 79 | 0.10 |
| Best of 10 | 14.52 | 69 | 0.22 | 68.15 | 93 | 1.55 | 46.36 | 96 | 0.07 | 12.14 | 77 | 0.10 |
| Best of 20 | 14.39 | 69 | 0.05 | 67.67 | 92 | 1.56 | 46.30 | 96 | 0.00 | 12.14 | 77 | 0.07 |

## 4   Experimental Results

To evaluate the adaptive inliner, we ran a set of experiments to measure the effectiveness of the inlining strategy and the effectiveness of the search strategy. In each experiment, we used the adaptive inliner to create a transformed source program, which we then compiled with gcc. We compared the results of our system against the original source code and against the results of the gcc inliner. We performed the experiments using the same computer setup that we described in Section 3. Due to space limitations, we will focus our discussion on four benchmark codes, vortex, bzip2, mcf and parser. Again, Waterman's dissertation provides more detailed results'[26].

To assess the potential impact of the adaptive inliner, we ran one hundred descents of the hillclimber on each benchmark and recorded both the running time and the condition string for each run. Using the hundred descents, we computed the average performance from a single descent (average over 100 descents), a best-of-5 run (average of 20 best-of-5 runs), a best-of-10 run (average of 10 best-of-10 runs), and a best-of-20 run (average of five best-of-20 runs). Table 3 shows these results, along with the running time for the code with no inlining and with gcc 3.3's inliner.[5] Improvements range from 4% to 31%.

On these four benchmarks, the gcc inliner always produces faster code than the original. (We saw one benchmark, gzip, where gcc's inliner produced a slowdown.) The adaptive inliner, in general, outperforms gcc's inliner. A single descent usually beats gcc; on mcf, the average single descent produced a slightly slower version than gcc's inliner. As a trend, more descents produce better results, although the returns appear to diminish beyond ten descents. The column labelled *Dev* shows the standard deviation in running time across the multiple "best-of-x" runs. While the *average* result from a single descent is close to that of a best-of-10 run, any single descent may well be far away from a better solution. Such variability is a natural result of using randomized greedy algorithms.

The improved performance and consistency from multiple descents strongly encourage such an approach. Of course, increasing the number of descents

---

[5] To maximize the performance of gcc's inliner, we moved all the source code for each application into a single file.

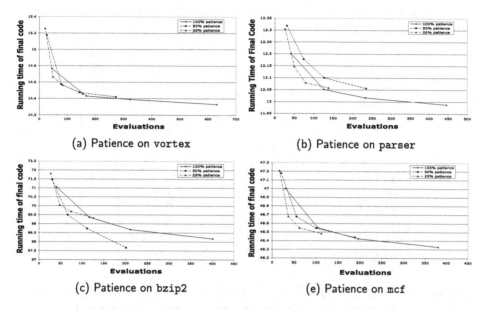

**Fig. 3.** Effects of patience on benchmark programs

increases the overall cost of finding a good heuristic. The hillclimber, at five to ten descents, seems to represent a good point on the cost/benefit curve. (Remember, the developer need not run the adaptive system on every compile. Because it returns the condition string, subsequent compiles can simply use that program-specific heuristic. The adaptive step need only be redone when program properties change in a significant way.)

To explore the tradeoff between the number of evaluations and the speed of the resulting executable, we conducted experiments with an *impatient hillclimber* [3]. A *patient hillclimber* examines each neighbor of the current point before it declares the current point to be a local minimum. An impatient hillclimber limits the number of neighbors that it will examine before deciding the current point is a local minimum. That limit, the *patience factor*, is expressed as a percentage of the neighbors. The implementation of an impatient hillclimber must select the neighbors in random order.

Because an impatient hillclimber can terminate its search prematurely, it will miss some good solutions. However, the lower cost per descent of an impatient hillclimber allows the compiler to perform more descents—to restart the search from another randomly chosen start point. We have shown elsewhere that impatient hillclimbers are effective in spaces that have a sufficient number of "good" solutions [3,15]. These experiments suggest that the search spaces in which the adaptive inliner operates have that property.

The graphs in Figure 3 show the effects of patience on both effort and solution quality for the adaptive inliner. For each benchmark, the graph shows behavior of a patient hillclimber (100% patience) and two impatient hillclimbers. We

**Table 4.** Frequency with which each neighbor was chosen as the downward step

| Step | vortex | parser | bzip2 | mcf |
|---|---|---|---|---|
| sc Increased | 7.88% | 11.17% | 15.74% | 9.30% |
| sc Decreased | 9.07% | 19.68% | 21.30% | 22.10% |
| Loop sc Increased | 8.11% | 10.64% | 0.93% | 1.16% |
| Loop sc Decreased | 8.35% | 8.51% | 1.85% | 3.49% |
| scc sc Increased | 13.60% | 10.11% | 23.15% | 20.93% |
| scc sc Decreased | 5.25% | 8.51% | 12.04% | 34.88% |
| clc Increased | 3.82% | 4.26% | 8.33% | 2.33% |
| clc Decreased | 3.82% | 2.12% | 2.78% | 2.33% |
| cpc Increased | 3.58% | 5.32% | 2.78% | 2.33% |
| cpc Decreased | 4.06% | 1.59% | 4.63% | 1.16% |
| cpc sc Increased | 6.44% | 3.19% | 0.00% | 0.00% |
| cpc sc Decreased | 3.34% | 0.53% | 0.00% | 0.00% |
| dcc Increased | 18.85% | 4.26% | 1.85% | 0.00% |
| dcc Decreased | 3.82% | 10.11% | 4.63% | 0.00% |

examine 50% and 25% patience since they provide sufficient savings to make limited patience worthwhile. Lower values would examine just one or two neighbors for each point. For these search spaces, those numbers are just too small.

The graphs show average results taken over 100 restarts. The graphs show a common and expected theme: if the system is limited to a fixed number of evaluations, an impatient hillclimber produces better results than a patient hillclimber. Multiple descents are more important to protect against a bad start point than is a thorough exploration of the neighborhood. If the number of evaluations is not a concern, multiple patient descents usually provide better results.

The results for bzip2 are an anomaly that demonstrates the noise involved in random greedy algorithms. For bzip2, we obtained better results with 50% patience than with 100% patience. We attribute the difference between the runs to the fact that they both used randomly selected starting points. Clearly, the runs at 50% patience found more effective starting points.

A final experiment that provides insight into the search space is shown in Table 4. We examined the fraction of the time that each neighbor was chosen as the downward step in the hillclimber, across the various benchmarks. Originally, we were looking for bias on which we could capitalize. The experiment showed little bias; in fact, every possible change occurs a significant percentage of the time for at least some benchmarks. This experiment produced two important conclusions. First, each parameter in the condition string plays a role in some set of decisions. This fact shows that the inliner should examine a variety of program properties. The condition string and the program metrics capture important aspects of the problem and its search spaces.

Second, the most frequently chosen parameters vary by benchmark. Thus, we should not bias the hillclimber, since trends do not carry across benchmarks. In itself, this observation is important. If the same parameters were adjusted in the same ratio across different benchmarks, then it would suggest the possibility of a universal solution to finding sets of inlining decisions. However, the wide variation in winning parameters across the benchmarks strongly supports the notion that different heuristics are needed for different programs. It reinforces our belief that adaptive inlining should outperform any static heuristic.

Taken together, these results demonstrate the efficacy of adaptive inlining. The adaptive inliner consistently outperforms the traditional inlining approach embodied in gcc; it also outperformed no inlining. In the one case where gcc's inliner degraded performance (gzip), the adaptive system discovered a heuristic that ran 15% faster than the original code. The quality of results varies based on the number of evaluations provided to the adaptive system, but good results can be obtained with a small number of evaluations using limited patience. Finally, examining the neighbors chosen by the hill climber's descent demonstrates that different sets of inlining decisions are appropriate for different programs and that an adaptive approach is necessary to capitalize fully on the potential of inlining.

## 5 Related Work

Our work touches upon two separate areas of compiler technology, adaptive control of optimization and inline substitution. Both have an extensive background in the literature. Space constraints prevent us from providing a complete related work section.

Adaptive control of optimization has been widely explored in recent years. Work has included profile-based optimization [6,13] and self-tuning libraries [27]. Several groups have looked at the problem of selecting and ordering optimizations [8,28,25,3,21]; those papers have used a variety of adaptive control mechanisms ranging from genetic algorithms [8,21] to feedback-driven search [25,3] to model-driven algorithms [28]. Other authors have looked at selecting command-line options for the compiler [14] and deriving parameters and heuristics for specific optimizations [19,24,9]. None of these studies examined flexible, expressive parameter schemes similar to ours.

Inlining has a long history in the literature, dating back to the early 1970's [2,20] [1,16,17,22]. Many authors have studied at the decision problem for inlining [4,10,7] [11,18,12,29]. The closest work to our own is by Cavazos and O'Boyle [5]. They used a genetic algorithm to tune the inlining heuristic in the Jikes RVM for new platforms. Their system derived a platform-specific, program-independent inlining heuristic; it was run once per platform as part of the process of porting the RVM. In contrast, our system uses impatient search to find reusable but program-specific inlining heuristics.

## 6 Conclusions

This paper presents the design of an adaptive inliner and results of an experimental validation of that tool. Our tool constructs a program-specific heuristic to make inlining decisions and applies that heuristic to produce a transformed version of the source compiler. Individual decisions are made by applying the heuristic on a call-site by call-site basis; the heuristic uses measured properties of the call site, caller, and callee. Our system measures seven specific program properties, but the scheme is easily extended to include new metrics.

To validate our ideas and our design, we compared the performance of the original programs, of those programs as optimized by gcc's inliner, and of those programs optimized in our system. All the versions were compiled with gcc, run, and measured. The results show that the adaptive system finds program-specific inlining heuristics that consistently outperform gcc's inliner and the original programs. Careful analysis of the adaptive system's behavior suggests that no single heuristic can achieve equivalent results across diverse programs.

Design and development of this system led to many insights. Two are particularly important. The parameterization used to express the decision heuristic lets the adaptive controller express and explore a huge decision space and allows it sufficiently precise control to obtain good results. In our experience, compilers and optimizations do not provide an interface that allows effective external control; parameter schemes similar to ours would be a substantial improvement. The techniques that we developed to deal with discretizing large integer spaces and to search them efficiently may help others as they develop adaptive controllers for other complex optimizations. Our solutions should provide a starting point for exploring those spaces and building new search algorithms.

# References

1. Allen, F., Carter, J., Fabri, J., Ferrante, J., Harrison, W., Loewner, P., Trevillyan, L.: The experimental compiling system. IBM Journal of Research and Development 24(6), 695–715 (1980)
2. Allen, F.E., Cocke, J.: A catalogue of optimizing transformations. In: Rustin, J. (ed.) Design and Optimization of a Compiler, pp. 1–30. Prentice-Hall, Englewood Cliffs (1972)
3. Almagor, L., Cooper, K.D., Grosul, A., Harvey, T.J., Reeves, S.W., Subramanian, D., Torczon, L., Waterman, T.: Finding effective compilation sequences. In: Proceedings of the 2004 ACM SIGPLAN/SIGBED Conference on Languages, Compilers and Tools for Embedded Systems, June 2004, pp. 231–239 (2004)
4. Ball, J.E.: Predicting the effects of optimization on a procedure body. In: Proceedings of the 1979 SIGPLAN Symposium on Compiler Construction, August 1979, pp. 214–220 (1979)
5. Cavazos, J., O'Boyle, M.F.P.: Automatic tuning of inlining heuristics. In: Proceedings of the 2005 ACM IEEE Conference on Supercomputing (SC 2005) (November 2005)
6. Chang, P.P., Mahlke, S.A., Hwu, W.W.: Using profile information to assist classic code optimizations. Software—Practice and Experience 21(12), 1301–1321 (1991)
7. Cooper, K.D., Hall, M.W., Torczon, L.: An experiment with inline substitution. Software—Practice and Experience 21(6), 581–601 (1991)
8. Cooper, K.D., Schielke, P.J., Subramanian, D.: Optimizing for reduced code space using genetic algorithms. In: Proceedings of the ACM SIGPLAN Workshop on Languages, Compilers, and Tools for Embedded Systems, May 1999, pp. 1–9 (1999)

9. Cooper, K.D., Waterman, T.: Investigating adaptive compilation using the MIP-Spro compiler. In: Proceedings of the 2003 LACSI Symposium, October 2003, Los Alamos Computer Science Institute, Santa Fe, NM (2003)
10. Davidson, J.W., Holler, A.M.: A study of a C function inliner. Software—Practice and Experience 18(8), 775–790 (1988)
11. Davidson, J.W., Holler, A.M.: Subprogram inlining: A study of its effects on program execution time. IEEE Transactions on Software Engineering 18(2), 89–102 (1992)
12. Dean, J., Chambers, C.: Towards better inlining decisions using inlining trials. In: Proceedings of the 1994 ACM Conference on LISP and Functional Programming, June 1994, pp. 273–282 (1994)
13. Fisher, J.A.: Trace scheduling: A technique for global microcode compaction. IEEE Transactions on Computers C-30(7), 478–490 (1981)
14. Granston, E., Holler, A.: Automatic recommendation of compiler options. In: Proceedings of the 4th Feedback Directed Optimization Workshop (December 2001)
15. Grosul, A.: Adaptive Ordering of Code Transformations in an Optimizing Compiler. PhD thesis, Rice University (2005)
16. Harrison, W.: A new strategy for code generation - the general purpose optimizing compiler. In: Proceedings of the 4th ACM SIGACT-SIGPLAN symposium on Principles of programming languages, January 1977, pp. 29–37 (1977)
17. Hecht, M.S.: Flow Analysis of Computer Programs. Elsevier North-Holland, New York (1977)
18. Hwu, W.W., Chang, P.P.: Inline function expansion for compiling C programs. In: Proceedings of the ACM SIGPLAN 1989 Conference on Programming Language Design and Implementation, June 1989, pp. 246–257 (1989)
19. Kisuki, T., Knijnenburg, P., O'Boyle, M.: Combined selection of tile sizes and unroll factors using iterative compilation. In: Proceedings of the 2000 International Conference on Parallel Architectures and Compilation Techniques, October 2000, pp. 237–248 (2000)
20. Knuth, D.E.: An empirical study of FORTRAN programs. Software—Practice and Experience 1(2), 105–133 (1971)
21. Kulkarni, P.A., Hines, S.R., Whalley, D.B., Hiser, J.D., Davidson, J.W., Jones, D.L.: Fast and efficient searches for effective optimization-phase sequences. ACM Trans. Archit. Code Optim. 2(2), 165–198 (2005)
22. Scheifler, R.W.: An analysis of inline substitution for a structured programming language. Communications of the ACM 20(9), 647–654 (1977)
23. Serrano, M.: Inline expansion: *when* and *how*? In: Serrano, M. (ed.) Proceedings of the Ninth International Symposium on Programming Languages, Implementations, Logics, and Programs, September 1997, pp. 143–147 (1997)
24. Stephenson, M., Amarasinghe, S., Martin, M., O'Reilly, U.-M.: Meta optimization: Improving compiler heuristics with machine learning. In: Proceedings of the ACM SIGPLAN 2003 Conference on Programming Language Design and Implementation (June 2003)
25. Triantafyllis, S., Vachharajani, M., Vachharajani, N., August, D.I.: Compiler optimization-space exploration. In: Proceedings of the International Symposium on Code Generation and Optimization: Feedback directed and runtime-optimization, March 2003, pp. 204–215 (2003)
26. Waterman, T.: Adaptive Compilation and Inlining. PhD thesis, Rice Univ. (2005)

27. Whaley, R.C., Petitet, A., Dongarra, J.J.: Automated empirical optimization of software and the ATLAS project. Parallel Computing 27(1–2), 3–25 (2001)
28. Zhao, M., Childers, B., Soffa, M.L.: Predicting the impact of optimizations for embedded systems. In: Proceedings of the 2003 ACM SIGPLAN Conference on Languages, Tools, and Compilers for Embedded Systems, June 2003, pp. 1–11 (2003)
29. Zhao, P., Amaral, J.N.: To inline or not to inline? enhanced inlining decisions. In: Proceedings of the 16th International Workshop on Languages and Compilers for Parallel Computing, October 2003, pp. 405–419 (2003)

# Automatic Transformation of Bit-Level C Code to Support Multiple Equivalent Data Layouts

Marius Nita and Dan Grossman

Department of Computer Science & Engineering
University of Washington, Seattle WA 98195-2350, USA
{marius,djg}@cs.washington.edu

**Abstract.** Portable low-level C programs must often support multiple equivalent in-memory layouts of data, due to the byte or bit order of the compiler, architecture, or external data formats. Code that makes assumptions about data layout often consists of multiple highly similar pieces of code, each designed to handle a different layout. Writing and maintaining this code is difficult and bug-prone: Because the differences among data layouts are subtle, implicit, and inherently low-level, it is difficult to understand or change the highly similar pieces of code consistently.

We have developed a small extension for C that lets programmers write concise declarative descriptions of how different layouts of the same data relate to each other. Programmers then write code assuming only one layout and rely on our translation to generate code for the others. In this work, we describe our declarative language for specifying data layouts, how we perform the automatic translation of C code to equivalent code assuming a different layout, and our success in applying our approach to simplify the code base of some widely available software.

## 1   Introduction

C is sometimes referred to as a "portable assembly language" because it is implemented for almost every platform and allows direct bit-level access to raw memory. It remains the *de facto* standard for writing low-level code such as debuggers and run-time systems that manipulate low-level data representations or process external file formats. It is therefore quite ironic that C is *not* well-suited to writing *portable* bit-level code.

In practice, for such code to be portable it must support multiple equivalent data formats. A ubiquitous example is big-endian and little-endian byte order. The order of bit-fields in a struct can also vary with compilers. Additional idiosyncratic examples arise with each unusual file format, compiler, or architecture. Though such code is occasionally performance-critical (e.g., network-packet processing), it usually is not (e.g., file-header processing).

Writing portable code is time-consuming and error-prone. Simple web searches reveal hundreds of (known) endianness bugs. Even for bug-free code, data-layout portability often leads to large amounts of code duplication; using Google

L. Hendren (Ed.): CC 2008, LNCS 4959, pp. 85–99, 2008.
© Springer-Verlag Berlin Heidelberg 2008

Code Search we found approximately one thousand open-source packages with near-identical code segments based on byte- or bit-order. Such code segments are often poorly documented and are difficult to maintain consistently, particularly because the code is inherently low-level.

## 1.1    Conventional Approaches

We believe the most common approach to supporting multiple equivalent data layouts is, indeed, code duplication and conditionals (typically with the preprocessor) to choose the correct variant. In our experience, a common approach to such duplication is that one version of the code is developed first (e.g., for a big-endian machine), then — perhaps much later when portability issues arise — the code is copied, one copy is edited, and an `#ifdef` chooses between copies. This process is error-prone and leads to maintenance problems as the copies must remain consistent.

A natural alternative is to abstract all data-layout assumptions into helper functions, confining code duplication to the smallest amount of code possible. We believe dismissing any code that does not follow this approach as "poorly written" is naive. First, if a nonportable code segment is already written, changing it to abstract out such assumptions could introduce bugs on mature platforms. Second, the resulting code can be much harder to read and understand: C *is* good at expressing bit-level operations directly so the code is often reasonably clear when specialized to a given data layout.

## 1.2    Our Approach

We have developed a tool that takes annotated C code and lets programmers (1) write one version of their code assuming one particular data layout and (2) declaratively specify multiple equivalent data layouts. We then perform a source-to-source transformation that automatically generates versions of the code for each data layout. In this way, we retain the coding effort and clarity of writing nonportable code while supporting portability. We simply use compiler technology to do what it does well: transform code to equivalent versions. Moreover, the declarative specifications are concise documentation of data-layout assumptions.

Our approach should fit well with typical software development. Programmers can still write nonportable code first and then add data-layout specifications and "port statements" (described later) to indicate where to perform our source-to-source transformation. Our tool can be used incrementally since only code executed in the lexical scope of a port statement needs transforming. By producing regular C code, the output of our tool can be distributed as open-source software, processed by conventional tools, or edited manually.

## 1.3    Outline

This paper describes our tool, how our transformation works, and our preliminary experience rewriting portions of the Gnu Debugger and Gnu Binary File

```
1     enum endian { BIG, LITTLE };
2     struct reloc { char idx[3]; char type; };
3     int idx, extern, pcrel, neg, length;
4     struct reloc *reloc;
      ...
5     if (bfd_header_endian(abfd) == BIG) {
6       reloc->idx[0] = idx >> 16;
7       reloc->idx[1] = idx >> 8;
8       reloc->idx[2] = idx;
9       reloc->type = ((extern ?  0x10 : 0) | (pcrel ?   0x80 : 0)
10                     | (neg ?    0x08 : 0) | (length << 5));
11    } else {
12      reloc->idx[2] = idx >> 16;
13      reloc->idx[1] = idx >> 8;
14      reloc->idx[0] = idx;
15      reloc->type = ((extern ?  0x08 : 0) | (pcrel ?   0x01 : 0)
16                     | (neg ?    0x10 : 0) | (length << 1));
17    }
```

**Fig. 1.** Example BFD code

Descriptor Library with our approach. Section 2 informally presents a real example to give a programmer's view of our extension. Section 3 then describes our language extensions completely. Section 4 describes our implementation, i.e., how we perform the source-to-source transformation. Section 5 describes some preliminary experience. Section 6 describes related work, and Section 7 concludes with several directions for future work.

## 2   Example

To give a flavor for how our tool works, we demonstrate its use on a code snippet from the Gnu Binary File Descriptor Library (BFD) [17], a library that facilitates working with binary formats such as a.out or ELF. Sections within some of these formats may be stored in either little- or big-endian order. Code that reads or writes these formats comes in two halves, each half handling one data layout.

Example 1 shows a snippet of such BFD code, rewritten slightly for conciseness. reloc->idx stores the three low-order bytes in idx either left-to-right (lines 6-8) or right-to-left (lines 12-14), depending on the byte order of the header section in the binary format being handled. The field reloc->type is an 8-bit piece of data holding six bit-flags and one 2-bit piece of data. Depending on the endianness of the header, the bit data is stored in either left-to-right (lines 9-10) or right-to-left (lines 15-16) order. Notice that the two representations of reloc->type are *not* related by the bitwise reverse function. The order of the two bits within length remains unchanged.

Changes to this code must be done simultaneously to both halves, taking into account the low-level details about how the representations differ. The bit

```
enum endian { BIG, LITTLE };
struct reloc {
  char idx[3] @ match endian,byte with BIG    -> 0:1:2
                                       | LITTLE -> 2:1:0;
  char type   @ match endian,bit  with BIG    -> 0:1:2:3:4:5:6:7
                                       | LITTLE -> 7:5:6:4:3:2:1:0;
};
  int idx, extern, pcrel, neg, length;
struct reloc *reloc;
  ...
port (bfd_header_endian(abfd), BIG) {
  reloc->idx[0] = idx >> 16;
  reloc->idx[1] = idx >> 8;
  reloc->idx[2] = idx;
  reloc->type = ((extern ?  0x10 : 0) | (pcrel ?    0x80 : 0)
             | (neg ?     0x08 : 0) | (length << 5));
}
```

**Fig. 2.** Figure 1, rewritten for use with our tool

constants 0x10, 0x08, and 0x80 correspond to bitwise reverse analogues in the opposite half: 0x08, 0x10, and 0x01. The left-shift and bitwise-or on line 9 place the two bits in `length` in `reloc->type`'s bits 6 and 7. Since the representation is reversed on the other endianness, these bits will occupy positions 2 and 3, so a left-shift by 5 on big-endian formats must be accompanied by a left-shift by 1 on little-endian formats. The programmer must understand all these details when writing and changing this code, and ensure that changes to one half are propagated into the other half in a way that respects these low-level implicit relationships between data layouts.

Figure 2 shows the code in Figure 1, rewritten for use with our tool. Two points are worth emphasizing. First, we write only half the code, assuming one data representation. Second, the relationships between the two data representations for each `reloc->idx` and `reloc->type` are made explicit in the field declarations within `struct reloc`.

The extra declaration sections (to the right of @) on the two fields define how equivalent data layouts of the same data relate to each other. `match`, `byte`, `bit`, and `with` are built-in keywords, `endian` is a C enumeration type defined by the programmer and inhabited by the constants `BIG` and `LITTLE`, and the colon-delimited sequences specify how positions of the bytes or bits within data change from one data layout to another. The specifications case over the type `endian` and provide a data layout for each of its constants. The keywords `bit` and `byte` define the granularity of the specification — whether the numbers in the colon-delimited sequence denote bits or bytes.

The specification on field `idx` says that `idx` is laid out in two ways, each corresponding to an `endian` constant. The two layouts are the reverse of the

```
enum endian { BIG, LITTLE };
struct reloc { char idx[3]; char type; };
int idx, extern, pcrel, neg, length;
struct reloc *reloc;
...

int tmp = bfd_header_endian(abfd);
switch (tmp) {
case LITTLE: flip₀(reloc->idx);
             flip₁(& reloc->type);
             break;
case BIG:    break;
}
reloc->idx[0] = idx >> 16;
reloc->idx[1] = idx >> 8;
reloc->idx[2] = idx;
reloc->type = ((extern ?  0x10 : 0) | (pcrel ?   0x80 : 0)
             | (neg ?      0x08 : 0) | (length << 5));
switch (tmp) {
case LITTLE: unflip₀(reloc->idx);
             unflip₁(& reloc->type);
             break;
case BIG:    break;
}
```

**Fig. 3.** Our translation applied to the code in Figure 2

other $(0:1:2$ vs $2:1:0)$, at a byte-level granularity. The declaration on field type is at the granularity of bits, but the two representations are not quite the reverse of each other. Bits 5 and 6, which represent the two length bits, remain in the same order.

The constants BIG and LITTLE associated with the layout declarations are used in the translation of the port statement. The port statement is written under the assumption that bfd_header_endian(abfd) evaluates to BIG. If it evaluates to LITTLE, our translation assumes that the bytes within reloc->idx should be represented in order $2:1:0$, i.e., the reverse of how they would be laid out when bfd_header_endian(abfd) evaluates to BIG. Therefore, when it evaluates to LITTLE, the bytes within reloc->idx are reversed prior to entering the body of the port. Likewise, the bits within reloc->type are shuffled according to the $7:5:6:4:3:2:1:0$ specification. When bfd_header_endian(abfd) evaluates to BIG, the body is simply executed. The end result is that the code in Figure 2 executes exactly as the code in Figure 1, but is shorter, better-documented, and easier to write and maintain.

Figure 3 shows the code generated by our translation for the program in Figure 2. When bfd_header_endian(abfd) evaluates to LITTLE, the layouts of reloc->idx and reloc->type are flipped by functions $flip_0$ and $flip_1$ in accord with the specifications attached to the corresponding field declarations. When control enters what used to be the body of the port block, the two fields are laid out as they would be when `bfd_header_endian(abfd)` evaluates to `BIG`, which matches the code's assumptions. When control exits this code, the layouts of the two fields are flipped back into their original forms by functions $unflip_0$ and $unflip_1$. The $flip$ and $unflip$ functions are automatically generated by our translation from the specifications on the two fields. The bodies of $flip_1$ and $unflip_1$ are shown in Figure 5 on page 94; the code for $flip_0$ and $unflip_0$ is straightforward. An analysis determines the data whose layouts should be flipped/unflipped, by inspecting all variable and field accesses and checking if their declarations contain a layout specification that cases over the type `endian`.

# 3    Description of the Extension

Having described our tool via an example, we now give a complete description of our annotations, their meaning, and how we perform our automatic translation to support multiple data layouts.

At the syntax level, our extension has two components. First, we extend C's declaration language to allow specifying multiple equivalent data layouts for variables and fields. Second, we introduce a new statement form `port(e,c){e'}` that allows programmers to write code assuming only one data representation. A translation takes code written with our extension and outputs code suitable for passing to a C compiler.

## 3.1    The Specification Language

A layout specification is written as

$$\texttt{match}\ \tau, g\ \texttt{with}\ c_1 \rightarrow s_1\ |\ c_2 \rightarrow s_2\ |\ \ldots\ |\ c_n \rightarrow s_n$$

Symbols $c_i$ are C enumeration constants belonging to enumeration type $\tau$ and $s_i$ are colon-delimited sequences containing either natural numbers (starting at 0) or the symbol '_'. $g$ denotes the granularity of the specification. Our system supports granularities `bit`, `byte`, and `nibble`. Others are easily added. Layout specifications can appear on local and global variables and struct fields of integral type (`char`, `int`, etc.) and arrays thereof.

A sequence $s$ assigns names to the underlying layout units in the data, according to the granularity $g$. For example, if the specification on a 4-byte piece of data has granularity `byte`, a sequence `0:1:2:3` assigns names 0 through 3 to the bytes within the data. In addition to numbers, sequences $s$ may contain '_' symbols, meaning that the corresponding layout units do not contain useful data and need not be named, e.g., pad bytes. For example, a sequence `0:1:_:_` represents a 4-byte sequence containing two named data bytes and two pad bytes.

A sequence $s$ is not useful in isolation. Two or more, however, can precisely describe how multiple equivalent layouts of the same data relate to each other. For example, the sequences `0:1:2` and `2:1:0` represent two layouts that are related by the reverse function. We say that they are *equivalent* because all the layout units (bits, bytes, nibbles) in one are present in the other.

Each sequence $s$ is associated with a constant $c$. The set of constants in a specification is used by the `port` block (described in the next section) to specify its assumptions about the layouts of variables and fields used in its body.

Given two layout specification sequences $s_1$ and $s_2$, we can generate a *flip* function that takes a piece of data assumed to be laid out as described by $s_1$ and shuffles it such that the result is laid out according to $s_2$. In our tool, we must also generate an *unflip* function that undoes this effect, flipping data that is laid out according to $s_2$ back into its original layout, $s_1$. Functionally, *flip* is an isomorphism and *unflip* is its inverse. It would be unexpected, from the point of view of the programmer, for either function to "forget" bits or bytes within the data, with the exception of "don't care" (_) layout units.

In order to ensure that *flip* and *unflip* functions respect this behavior and to facilitate C code generation, we restrict the set of layout specifications that can be written to those that are *well-formed*. A specification (`match` $\tau, g$ `with` $c_1$ `->` $s_1$ | ... | $c_n$ `->` $s_n$) is well-formed if:

1. Constants do not overlap: $c_i \neq c_j$ when $i \neq j$.
2. All constants inhabiting type $\tau$ must be included in the specification.
3. All $s_i$'s are equal in length. The lengths are multiples of 8 bits.
4. For all $s_i$, no number within $s_i$ appears more than once.
5. Any number that occurs in an $s_i$ must occur in all others.

The first two requirements ensure that specifications are complete and deterministic. Given a constant $c$, there is exactly one layout per variable or field associated with it. The rest of the requirements ensure that well-formed specifications do not contain any layout sequences that forget or add data. We also assume that the sequence lengths are multiples of 8 bits, as C types have sizes that are multiples of bytes. The assumption aids our code generation, which breaks layouts into bytes.

## 3.2   The `port` Statement

In addition to layout specifications on declarations, our extension provides a new `port` statement. The statement is provided as a means for programmers to delimit code that probes the in-memory layout of data with multiple possible layouts. Programmers write the body of `port` assuming one layout and the compiler generates code that will work as intended for the other layouts.

A `port` block is written as

$$\texttt{port}(e,\ c)\ \{\ e'\ \}$$

where $c$ is a constant with enumeration type $\tau$. The enumeration type and associated constants $c_i$ in the layout specification language provide the connection between specifications and the `port` statement. For each piece of data used in $e'$ whose declarations carry associated layout specifications at type $\tau$ (meaning the specifications case over $\tau$), the constants inhabiting $\tau$ represent different ways to lay out the bytes, bits, and nibbles in that data. (Recall that each sequence $s_k$ in a layout specification corresponds to a constant $c_k$.) The programmer writes the body of the port block, $e'$, under the assumption that variables and fields used in $e'$ are laid out according to $c$. This is assumed to be the case when $e$ evaluates to $c$. If $e$ evaluates to a constant $c' \neq c$, the programmer's assumptions no longer hold. The compiler will then ensure that before $e'$ is executed, the layouts of the variables and fields within $e'$ are laid out according to $c$, and when control exits $e'$, they are laid out as they were before control reached the port block.

Consider the following code, which prints the high-order byte within the layout of a 32-bit integer:

```
int x @ match endian,byte with BIG     -> 0:1:2:3
                             | LITTLE -> 3:2:1:0;
...
port(endianness(), BIG) { printf("%x", ((char*)&x)[0]); }
```

Here, the programmer assumes that endianness() evaluates to BIG and writes code that is correct for big-endian machines. If endianness() evaluates to LITTLE, the body of the port block is obviously incorrect — it does not print the high-order byte. In this case, the compiler uses the specification attached to x to ensure that its bytes are laid out according to the block's assumptions. In this case, the bytes within x are reversed.

More precisely, the semantics of port$(e,c)\{e'\}$ is as follows:

- If $e$ evaluates to $c$, no further action is required and the body $e'$ is executed.
- If $e$ evaluates to $c' \neq c$, the layout of every variable and field used within $e'$ with a specification at the type of $c$ will be "flipped" to match the assumption that they are laid out according to $c$. The layouts are "unflipped" to their original states after $e'$ is executed.

We allow nesting of port blocks as long as their associated constants $c$ are of different types, to avoid re-flipping data that was already flipped by an outer port block. While we could allow arbitrary nesting and use a simple analysis to avoid re-flipping, in practice it makes little sense to nest blocks in this manner. (E.g., it is akin to nesting a block guarded by #ifdef LITTLE within one guarded by #ifdef BIG.)

### 3.3   Translation

Given a program written using our extensions, a translation produces plain C code that respects the semantics outlined in the previous section. The translation transforms the code in the following ways:

- It erases the data-representation specifications from variable and field declarations.
- If a variable or field with multiple layouts is accessed within a port block, the translation generates a *flip* function and an *unflip* function. The first flips the layout of the data to accord with the block's assumptions and the latter flips its layout back into its original form.

```
int tmp = e;
switch(tmp) {
  case c₁: flip₁₁(& x₁); ... flip₁ₘ(& xₘ); break;        /* from c₁ to c */
  ...
  case c: break;                                          /* already in c */
  ...
  case cₙ: flipₙ₁(& x₁); ... flipₙₘ(& xₘ); break;         /* from cₙ to c */
}
e';
switch(tmp) {
  case c₁: unflip₁₁(& x₁); ... unflip₁ₘ(& xₘ); break;     /* from c to c₁ */
  ...
  case c: break;                                          /* already in c */
  ...
  case cₙ: unflipₙ₁(& x₁); ... unflipₙₘ(& xₘ); break;     /* from c to cₙ */
}
```

**Fig. 4.** Translation of `port(e,c){e'}`

- It rewrites `port(e,c){e'}` statements to plain C code that calls *flip* functions prior to entering $e'$, executes $e'$, and calls *unflip* functions upon exiting $e'$.

Given a statement `port(e,c){e'}` where $c$ has enumeration type $\tau$, the translation proceeds as follows. First, we gather all the variables and field accesses $x_1, x_2, \ldots, x_m$ that are used in $e'$ and have associated layout specifications at type $\tau$. Let the set of constants inhabiting $\tau$ be $c_1, c_2, \ldots, c_n$. Each of the variables and field accesses $x_i$ will have an associated layout specification that assigns a layout to each constant $c_i$.

The translation scheme is shown in Figure 4. First, we generate code that evaluates $e$ and saves the result in a fresh temporary $tmp$. Then we generate code that, depending on the result of $e$, flips the layouts of $x_1, \ldots, x_m$ so that they match the assumptions in $e'$ — that the $x_i$ are laid out according to the specifications corresponding to constant $c$. We then generate $e'$ unchanged. After $e'$, we generate code that flips the layouts of $x_i$ back to their original forms. For each constant $c_i$, each variable and field access $x_j$ will have $c_i$ -> $s_i$ and $c$ -> $s$ included in its associated specification. The function *flip*$_{ij}$ changes the layout of $x_i$ from $s_i$ into $s$ and and *unflip*$_{ij}$ changes it back from $s$ into $s_i$.

The translation calls flip/unflip functions for exactly the variables that (1) have multiple data layouts and (2) are accessed in the lexical scope of the port block. Notice any references to such variables passed to functions called in the port block will refer to flipped data, i.e., the flipping happens in place.[1] In theory, if two items that need flipping might alias, we need to check for aliasing dynamically to avoid double-flipping (and unflipping). In practice, we have not

---

[1] Conversely, we do not flip any data that is accessed in a callee but not mentioned directly in the port block. This can be an issue only with global variables or extremely convoluted code and this has not been a problem in practice.

```
void flip₁(void * input) {              void unflip₁(void * input) {
    char* t₀ = (char*)input;                char* t₀ = (char*)input;
    char t₁ = t₀[0];                        char t₁ = t₀[0];
    t₀[0] = 0;                              t₀[0] = 0;
    t₀[0] |= ((t₁ << 7) & 0x80);            t₀[0] |= ((t₁ << 7) & 0x80);
    t₀[0] |= ((t₁ << 4) & 0x40);            t₀[0] |= ((t₁ << 5) & 0x40);
    t₀[0] |= ((t₁ << 4) & 0x20);            t₀[0] |= ((t₁ << 3) & 0x20);
    t₀[0] |= ((t₁ << 1) & 0x10);            t₀[0] |= ((t₁ << 1) & 0x10);
    t₀[0] |= ((t₁ >> 1) & 0x08);            t₀[0] |= ((t₁ >> 1) & 0x08);
    t₀[0] |= ((t₁ >> 3) & 0x04);            t₀[0] |= ((t₁ >> 4) & 0x04);
    t₀[0] |= ((t₁ >> 5) & 0x02);            t₀[0] |= ((t₁ >> 4) & 0x02);
    t₀[0] |= ((t₁ >> 7) & 0x01);            t₀[0] |= ((t₁ >> 7) & 0x01);
}                                       }
```

**Fig. 5.** Flip and unflip functions for `reloc->type` in Figure 2

encountered any code where such aliasing occurred, suggesting it may instead be reasonable and in the spirit of C to make such aliasing an unchecked error.

### 3.4 Generation of Flip Functions

Our tool generates *flip* and *unflip* functions that mutate the layouts of their input data in-place. The prototype of every flip function has the form void *flip*(void*). Variables and fields whose layouts must be flipped are passed to their corresponding flip functions by address.

The body of a flip function breaks its input into bytes, via a cast to `char*`, and saves them in temporary variables. If the specified granularity is `byte`, flipping is a matter of assigning the temporaries into their new locations in the input. For smaller granularities, we generate bit-shifting and masking code to fetch the bits or nibbles from within the temporaries holding bytes and code to assign them to their new locations.

Figure 5 shows the *flip* and *unflip* functions generated by our translation from the specification on field `type` in Figure 2. For each bit in the input layout, we generate code that shifts it to the position specified by the output sequence and masks out the rest of the bits. The result is added to the output sequence by a bitwise-or. Code generation at `nibble` granularity is similar, except the only possible masks are `0xf0` and `0x0f`, and we shift by either 4 or 0 bits.

## 4    Implementation

Our prototype is implemented as a modification of the CIL frontend for C [14]. CIL inputs a C program, performs a series of transformations to simplify the code into a uniform subset of C, and outputs equivalent, human-readable C code. In addition, one can provide custom transformations that are applied to the intermediate representations before the output phase.

We modified CIL's parser, lexer, and abstract syntax to allow **port** statements and layout specifications in the input language. We then implemented a custom transformation that erases layout specifications and rewrites **port** blocks according to the translation scheme in Figure 4. In addition, *flip* and *unflip* functions are generated and inserted into the output program. We have also experimented with generating preprocessor macros instead of functions.

The tool outputs clean C code suitable for passing to a C compiler. As discussed more thoroughly in Section 5, a standard optimizing compiler is capable of entirely optimizing away byte-level flips when flips are generated as macros, and the overhead induced by bit- and nibble-level flips is manageable.

In our implementation, the annotation language is a syntactic extension to the C language. However, should it be desired, it is easy to encode annotations in stylized comments or empty preprocessor macros, such that an annotated program is still legal (but nonportable) C.

# 5   Experience

To assess the usefulness of the tool, we applied it to subsets of two pieces of software: the Gnu Debugger (GDB) [16] and the BFD library, which ship together as part of the GDB distribution. Preliminary experience suggests that our tool is a valuable addition to the developer's toolset. It improves readability, shrinks the code base, and aids in minimizing development and maintenance issues associated with code that is duplicated for the purpose of handling multiple data layouts. In the rest of this section, we describe how we simplified part of the GDB/BFD code base, present some quantitative results, discuss the limitations of our tool, and share our experiences modifying GDB/BFD code.

*Simplifying the Code Base:* To estimate the extent of the code-duplication problem in GDB/BFD, we manually examined 120 files in a source base of roughly 1700 C files and 1 million lines of code. In these files, we recorded 407 occurrences of snippets where multiple versions of the same code were specialized to particular data layouts. We counted roughly 3600 lines of duplicated code: code that could be potentially eliminated with our tool. While we focused on the part of the source base that we believe contains a lot of code doing low-level data processing, there is surely more such code in the part of the enormous source base that we have not inspected.

We applied our tool to 10 of these files, chosen in no particular fashion. Across the 10 files, we found 31 occurrences of highly similar code-pairs with each half specialized to a particular endianness. We used the **port** statement to eliminate half the code in each of these occurrences, totaling 188 lines (2,465 lexical tokens) of code. To ensure that the new code behaved the same as the old handwritten code, 11 data-layout annotations were required, each specifying two possible data layouts.

Two of the annotations (the ones shown in Figure 2) sufficed for 21 of the 31 **port** statements and contributed to eliminating 124 lines (1,894 lexical tokens) of code. The struct type with which they are associated is used by many files in the BFD code base. Many of the other annotations were localized, on local variables within functions in which the `port` blocks were placed, and affected one or two occurrences of `port`. In one case, 3 annotations affected 2 blocks.

In addition to code being eliminated directly by `port` blocks, some related "scaffolding code" became superfluous. Developers tuck hard-to-understand bit-masks and flags into pairs of macro definitions, such as:

```
#define RELOC_STD_BITS_LENGTH_BIG        0x60
#define RELOC_STD_BITS_LENGTH_LITTLE     0x06
#define RELOC_STD_BITS_LENGTH_SH_BIG     5
#define RELOC_STD_BITS_LENGTH_SH_LITTLE 1
```

The former two are bit-masks used to identify the two `length` bits from Figure 1 in a byte. The latter two are amounts by which to shift left to place the `length` bits in a byte. In each case, big- and little-endian versions of the constants are provided. After applying our tool, half these constants were no longer needed.

*Performance:* None of our changes had an observable performance impact on GDB. First, none of the code blocks we found and changed were in inner loops or other performance-critical sections. Second, the overhead of our translation is small, as the underlying compiler optimizes our code efficiently.

To gain a preliminary understanding of the performance impact of the generated *flip* code currently generated by our system, we picked `port` statements from the ported BFD source and compared the quality of the generated code to the previous handwritten code. Since our generated code consists of flipping some layouts, executing handwritten code, then unflipping the layouts, the performance overhead consists entirely of executing flip and unflip functions. Of the 31 blocks we ported, the average number of required flips/unflips was 1.5 and the maximum was 3.

We noticed that if we generate preprocessor macros instead of functions, byte-level flips are entirely optimized away by `gcc -O3`. For example, `gcc` produces the same assembly code for `flip(x); y=x[0]; unflip(x);` as it does for `y=x[3];`. This is hardly surprising, as all that is needed for this optimization is copy propagation and dead-code elimination. In their current form, bit- and nibble-level flips are not optimized as efficiently and can add 50%–100% overhead in number of executed instructions. This is expected, as most of the time, the code executed between flips and unflips is roughly the size of a flip body.

*Limitations:* There were two low-level code-pairs that we could not port to our tool. Take, for example, the following snippet:

```
char valbuf[4];
...
if (TARGET_BYTE_ORDER == BFD_ENDIAN_BIG)
  memcpy (valbuf + (4 - len), val, len);
else
  memcpy (valbuf, (char *) val, len);
```

The code copies `val` into `valbuf` such that the bytes in `val` are right-justified on big-endian targets and left-justified on little-endian ones. Assuming the bytes within `val` are not already reversed on big-endian machines, we cannot write a static specification that handles this pattern, since `len` is a dynamic value. This makes clear the main limitation of our approach: it does not apply when the two equivalent data layouts cannot be specified statically.

*Discussion:* The process of determining relationships between equivalent data layouts by reading the code was difficult. First, bit-masks and shift constants are hidden under macros that are scattered across header files far away from the code that uses them. Second, code-pairs that touch the layout of data usually only inspect a subset of the underlying bits and bytes, so one must inspect several code-pairs before gaining a thorough understanding of the layout relationships. Third, identifying the code-pairs themselves is a problem, as there are many ways to express conditionals that run code depending on a particular layout. One may use `#ifdefs` or `if` statements, and in each case the predicate may be different (e.g., `bfd_header_endian()` vs. `TARGET_BYTE_ORDER == BFD_ENDIAN_BIG`).

We believe our rewritten code is much easier to understand than the original: Bit-level code is clearly delimited by port statements and the relationships between equivalent layouts are explicit. We do not necessarily advocate rewriting mature subtle bit-level code unless it is already being maintained or modified for other reasons; we did so to evaluate our research on real code used in practice that we did not write. We definitely do advocate using our approach for new code or when making code portable for the first time.

## 6    Related Work

We are unaware of any prior work that automatically translates bit-level C code to work for multiple data layouts. Our own recent prior work [15] was designed to find type-casts that rely on platform-specific assumptions to be memory-safe. That work, while useful for finding certain classes of bugs related to structure padding and word size, does not address the issues associated with multiple data layouts. More significantly, for bit-level differences such as endianness, our prior work will never find bugs, since assuming the wrong endianness does not violate memory safety — it just produces the wrong answer.

CCured [13], Deputy [3], SAFECode [4], and Cyclone [9] are projects that aim to make C safer and more expressive, in some cases enriching it with new programming abstractions, and compiling it in a way that prevents unchecked errors. These systems are similar to ours in that they perform source-to-source transformations and pass the output to a C compiler. However, they do not facilitate working with multiple data layouts. Programmers must resort to specializing code to each endianness as they would in plain C.

Some analyses over C programs (e.g. [12,19]) assume one bit-level layout for any piece of data, which is useful for precision, but not for writing portable code.

PADS [7], PacketTypes [10], and DataScript [1] are projects that facilitate working with data formats. PacketTypes lets programmers specify the layout of network packets using a declarative language. Similarly, PADS uses a declarative language to allow specifying arbitrary ad-hoc data formats, both textual and binary, and automatically generates parsers that process the data. Like PADS, DataScript takes declarative specifications for binary formats and generates code that loads and processes binary files. It may be possible to modify software like BFD to use PADS or DataScript for processing binary formats. However, these projects do not handle discrepancies arising from how compilers/architectures lay out data in memory and leave it up to the programmer to handle multiple layouts of the same data.

Other work has focused on making it easier to work with bit-level data. Diatchki *et al.* [5] augment a Haskell-like language with *bitdata*: bit-level entities that can be manipulated in various high-level ways in a type-safe manner. Erlang bit patterns [8] allow pattern matching on binary data. Other projects (e.g. [6]) augment C and C++ with libraries that facilitate working with bit-level data. These projects do not facilitate working with multiple bit-level layouts.

Our *flip* and *unflip* functions are similar to relational lenses [2]. A lens is a pair of functions, *get* and *putback*. One extracts a representation (e.g., XML data) of an element in a concrete domain (e.g., a database entry) and the other puts the representation back into the concrete domain. Unlike *flip* and *unflip*, *get* and *putback* are not exact inverses of each other. That is, *get* is allowed to forget part of the data in the concrete domain.

Finally, some prior work has focused on making it easier to handle similar blocks of code (e.g., Simultaneous Editing [11] and Linked Editing [18]). These systems allow programmers to link together blocks of code that share a high-degree of syntactic similarity, such that modifications to certain regions of one block are automatically propagated to the others. However, they are unaware of semantic relationships: e.g., one cannot cause an index of "0" in a big-endian code block to be propagated as "3" to the corresponding little-endian block.

# 7   Conclusions and Future Work

We have designed, implemented, and evaluated a tool that provides direct support for writing code that is portable to multiple bit-level data representations. The key novelty is an approach where programmers write their algorithm in C with one representation in mind and declaratively specify what the equivalent representations are. A source-to-source transformation then produces C code with one version of the algorithm for each representation.

While we view our tool as successful, there are improvements that could make it more widely applicable. First, its current requirement that all data layouts be equivalent is too strong for scenarios where word size varies (e.g., 32-bit versus 64-bit machines). Second, for short, performance-critical code segments, our "flip on entry / unflip on exit" implementation strategy may be inferior to a more sophisticated transformation that modified the code segments. However, optimizing byte-endian code like `flip(x); y=x[3]; unflip(x);` into `y=x[0];` is within the capabilities of an optimizing C compiler, as discussed in Section 5.

We would also like to consider automating or semi-automating tasks we still leave with the programmer, such as identifying where port statements are necessary or editing legacy code to use our tool.

# References

1. Back, G.: DataScript - A specification and scripting language for binary data. In: ACM Conference on Generative Programming and Component Engineering 2002 (2002)
2. Bohannon, A., Vaughan, J.A., Pierce, B.C.: Relational lenses: A language for updateable views. In: Principles of Database Systems 2006 (2006)
3. Condit, J., Harren, M., Anderson, Z., Gay, D., Necula, G.: Dependent types for low-level programming. In: European Symposium on Programming 2007 (2007)
4. Dhurjati, D., Kowshik, S., Adve, V.: SAFECode: Enforcing alias analysis for weakly typed languages. In: ACM Conference on Programming Language Design and Implementation (2006)
5. Diatchki, I.S., Jones, M.P., Leslie, R.: High-level views on low-level representations. In: ACM International Conference on Functional Programming (2005)
6. Dipperstein, M.: ANSI C and C++ bit manipulation libraries, http://michael.dipperstein.com/bitlibs/
7. Fisher, K., Mandelbaum, Y., Walker, D.: The next 700 data description languages. In: ACM Symposium on Principles of Programming Languages (2006)
8. Gustafsson, P., Sagonas, K.: Efficient manipulation of binary data using pattern matching. J. Funct. Program. 16(1) (2006)
9. Jim, T., Morrisett, G., Grossman, D., Hicks, M., Cheney, J., Wang, Y.: Cyclone: A safe dialect of C. In: USENIX Annual Technical Conference (2002)
10. McCann, P.J., Chandra, S.: Packet types: abstract specification of network protocol messages. In: Proceedings of the Conference on Applications, Technologies, Architectures, and Protocols for Computer Communication (2000)
11. Miller, R.C., Myers, B.A.: Interactive simultaneous editing of multiple text regions. In: USENIX Annual Technical Conference (2002)
12. Miné, A.: Field-sensitive value analysis of embedded C programs with union types and pointer arithmetics. In: ACM Conference on Language, Compilers, and Tool Support for Embedded Systems (2006)
13. Necula, G., Condit, J., Harren, M., McPeak, S., Weimer, W.: CCured: Type-safe retrofitting of legacy software. ACM Transactions on Programming Languages and Systems 27(3) (2005)
14. Necula, G., McPeak, S., Rahul, S.P., Weimer, W.: CIL: Intermediate language and tools for analysis and transformation of C programs. In: International Conference on Compiler Construction (2002)
15. Nita, M., Grossman, D., Chambers, C.: A theory of platform-dependent low-level software. In: ACM Symposium on Principles of Programming Languages (2008)
16. The GNU Project. GDB, The GNU Debugger, http://sourceware.org/gdb/
17. The GNU Project. GNU Binutils, http://sources.redhat.com/binutils/
18. Toomim, M., Begel, A., Graham, S.L.: Managing duplicated code with linked editing. In: IEEE Symposium on Visual Languages - Human Centric Computing (2004)
19. Wilson, R.P., Lam, M.S.: Efficient context-sensitive pointer analysis for C programs. In: ACM Conference on Programming Language Design and Implementation (1995)

# Control Flow Emulation on Tiled SIMD Architectures

Ghulam Lashari, Ondřej Lhoták, and Michael McCool

D. R. Cheriton School of Computer Science, University of Waterloo

**Abstract.** Heterogeneous multi-core and streaming architectures such as the GPU, Cell, ClearSpeed, and Imagine processors have better power/performance ratios and memory bandwidth than traditional architectures. These types of processors are increasingly being used to accelerate compute-intensive applications. Their performance advantage is achieved by using multiple SIMD processor cores but limiting the complexity of each core, and by combining this with a simplified memory system. In particular, these processors generally avoid the use of cache coherency protocols and may even omit general-purpose caches, opting for restricted caches or explictly managed local memory.

We show how control flow can be emulated on such tiled SIMD architectures and how memory access can be organized to avoid the need for a general-purpose cache and to tolerate long memory latencies. Our technique uses streaming execution and multipass partitioning. Our prototype targets GPUs. On GPUs the memory system is deeply pipelined and caches for read and write are not coherent, so reads and writes may not use the same memory locations simultaneously. This requires the use of double-buffered streaming. We emulate general control flow in a way that is transparent to the programmer and include specific optimizations in our approach that can deal with double-buffering.

## 1 Introduction

GPUs are high-performance processors originally designed for graphics acceleration. However, they are programmable and capable of accelerating a variety of demanding floating-point applications. They can often achieve performance that is more than an order of magnitude faster than corresponding CPU implementations [1]. Application areas for which implementations have been performed include ray tracing, image and signal processing, computational geometry, financial option pricing, sequence alignment, protein folding, database search, and many other problems in scientific computation including solving differential equations and optimization problems.

These processors are best suited to massively parallel problems, and internally make extensive use of SIMD (single instruction, multiple data) parallelism. These processors do have multiple cores with separate threads of control, but each core uses SIMD execution. We will refer to such an architecture as a *tiled SIMD architecture*. Although we will focus on the GPU in this paper, even on the Cell

L. Hendren (Ed.): CC 2008, LNCS 4959, pp. 100–115, 2008.
© Springer-Verlag Berlin Heidelberg 2008

processor and other general-purpose multi-core processors, higher performance can be achieved by a tiled SIMD approach to vectorization.

The simplicity of the tiled SIMD architecture enables a number of optimizations that result in higher performance. The techniques we will present can also apply to pure SIMD machines, such as the ClearSpeed processor. A tiled SIMD architecture can be emulated on a pure SIMD machine, simply by executing the per-tile computations serially instead of in parallel, just as concurrent threads can be emulated on a serial machine.

A major difficulty with pure SIMD machines is the efficient implementation of control flow. In a pure SIMD machine, control flow can be naively emulated by taking all paths of execution and then conditionally discarding results. However, this approach can result in arbitrarily poor efficiency. We show how to automatically and efficiently emulate general control flow on a tiled SIMD architecture.

We use GPUs as our test platform. This means that we have to deal with several other issues that are specific to GPUs, in particular double-buffering. However, our general approach can apply to any other tiled SIMD architecture.

We assume the processors are programmed using a stream processing model [1,2,3]. The model is based on applying a simple program, called a kernel, to each element of an input array. Conceptually all invocations of the kernel execute in parallel on each element. Kernel invocations cannot retain state or communicate with each other during computation. The order of execution of kernel invocations is also unspecified. In practice, for execution on a tiled SIMD machine, the arrays are strip-mined and the kernels are executed over small subsets (tiles) of the input arrays, using a combination of parallel and serial execution.

In the SPMD (single program, multiple data) variant of the stream processing model, the kernels can contain control flow; in the SIMD variant, they cannot. Our goal is to transform an SPMD kernel into a schedule of SIMD kernels over tiles, so that SPMD kernels can be executed on (tiled) SIMD machines.

We assume SIMD kernel execution is guarded; a guard is a predicate which controls whether the kernel will execute based on a data-dependent condition. If the guard fails for all the elements in a tile then computation on that tile is aborted, *actually avoiding work*. Aborted tiles do not write any output. However, if only some guards fail then the computation proceeds in SIMD fashion over the tile, but the outputs are masked: no output is written for elements for which the guard failed. We also assume that the hardware provides a count of the guards that did not fail across the entire stream after a kernel is executed over that stream. We will call this the completion count (CC). Finally, we assume the hardware uses deep memory pipelining and that reads and writes to the same memory location are not permitted during a single kernel invocation. This requires double-buffering of inputs and outputs.

We prototyped our multi-pass partitioning (MPP) technique on a GPU as GPUs have all the above-mentioned features; the guard can be implemented with a discard or early z-cull operation and the completion count with an occlusion count. In the conclusions we will discuss two modifications that could be made to tiled SIMD architectures to simplify control flow emulation.

Our contribution is a technique to efficiently emulate the SPMD stream processing model on a tiled SIMD machine. Our technique automatically partitions SPMD kernels with arbitrarily complex control flow into a set of SIMD sub-kernels without any internal control flow, only guards. We show how to automatically generate and run an efficient data-dependent schedule of these SIMD sub-kernels.

## 2    Previous Work

Our work is related to previous work on partitioning large computations with unbounded resource usage into multiple passes that respect hardware resource limits, and to prior approaches for the control flow emulation on SIMD machines.

Several algorithms have been suggested to virtualize limited hardware resources by partitioning GPU programs. However, existing algorithms partition only straight-line programs comprised of a single basic block. Chan [4] and Foley [5] devised the RDS (Recursive Dominator Split) and MRDS algorithms, respectively, that greedily merge operations in the dependence DAG into passes. Riffel [6] redefined the partitioning problem as a job shop scheduling problem and devised a greedy list scheduling algorithm called MIO. Heirich [7] presented an optimal algorithm based on dynamic programming for the MPP problem. However, none of these algorithms handle input programs with data dependent loops. Therefore, they do not work in the presence of control flow.

If-conversion is a technique that has been widely used in the context of vector machines to transform control dependence into data dependence. Both branches of the if statement are executed, but the writes are selectively performed, for components of the vector operand, to preserve the original results of the if statement. Our technique is more general than if-conversion in that it handles arbitrary control constructs including loops.

Purcell [8] manually partitioned a ray tracing algorithm composed of three nested loops into a set of conditionally executed blocks so it could run on a GPU that had no native control flow. The ray tracer was split into four kernels: ray generation, grid traversal, intersection, and shading. The execution of kernels on rays was controlled by a state variable that was maintained for each ray. The states corresponded to the kernels; for example, the traversing kernel would only run on those rays that were in the *traversing* state. Purcell then created a static schedule of the kernels that included running the ray generation kernel once, then repeatedly running traversal and intersection kernels, and then invoking the shading kernel once.

We generalize Purcell's approach and automate the partitioning so it can work on any control flow graph. Also, in the implementations we have studied, Purcell terminated the computation based on a user-provided number of iterations. Our approach instead automatically terminates the computation when all the stream elements have terminated. We also automatically handle the double buffering required by the fact that inputs cannot be bound as outputs in a single pass due to read-write hazards. We will compare our results directly to Purcell's ray-tracing implementation to evaluate performance but our techniques apply to any algorithm that requires control flow.

The idea that an arbitrary control flow graph can be implemented by predicating each basic block and wrapping all the basic blocks inside a single iteration is quite old (at least forty years [9]). Harel calls it a "folk theorem" and surveys many proofs [10]. This approach to implementing control flow has also been used to show that goto is unnecessary, since in fact all programs can be implemented using a "flow-chart simulator" that uses only structured control flow [11].

An alternative way to efficiently execute conditionals on SIMD machines is to use conditional streams [12,13]. A single input stream is routed into multiple output streams and a separate kernel is then applied to each output stream. Similarly multiple input streams can be merged into a single output stream and a single kernel applied to the output stream. This however requires special hardware for stream compaction and expansion and also reorders the stream elements. Our mechanism does not reorder the stream and requires much simpler hardware support. Our technique is based on guarded kernels and tiling of the input stream. If the individual tiles are coherent, this will result in avoiding work for an entire tile for which the guard fails.

It should be noted here that the most recent generation of GPUs do support internal control flow on tiles; they do this by maintaining a hardware stack of conditional masks and temporary values for each SIMD tile. However, our approach permits simpler hardware and can potentially be used on pure SIMD machines (such as the ClearSpeed processor) as well. Even if control flow is implemented using a hardware mechanism, some resource may be limited, such as loop nesting depth, number of registers, or amount of local memory. In this case kernel partitioning will be needed. If control flow is present the kernel will have to be partitioned using techniques similar to those presented here even if the control flow is not itself directly limited.

# 3 Control Flow Emulation on SIMD Machines

Our approach consists of three components: program partitioning, handling of state retained between partitions, and dynamic scheduling.

## 3.1 Program Partitioning

Our technique is capable of handling programs with arbitrary control flow constructs with arbitrary nesting depth and iteration counts. We first create a control flow graph of such programs that is then passed as input to our partitioning algorithm.

The basic idea behind our partitioning algorithm is to split the control flow graph of the program on the basic block level. A kernel is created for each basic block. For each element of the input array, we maintain (in a separate array) a program counter that indicates the next basic block to execute. Each kernel is predicated to run the basic block code only if the program counter matches the basic block number; otherwise, the basic block code is skipped. To mimic

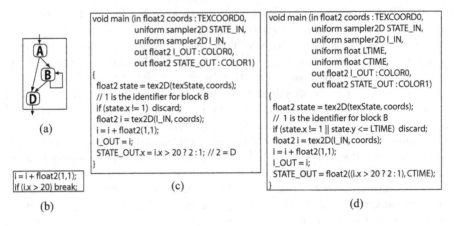

```
void main (in float2 coords : TEXCOORD0,
          uniform sampler2D STATE_IN,
          uniform sampler2D I_IN,
          out float2 I_OUT : COLOR0,
          out float2 STATE_OUT : COLOR1)
{
  float2 state = tex2D(texState, coords);
  // 1 is the identifier for block B
  if (state.x != 1) discard;
  float2 i = tex2D(I_IN, coords);
  i = i + float2(1,1);
  I_OUT = i;
  STATE_OUT.x = i.x > 20 ? 2 : 1; // 2 = D
}
```

(a)

```
i = i + float2(1,1);
if (i.x > 20) break;
```

(b)

(c)

```
void main (in float2 coords : TEXCOORD0,
          uniform sampler2D STATE_IN,
          uniform sampler2D I_IN,
          uniform float LTIME,
          uniform float CTIME,
          out float2 I_OUT : COLOR0,
          out float2 STATE_OUT : COLOR1)
{
  float2 state = tex2D(texState, coords);
  // 1 is the identifier for block B
  if (state.x != 1 || state.y <= LTIME) discard;
  float2 i = tex2D(I_IN, coords);
  i = i + float2(1,1);
  I_OUT = i;
  STATE_OUT = float2((i.x > 20 ? 2 : 1), CTIME);
}
```

(d)

**Fig. 1.** (a): A simple GPU program with a loop. (b): Basic block B of the program. (c): Kernel for basic block B that discards an array element if the state (i.e. program counter) does not match with the basic block identifier. (d): Kernel for basic block B that uses timestamped program counter.

the execution of the original program, we run a schedule of these kernels. The schedule is maintained on the host CPU that repeatedly takes a kernel off the schedule and invokes it on the SIMD device. In later sections, we will show how an efficient schedule can be derived.

Figure 1(a) shows the control flow graph of a simple program we will use as an example. Figure 1(b) shows the code of basic block B from the original program, and Figure 1(c) shows the corresponding kernel for that block after the program has been partitioned.

Application of the original program to an array results in individual activations of the program taking different paths in the graph. Each activation may also perform a different number of loop iterations. In contrast, after partitioning we schedule individual basic block kernels in some particular order, running some of them repeatedly. Predication is used to ensure that execution of a given kernel processes only those array elements on which the code should execute according to the original program. We implemented predicates using the GPUs' conditional *discard* feature, although it might also be possible to use the early z-cull feature or a GPU if statement.

In order to ensure that the transformed code has the same semantics as the original program, we must capture the control flow decisions of individual array elements as they flow along the control flow edges. We do so using "program counters" (maintained in the SIMD device memory). We assign a unique identifier to each basic block. Before the schedule is run, the program counters for all the array elements are initialized to the identifier of the entry node in the control flow graph. Upon invocation of a kernel, only array elements whose predicates are true execute the corresponding basic block. The predicate inside the kernel ensures the program counter of the array element matches the identifier of the corresponding basic block. At the end of the basic block execution, the program counters are updated to reflect which basic block to execute next, possibly based on data-dependent information specific to each array element being processed. If the program counter of an array element does not match the currently executing kernel, the array element is not processed, and its program counter remains unchanged; the array element will be processed the next time the kernel matching its program counter is executed. The exit nodes in the control flow graph set the program counter to a unique identifier $\infty$ indicating that the array element has completed. Figure 1(c) shows Cg code that implements the predicate and updates the program counters to capture the control flow decisions.

The target hardware cannot read and write from the same array in one pass, but program counter arrays must be read, modified, and written in each kernel. Therefore, we must allocate two arrays $\alpha$ and $\beta$ to double-buffer program counters. At each kernel invocation, one of these arrays is bound as input and the other as output. As a kernel finishes execution, the newly computed program counters for the executed array elements are written to $\alpha$ or $\beta$, whichever is bound as output to the kernel.

## 3.2 Temporary Variables

When the program is split into separate kernels, the values of temporary variables must be communicated from one kernel to the next. Like program counters, these temporary variables reside in the SIMD device memory across all passes in order to avoid data transfer overhead to and from the host CPU.

We identify three kinds of temporary variables in the original program: *BB variables* are those that are never live across a basic block boundary, *exposed variables* are those that are live across a basic block boundary but are never read and then written in the same block, and *RW variables* are those that are live across a basic block boundary and are read and then written in the same basic block. BB variables need no special treatment after program partitioning. Exposed and RW variables, however, must be saved into array memory after they are defined and restored before they are used. Exposed variables do not require double-buffering, so a single array suffices for each exposed variable. For each RW variable, we allocate two arrays for double-buffering. Each exposed or RW variable is turned into an array input, output, or both for kernels in which it is read or written.

We now show how these kinds of variables are identified. For each basic block in the original program, we compute two sets of variables: upward exposed *uses* (UEU) and downward exposed *defs* (DED) [14]. These variables become the array inputs and outputs, respectively, of the corresponding kernel. The UEUs for each basic block are those variables that are live at the beginning of the block; they are computed using a local liveness analysis. The DEDs for each basic block are variables that are written inside the block and live at the end of the block, as computed by a global liveness analysis of the whole program. Each variable that is both a UEU and a DED for the same block is a RW variable; every other variable that is a UEU or a DED for some block is an exposed variable.

Simply turning all variables that are live at the beginning and end of a basic block into inputs and outputs, respectively, would give correct semantics, but would require reading and writing every variable that is live across a basic block, even if it is not used within the block. Using UEUs and DEDs instead avoids this inefficiency.

Unlike program counters, RW variables need not be double-buffered in all kernels, but only in those in which they are read and then written. We will discuss the binding of RW variable arrays to kernels in Section 3.4 and 4.2. The Cg code in Figure 1(c) shows how to save and restore the RW variable $i$.

## 3.3   Dynamic Scheduling Using a Worklist

To decide which kernels to execute and with which program counter bindings, the host CPU maintains a dynamic worklist that is updated based on the completion counts. Each element of the worklist is a kernel with either a left or right arrow. For example, $\overrightarrow{B}$ indicates that kernel $B$ should be executed with $\alpha$ as input and $\beta$ as output, while $\overleftarrow{B}$ indicates the opposite bindings. The worklist is initialized with the initial basic block $\overrightarrow{A}$. In each pass, a kernel is taken off the worklist and executed. If the resulting completion count is not zero (i.e. the guard succeeded for at least one array element), all immediate static successors (as given by the control flow graph) are added to the worklist, with a program counter binding that is the opposite of the current pass.

The worklist ensures that a kernel $X$ will not execute unless one of its predecessors was run since the last run of $X$. In our running example, $A$ will run only once, since it has no predecessors.

If kernels $X$ and $Y$ need to be executed and there is a control flow path from $X$ to $Y$ but not from $Y$ to $X$, $X$ should be executed before $Y$, since executing $X$ will require executing $Y$ after it. To ensure this, of all the kernels appearing on the worklist, we always execute the kernel that appears earliest in a reverse post-order traversal of the control flow graph. This order is precomputed before execution begins. In our running example, this order delays execution of $D$ until all iterations of $B$ have completed, so that $D$ is only run once on all array elements together.

## 3.4   Stale State

When an array element is discarded, no output is written for it. Therefore, if kernels discard array elements that are skipped, program counters for skipped elements cannot be updated in the output array. After executing a kernel that inputs program counter array $\alpha$ and outputs program counter array $\beta$, up-to-date program counters will be in array $\beta$ for those elements that were executed, and in array $\alpha$ for those elements that were skipped. Neither array will have up-to-date program counters for every array element.

Stale program counters may cause extraneous execution of basic blocks and even prevent the computation from terminating in some cases. Figure 2(a) illustrates this with an example of the execution of the program from Figure 1.

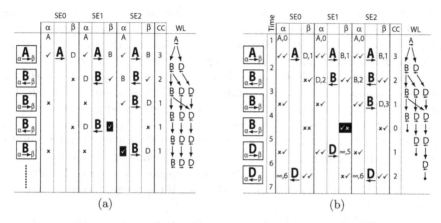

(a)                                             (b)

**Fig. 2.** (a): A stale program counter causes extraneous execution of block $B$–resulting in non-termination. (b): Timestamp identifies a stale program counter and prevents extraneous execution of block $B$.

The control flow graph consists of three basic blocks $A$, $B$, and $D$, where $B$ is a self-loop. The program is run on three array elements SE0, SE1, and SE2, making zero, one, and two loop iterations, respectively. The first column shows the kernel executed in each pass. The arrow under the kernel name indicates whether the program counter is read from array $\alpha$ and written to $\beta$, or vice versa. The column labeled CC shows the completion count for each kernel executed. The last column shows the contents of the worklist, in reverse post order, between passes. The columns in the middle show the progress of each of the array elements. Each of them is further subdivided into three sub-columns. Each middle sub-column shows the basic blocks that execute. The left and right sub-columns show the values of the two program counter arrays $\alpha$ and $\beta$. A ✓ indicates that the current program counter matches the kernel being executed, so the basic block appears in the middle sub-column, and the new program counter appears in the opposite program counter array. A × indicates that the current program counter does not match the kernel, so the basic block is not executed, and the opposite program counter array is not updated.

In the first pass, all three array elements execute block $A$, and the new program counters ($D$ or $B$) are written to $\beta$. Kernels $\overleftarrow{B}$ and $\overleftarrow{D}$ are added to the worklist. In the second pass, SE0 discards while SE1 and SE2 execute $B$ and kernels $\overrightarrow{B}$ and $\overrightarrow{D}$ are added to the worklist. In the third pass, SE2 completes the second iteration of $B$, adding $\overleftarrow{B}$ to the worklist while both SE0 and SE2 discard. In the fourth pass, the stale program counter $B$ is found in $\beta$ for SE1, causing $B$ to be executed again, even though it was already executed in the second pass. This is an extra execution of $B$ that was not specified by the original program. In addition, it results in addition of $\overrightarrow{B}$ to the worklist, triggering another execution of B. Finally, because $\beta$ is not updated, the same thing will continue to happen in every second future pass, so the kernels will loop indefinitely.

In order to prevent the above problems caused by stale program counters, we add timestamps. With each kernel execution, we increment a global clock (maintained on the host CPU). We maintain a timestamp (in array memory) for each program counter, and two timestamps (in CPU memory) for each kernel, one for each program counter array binding (i.e. $\overrightarrow{A}$ and $\overleftarrow{A}$). Each program counter is stamped when it is generated, and a kernel is stamped when it is executed with the corresponding binding. The key idea is that a program counter $A$ in $\alpha$ is stale if and only if it was generated earlier than the most recent execution of kernel $\overrightarrow{A}$ (since that execution will have generated a more up-to-date program counter in $\beta$). Thus, to avoid extraneous execution due to stale program counters, we need only modify the predicate of each kernel to skip the basic block if the program counter is stale, even if the program counter matches the basic block.

The code applying timestamps to our running example is given in Figure 1(d). Figure 2(b) shows the execution of schedule with timestamped program counters. The global clock appears in the column labeled Time. The first three passes of the schedule are the same as in Figure 2(a). In fourth pass, however, SE1 is discarded in kernel $\overleftarrow{B}$ because the timestamp of the program counter in $\beta$ (1) is lower than the most recent execution time of $\overleftarrow{B}$ (2). Thus, the extraneous execution is avoided, and computation terminates in six passes as the worklist becomes empty.

Timestamps prevent the extraneous execution and non-termination caused by stale program counters. However, the schedule is still inefficient: we must execute block D twice. We will show an improvement in the next section.

RW temporary variables suffer from the staleness problem as well, as they are double-buffered. We solve the RW variable staleness problem by keeping the RW variable array bindings synchronized with the program counter array bindings (i.e. always copy all RW variables in every kernel). Since the timestamps prevent execution when the program counter is stale, and double-buffering of variables is synchronized with double-buffering of the program counter, the same timestamps also prevent use of stale variables. However, copying all variables in every kernel is inefficient; we will describe a better approach in the following section.

## 4   Optimizations

Two important optimizations can significantly reduce extraneous execution of kernel partitions and data copying: graph bipartization and node bypassing.

### 4.1   Graph Bipartization

When a block is reached with two different program counter array bindings, it must be executed twice, once for each binding. Moreover, the resulting program counters will again be split between both arrays, so blocks that come after it must also be executed twice. We would like to transform the control flow graph to avoid this double execution of blocks.

Specifically, we must transform the graph to be 2-colourable (equivalently, bipartite or containing no odd cycles). At run time, a kernel must be executed with a given binding if one of its predecessors has been executed with the opposite binding. If it is possible to statically assign bindings to the basic blocks such that the binding for a block is the opposite of the bindings of all its predecessors, then at run time, each kernel only ever needs to be executed with its statically assigned binding. Since the bindings can be thought of as colours for nodes, this is possible exactly when the graph is 2-colourable.

We make the graph 2-colourable by inserting additional *copying nodes* on existing edges of the graph. Each copying node simply copies program counters from its input array to its output array. Although copying takes some time, the cost of running a copying node is likely to be cheaper than having to run a possibly large basic block twice, along with all blocks executed after it. Still, we want to minimize the number of copying nodes.

To determine where to place copying nodes, we must find the smallest subset of edges that must be removed from the control flow graph in order to make it 2-colourable. This problem, Bipartite Subgraph, is a dual of Max-Cut and is NP-complete [15]. Each of the removed edges must join vertices of the same colour in the resulting 2-colouring; otherwise, it would not have to be removed, contradicting the optimality of the subset. Therefore, placing a copying node on each edge that is to be removed is equivalent to removing it. The minimal set of edges on which copying nodes must be placed is exactly the solution of Bipartite Subgraph.

To make bipartization computationally tractable we use an approximation algorithm for Max-Cut. Fortunately, a well-known approximation algorithm is available that runs in linear time, is easy to implement, and achieves a $\frac{1}{2}$-approximation [16].

Once the graph has been made 2-colourable, colours can be assigned in a simple traversal of the graph. Figure 3 shows a version of our running example made 2-colourable by adding copying nodes $C_1$ and $C_2$, and the corresponding multipass execution of the basic blocks. Block $D$ is now executed only once, and the number of executions for block B have reduced from three to two.

## 4.2  Node Bypassing

As explained in Section 3.2, temporary variables are divided into BB variables, exposed variables, and RW variables. Only RW variables are double-buffered. Just like program counters, the values of RW variables could be stale. As described in Section 3.4, a simple but inefficient way to avoid the problems caused by staleness is to keep the variable double-buffering synchronized with program counter double-buffering, so that the same timestamp can be used for both. Unfortunately, this requires extra data copying.

One way to avoid copying all RW variables in all kernels is to add a separate timestamp for each RW variable, to avoid the need to synchronize with program counter double-buffering. However, if a cycle in the control flow graph contains an odd number of nodes that read and write the variable, the nodes in this cycle

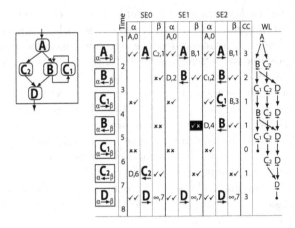

**Fig. 3.** Bipartization avoids double execution of block $D$

would have to be executed twice, once for each array binding for the variable. A program with $n$ double-buffered variables could require $2^n$ combinations of variable array bindings. Requiring a basic block to be executed $2^n$ times is not practical.

We propose a more efficient solution that reduces the wasted memory bandwidth without requiring additional timestamps. For each variable, we define *RW blocks* as those that contain a read followed by a write of the variable, and *free blocks* as those that do not. The problem is then to find a subset of free blocks in which to copy the variable so that in every cycle, the total number of RW blocks and copies is even. This property, which we call the *Node Bypass Property*, makes it possible to statically assign variable array bindings to each basic block. Since we have made the control flow graph bipartite, we know that the set of all free blocks is one solution. To improve efficiency, we would like to minimize the number of copies (i.e. maximize the number of bypassed copy nodes). We have shown this problem to be NP-complete (by reducing Max-Cut to it). In the opposite direction, we have also reduced it to Weighted Max-Cut, so heuristics for Weighted Max-Cut can be used to find approximate solutions to Max Node Bypass. Sketches of both constructions appear in the appendix.

## 5    Experimental Results

We implemented our partitioning technique in the OpenGL backend of the Sh code generator [17]. Sh is a shader metaprogramming language and a precursor to the RapidMind development platform [18]. The hardware used for the experiment consisted of a 3.0GHz Intel Pentium4 with 1.0GB of RAM and an NVIDIA GeForce 8800 GTS GPU with 320MB of memory. The software was tested under the Windows XP operating system with NVIDIA video driver version 97.73 and Cg compiler version 1.5.

**Table 1.** For each scene, the number of triangles and voxels and the size of the triangle list is shown. Also the number of iterations of the ray tracing loop required by the hand-partitioned (HP) and auto-partitioned (AP) ray tracer program is shown. The last five columns show absolute and relative execution times of the three versions of the ray tracer: hand-partitioned using 4 outputs (HP), auto-partitioned using only 4 outputs (AP4), and auto-partitioned using all 8 outputs (AP8).

| Scenes | Tris | Voxs | TriList Size | Iter (HP) | Iter (AP) | Time (HP) | Time (AP4) | Time (AP8) | Time (HP/AP4) | Time (HP/AP8) |
|---|---|---|---|---|---|---|---|---|---|---|
| Glassner04 | 840 | 140 | 1618 | 339 | 681 | 5222 | 5847 | 4311 | 89% | 121% |
| Glassner05 | 840 | 315 | 2142 | 279 | 563 | 4196 | 4842 | 3580 | 87% | 117% |
| Glassner10 | 840 | 2340 | 3886 | 111 | 227 | 1647 | 2096 | 1545 | 81% | 107% |

We used a ray tracer with a number of scenes to evaluate the quality of partitions and schedule generated by our partitioning technique. We took the hand-partitioned ray tracer implementation bundled with the distribution of BrookGPU [19] and ported it to Sh. We also rewrote the ray tracer as a single GPU program with nested loops. The rewritten ray tracer was then passed as input to our partitioning algorithm. For comparison, our algorithm then automatically partitioned the ray tracer and executed the resulting kernels using dynamic scheduling. We compared the performance of the hand-partitioned ray tracer against that of our automatically partitioned implementation (see Table 1).

The hand-partitioned ray tracer consists of seven kernels: Three of them generate eye rays and static and dynamic data for traversal, the fourth traverses the voxels, the fifth computes ray-triangle intersections, the sixth validates the intersections, and the seventh performs shading for the intersection points. The traversal, intersection, and intersection validation kernels run repeatedly using a host CPU loop. Unlike the automatically partitioned version, the hand-partitioned version provides no automated way to determine when computation has completed. We determined the minimum number of iterations required for each scene manually by comparing the output of runs with different numbers of iterations. The render times shown in Table 1 for the hand-partitioned ray tracer are for the minimum number of iterations required for each scene.

The control flow graph of the ray tracer originally contained 12 basic blocks. To give each kernel a reasonable amount of computation, we automatically merged basic blocks that were split only due to *if* statements (not loops) using conditional assignments. This reduced the number of basic blocks to 5.

Our partitioning algorithm automatically partitioned the ray tracer into five kernels. The algorithm employed all the techniques presented in Sections 3.3, 3.4, 4.1, and 4.2. The Graph Bipartization algorithm introduced two copying nodes, increasing the number of kernels to seven. The liveness analysis revealed eleven temporary variables that were live across basic block boundaries in the control flow graph. Seven of them were exposed variables while four were RW variables that required double-buffering. The max-node-bypass approximation algorithm then detected that all but one node for each of these four variables could be bypassed. Hence only one extra kernel was needed to read and write these RW variables in order to keep them synchronized with the program counters.

Note that automatic partitioning can take advantage of any hardware improvements, but hand-partitioned code must be rewritten to do so. For example, the hand-partitioned ray tracer was optimized for an older GPU, so it utilized only four of the eight available outputs of the improved hardware. Our automatically partitioned ray tracer utilized all eight, saving us from further partitioning the kernels to virtualize the hardware's output resources. We also evaluated a version of the auto-partitioning algorithm limited to using four outputs for a fair comparison with the hand-partitioned algorithm.

We ran the hand-partitioned and the automatically partitioned ray tracers on three different scenes that consisted of different number of voxels and triangles. The details about the scenes are given in Table 1. When allowed to use all eight outputs, our auto-partitioned ray tracer was 7% to 21% faster than the hand-partitioned one. However, even when artificially limited to four outputs, our auto-partitioned ray tracer was only 11% to 19% slower than the hand-partitioned version. In general the auto-partitioned ray tracer also performed more repetitions than the hand-partitioned implementation. We attribute this to the generality of our solution. The hand-partitioned ray tracer was written by experts in the ray tracing area who were able to structure the ray tracing kernels so that more work could be done in fewer executions of the kernels, but our auto-partitioning algorithm has little knowledge about the algorithm implemented in the program being partitioned. Moreover, some overhead is due to the occlusion query that determines when execution has terminated; in the hand-partitioned implementation, the number of iterations to execute must be determined manually. Finally, use of the occlusion query requires adding timestamps to handle stale program counters, which uses additional memory bandwidth.

## 6    Conclusions and Future Work

This paper presented a mechanism to emulate SPMD stream processing behaviour on a tiled SIMD machine using the GPU as a test platform. We showed how to automatically partition programs containing arbitrary control flow and to schedule the resulting partitions. We showed how to automatically detect the termination of computation using a completion count mechanism (implemented using an occlusion count feature on the GPU) and presented solutions to stale state problems that arose from double-buffering. The solutions to stale state included timestamps, graph bipartization, and a node-bypass optimization. A worklist-based algorithm was also presented for dynamically scheduling the partitions. A ray tracer performed 7% to 21% faster when partitioned using our automatic technique than a hand-tuned manually partitioned version, because our automatic technique took advantage of all available hardware resources, while the manually partitioned version was optimized for an older GPU. Even when artificially limited to using the same resources as the manually partitioned version, the automatically partitioned ray tracer was only 11% to 19% slower—although it was also more general in that it was automatically checking for completion.

We realized during this work that the complications arising from stale state could be avoided if the hardware implementing the guard allowed writing to the outputs before the guard was evaluated. Unfortunately, on current GPUs, the discard operation masks out all outputs, including writes that occurred before the discard. Thus, when the guard fails, we cannot copy state from the input arrays to the output arrays, resulting in stale state. Avoiding stale state by using a different strategy for predication might eliminate the need for timestamps, graph bipartization, and solving the max node bypassing problem.

Another way to avoid stale state would be to remove the hardware restriction that prevents both reading and writing the same memory location in a kernel. If double buffering was not required, we could keep the state of the stream elements in one set of arrays, again avoiding stale state. In fact, either one of these modifications, on its own, would suffice to eliminate stale state and its associated complication.

In the future, we would like to explore additional optimization techniques. A better scheduling technique that prioritized the kernels for scheduling based on the amount of work accumulated for them could deliver better performance. The use of the completion count could also be limited to only some passes instead of all of them. A major performance improvement can be achieved by packing the intermediate results into different components of the same tuple of an array, but this is not easy to implement because of the double-buffering. We statically inserted copying nodes to avoid running certain kernels twice, but dynamically inserting the copying nodes, when needed, could result in less copying. Moreover, one should probably insist on adding copying nodes that will do the least amount of work as opposed to the minimum number of nodes. For example, if a path on the control graph is taken 90% of the time and the other is taken 10% of the time, it is better to insert two nodes on the latter rather than one on the former.

As current GPUs and other high-throughput targets are actually SPMD machines and can handle limited control flow, it would be useful to generalize our approach and use it as part of a resource virtualization framework. In the general context it is important to merge control flow and generate larger SPMD kernels to avoid the overhead of invoking a large number of small kernels. Additional transformations should be explored to restructure the program so that it fits within hardware limits, while maximizing efficiency and advantage of the limited control flow provided by the GPU.

# References

1. Owens, J.D., Luebke, D., Govindaraju, N., Harris, M., Lefohn, J.K.A.E., Purcell, T.J.: A survey of general-purpose computation on graphics hardware. In: Eurographics 2005: State of the Art Reports, pp. 21–51 (2005)
2. Das, A., Dally, W.J., Mattson, P.: Compiling for stream processing. In: PACT 2006: Parallel Architectures and Compilation Techniques, pp. 33–42. ACM, New York (2006)
3. McCool, M.D.: Scalable Programming Models for Massively Multi-Core Processors. In: Proc. IEEE (January 2008)

4. Chan, E., Ng, R., Sen, P., Proudfoot, K., Hanrahan, P.: Efficient partitioning of fragment shaders for multipass rendering on programmable graphics hardware. In: HWWS 2002: Proceedings of the ACM SIGGRAPH/EUROGRAPHICS conference on Graphics hardware, pp. 69–78 (2002)
5. Foley, T., Houston, M., Hanrahan, P.: Efficient partitioning of fragment shaders for multiple-output hardware. In: HWWS 2004: Proceedings of the ACM SIG-GRAPH/EUROGRAPHICS conference on Graphics hardware, pp. 45–53 (2004)
6. Riffel, A., Lefohn, A.E., Vidimce, K., Leone, M., Owens, J.D.: Mio: fast multipass partitioning via priority-based instruction scheduling. In: HWWS 2004: ACM SIG-GRAPH/EUROGRAPHICS conference on Graphics hardware, pp. 35–44 (2004)
7. Heirich, A.: Optimal automatic multi-pass shader partitioning by dynamic programming. In: HWWS 2005: Proceedings of the ACM SIG-GRAPH/EUROGRAPHICS conference on Graphics hardware, pp. 91–98 (2005)
8. Purcell, T.J., Buck, I., Mark, W.R., Hanrahan, P.: Ray tracing on programmable graphics hardware. ACM Transactions on Graphics 21(3), 703–712 (2002)
9. Cooper, D.C.: Böhm and Jacopini's reduction of flow charts. Commun. ACM 10(8), 463 (1967)
10. Harel, D.: On folk theorems. Commun. ACM 23(7), 379–389 (1980)
11. Knuth, D.E.: Structured programming with go to statements. ACM Comput. Surv. 6(4), 261–301 (1974)
12. Kapasi, U.J., Dally, W.J., Rixner, S., Mattson, P.R., Owens, J.D., Khailany, B.: Efficient conditional operations for data-parallel architectures. In: 33rd Annual IEEE/ACM International Symposium on Microarchitecture, pp. 159–170 (2000)
13. Popa, T.S.: Compiling Data Dependent Control Flow on SIMD GPUs. Master's thesis, University of Waterloo (2004)
14. Marlowe, T.J., Ryder, B.G.: Properties of data flow frameworks: a unified model. Acta Inf. 28(2), 121–163 (1990)
15. Garey, M.R., Johnson, D.S.: Computers and Intractability. W. H. Freeman and Company, San Francisco (1979)
16. Sahni, S., Gonzalez, T.: P-complete approximation problems. Journal of the ACM 23(3), 555–565 (1976)
17. McCool, M.D., Qin, Z., Popa, T.S.: Shader Metaprogramming. In: Proc. Graphics Hardware, September 2002, pp. 57–68 (2002)
18. McCool, M.D.: Data-Parallel Programming on the Cell BE and the GPU using the RapidMind Development Platform. In: Proc. GSPx Multicore Applications Conference (October–November 2006)
19. Buck, I.: BrookGPU (2003), http://graphics.stanford.edu/projects/-brookgpu/

# A   Complexity of Max Node Bypassing

**Theorem 1.** *The Max Node Bypassing Problem is NP-hard.*

*Proof (Proof Sketch). We show a reduction from an instance of Max-Cut to an instance of Max Node Bypassing. Given an instance of Max-Cut $G \langle V, E \rangle$, create a control flow graph $G'$ using the "gadgets" shown in Figure 4 as follows.*

- *For each node $v \in V$, create a gadget A as shown in Figure 4 with both $\bigcirc$ and $\bigtriangledown$ labeled $v$.*
- *For each edge $v \to w \in E$, create a gadget B as shown in Figure 4 with both $\Diamond$ and $\square$ labeled "$v \to w$", and connect the $\square$ labeled "$v \to w$" to the $\bigcirc$ labeled $w$ and the $\bigtriangledown$ labeled $v$ to the $\Diamond$ labeled "$v \to w$".*

*The resulting control flow graph $G'$ is an instance of the Max Node Bypassing Problem with the $\square$s as free nodes, and $\bigtriangledown$s, $\Diamond$s, $\bigcirc$s as RW nodes. $G'$ is bipartite. It can be proved that a set $C \subseteq E$ is a cut if and only if the corresponding $\square$s labeled with edges in $C$ satisfy the Node Bypassing Property in $G'$. Therefore the maximal cut in $G$ corresponds to the maximal node-bypass in $G'$.*

To approximately solve an instance of the Max Node Bypassing Problem, we reduce in the **opposite** direction, from Max Node Bypassing Problem to Weighted Max-Cut. We can then solve the Weighted Max-Cut using known approximation algorithms, such as a variant of [16].

Given an instance of Max Node Bypassing, a bipartite control flow graph $G \langle V, E \rangle$ and set of free nodes $S \subseteq V$, we create an instance of Weighted Max-Cut $G' \langle V', E' \rangle$ as follows. For each node $v \in S$, we create gadget C shown in Figure 4. For each node $v \notin S$, we create gadget D. For each edge $v \to w \in E$, we merge $v_3 \in V'$ with $w_1 \in V'$. We assign weights to all the edges as follows: each dashed edge has weight 1, the weight of each solid edge is the total number of dashed edges plus 1. It can be shown that the set of solid edges in $G'$ make a cut. The Max-Cut in $G'$ must therefore include at least the solid edges and possibly some dotted edges. It can also be shown that a subset $\sigma \subset S$ of free nodes satisfy the Node Bypassing Property if and only if the set of dashed edges in gadgets C corresponding to nodes in $\sigma$, combined with the set of all solid edges, is a cut in $G'$. Therefore, the maximal subset satisfying the Node Bypassing Property corresponds to the Max-Cut in $G'$. Thus, an approximation to the Max-Cut in $G'$ can be mapped back to an approximately maximal node bypass in $G$.

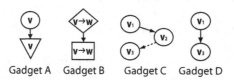

Gadget A    Gadget B    Gadget C    Gadget D

**Fig. 4.** Gadget graphs

# Generating SIMD Vectorized Permutations

Franz Franchetti and Markus Püschel*

Electrical and Computer Engineering,
Carnegie Mellon University,
5000 Forbes Avenue, Pittsburgh, PA 15213
{franzf,pueschel}@ece.cmu.edu
http://www.spiral.net

**Abstract.** This paper introduces a method to generate efficient vectorized implementations of small stride permutations using only vector load and vector shuffle instructions. These permutations are crucial for high-performance numerical kernels including the fast Fourier transform. Our generator takes as input only the specification of the target platform's SIMD vector ISA and the desired permutation. The basic idea underlying our generator is to model vector instructions as matrices and sequences of vector instructions as matrix formulas using the Kronecker product formalism. We design a rewriting system and a search mechanism that applies matrix identities to generate those matrix formulas that have vector structure and minimize a cost measure that we define. The formula is then translated into the actual vector program for the specified permutation. For three important classes of permutations, we show that our method yields a solution with the minimal number of vector shuffles. Inserting into a fast Fourier transform yields a significant speedup.

## 1 Introduction

Most current instruction set architectures (ISAs) or ISA extensions contain single instruction multiple data (SIMD) vector instructions. These instructions operate in parallel on subwords of a large vector register (typically 64-bit or 128-bit wide). Typically SIMD vector ISA extensions support 2-way–16-way vectors of floating-point or integer type. The most prominent example is Intel's SSE family.

From a software development point of view the most challenging difference across vector extensions is their widely varying capability in reorganizing data with in-register shuffle instructions. To obtain highest performance it is crucial to limit memory accesses to transfers of entire vectors and to perform any data reordering within the register file, ideally using the minimal number of shuffle instructions. Unfortunately, the optimal solution is difficult to find and depends on the target architecture.

The above optimizations are most relevant for highly optimized numerical kernels where the slowdown suffered from "useless" instructions can be punishing. For instance, on a Core2 Duo loading an aligned unit-stride 16-way vector of

---

* This work was supported by NSF through awards 0234293, 0325687, and by DARPA through the Department of Interior grant NBCH1050009.

8-bit elements costs one vector load, while gathering the same data at a stride costs at least 24 instructions, some of them particularly expensive. However, finding a short instruction sequence that reorganizes data in-register in a desired way is akin to solving puzzles.

**Contribution.** In this paper we automatically generate vector programs for an important class of permutations called stride permutations or matrix transpositions, given only the specification of the permutation and the specification of the target vector instruction set architecture (ISA).

The basic idea is that we model both instructions and permutations as matrices, and instruction sequences as matrix formulas using the Kronecker product formalism [1]. We design a rewriting system that applies matrix identities to generate, using a dynamic programming backtracking search, vectorized matrix formulas that minimize a cost measure that we define. The formula is then translated into the actual vector program implementing the specified permutation. For 3 important classes of permutations, we show that our method yields a solution with the minimal number of vector shuffles. We also demonstrate a significant speedup when inserting the generated permutation into small unrolled fast Fourier transform (FFT) kernels generated by Spiral [2].

**Related Work.** The motivation of this work arose from generating optimized programs for the discrete Fourier transform (DFT) in Spiral [2]. Spiral automates the entire code generation and optimization process, including vectorization [3,4], but, for FFTs, relies on three classes of in-register permutations [3]. These had to be implemented by hand for each vector extension. This paper closes the loop by generating these basic blocks for complete automatic porting across vector extensions. While our method is domain specific, it could in principle be applied to optimize vectorization of strided data access in a general purpose compiler, in an application similar to the approach in [5].

Reference [6] served as inspiration for our approach. Reference [7] derives the number of block transfers and [8] an optimal algorithm for transpositions on multi-level memories. Both index computation time and I/O time are considered in [9], and [10] optimizes matrix transpositions using a combination of analytical and empirical approaches. In contrast to prior work, we generate vectorized programs for small stride permutations that are optimized specifically for the peculiarities of current SIMD extensions.

General compiler vectorization techniques such as loop vectorization [11] or extraction of instruction-level parallelism and data reorganization optimization [12,5] operate on input programs while we generate programs for a very specific functionality using a declarative language and rewriting.

## 2 Background

We briefly overview SIMD vector instructions and introduce our mathematical framework to describe, manipulate, and vectorize stride permutations.

### 2.1 Vector SIMD Extensions

Most current general purpose and DSP architectures include short vector SIMD (single instruction, multiple data) extensions. For instance, Intel and AMD defined over the years MMX, Wireless MMX, SSE, SSE2, SSE3, SSSE, SSE4, SSE5, 3DNow!, Extended 3DNow!, and 3DNow! Professional as x86 SIMD vector extensions. On the PowerPC side AltiVec, VMX, the Cell SPU, and BlueGene/L's custom floating-point unit define vector extensions. Additional extensions are defined by PA-RISC, MIPS, Itanium, XScale, and many VLIW DSP processors.

Common to all vector extensions are stringent memory transfer restrictions. Only naturally aligned vectors can be loaded and stored with highest efficiency. Accessing unaligned or strided data can be extremely costly. For performance this requires that data be reordered (shuffled) inside the register file, using *vector shuffle instructions*. However, the available vector shuffle instructions vastly differ across SIMD extensions.

We mainly base our discussion on Intel's SSE2 extension, which defines six 128-bit *modes*: 4-way single-precision and 2-way double-precision vectors, and 2-way 64-bit, 4-way 32-bit, 8-way 16-bit, and 16-way 8-bit integer vectors. We denote the vector length of a SIMD extension mode with $\nu$.

**C intrinsic interface.** Compilers extend the C language with vector data types and intrinsic functions for vector instructions. This way, the programmer can perform vectorization and instruction selection while register allocation and instruction scheduling are left to the C compiler. We use the C extension defined by the Intel C++ compiler (also supported by Microsoft Visual Studio and the GNU C compiler).

**SSE2 vector shuffle instructions.** Intel's SSE2 extension provides one of the richest sets of vector shuffle instructions among the currently available SIMD extensions. Table 1 summarizes the instructions native to SSE2's 6 modes.

For example, _mm_shuffle_pd is a parameterized binary shuffle instruction for the 2-way 64-bit floating-point mode. It shuffles the entries of its two operand vectors according to a compile time constant (a 2-bit integer). _mm_unpacklo_ps is a 4-way 32-bit floating-point shuffle instruction that interleaves the lower halves of its two operands.

We observe some intricacies of the SSE2 instruction set that considerably complicate its usability in general and the vectorization of permutations in particular: 1) The floating-point modes of SSE2 extend SSE while the integer modes extend MMX. This leads to inconsistencies among the available operations and naming conventions. 2) The parameterized shuffle instructions like _mm_shuffle_ps are not as general as in AltiVec. 3) Integer vector instructions for coarser granularity

**Table 1.** SSE2 shuffle instructions. $\{\ldots\}$ denotes a vector value. a and b are vectors, a.i and b.i vector elements. $<\ldots>$ denotes an integer compile time parameter derived from the constants inside $<>$. $0 \leq$ j, k, m, n $< 4 \leq$ t, u, v, w $< 8$, and $0 \leq$ r, s $< 2$.

---

*2-way 64-bit floating-point*
```
_mm_unpacklo_pd(a, b) → {a.0, b.0}
_mm_unpackhi_pd(a, b}) → {a.1, b.1}
_mm_shuffle_pd(a, b, <r, s>) → {a.r, b.s}
```
*4-way 32-bit floating-point*
```
_mm_unpacklo_ps(a, b) → {a.0, b.0, a.1, b.1}
_mm_unpackhi_ps(a, b) → {a.2, b.2, a.3, b.3}
_mm_shuffle_ps(a, b, <j, k, m, n>), → {a.j, a.k, b.m, b.n}
```
*2-way 64-bit integer*
```
_mm_unpacklo_epi64(a, b) → {a.0, b.0}
_mm_unpackhi_epi64(a, b) → {a.1, b.1}
```
*4-way 32-bit integer*
```
_mm_unpacklo_epi32(a, b) → {a.0, b.0, a.1, b.1}
_mm_unpackhi_epi32(a, b) → {a.2, b.2, a.3, b.3}
_mm_shuffle_epi32(a, <j, k, m, n>)→ {a.j, a.k, a.m, a.n}
```
*8-way 16-bit integer*
```
_mm_unpacklo_epi16(a, b) → {a.0, b.0, a.1, b.1, a.2, b.2, a.3, b.3}
_mm_unpackhi_epi16(a, b) → {a.4, b.4, a.5, b.5, a.6, b.6, a.7, b.7}
_mm_shufflelo_epi16(a, <j,k,m,n>) → {a.j,a.k,a.m,a.n,a.4,a.5,a.6,a.7}
_mm_shufflehi_epi16(a, <t,u,v,w>) → {a.0,a.1,a.2,a.3,a.t,a.u,a.v,a.w}
```
*16-way 8-bit integer*
```
_mm_unpacklo_epi8(a, b) → {a.0, b.0, a.1, b.1,...,a.7, b.7}
_mm_unpackhi_epi8(a, b) → {a.8, b.8, a.9, b.9,...,a.15, b.15}
```

---

(for instance, 4-way 32-bit) can be used with vectors of finer granularity (for instance, 8-way 16-bit and 16-way 8-bit).

**Gather vs. vectorized permutation.** Data permutations can be implemented in two ways:

- using vector shuffle instructions, or
- using gather/scatter operations that load/store $\nu$ scalars from/to non-contiguous memory locations.

The goal of this paper is to generate fast implementations of the former and evaluate against the latter. We focus on small permutations where no cache effects are visible. Vector shuffle operations increase the instruction count without doing "useful" computation and may be executed on the same execution units as vector arithmetic operations. However, once loaded, data stays in the register file provided no spilling is necessary. Conversely, implementing vector gathers and scatters can become costly: On SSE2, 2, 7, 16, and 24 instructions are needed per gather/scatter for 2-way, 4-way, 8-way, and 16-way vectors, respectively. On the Cell SPU it is even more costly, even though scalar loads are supported.

## 2.2   Mathematical Background

We introduce the mathematical formalism used in this paper. For more details, we refer the reader to [1,2,6]. All vectors in this paper are column vectors.

**Direct sum of vectors.** The direct sum $x \oplus y \in \mathbb{R}^{m+n}$ of two vectors $x \in \mathbb{R}^m$ and $y \in \mathbb{R}^n$ is the concatenation of their elements.

**Permutations and permutation matrices.** The goal of this paper is to generate vectorized data permutations. We represent permutations as *permutation matrices* $P \in \mathbb{R}^{n \times n}$.

We define two basic permutation matrices: the $n \times n$ *identity matrix* $I_n$ and the *stride permutation matrix* $L_m^{mn}$, which permutes an input vector $x$ of length $mn$ as $in + j \mapsto jm + i$, $0 \le i < m$, $0 \le j < n$. For example ("." represents "0"),

$$L_2^6 \begin{pmatrix} x_0 \\ x_1 \\ x_2 \\ x_3 \\ x_4 \\ x_5 \end{pmatrix} = \begin{pmatrix} x_0 \\ x_2 \\ x_4 \\ x_1 \\ x_3 \\ x_5 \end{pmatrix}, \quad \text{with } L_2^6 = \begin{pmatrix} 1 & \cdot & \cdot & \cdot & \cdot & \cdot \\ \cdot & \cdot & 1 & \cdot & \cdot & \cdot \\ \cdot & \cdot & \cdot & \cdot & 1 & \cdot \\ \cdot & 1 & \cdot & \cdot & \cdot & \cdot \\ \cdot & \cdot & \cdot & 1 & \cdot & \cdot \\ \cdot & \cdot & \cdot & \cdot & \cdot & 1 \end{pmatrix}.$$

If $x$ is viewed as an $n \times m$ matrix, stored in row-major order, then $L_m^{mn}$ performs a transposition of this matrix.

**Matrix operators.** We need three matrix operators. The matrix *product* $C = AB$ is defined as usual. The *tensor* (or Kronecker) product of matrices is defined by

$$A \otimes B = (a_{i,j}B)_{i,j} \quad \text{with} \quad A = (a_{i,j})_{i,j}.$$

In particular,

$$I_n \otimes A = \begin{pmatrix} A & & \\ & \ddots & \\ & & A \end{pmatrix}.$$

Finally, the *stacking* of two matrices $A$ and $B$ is defined in the obvious way:

$$C = \begin{pmatrix} A \\ B \end{pmatrix}.$$

**Permutation matrix identities.** Our approach uses factorization properties of stride permutation matrices. We summarize those that we use throughout this paper. Intuitively, these identities express performing a matrix transposition by two passes instead of using a single pass. They are including blocked matrix transposition.

Identity matrices can be split into tensor products of identity matrices if their sizes are composite numbers, $I_{mn} = I_m \otimes I_n$. Further, we use four factorizations of stride permutations:

$$L_n^{kmn} = \left( L_n^{kn} \otimes I_m \right) \left( I_k \otimes L_n^{mn} \right) \tag{1}$$

$$L_n^{kmn} = L_{kn}^{kmn} L_{mn}^{kmn} \tag{2}$$

$$L_{km}^{kmn} = \left( I_k \otimes L_m^{mn} \right) \left( L_k^{kn} \otimes I_m \right) \tag{3}$$

$$L_{km}^{kmn} = L_k^{kmn} L_m^{kmn}. \tag{4}$$

**Table 2.** Translating matrix formulas into Matlab style code. $x$ denotes the input and $y$ the output vector. The subscript of $A$ and $B$ specifies the size of the matrix. $\mathtt{x[b:s:e]}$ denotes the subvector of $x$ starting at b, ending at e and extracted at stride s.

| Matrix formula | Code |
|---|---|
| $y = (A_n B_n)x$ | ```t[0:1:n-1] = B(x[0:1:n-1]);```<br>```y[0:1:n-1] = A(t[0:1:n-1];)``` |
| $y = (I_m \otimes A_n)x$ | ```for (i=0;i<m;i++)```<br>```    y[i*n:1:i*n+n-1] = A(x[i*n:1:i*n+n-1]);``` |
| $y = (A_m \otimes I_n)x$ | ```for (i=0;i<m;i++)```<br>```    y[i:n:i+m-1] = A(x[i:n:i+m-1]);``` |
| $y = L_m^{mn}\, x$ | ```for (i=0;i<m;i++)```<br>```    for (j=0;j<n;j++)```<br>```        y[i+m*j]=x[n*i+j];``` |
| $y = \begin{pmatrix} A_{m \times k} \\ B_{n \times k} \end{pmatrix} x$ | ```y[0:1:m-1]   = A(x[0:1:k-1]);```<br>```y[m:1:m+n-1] = B(x[0:1:k-1]);``` |

**Translating matrix expressions into programs.** Matrix formulas, constructed using the above formalism, can be recursively translated into standard scalar programs by applying the translation rules in Table 2 [13].

# 3    Vector Programs and Matrix Expressions

In this section we explain how we model vector instructions as matrices, sequences of vector instructions as matrix expressions, and how these are translated into programs.

## 3.1    Modeling Vector Shuffle Instructions as Matrices

We consider only unary and binary vector shuffle instructions. (AltiVec's `vec_perm` is a three-operand instruction but the third operand is a parameter.) The basic idea is to view each such instruction, when applied to its input vector(s), as a matrix-vector product. The matrix becomes a declarative representation of the instruction. As an example, consider the instruction `_mm_unpacklo_ps`, which performs the operation (see Table 1).

```
_mm_unpacklo_ps(a, b) -> {a.0, b.0, a.1, b.1}
```

Setting $x_0 = (a_0, a_1, a_2, a_3)^T$ and $x_1 = (b_0, b_1, b_2, b_3)^T$, this shuffle becomes the the matrix-vector product

$$y = M^4_{\_mm\_unpacklo\_ps}(x_0 \oplus x_1), \quad \text{with } M^4_{\_mm\_unpacklo\_ps} = \begin{pmatrix} 1 & \cdot & \cdot & \cdot & \cdot & \cdot & \cdot & \cdot \\ \cdot & \cdot & \cdot & \cdot & 1 & \cdot & \cdot & \cdot \\ \cdot & 1 & \cdot & \cdot & \cdot & \cdot & \cdot & \cdot \\ \cdot & \cdot & \cdot & \cdot & \cdot & 1 & \cdot & \cdot \end{pmatrix}.$$

Hence, the instruction `_mm_unpacklo_ps` is represented by the matrix $M^4_{\text{\_mm\_unpacklo\_ps}}$. The subscript indicates the instruction and the superscript the vector length $\nu$.

**Unary and binary instructions.** In general, for a $\nu$-way mode, unary instructions are represented as $\nu \times \nu$ matrices and binary instructions as $\nu \times 2\nu$ matrices. Further, each binary instruction induces a unary instruction by setting both of its inputs to the same value. The exact form of these matrices follow directly from Table 1.

**Polymorphic instructions.** Some instructions can be used with multiple data types, which produces different associated matrices. For example, in 2-way 64-bit integer mode and 4-way 32-bit integer mode, `_mm_unpacklo_epi64` is respectively represented by

$$M^2_{\text{\_mm\_unpacklo\_epi64}} = \begin{pmatrix} 1 & \cdot & \cdot & \cdot \\ \cdot & \cdot & 1 & \cdot \end{pmatrix} \quad \text{and} \quad M^4_{\text{\_mm\_unpacklo\_epi64}} = \begin{pmatrix} 1 & \cdot & \cdot & \cdot & \cdot & \cdot & \cdot & \cdot \\ \cdot & 1 & \cdot & \cdot & \cdot & \cdot & \cdot & \cdot \\ \cdot & \cdot & \cdot & \cdot & 1 & \cdot & \cdot & \cdot \\ \cdot & \cdot & \cdot & \cdot & \cdot & 1 & \cdot & \cdot \end{pmatrix}.$$

`_mm_unpacklo_epi64` can also be used in 8-way 16-bit and 16-way 8-bit integer mode as well as in 2-way 64-bit and 4-way 32-bit floating-point mode.

**Parameterized instructions.** We treat parameterized instructions as one instruction instance per possible parameter value. For instance, `_mm_shuffle_ps` is parameterized by four 2-bit constants, leading to 256 instruction instances. We assume that all parameters are fixed at compile time, even if the instruction set does support variable parameters (as AltiVec's `vec_perm`).

**Building matrices from ISA definition.** Our system generates the matrices for the given instruction set automatically. To do this, we first collect the instruction description from ISA and compiler manuals and basically copy them verbatim into a database. Each instruction is represented by a record including the vector length $\nu$, the *semantics* function that takes up to three lists (two input vectors and one parameter vector) and produces a list, and the *parameters* list that contains all possible parameter values. Unary instructions ignore the second input and unparameterized instructions ignore the third input. For instance, `_mm_shuffle_ps` is represented by

```
Intel_SSE2.4_x_float._mm_shuffle_ps := rec(
  v := 4,
  semantics := (x, y, p) -> [x[p[1]], x[p[2]], y[p[3]], y[p[4]]],
  parameters := Cartesian([[1..4],[1..4], [1..4], [1..4]])
);
```

The matrix generation is straightforward by "applying" the instruction to the canonical base vectors; the results are the columns of the desired matrix. More formally, if $e^\nu_i \in \mathbb{R}^\nu$ is the canonical basis vector with the "1" at the $i$th position and $0^\nu \in \mathbb{R}^\nu$ the zero vector, then the matrix $M_p$ for an instruction with semantics function $s(\cdot, \cdot, \cdot)$ and parameter $p$ is given by

$$M^{\nu}_{\text{instr},p} = \left( s(e^{\nu}_0, 0^{\nu}, p) | \ldots | s(e^{\nu}_{\nu-1}, 0^{\nu}, p) | s(0^{\nu}, e^{\nu}_0, p) | \ldots | s(e^{\nu}_{0^{\nu}, \nu-1}, p) \right).$$

## 3.2 Translating Matrix Formulas into Vector Programs

In Table 2, we summarized how matrix formulas are recursively translated into scalar code. To obtain vector programs for formulas representing permutations, we expand this table with three cases: instruction matrices, vector permutations, and half-vector permutations. Then we define the class of all formulas that we translate into vector programs and define a cost measure for these formulas.

**Instruction matrices.** If a matrix, such as $M^4_{\text{mm\_unpacklo\_ps}}$, corresponds to a vector instruction it is translated into this instruction.

**Vector permutations.** If a permutation is of the form $P \otimes I_{\nu}$, $P$ a permutation matrix, it permutes blocks of data of size $\nu$. Hence, we translate $P \otimes I_{\nu}$ into vector code by first translating $P$ into scalar code, and then replacing the scalar data type to the corresponding vector data type.

For example, $y = (L^4_2 \otimes I_4) x$ is implemented for 4-way 32-bit floating point SSE2 in two steps. First, $y = L^4_2 x$ is translated into the scalar program.

```
float x[2], y[2]; y[0] = x[0]; y[1] = x[2]; y[2] = x[1]; y[3] = x[3];
```

Then the scalar data type `float` is replaced by the vector data type `__m128` to get the final program

```
__m128 x[2], y[2]; y[0] = x[0]; y[1] = x[2]; y[2] = x[1]; y[3] = x[3];
```

**Half-vector permutation.** Permutations $P \otimes I_{\nu/2}$ are implemented using the same instructions `i1` and `i2` that implement, if possible, $L^4_2 \otimes I_{\nu/2}$. Otherwise, $P \otimes I_{\nu/2}$ cannot be implemented.

**Vectorized matrix formulas.** We define *vectorized matrix formulas* ⟨vmf⟩ as matrix formulas that can be translated into vector programs as explained above. The exact form depends on the vector extension and mode used. Formally, in BNF

$$\langle \text{vmf} \rangle ::= \langle \text{vmf} \rangle \langle \text{vmf} \rangle \mid I_m \otimes \langle \text{vmf} \rangle \mid \binom{\langle \text{vmf} \rangle}{\langle \text{vmf} \rangle} \mid \langle \text{perm} \rangle \otimes I_{\nu} \mid$$

$$\langle \text{perm} \rangle \otimes I_{\nu/2} \text{ if } L^4_2 \otimes I_{\nu/2} \text{ possible} \mid M_{\text{instr}} \text{ with instr in ISA}$$
$$\langle \text{perm} \rangle ::= L^{mn}_m \mid I_m \otimes \langle \text{perm} \rangle \mid \langle \text{perm} \rangle \otimes I_m \mid \langle \text{perm} \rangle \langle \text{perm} \rangle$$

**Cost measure.** We define a cost measure for vectorized matrix formulas recursively through (5)–(11). (6) assigns a constant cost $c_{\text{instr}}$ to each instruction `instr`. (7) states that permutations of vectors are for free, as they do not incur any vector shuffle instructions. (9)–(11) makes our cost measure additive with respect to matrix operators ".", "$\binom{\cdot}{\cdot}$", and "$\otimes$". The instructions `i1` and `i2` in (8) are the same that implement $L^4_2 \otimes I_{\nu/2}$.

$$\text{Cost}_{\text{ISA},\nu}(P) = \infty, \quad P \text{ not a } \langle \text{vmf} \rangle \tag{5}$$

$$\text{Cost}_{\text{ISA},\nu}(M_{\text{instr}}^{\nu}) = c_{\text{instr}} \tag{6}$$

$$\text{Cost}_{\text{ISA},\nu}(P \otimes I_{\nu}) = 0, \quad P \text{ permutation} \tag{7}$$

$$\text{Cost}_{\text{ISA},\nu}(P \otimes I_{\nu/2}) = \lfloor n/2 \rfloor c_{\text{i}1} + \lceil n/2 \rceil c_{\text{i}2}, \quad P \ 2n \times 2n \text{ permutation} \tag{8}$$

$$\text{Cost}_{\text{ISA},\nu}(A B) = \text{Cost}_{\text{ISA},\nu}(A) + \text{Cost}_{\text{ISA},\nu}(B) \tag{9}$$

$$\text{Cost}_{\text{ISA},\nu}\left(\begin{pmatrix} A \\ B \end{pmatrix}\right) = \text{Cost}_{\text{ISA},\nu}(A) + \text{Cost}_{\text{ISA},\nu}(B) \tag{10}$$

$$\text{Cost}_{\text{ISA},\nu}(I_m \otimes A) = m\text{Cost}_{\text{ISA},\nu}(A) \tag{11}$$

To minimize the instruction count $c_{\text{instr}} = 1$ is chosen. Using values of $c_{\text{instr}}$ that depend on $\text{instr}$ allows for fine-tuning of the instruction selection process when multiple solutions with minimal instruction count exist. For example, for SSE2 we set $c_{\text{instr}} = 1$ for binary instructions and $c_{\text{instr}} = 0.9$ to unary instructions. This slightly favors unary instructions which require one register less. Other refinements are possible.

# 4    Generating Vectorized Permutation Programs

Our goal is to generate efficient vector programs that implement stride permutations $L_k^{n\nu}$. The parameters of the stride permutation imply that we permute data that can be stored in an array of $n$ SIMD vectors and that $k \mid n\nu$.

**Problem statement.** *Input:* The permutation $L_k^{n\nu}$ to be implemented, the vector length $\nu$, and a list of vector instruction instances $\text{instr}$ for the ISA considered and their associated costs $c_{\text{instr}}$.

*Output:* A vectorized matrix formula for $L_k^{n\nu}$ with minimized cost and the implementation of the formula.

Our algorithm for solving the problem uses a rewriting system that is used in tandem with a dynamic programming search using backtracking. For important cases the solution is proven optimal.

## 4.1    Rewriting Rule Set

We use a rewriting system [14] to recursively translate the given stride permutation $L_k^{n\nu}$ into a vectorized matrix formula. In each rewriting step, the rewriting system finds one of the rules (12)–(22) and suitable parameters (a subset of $k$, $\ell$, $m$, $n$, $r$, $\text{instr}$, $\text{i}1$, and $\text{i}2$) for that rule so that its left side matches a subformula in the current matrix formula. This matching subformula is then replaced by the right side of the rule.

Note that there may be degrees of freedom, as the matching of the left side may, for instance, involve factorizing the integer $kmn$ into three integers $k$, $m$, and $n$, or involve the picking of a suitable, non-unique instruction $\text{instr}$. Also, it is not guaranteed that one of the rules is applicable, which may lead to dead ends. However, Section 4.3 shows that under relatively weak conditions (that are met by most current vector extension modes) there exists a solution for any $L_k^{n\nu}$.

The best solution has no obvious closed form; we use a dynamic programming search with backtracking to find it. The remainder of this section discusses the rewriting rule set while Section 4.2 discusses the search.

**Recursive rules.** Rules (12)–(17) are recursive rules. (12) is the entry rule, normalizing $L_k^{n\nu}$ into the shape $I_\ell \otimes L_m^{mn} \otimes I_r$ to simplify pattern matching. (13)–(16) mirror identities (1)–(4) and have the factorization $kmn$ as degree of freedom. (17) extracts candidates for vector instruction matrices and may be followed by application of (20)–(22).

$$L_m^{mn} \to I_1 \otimes L_m^{mn} \otimes I_1 \tag{12}$$

$$I_\ell \otimes L_n^{kmn} \otimes I_r \to \left( I_\ell \otimes L_n^{kn} \otimes I_{mr} \right)\left( I_{\ell k} \otimes L_n^{mn} I_r \right) \tag{13}$$

$$I_\ell \otimes L_n^{kmn} \otimes I_r \to \left( I_\ell \otimes L_{kn}^{kmn} \otimes I_r \right)\left( I_\ell \otimes L_{mn}^{kmn} \otimes I_r \right) \tag{14}$$

$$I_\ell \otimes L_{km}^{kmn} \otimes I_r \to \left( I_{k\ell} \otimes L_m^{mn} \otimes I_r \right)\left( I_\ell \otimes L_k^{kn} \otimes I_m \right) \tag{15}$$

$$I_\ell \otimes L_{km}^{kmn} \otimes I_r \to \left( I_\ell \otimes L_k^{kmn} \otimes I_r \right)\left( I_\ell \otimes L_m^{kmn} \otimes I_r \right) \tag{16}$$

$$I_{k\ell} \otimes L_m^{mn} \otimes I_r \to I_k \otimes \left( I_\ell \otimes L_m^{mn} \otimes I_r \right) \quad \text{if } \ell mnr \in \{\nu, 2\nu\} \tag{17}$$

**Base cases.** Rules (18)–(22) translate constructs $I_\ell \otimes L_m^{mn} \otimes I_r$ into vectorized matrix formulas. Rule (19) is only applied if $L_2^4 \otimes I_{\nu/2}$ can be done using two instructions.

$$I_\ell \otimes L_m^{mn} \otimes I_{r\nu} \to \left( I_\ell \otimes L_m^{mn} \otimes I_r \right) \otimes I_\nu \tag{18}$$

$$I_\ell \otimes L_m^{mn} \otimes I_{r\nu/2} \to \left( I_\ell \otimes L_m^{mn} \otimes I_r \right) \otimes I_{\nu/2} \tag{19}$$

$$I_\ell \otimes L_m^{mn} \otimes I_r \to M_{\text{instr}}^\nu \quad \text{if } \exists \text{ instr}: I_\ell \otimes L_m^{mn} \otimes I_r = M_{\text{instr}}^\nu \tag{20}$$

$$I_\ell \otimes L_m^{mn} \otimes I_r \to M_{\text{i1}}^\nu M_{\text{i2}}^\nu \quad \text{if } \exists \text{ i1, i2}: I_\ell \otimes L_m^{mn} \otimes I_r = M_{\text{i1}}^\nu M_{\text{i2}}^\nu \tag{21}$$

$$I_\ell \otimes L_m^{mn} \otimes I_r \to \begin{pmatrix} M_{\text{i1}}^\nu \\ M_{\text{i2}}^\nu \end{pmatrix} \quad \text{if } \exists \text{ i1, i2}: I_\ell \otimes L_m^{mn} \otimes I_r = \begin{pmatrix} M_{\text{i1}}^\nu \\ M_{\text{i2}}^\nu \end{pmatrix} \tag{22}$$

The right-hand side of (18) can be implemented solely using vector assignments (see Section 3.2). (19) introduces half-vector permutations which are necessary if $mn$ is not a two-power. (20) matches if a (necessarily unary) vector instruction (instance) instr exists, which implements the left-hand side. As example,

```
y = _mm_shuffle_ps(x, x, _MM_SHUFFLE(0,2,1,3));
```

implements $y = (I_1 \otimes L_2^4 \otimes I_1)\, x$ for 4-way single-precision floating-point SSE2. (21) matches if two (necessarily unary) vector instruction (instances) i1 and i2 exist, which implement its left-hand side when applied consecutively. As example,

```
y = _mm_shufflehi_epi16(_mm_shufflelo_epi16(x,
    _MM_SHUFFLE(0,2,1,3)), _MM_SHUFFLE(0,2,1,3));
```

implements $y = (I_2 \otimes L_2^4 \otimes I_2)\, x$ for 16-way 8-bit integer SSE2. (22) matches if two (necessarily binary) vector instruction (instances) i1 and i2 exist, which implement its left-hand side when applied to the input in parallel. As example,

```
y[0] = _mm_unpacklo_epi64(x[0], x[1]);
y[1] = _mm_unpacklo_epi64(x[0], x[1]);
```

implements $y = (I_1 \otimes L_2^4 \otimes I_4)\, x$ for 8-way 16-bit integer SSE2.

**Base case library.** To speed up the pattern matching required in (20)–(22), we perform a one-time initialization for each new vector architecture (instruction set and mode), and build a base case library that caches the instruction sequences that implement $I_\ell \otimes L_m^{mn} \otimes I_r$ for all values $\ell$, $m$, $n$, and $r$ with $\ell m n r \in \{\nu, 2\nu\}$ or stores that no such instruction(s) exist. We build this table in a five-step procedure.

- First we create the matrices associated with each instance of each instruction (for all modes and parameters).
- Next we filter out all matrices that have more than one "1" per column, as these matrices cannot be used to build permutations.
- To support (19), we search for a pair of binary instructions that implement $L_2^4 \otimes I_{\nu/2}$.
- To support (20), we find all unary instruction (instances) that implement $I_\ell \otimes L_m^{mn} \otimes I_r$ with $\nu = \ell m n r$ and save them in the cache.
- To support (21), we find all sequences of two unary instruction (instances) that implement $I_\ell \otimes L_m^{mn} \otimes I_r$ with $\nu = \ell m n r$ and save them in the cache.
- To support (22), we find all pairs binary instruction (instances) that implement $I_\ell \otimes L_m^{mn} \otimes I_r$ with $2\nu = \ell m n r$ and save them in the cache.

## 4.2 Dynamic Programming Search

The rule set (12)–(22) contains recursive and base rules with choices. We want to find a (not necessarily unique) vectorized matrix formula for $L_k^{n\nu}$ with minimal cost. We use dynamic programming with backtracking, which finds the optimal solution within the space of possible solutions spanned by the rewriting rules.

**Dynamic Programming (DP).** For a formula $F$, let $E(F)$ be the set of formulas that can be reached by applying one rewriting step using (12)–(22). Assume $A \in E(F)$ is not yet a vectorized matrix formula. We define $X(A)$ as the optimal vectorized matrix formula, computed recursively together with its cost, or cost $= \infty$ is it does not exist. DP computes $X(F)$ as

$$X(F) = \arg\min \{\text{Cost}_{\text{ISA},\nu} (X(A)) \,|\, A \in E(F)\}. \tag{23}$$

All computed optimal costs and associated formulas are stored in a table. DP is started by evaluating $\text{Cost}_{\text{ISA},\nu} (X(L_k^{n\nu}))$.

**Backtracking.** Not all formulas $I_\ell \otimes L_m^{mn} \otimes I_r$ with $\ell m n r \in \{\nu, 2\nu\}$ can be necessarily translated into a vectorized matrix formula using (20)–(22). Thus, randomly picking elements $A \in E(F)$ during the rewriting process may not yield a vectorized matrix formula at termination; hence, DP needs to backtrack and in the worst case will generates all formulas that can be obtained using our rewriting rules.

Existence and optimality of the solution are discussed in Section 4.3.

**Cycles in rewriting.** (14) and (16) produce an infinite cycle. To avoid that problem, we actually run two DPs—once without (14) and once without (16)—and take the minimum value of both answers.

**Runtime of algorithm.** The generation of vectorized base cases consists of two components: one-time generation of the base case library, and a DP for each stride permutation to be generated.

- *Base case library.* For an instruction set extension mode with $n$ instruction instances, $O(n^2)$ matrix comparisons are required to build the base case library. On a current machine the actual runtime is a few seconds to minutes.
- *DP.* Let $n\nu = \prod_{i=0}^{k-1} p_i^{r_i}$ be the prime factorization of $n\nu$. For a stride permutation $L_k^{n\nu}$, DP with backtracking is in exponential in $\sum_i r_i$. However, $k$ and $r_i$ are small as we are only handling basic blocks. On a current machine the actual runtime is a few seconds.

## 4.3 Existence and Optimality

Since we model both permutations and instructions using matrices, we can use mathematics to answer existence and optimality questions. Specifically, we give conditions under which our rewriting system finds a solution, i.e., a vectorized matrix formula, at all.

Further, we show vectorized matrix formulas for $L_\nu^{\nu^2}$ generated for all modes of SSE2 and the Cell BE and establish their optimality. We also discuss the optimality of solutions for $L_2^{2\nu}$, and $L_\nu^{2\nu}$. These three permutations are the ones needed, for example, in the short-vector Cooley-Tukey FFT [4]; $L_\nu^{\nu^2}$ is an ubiquitous algorithmic building block and crucial in matrix-matrix and matrix-vector multiplication for some vector extensions.

**Existence of solution.** Under the most general conditions, our algorithm does not necessarily return a solution. However, under relatively weak conditions imposed on the ISA, a solution can be guaranteed. The conditions are met by most current SIMD extensions. One notable exception is 16-way 8-bit integer in SSE2, for which the second condition does not hold.

- For $\nu \mid k \mid n$, a $\langle vmf \rangle$ for $L_2^{2\nu}$ must exist.
- For $\nu \nmid k$ or $k \nmid n$, $\langle vmf \rangle$ for $L_2^{2\nu}$, $L_2^\nu$, and $L_2^4 \otimes I_{\nu/2}$ must exist.

The proof explicitly constructs a (suboptimal) vectorized formula using rules (1)–(4). We omit the details.

**Optimality of generated implementations.** Floyd [7] derived the exact number of block transfers required to transpose an arbitrary matrix on a two-level memory where the small memory can hold two blocks. We can apply his theorem to our situation by identifying binary vector instructions with the two-element memory in his formulation. The number of block transfer operations then yields a lower bound on the number of binary vector instructions required to perform a stride permutation. Specifically, if $\mathcal{C}_\nu(P)$ is the minimal number of vector shuffle instructions required to perform $P$, then

$$\mathcal{C}_\nu(\mathrm{L}_k^{2\nu}) \geq 2, \quad \text{for } k \neq 1, 2\nu, \quad \text{and} \quad \mathcal{C}_\nu(\mathrm{L}_\nu^{\nu^2}) \geq \nu \log_2 \nu. \tag{24}$$

For example, for $\mathrm{L}_\nu^{\nu^2}$ our method generates the following vectorized matrix formulas. On SSE2 and on Cell the corresponding instructions counts match the lower bounds on (24) for all modes and are hence optimal.

$$\mathrm{L}_4^{16} = \left(\mathrm{L}_4^8 \otimes \mathrm{I}_2\right)\left(\mathrm{I}_2 \otimes \mathrm{L}_4^8\right)$$

$$\mathrm{L}_8^{64} = \left(\mathrm{I}_4 \otimes (\mathrm{L}_2^4 \otimes \mathrm{I}_4)\right)\left(\mathrm{L}_4^8 \otimes \mathrm{I}_8\right)\left(\mathrm{I}_4 \otimes (\mathrm{L}_4^8 \otimes \mathrm{I}_2)\right)\left((\mathrm{I}_2 \otimes \mathrm{L}_2^4) \otimes \mathrm{I}_8\right)\left(\mathrm{I}_4 \otimes \mathrm{L}_8^{16}\right)$$

$$\mathrm{L}_{16}^{256} = \left(\mathrm{I}_8 \otimes (\mathrm{L}_2^4 \otimes \mathrm{I}_8)\right)\left(\mathrm{L}_8^{16} \otimes \mathrm{I}_{16}\right)\left(\mathrm{I}_8 \otimes (\mathrm{L}_4^8 \otimes \mathrm{I}_4)\right)\left((\mathrm{I}_4 \otimes \mathrm{L}_2^4) \otimes \mathrm{I}_{16}\right)$$

$$\left((\mathrm{I}_2 \otimes \mathrm{L}_2^4 \otimes \mathrm{I}_2) \otimes \mathrm{I}_{16}\right)\left(\mathrm{I}_8 \otimes (\mathrm{L}_8^{16} \otimes \mathrm{I}_2)\right)\left((\mathrm{I}_4 \otimes \mathrm{L}_2^4) \otimes \mathrm{I}_{16}\right)\left(\mathrm{I}_8 \otimes \mathrm{L}_{16}^{32}\right)$$

The formula for $\mathrm{L}_8^{64}$ yields the following implementation in 8-way 16-bit integer SSE2. All variables are of type __m128i.

```
t3 = _mm_unpacklo_epi16(X[0], X[1]); t4 = _mm_unpackhi_epi16(X[0], X[1]);
t7 = _mm_unpacklo_epi16(X[2], X[3]); t8 = _mm_unpackhi_epi16(X[2], X[3]);
t11 = _mm_unpacklo_epi16(X[4], X[5]);t12 = _mm_unpackhi_epi16(X[4], X[5]);
t15 = _mm_unpacklo_epi16(X[6], X[7]);t16 = _mm_unpackhi_epi16(X[6], X[7]);
t17 = _mm_unpacklo_epi32(t3, t7);    t18 = _mm_unpackhi_epi32(t3, t7);
t19 = _mm_unpacklo_epi32(t4, t8);    t20 = _mm_unpackhi_epi32(t4, t8);
t21 = _mm_unpacklo_epi32(t11, t15);  t22 = _mm_unpackhi_epi32(t11, t15);
t23 = _mm_unpacklo_epi32(t12, t16);  t24 = _mm_unpackhi_epi32(t12, t16);
Y[0] = _mm_unpacklo_epi64(t17, t21); Y[1] = _mm_unpackhi_epi64(t17, t21);
Y[2] = _mm_unpacklo_epi64(t18, t22); Y[3] = _mm_unpackhi_epi64(t18, t22);
Y[4] = _mm_unpacklo_epi64(t19, t23); Y[5] = _mm_unpackhi_epi64(t19, t23);
Y[6] = _mm_unpacklo_epi64(t20, t24); Y[7] = _mm_unpackhi_epi64(t20, t24);
```

Further, $\mathrm{L}_\nu^{2\nu}$ can be implemented optimally on all considered vector architectures using 2 binary vector instructions. However, $\mathrm{L}_2^{2\nu}$ *cannot* be implemented optimally on 8-way and 16-way SSE2 due to restrictions in the instruction set.

## 5   Experimental Results

We generated and evaluated vectorized permutations for a single core of a 2.66 GHz Intel Core2 Duo and one SPE of a 3.2 GHz IBM Cell BE processor. We used the Intel C++ compiler 9.1 for SSE and the GNU C compiler 4.1.1 for the Cell BE. The small sizes of the code generated by our approach makes it infeasible to compare our generated programs to any optimized matrix transposition library.

**Implementation in Spiral.** We implemented our approach as part of Spiral [2], a program generator that autonomously implements and optimizes DSP transforms. In particular, Spiral generates high performance vectorized DFT implementations [4]. These implementations require vectorized basic blocks for stride permutations $L_\nu^{\nu^2}$, $L_2^{2\nu}$, and $L_\nu^{2\nu}$, which were hand-supplied in [4]. Using the approach presented in this paper, we automate this last manual step to enable automatic porting to new vector architectures.

**Stand-alone stride permutation.** In the first experiment, we generated implementations for $y = L_\nu^{\nu^2} x$ for SSE2 2-way, 4way, 8-way, and 16-way, as well as one 4-way Cell SPU. We compare our generated vectorized shuffle-based implementation against the one based on vector gathers (see Section 2.1). The shuffle-based implementations require $\nu$ vector loads, $\nu$ vector stores, and $\nu \log_2 \nu$ shuffle operations. The gather-based implementations require $\nu$ vector gathers and $\nu$ vector stores. We measured the cycles required for the data to get permuted from L1 cache to L1 cache, measuring many iterations to compensate for the timing overhead and to get a throughput measure.

Table 3 summarizes the results. In this setting, the shuffle-based implementation is much cheaper than the gather-based implementation. The reason is that sustained subword memory access is particularly costly on modern CPUs, which are optimized for wide words.

**Table 3.** Runtime and number of instructions needed for the stride permutations $y = L_\nu^{\nu^2} x$ when implemented using vector shuffles (generated by our method) or gather-based (the usual approach)

|  | Core2 SSE2 | | | | Cell SPU | |
|---|---|---|---|---|---|---|
|  | $\nu = 2$ | $\nu = 4$ | $\nu = 8$ | $\nu = 16$ | $\nu = 2$ | $\nu = 4$ |
| *vector shuffle* | | | | | | |
| shuffle instructions | 2 | 8 | 24 | 64 | 2 | 8 |
| move instructions | 4 | 8 | 16 | 32 | 6 | 10 |
| cycles | 4 | 13 | 35 | 106 | 15 | 22 |
| *vector gather* | | | | | | |
| gather instructions | 4 | 28 | 128 | 384 | 14 | 62 |
| store instructions | 2 | 4 | 8 | 16 | 2 | 4 |
| cycles | 15 | 60 | 94 | 407 | 32 | 112 |

**Permutations within numerical kernels.** In the second experiment we investigated the impact of our generated vectorized permutations versus vector gathers inside DFT kernels. For proper evaluation, we used Spiral-generated DFT kernels using the split complex format; these kernels are very fast (equal or better than FFTW 3.1.2 and Intel IPP 5.1) since they consist exclusively of vector arithmetic, vector memory access, and stride permutations $L_\nu^{\nu^2}$.

For $n = k\nu^2 \leq 128$, $1 \leq k \leq 8$, a split complex $DFT_n$ requires between $\frac{3}{\nu} n \log_2 n$ and $\frac{8}{\nu} n \log_2 n$ vector arithmetic operations and $k$ stride permutations

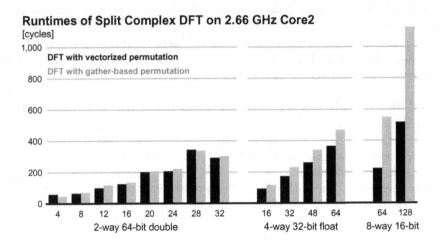

**Fig. 1.** Vectorized split complex DFT for various small sizes

$L_\nu^{\nu^2}$. Hence, the majority of vector instructions are arithmetic operations, but the number of vector shuffles and vector gathers still make up between 5% and 15% and between 15% to 50% of all instructions in their respective implementations. The overhead is largest for long vector lengths $\nu$ and small problem sizes $n$.

Figure 1 shows the cycle counts of Spiral-generated FFT code in both cases. For 2-way double-precision SSE2 the difference is negligible. For 4-way single-precision SSE2, the difference is up to 35%, due to a relative higher vector shuffle operations count and since expensive 4-way shuffle instructions are relatively more expensive. In the 8-way case these arguments become even more pronounced and the shuffle-based implementation is more than twice as fast as the gather-based implementation.

## 6  Conclusion

In this paper we show how to generate efficient vector programs for small stride permutations, which are important building blocks for numerical kernels. Even though this is a very specific class, we think we put forward an interesting approach that may have broader applicability. Namely, we have shown how to model vector instructions as matrices and then use matrix algebra for both generating and optimizing algorithm and implementation for the desired permutation and analyzing the quality of the result. On the practical side, our method enables us to quickly generate the building blocks that Spiral needs to generate FFTs for a given vector architecture. This enables us to port Spiral to new vector architectures without creative human effort.

# References

1. van Loan, C.: Computational Framework of the Fast Fourier Transform. SIAM, Philadelphia (1992)
2. Püschel, M., Moura, J.M.F., Johnson, J., Padua, D., Veloso, M., Singer, B.W., Xiong, J., Franchetti, F., Gačić, A., Voronenko, Y., Chen, K., Johnson, R.W., Rizzolo, N.: SPIRAL: Code generation for DSP transforms. Proceedings of the IEEE 93(2), 232–275 (2005); Special issue on Program Generation, Optimization, and Adaptation
3. Franchetti, F., Voronenko, Y., Püschel, M.: A rewriting system for the vectorization of signal transforms. In: Proc. High Performance Computing for Computational Science (VECPAR) (2006)
4. Franchetti, F., Püschel, M.: Short vector code generation for the discrete Fourier transform. In: Proc. IEEE Int'l Parallel and Distributed Processing Symposium (IPDPS), pp. 58–67 (2003)
5. Nuzman, D., Rosen, I., Zaks, A.: Auto-vectorization of interleaved data for SIMD. In: Proc. Programming Language Design and Implementation (PLDI), pp. 132–143 (2006)
6. Johnson, J.R., Johnson, R.W., Rodriguez, D., Tolimieri, R.: A methodology for designing, modifying, and implementing FFT algorithms on various architectures. Circuits Systems Signal Processing 9, 449–500 (1990)
7. Floyd, R.W.: Permuting information in idealized two-level storage. Complexity of Computer Calculations, 105–109 (1972)
8. Vitter, J.S., Shriver, E.A.M.: Algorithms for parallel memory I: Two-level memories. Algorithmica 12(2/3), 110–147 (1994)
9. Suh, J., Prasanna, V.: An efficient algorithm for out-of-core matrix transposition. IEEE Transactions on Computers 51(6), 420–438 (2002)
10. Lu, Q., Krishnamoorthy, S., Sadayappan, P.: Combining analytical and empirical approaches in tuning matrix transposition. In: Proc. Parallel Architectures and Compilation Techniques (PACT), pp. 233–242 (2006)
11. Zima, H., Chapman, B.: Supercompilers for parallel and vector computers. ACM Press, New York (1990)
12. Ren, G., Wu, P., Padua, D.: Optimizing data permutations for SIMD devices. In: Proc. Programming Language Design and Implementation (PLDI), pp. 118–131 (2006)
13. Xiong, J., Johnson, J., Johnson, R., Padua, D.: SPL: A language and compiler for DSP algorithms. In: Proc. Programming Language Design and Implementation (PLDI), pp. 298–308 (2001)
14. Dershowitz, N., Plaisted, D.A.: Rewriting. In: Robinson, A., Voronkov, A. (eds.) Handbook of Automated Reasoning, vol. 1, pp. 535–610. Elsevier, Amsterdam (2001)

# Automatic Transformations for Communication-Minimized Parallelization and Locality Optimization in the Polyhedral Model

Uday Bondhugula[1], Muthu Baskaran[1], Sriram Krishnamoorthy[1],
J. Ramanujam[2], Atanas Rountev[1], and P. Sadayappan[1]

[1] Dept. of Computer Science and Engineering, The Ohio State University, Columbus, OH, USA
{bondhugu,baskaran,krishnsr,rountev,saday}@cse.ohio-state.edu
[2] Dept. of Electrical and Computer Engg., Louisiana State University, Baton Rouge, LA , USA
jxr@ece.lsu.edu

**Abstract.** The polyhedral model provides powerful abstractions to optimize loop nests with regular accesses. Affine transformations in this model capture a complex sequence of execution-reordering loop transformations that can improve performance by parallelization as well as locality enhancement. Although a significant body of research has addressed affine scheduling and partitioning, the problem of automatically finding good affine transforms for communication-optimized coarse-grained parallelization together with locality optimization for the general case of arbitrarily-nested loop sequences remains a challenging problem.

We propose an automatic transformation framework to optimize arbitrarily-nested loop sequences with affine dependences for parallelism and locality simultaneously. The approach finds good tiling hyperplanes by embedding a powerful and versatile cost function into an Integer Linear Programming formulation. These tiling hyperplanes are used for communication-minimized coarse-grained parallelization as well as for locality optimization. The approach enables the minimization of inter-tile communication volume in the processor space, and minimization of reuse distances for local execution at each node. Programs requiring one-dimensional versus multi-dimensional time schedules (with scheduling-based approaches) are all handled with the same algorithm. Synchronization-free parallelism, permutable loops or pipelined parallelism at various levels can be detected. Preliminary studies of the framework show promising results.

## 1 Introduction and Motivation

Current trends in architecture are increasingly towards larger number of processing elements on a chip. This has led to multi-core architectures becoming mainstream along with the emergence of several specialized parallel architectures or accelerators. The difficulty of programming these architectures to effectively tap the potential of multiple on-chip processing units is a well-known challenge. Among several approaches to addressing this issue, one that is very promising but simultaneously very challenging is automatic parallelization.

Many compute-intensive applications often spend most of their running time in nested loops. This is particularly common in scientific and engineering applications. The polyhedral model [6,10,12] provides a powerful abstraction to reason about transformations

L. Hendren (Ed.): CC 2008, LNCS 4959, pp. 132–146, 2008.
© Springer-Verlag Berlin Heidelberg 2008

on such loop nests by viewing a dynamic instance (iteration) of each statement as an integer point in a well-defined space which is the statement's *polyhedron*. With such a representation for each statement and a precise characterization of inter or intra-statement dependences, it is possible to reason about the correctness and goodness of a sequence of complex loop transformations using machinery from Linear Algebra and Integer Linear Programming. The polyhedral model is applicable to loop nests in which the data access functions and loop bounds are affine combinations (linear combination with a constant) of the enclosing loop variables and parameters. While a precise characterization of data dependences is feasible for programs with static control structure and affine references/loop-bounds, code with non-affine array access functions or dynamic control can also be handled, using conservative assumptions.

Early approaches to automatic parallelization applied only to perfectly nested loops and involved the application of a sequence of transformations to the program's attributed abstract syntax tree. The polyhedral model has enabled much more complex programs to be handled, and easy composition and application of more sophisticated transformations [6,12]. The task of program optimization in the polyhedral model may be viewed in terms of three phases: (1) static dependence analysis of the input program, (2) transformations in the polyhedral abstraction, and (3) generation of efficient loop code. Despite the progress in these techniques, several scalability challenges limited applicability to small loop nests. Significant recent advances in dependence analysis [28] and code generation [2,23,27] have demonstrated the applicability of the polyhedral techniques to real applications. However, current state-of-the-art polyhedral implementations still apply transformations manually and significant time is spent by an expert to determine the best set of transformations [6,12]. An important open issue is the choice of transformations from the huge space of valid transforms. Our work addresses this problem, by formulating a way to obtain good transformations fully automatically.

Tiling is a key transformation and has been studied from two perspectives — data locality optimization and parallelization. Tiling for locality requires grouping points in an iteration space into smaller blocks (tiles) allowing reuse in multiple directions when the block fits in a faster memory (registers, L1, or L2 cache). Tiling for coarse-grained parallelism fundamentally involves partitioning the iteration space into tiles that may be concurrently executed on different processors with a reduced frequency and volume of inter-processor communication: a tile is atomically executed on a processor with communication required only before and after execution. Hence, one of the key aspects of an automatic transformation framework is to find good ways of performing tiling.

Existing automatic transformation frameworks [1,13,17,18,19] have one or more drawbacks or restrictions that do not allow them to effectively parallelize/optimize loop nests. All of them lack a realistic cost model that is suitable for coarse-grained parallel execution as is used in practice with manually developed parallel applications. With the exception of Griebl [13], previous work generally focuses on one or the other of the complementary aspects of parallelization and locality optimization. The approach we develop answers the following question: What is a good way to tile imperfectly nested loop sequences to minimize the volume of communication between tiles (in processor space) as well as improve data reuse at each processor?

The rest of this paper is organized as follows. Section 2 provides an overview of the polyhedral model. In Section 3 describes our automatic transformation framework. Section 4 shows step-by-step application of our approach through an example. Section 5 provides a summary of the implementation and initial results. Section 6 discusses related work and conclusions are presented in Section 7. Full details of the framework, transformations and optimized code for various examples, and experimental results are available in extended reports [3,4].

## 2   Overview of the Polyhedral Framework

The set $X$ of all vectors $x \in \mathbf{Z}^n$ such that $\mathbf{h}.x = k$, for $k \in \mathbf{Z}$, forms an *affine hyperplane*. The set of parallel *hyperplane instances* corresponding to different values of $k$ is characterized by the vector $\mathbf{h}$ which is normal to the hyperplane. Each instance of a hyperplane is an $n - 1$ dimensional affine sub-space of the $n$-dimensional space. Two vectors $x_1$ and $x_2$ lie in the same hyperplane if $\mathbf{h}.x_1 = \mathbf{h}.x_2$.

The set of all vectors $x \in \mathbf{Z}^n$ such that $Ax + b \geq 0$, where $A$ is an integer matrix, defines a (convex) integer *polyhedron*. A *polytope* is a bounded polyhedron. Each runtime instance of a statement $S$ is identified by its iteration vector $i$, of dimensionality $m_{S_k}$, containing values for the indices of the loops surrounding it from outermost to innermost. Hence, a statement $S$ is associated with a polytope characterized by a set of bounding hyperplanes or faces. This is true when the loop bounds are affine combinations of outer loop indices and program parameters (typically, symbolic constants representing the problem size). Let $p$ be the vector of the program parameters.

A well-known known result useful for polyhedral analyses is the following [26]:

**Lemma 1 (Affine form of Farkas Lemma).** *Let $\mathcal{D}$ be a non-empty polyhedron defined by $s$ affine inequalities or faces: $\mathbf{a_k}.x + b_k \geq 0$, $1 \leq k \leq s$. An affine form $\psi(x)$ is non-negative everywhere in $\mathcal{D}$ iff it is a positive affine combination of the faces:*

$$\psi(x) \equiv \lambda_0 + \sum_k \lambda_k(\mathbf{a_k}x + b_k), \quad \lambda_k \geq 0 \tag{1}$$

The non-negative constants $\lambda_k$ are referred to as Farkas multipliers.

*Polyhedral Dependences.* Our dependence model is of exact affine dependences and same as the one used in [6,18,22,28]. Dependences are determined precisely through array dataflow analysis [9], but the input need not be in single-assignment form. All dependences including anti (write-after-read), output (write-after-write) and input (read-after-read) dependences are considered. The Data Dependence Graph (DDG) is a directed multi-graph with each vertex representing a statement, and an edge, $e \in E$, from node $S_i$ to $S_j$ representing a polyhedral dependence from a dynamic instance of $S_i$ to one of $S_j$: it is characterized by a polyhedron, $\mathcal{P}_e$, called the *dependence polyhedron* that captures the exact dependence information corresponding to edge, $e$ (see Fig. 1(b) for an example). The dependence polyhedron is in the sum of the dimensionalities of the source and target statement's polyhedra (with dimensions for program parameters as well). Though the equalities in $\mathcal{P}_e$ typically represent the affine function mapping the target iteration vector $t$ to the particular source $s$ that is the last access to the conflicting

```
for (i=0; i<N; i++)
  for (j=0; j<N; j++)
    S1: A[i,j] = A[i,j]+u[i]*v[j];
for (i=0; i<N; i++)
  for (j=0; j<N; j++)
    S2: x[i] = x[i]+A[j,i]*y[j];
```

(a) original code

$$
\mathcal{P}_{e_1}: \begin{bmatrix} 1 & 0 & 0 & 0 & 0 & 0 \\ 0 & -1 & 0 & 0 & 1 & -1 \\ 0 & 0 & 1 & 0 & 0 & 0 \\ 0 & 0 & 0 & -1 & 1 & -1 \\ 1 & 0 & 0 & -1 & 0 & 0 \\ 0 & 1 & -1 & 0 & 0 & 0 \end{bmatrix} \begin{bmatrix} i \\ j \\ i' \\ j' \\ N \\ 1 \end{bmatrix} \begin{matrix} \geq 0 \\ \geq 0 \\ \geq 0 \\ \geq 0 \\ = 0 \\ = 0 \end{matrix}
$$

(b) Dependence polyhedron for the inter-statement dependence on A

|        | S1    |       |       | S2    |       |       |
|--------|-------|-------|-------|-------|-------|-------|
|        | i | j | const | i | j | const |
| $c_1$  | 0 | 1 | 0 | 1 | 0 | 0 |
| $c_2$  | 1 | 0 | 0 | 0 | 1 | 0 |
| $c_3$  | 0 | 0 | 0 | 0 | 0 | 1 |

(c) transformation

```
for (c1=0; c1<N; c1++)
  for (c2=0; c2<N; c2++)
    A[c2,c1] = A[c2,c1]+u[c2]*v[c1];
    x[c1] = x[c1]+A[c2,c1]*y[c1];
```

(d) transformed code

**Fig. 1.** Polyhedral transformation and dependences

memory location, also known as the *h-transformation* [10], the last access condition is not necessary; in general, the equalities can be used to eliminate variables from $\mathcal{P}_e$. In the rest of this section, we assume for convenience that $s$ can be completely eliminated using $h_e$, being substituted by $h_e(t)$.

A one-dimensional affine transform for statement $S_k$ is defined by:

$$
\phi_{s_k} = \begin{bmatrix} f_1 & \cdots & f_{m_{S_k}} \end{bmatrix} (i) + f_0, \quad f_i \in \mathbf{Z}
$$

A multi-dimensional affine transformation for a statement can now be represented by a matrix with each row being an affine hyperplane/transform. If such a transformation matrix has full column rank, it completely specifies when and where an iteration executes (one-to-one mapping from source to target). The total number of rows in the matrix may be much larger as some special rows, *splitters*, may represent unfused loops at a level. Fig. 1 shows application of a transformation. Such transformations capture the fusion structure as well as compositions of permutation, reversal, relative shifting, and skewing transformations. This representation for transformations has been used by many researchers [6,11,12,15], and directly fits with scattering functions that a code generator like CLooG [2] supports. Our problem is thus to find the the transformation matrices that are best for parallelism and locality.

## 3 Finding good transformations

### 3.1 Legality of Tiling Imperfectly-Nested Loops

**Theorem 1.** *Let $\phi_{s_i}$ be a one-dimensional affine transform for statement $S_i$. For $\{\phi_{s_1}, \phi_{s_2}, \ldots, \phi_{s_k}\}$ to be a legal (statement-wise) tiling hyperplane, the following should hold for each edge $e$ from $S_i$ to $S_j$:*

$$\phi_{s_j}(t) - \phi_{s_i}(s) \geq 0, \quad \mathcal{P}_e \tag{2}$$

*Proof.* Tiling of a statement's iteration space defined by a set of tiling hyperplanes is said to be legal if each tile can be executed atomically and a valid total ordering of the tiles can be constructed. This implies that there exists no two tiles such that they both influence each other. Let $\{\phi_{s_1}^1, \phi_{s_2}^1, \ldots, \phi_{s_k}^1\}$, $\{\phi_{s_1}^2, \phi_{s_2}^2, \ldots, \phi_{s_k}^2\}$ be two statement-wise 1-d affine transforms that satisfy (2). Consider a tile formed by aggregating a group of hyperplane instances along $\phi_{s_i}^1$ and $\phi_{s_i}^2$. Due to (2), for any dynamic dependence, the target iteration is mapped to the same hyperplane or a greater hyperplane than the source, i.e., the set of all iterations that are outside of the tile and are influenced by it always lie in the forward direction along one of the independent tiling dimensions ($\phi^1$ and $\phi^2$ in this case). Similarly, all iterations outside of a tile influencing it are either in that tile or in the backward direction along one or more of the hyperplanes. The above argument holds true for both intra- and inter-statement dependences. For inter-statement dependences, this leads to an interleaved execution of tiles of iteration spaces of each statement when code is generated from these mappings. Hence, $\{\phi_{s_1}^1, \phi_{s_2}^1, \ldots, \phi_{s_k}^1\}$, $\{\phi_{s_1}^2, \phi_{s_2}^2, \ldots, \phi_{s_k}^2\}$ represent rectangularly tilable loops in the transformed space. If such a tile is executed on a processor, communication would be needed only before and after its execution. From locality point of view, if such a tile is executed with the associated data fitting in a faster memory, reuse is exploited in multiple directions. $\square$

The above condition was well-known for the case of a single-statement perfectly nested loops from the work of Irigoin and Triolet [14] (as $h^T.R \geq 0$). We have generalized it above for multiple iteration spaces with exact affine dependences with possibly different dimensionalities and imperfect nestings for statements.

*Tiling at an arbitrary depth.* Note that the legality condition as written in (2) is imposed on all dependences. However, if it is imposed only on dependences that have not been carried up to a certain depth, the independent $\phi$'s that satisfy the condition represent tiling hyperplanes at that depth, i.e., rectangular blocking (stripmine/interchange) at that level in the transformed program is legal.

Consider the perfectly nested version of 1-d Jacobi shown in Fig. 2(a). The discussion that follows also applies to the imperfectly nested version, but for convenience we first consider the perfectly nested version. We first describe solutions obtained by existing state-of-the-art approaches: Lim and Lam's affine partitioning [18,19] and Griebl's space and time tiling with Forward Communication-Only (FCO) placement [13].

Lim et al. [19] define legal time partitions which have the same property of tiling hyperplanes as described above. Their algorithm obtains affine partitions that minimize

```
for (t=1; t<T; t++)
  for (i=2; i<N−1; i++)
    a[t,i] = 0.33*(a[t−1,i] +
             a[t−1,i−1] + a[t−1,i+1]);

      (a) 1-d Jacobi: perfectly nested
```

```
for (t=1; t<T; t++)
  for (i=2; i<N−1; i++)
    S1: b[i] = 0.33*(a[i−1]+ a[i]+a[i+1]);
  for (i=2; i<N−1; i++)
    S2: a[i] = b[i];

      (b) 1-d Jacobi: imperfectly nested
```

**Fig. 2.** 1-d Jacobi

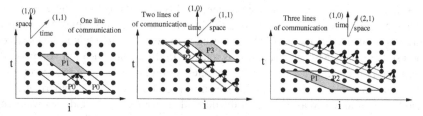

**Fig. 3.** Communication volume with different valid hyperplanes for perfectly nested 1-d Jacobi

the *order* of communication while maximizing the *degree* of parallelism. Equation (2) gives legality constraints $c_t \geq 0$, $c_t + c_i \geq 0$, and $c_t - c_i \geq 0$ corresponding to dependences $(1,0)$, $(1,1)$, and $(1,-1)$. There are infinitely many valid solutions with the same order complexity of synchronization, but with different communication volumes that may impact performance. Although it may seem that the volume may not affect performance, considering the fact that communication startup time on modern interconnects is significant, for higher dimensional problems such as $n$-d Jacobi, the ratio of communication to computation increases (proportional to tile size raised to $n - 1$). Existing work on tiling [24,25,30] can find near communication-optimal tiles for perfectly nested loops with constant dependences, but cannot handle arbitrarily nested loops. For 1-d Jacobi, all solutions within the cone formed by vectors $(1,1)$ and $(1,-1)$ are valid tiling hyperplanes. For the imperfectly nested version of 1-d Jacobi, the valid cone is $(2,1)$ and $(2,-1)$ (discussed later). For imperfectly nested Jacobi, Lim's algorithm [19] finds two valid independent solutions without optimizing for any particular criterion. In particular, the solutions found by their algorithm (Algorithm A in [19]) are $(2,-1)$ and $(3,-1)$ which are clearly not the best tiling hyperplanes to minimize communication volume, though they do minimize the *order* of synchronization which is $O(N)$; in this case any valid hyperplane has $O(N)$ synchronization. Figure 3 shows that the required communication increases as the hyperplane gets more and more oblique. For a hyperplane with normal $(k,1)$, one would need $(k+1)T$ values from the neighboring tile.

Using Griebl's approach, we first find that only space tiling is enabled with Feautrier's schedule being $\theta(t,i) = t$, i.e., using $(1,0)$ as the scheduling hyperplane. With forward communication-only (FCO) placement, an allocation is found such that dependences have positive components along space dimensions thereby enabling tiling of the time dimension; this decreases the frequency of communication. In this case, time tiling is enabled with FCO placement along $(1,1)$. However, note that communication in the processor space occurs along $(1,1)$, i.e., two lines of the array are required. However, using $(1,0)$ and $(1,1)$ as tiling hyperplanes with $(1,0)$ as space and $(1,1)$ as inner time and a tile space schedule of $(2,1)$ leads to only one line of communication along $(1,0)$. Our algorithm finds such a solution. Below we develop a cost function for an affine transform that captures communication volume and reuse distance.

### 3.2 Cost Function

Consider the following affine form:

$$\delta_e(t) = \phi_{s_i}(t) - \phi_{s_j}(h_e(t)), \quad t \in \mathcal{P}_e \tag{3}$$

The affine form $\delta_e(t)$ holds much significance. This function is the number of hyperplanes the dependence $e$ traverses along the hyperplane normal. It gives us a measure of the reuse distance if the hyperplane is used as time, i.e., if the hyperplanes are executed sequentially. Also, this function is a factor in the communication volume if the hyperplane is used to generate tiles for parallelization and used as a processor space dimension. An upper bound on this function means that the number of hyperplanes that would be communicated as a result of the dependence at the tile boundaries would not exceed this bound. We are particularly interested in whether this function can be reduced to a constant value or zero by choosing a suitable direction for $\phi$: if possible, that particular dependence leads to constant or no communication for this hyperplane. Note that each $\delta_e$ is an affine function of the loop indices. The challenge is to use this function to obtain a suitable objective for optimization in the affine framework.

*Challenges.* The constraints obtained from (2) only guarantee legality of tiling (permutability). However, several problems are encountered when one tries to apply a performance factor to find a good tile shape out of the several possibilities. Farkas Lemma has been used by many approaches [10,11,13,19] to eliminate loop variables from constraints by getting equivalent linear inequalities. The affine form in the loop variables is represented as a positive linear combination of the faces of the dependence polyhedron. When this is done, the coefficients of the loop variables on the left and right hand side are equated to eliminate the constraints of variables. This is done for each of the dependences, and the constraints obtained are aggregated. The resulting constraints are entirely in the coefficients of the tile mappings and Farkas multipliers. All Farkas multipliers can be eliminated, some by Gaussian elimination and the rest by Fourier-Motzkin elimination [19,26]. However, an attempt to minimize communication volume ends up in an objective function involving both loop variables and hyperplane coefficients. For example, $\phi(t) - \phi(h_e(t))$ could be $c_1 i + (c_2 - c_3)j$, where $1 \leq i \leq N \wedge 1 \leq j \leq N \wedge i \leq j$. One ends up with such a form when a dependence is not uniform or for an inter-statement dependence, making it hard to construct an objective function involving only the unknown hyperplane coefficients.

### 3.3   Cost Function Bounding and Minimization

**Theorem 2.** *If all iteration spaces are bounded, there exists an affine form $v(p) = u.p + w$ that bounds $\delta_e(t)$ for every dependence edge $e$:*

$$v(p) - \left(\phi_{s_i}(t) - \phi_{s_j}(h_e(t))\right) \geq 0, \quad t \in \mathcal{P}_e, \quad \forall e \in E \qquad (4)$$
$$i.e., \qquad v(p) - \delta_e(t) \geq 0, \quad t \in \mathcal{P}_e, \quad \forall e \in E$$

Even if $\delta_e$ involves loop variables, one can find large enough constants in $u$ that would be sufficient to bound $\delta_e(s)$. Note that the loop variables themselves are bounded by affine functions of the parameters, and hence the maximum value taken by $\delta_e(s)$ will be bounded by such an affine form. Also, since $v(p) \geq \delta_e(s) \geq 0$, $v$ should increase with an increase in the structural parameters, i.e., the coordinates of $u$ are positive. The reuse distance or communication volume for each dependence is bounded in this fashion by the same affine form. Such a bounding function was used by Feautrier [10] to find minimum latency schedules.

Now we apply Farkas Lemma to (4):

$$v(p) - \delta_e(t) \equiv \lambda_{e0} + \sum_{k=1}^{m_e} \lambda_{ek}\mathcal{P}_e^k, \qquad \lambda_{ek} \geq 0 \qquad (5)$$

where $\mathcal{P}_e^k$ is a face of $\mathcal{P}_e$. The above is an identity and the coefficients of each of the loop indices in $i$ and parameters in $p$ on the left and right hand side can be gathered and equated. We now get linear inequalities entirely in coefficients of the affine mappings for all statements, components of row vector $u$, and $w$. The above inequalities can at once be solved by finding a lexicographic minimal solution with $u$ and $w$ in the leading position, and the other variables following in any order. Let $\mathbf{u} = (u_1, u_2, \ldots u_k)$.

$$\text{minimize}_{\prec} \{u_1, u_2, \ldots, u_k, w, \ldots, c_i's, \ldots\} \qquad (6)$$

Finding the lexicographic minimal solution for a system of linear inequalities is within the reach of the simplex algorithm and can be handled by the Parametric Integer Programming (PIP) software [8]. Since the structural parameters are quite large, we first want to minimize their coefficients. We do not lose the optimal solution since an optimal solution would have the smallest possible values for $u$'s.

The solution gives a hyperplane for each statement. Note that the application of the Farkas Lemma to (4) is not required when a dependence is uniform, since the corresponding $\delta_e$ is independent of any loop variables. In such cases, we just have $w \geq \delta_e$.

### 3.4 Iteratively Finding Independent Solutions

Solving the ILP formulation in the previous section gives us a single solution to the coefficients of the best mappings for each statement. We need at least as many independent solutions as the dimensionality of the polytope associated with each statement. Hence, once a solution is found, we augment the ILP formulation with new constraints and obtain the next solution; the new constraints ensure linear independence with solutions already found. Let the rows of $H_S$ represent the solutions found so far for a statement $S$. Then, the sub-space orthogonal to $H_S$ [16,21] is given by:

$$H_S^\perp = I - H_S^T \left(H_S H_S^T\right)^{-1} H_S \qquad (7)$$

Note that $H_S^\perp . H_S^T = \mathbf{0}$, i.e., the rows of $H_S$ are orthogonal to those of $H_S^\perp$. Let $h_S^*$ be the next row (linear portion of the hyperplane) to be found for statement $S$. Let $H^i{}_S^\perp$ be a row of $H_S^\perp$. Then, any *one* of the inequalities given by $\forall i$, $H^i{}_S^\perp . h_S^* > 0, H^i{}_S^\perp . h_S^* < 0$ gives the necessary constraint to be added for statement $S$ to ensure that $h_S^*$ has a non-zero component in the sub-space orthogonal to $H_S$. This leads to a non-convex space, and ideally, all cases have to be tried and the best among those kept. When the number of statements is large, this leads to a combinatorial explosion. In such cases, we restrict ourselves to the sub-space of the orthogonal space where all the constraints are positive, i.e., the following constraints are added to the ILP formulation for linear independence:

$$\forall i, H^i{}_S^\perp . h^*{}_S \geq 0 \quad \wedge \quad \sum_i H^i{}_S^\perp h^*_S \geq 1 \qquad (8)$$

By just considering a particular convex portion of the orthogonal sub-space, we discard solutions that usually involve loop reversals or combination of reversals with other transformations; however, we believe this does not make a difference in practice. The mappings found are independent on a per-statement basis. When there are statements with different dimensionalities, the number of such independent mappings found for each statement is equal to the number of outer loops it has. Hence, no more orthogonality constraints need be added for statements for which enough independent solutions have been found (the rest of the rows get automatically filled with zeros or linearly dependent rows). The number of rows in the transformation matrix is the same for each statement, and the depth of the deepest loop nest in the target code is the same as that of the source loop nest. Overall, a hierarchy of fully permutable loop nest sets is found, and a lower level in the hierarchy will not be obtained unless constraints corresponding to dependences that have been carried by the parent permutable set have been removed.

### 3.5 Communication and Locality Optimization Unified

The above algorithm finds both synchronization-free and pipelined parallelism. The best possible solution to (6) is with $(u = 0, w = 0)$ and this happens when we find a hyperplane that has no dependence components along its normal, which is a fully parallel loop requiring no synchronization if it is at the outer level (*outer parallel*); it could be an inner parallel loop if some dependences were removed previously and so a synchronization is required after the loop is executed in parallel. Thus, in each of the steps where we find a new independent hyperplane, we end up first finding all synchronization-free hyperplanes; these are followed by a set of fully permutable hyperplanes that are tilable and pipelined parallel requiring constant boundary communication $(u = 0, w > 0)$ w.r.t. the tile sizes. In the worst case, a hyperplane with $u > 0, w \geq 0$ results in long communication from non-constant dependences. It is important to note that the latter are pushed to the innermost level. By considering communication volume and its minimization, all degrees of parallelism are found in the order of their preference.

From the point of view of data locality, the hyperplanes that are used to scan the tile space are the same as the ones that scan points in a tile. Hence, data locality is optimized from two angles: (1) cache misses at tile boundaries are minimized for local execution (as cache misses at local tile boundaries are equivalent to communication along processor tile boundaries); (2) by reducing reuse distances, we increase the local cache tile sizes. The former is due to selection of good tile shapes and the latter by the right permutation of hyperplanes (implicit in the order in which we find them).

### 3.6 Space and Time in Transformed Iteration Space

By minimizing $\phi(t) - \phi(s)$ as we find hyperplanes from outermost to innermost, we push dependence carrying to inner loops and also ensure that loops do not have negative dependence components (to the extent possible) so that target loops can be tiled. Once this is done, if the outer loops are used as space (any number desired, say $k$), and the rest are used as time (at least one time loop is required unless all loops are synchronization-free parallel), communication in the processor space is optimized as the outer space loops are the $k$ best ones. Whenever the loops can be tiled, they result in coarse-grained parallelism as well as better reuse within a tile.

**Input** Generalized dependence graph $G = (V, E)$ (includes dependence polyhedra $\mathcal{P}_e, e \in E$)

1: $S_{max}$: statement with maximum domain dimensionality
2: **for** each dependence $e \in E$ **do**
3:     Build legality constraints: apply Farkas Lemma on $\phi(t) - \phi(h_e(t)) \geq 0$ under $t \in \mathcal{P}_e$, and eliminate all Farkas multipliers
4:     Build communication volume/reuse distance bounding constraints: apply Farkas Lemma to $v(p) - (\phi(t) - \phi(h_e(t))) \geq 0$ under $\mathcal{P}_e$, and eliminate all Farkas multipliers
5:     Aggregate constraints from both into $C_e(i)$
6: **end for**
7: **repeat**
8:     $C = \emptyset$
9:     **for** each dependence edge $e \in E$ **do**
10:        $C \leftarrow C \cup C_e(i)$
11:    **end for**
12:    Compute lexicographic minimal solution with $u's$ coefficients in the leading position followed by $w$ to iteratively find independent solutions to $C$ (orthogonality constraints are added as each solution is found)
13:    **if** no solutions were found **then**
14:        Cut dependences between two strongly-connected components in the GDG and insert the appropriate *splitter* in the transformation matrices of the statements
15:    **end if**
16:    Compute $E_c$: dependences carried by solutions of Step 12/14
17:    $E \leftarrow E - E_c$; update the GDG $(V, E)$
18: **until** $H^\perp_{S_{max}} = 0$ and $E = \emptyset$

**Output** A transformation matrix for each statement (with the same number of rows)

**Fig. 4.** Overall algorithm

## 3.7 Fusion

The algorithm described in the previous section can also enable fusion across multiple iteration spaces that are weakly connected, as in sequences of producer-consumer loops. Solving for hyperplanes for multiple statements leads to a schedule for each statement such that all statements in question are *finely* interleaved: this is indeed fusion. This generalization of fusion is same as the one proposed in [6,12], and naturally integrates into our algorithm. A detailed description can be found in an extended report [3].

*Summary.* The overall algorithm is summarized in Fig. 4. It can be viewed as transforming to a tree of permutable loop nest sets/bands — each node of the tree is a good permutable loop nest set. Step 12 finds such a band of permutable loops. If all loops are tilable, there is just one node containing all the loops that are permutable. On the other extreme, if no loops are tilable, each node of the tree has just one loop and no tiling is possible. At least two hyperplanes should be found at any level (without dependence removal/cutting) to enable tiling. Dependences from previously found solutions are thus not removed unless they have to be (step 17) to allow the next permutable band to be found, and so on. Hence, partially tilable or untilable input is handled. Loops in each

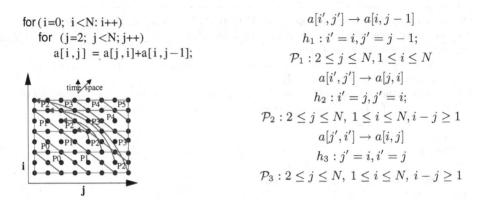

```
for(i=0; i<N: i++)
  for (j=2; j<N;j++)
    a[i,j] = a[j,i]+a[i,j-1];
```

$$a[i',j'] \rightarrow a[i,j-1]$$
$$h_1 : i' = i, j' = j - 1;$$
$$\mathcal{P}_1 : 2 \leq j \leq N, 1 \leq i \leq N$$
$$a[i',j'] \rightarrow a[j,i]$$
$$h_2 : i' = j, j' = i;$$
$$\mathcal{P}_2 : 2 \leq j \leq N, \ 1 \leq i \leq N, i - j \geq 1$$
$$a[j',i'] \rightarrow a[i,j]$$
$$h_3 : j' = i, i' = j$$
$$\mathcal{P}_3 : 2 \leq j \leq N, \ 1 \leq i \leq N, \ i - j \geq 1$$

**Fig. 5.** An example with non-uniform dependences

node of the target tree can be stripmined/interchanged when there are at least two of them; however, it is illegal to move a stripmined loop across different levels in the tree.

## 4   Example

Figure 5 shows an example from the literature [7] with affine non-uniform dependences, together with the corresponding dependence polyhedra (the source iteration vector has been eliminated). For the first dependence, the tiling legality constraint is

$$c_i i + c_j j - c_i i - c_j (j - 1) \geq 0 \quad \Rightarrow \quad c_j \geq 0$$

Since this is a constant dependence, the volume bounding constraint gives $w - c_j \geq 0$. For the second dependence, the tiling legality constraint is

$$(c_i i + c_j j) - (c_i j + c_j i) \geq 0$$

Applying Farkas Lemma (with $\mathcal{P}_2$), we have:

$$(c_i - c_j)i + (c_j - c_i)j \equiv \lambda_0 + \lambda_1(N - i) + \lambda_2(N - j)$$
$$+\lambda_3(i - j - 1) + \lambda_4(i - 1) + \lambda_5(j - 1) \quad (9)$$
$$\lambda_0, \lambda_1, \lambda_2, \lambda_3, \lambda_4, \lambda_5 \geq 0$$

Equating LHS and RHS coefficients for $i, j, N$ and the constants in (9), and eliminating Farkas multipliers through Fourier-Motzkin elimination, we obtain $c_i - c_j \geq 0$. The volume bounding constraint is

$$u_1 N + w - (c_i j + c_j i - c_i i - c_j j) \geq 0$$

A similar application of Farkas Lemma, and elimination of the multipliers yields $u_1 \geq 0, u_1 - c_i + c_j \geq 0$, and $3u_1 + w - c_i + c_j \geq 0$. Due to the symmetry with respect to $i$

and $j$, the third dependence does not lead to any new constraints. Aggregating legality and volume bounding constraints for all dependences, we get the formulation:

$$\text{minimize}_{\prec} \ (u_1, w, c_i, c_j)$$

subject to:
$$c_j \geq 0 \qquad\qquad\qquad w - c_j \geq 0$$
$$c_i - c_j \geq 0 \qquad\qquad\qquad u_1 \geq 0$$
$$u_1 - c_i + c_j \geq 0 \qquad\qquad 3u_1 + w - c_i + c_j \geq 0$$

The lexicographic minimal solution for the vector $(u_1, w, c_i, c_j)$ is $(0, 1, 1, 1)$ (the zero vector is a trivial solution and is avoided). Hence, we get $c_i = c_j = 1$. Note that $c_i = 1$ and $c_j = 0$ is not obtained even though it is a valid tiling hyperplane as it involves more communication: it requires $u_1$ to be positive.

The next solution is forced to have a positive component in the subspace orthogonal to $(1, 1)$ given by (7) as $(1,-1)$. This leads to the addition of the constraint $c_i - c_j \geq 1$ or $c_i - c_j \leq -1$ to the existing formulation. Adding $c_i - c_j \geq 1$ to (10), the lexicographic minimal solution is $(1, 0, 1, 0)$, i.e., $u_1 = 1, w = 0, c_i = 1, c_j = 0$ ($u_1 = 0$ is no longer valid). Hence, $(1, 1)$ and $(1, 0)$ are the tiling hyperplanes obtained. $(1,1)$ is used as space with one line of communication between processors, and the hyperplane $(1,0)$ is used as time in a tile. The outer tile schedule is $(2,1)$ ( = $(1,1) + (1,0)$).

This transformation is in contrast to other approaches based on schedules which obtain a schedule and then the rest of the transformation matrix. Feautrier's greedy heuristic gives the schedule $\theta(i, j) = 2i + j - 3$ which carries all dependences. However, using this as either space or time does not lead to communication or locality optimization. The $(2,1)$ hyperplane has non-constant communication along it. In fact, the only hyperplane that has constant communication along it is $(1,1)$. This is the best hyperplane to be used as a space loop if the nest is to be parallelized, and is the first solution that our algorithm finds. The $(1,0)$ hyperplane is used as time leading to a solution with one degree of pipelined parallelism with one line per tile of near-neighbor communication (along $(1,1)$) as shown in Fig. 4. Hence, a good schedule that tries to carry all dependences (or as many as possible) is not necessarily a good loop for the transformed iteration space.

## 5    Implementation and Preliminary Results

We have implemented our transformation framework using PipLib 1.3.3 [8]. Our tool takes as input dependence information (dependence polyhedra and h-transformations) from LooPo's [20] dependence tester and generates statement-wise affine transformations. Though in theory the approach, relying on integer programming, has worst-case exponential time complexity, we observe that it runs extremely fast in practice. The transformations generated are provided to CLooG [2] as scattering functions. The goal is to obtain tiled shared memory parallel code, for example, OpenMP code for multicore architectures. Table 1 summarizes the performance of transformed codes. The state-of-the-art from the research community is represented by [13,17,18,19], while ICC 10.1 with '-fast -parallel' was used as the native compiler. The results were obtained on an Intel Core 2 Quad (Q6600 2.4 GHz). Due to space constraints, detailed experimental evaluation can be found elsewhere [4].

**Table 1.** Initial results: speedup over state-of-the-art research

| Benchmark | Single core speedup | | Multi-core speedup (4 cores) | |
|---|---|---|---|---|
| | over native compiler | over state-of-the-art research | over native compiler | over state-of-the-art research |
| 1-d Jacobi (imperfect nest) | 5.23x | 2.1x | 20x | 1.7x |
| 2-d FDTD | 3.7x | 3.1x | 7.4x | 2.5x |
| 3-d Gauss-Seidel | 1.6x | 1.1x | 4.5x | 1.5x |
| LU decomposition | 5.6x | 5.7x | 14x | 3.8x |
| Matrix Vec Transpose | 9.3x | 5.5x | 13x | 7x |

## 6   Related Work

Iteration space tiling [14,24,29] is a standard approach for aggregating a set of loop iterations into tiles, with each tile being executed atomically. In addition, researchers have considered the problem of selecting tile shape and size to minimize communication, improve locality or minimize finish time [24,30]. These works are restricted to a single perfectly nested loop nest with uniform dependences.

Loop parallelization has been studied extensively. The reader is referred to the survey of Boulet et al. [5] for a detailed summary of older parallelization algorithms which accepted restricted input and/or are based on weaker dependence abstractions than exact polyhedral dependences. Scheduling with affine functions using faces of the polytope by application of the Farkas algorithm was first proposed by Feautrier [10]. Feautrier explored various possible approaches to obtain good affine schedules that minimize latency. The schedules carry all dependences and so all the inner loops can be parallel. However, transforming to permutable loops that are amenable to tiling was not addressed. Though schedules yield inner parallel loops, the time loops cannot be tiled unless communication in the space loops is in the forward direction (dependences have positive components along all dimensions). Several works [6,13,22] make use of such schedules. Overall, Feautrier's classic works [10,11] are geared towards finding maximum fine-grained parallelism as opposed to tilability for coarse-grained parallelization with minimized communication and better locality.

Lim and Lam [18,19] proposed an affine partitioning framework that identifies outer parallel loops (communication-free space partitions) and pipelined parallel permutable loops to maximize the degree of parallelism and minimize the order of synchronization. They employ the same machinery for blocking [17]. Several (infinitely many) solutions equivalent in terms of the criterion they optimize for result from their algorithm, and these significantly differ in communication cost and locality; no metric is provided to differentiate between these solutions. As seen in Sec. 3, without a cost function, the solutions obtained even for the simplest input are not satisfactory.

Ahmed et al. [1] proposed a framework for locality optimization of imperfectly nested loops for sequential execution. The approach embeds each statement into a product space, which is then transformed for locality. Their heuristic sets reuse distances in the target space for some dependences to zero (or a constant) to obtain coefficients of the embedding/transformation matrix. However, there is no concrete procedure to determine choice of the dependences and the number.

Griebl [13] presents an integrated framework for optimizing locality and parallelism with space and time tiling. Griebl's approach enables time tiling by using a forward communication-only placement with an existing schedule. As described in Sec. 3, using schedules as time loops may not lead to communication or locality-optimized solutions.

Cohen et al. [6] and Girbal et al. [12] developed a framework to compose sequences of transformations semi-automatically. Transformations are applied automatically, but specified manually by an expert. Pouchet et al. [22] searches the space of transformations (one-dimensional schedules) to find good ones through iterative optimization by employing performance counters. On the other hand, our approach is fully automatic. However, some empirical and iterative optimization is required to choose transforms that work best in practice. This is true when several fusion choices exist, or optimal tile sizes and unroll factors have to be determined. A combination of our algorithm and empirical search in a smaller space is an interesting approach to pursue.

## 7    Conclusions

We present a single framework that addresses automatic parallelization and data locality optimization in the polyhedral model. The proposed algorithm finds communication-minimized tiling hyperplanes for parallelization of a sequence of arbitrarily nested loops. The same hyperplanes also minimize reuse distances and improve data locality. The approach also enables fusion in the presence of producing-consuming loops. To the best of our knowledge, this work is the first to propose a practical cost model to drive automatic transformation in the polyhedral model. The framework has been implemented in a fully-automatic tool for transforming C/Fortran code using the LooPo infrastructure and CLooG. Preliminary experiments show very promising results.

## Acknowledgments

We would like to thank Martin Griebl and his team (FMI, Universität Passau, Germany) for the LooPo infrastructure. We would also like to thank Cédric Bastoul (Paris-Sud XI University) and all other contributors of CLooG and PipLib. This work was supported in part by a State of Ohio Development Fund and the National Science Foundation through grants 0121676, 0121706, 0403342, 0508245, 0509442, 0509467 and 0541409.

## References

1. Ahmed, N., Mateev, N., Pingali, K.: Synthesizing transformations for locality enhancement of imperfectly-nested loop nests. IJPP 29(5) (October 2001)
2. Bastoul, C.: Code generation in the polyhedral model is easier than you think. In: IEEE PACT, pp. 7–16 (September 2004)
3. Bondhugula, U., Baskaran, M., Krishnamoorthy, S., Ramanujam, J., Rountev, A., Sadayappan, P.: Affine transformations for communication minimal parallelization and locality optimization for arbitrarily-nested loop sequences. Technical Report OSU-CISRC-5/07-TR43, The Ohio State University (May 2007)
4. Bondhugula, U., Ramanujam, J., Sadayappan, P.: PLuTo: A practical and fully automatic polyhedral parallelizer and locality optimizer. Technical Report OSU-CISRC-5/07-TR70, The Ohio State University (October 2007)

5. Boulet, P., Darte, A., Silber, G.-A., Vivien, F.: Loop parallelization algorithms: From parallelism extraction to code generation. Parallel Computing 24(3–4), 421–444 (1998)
6. Cohen, A., Girbal, S., David,, Parello, M.S., Temam, O., Vasilache, N.: Facilitating the search for compositions of program transformations. In: ICS, pp. 151–160 (June 2005)
7. Darte, A., Vivien, F.: Optimal fine and medium grain parallelism detection in polyhedral reduced dependence graphs. IJPP 25(6), 447–496 (1997)
8. Feautrier, P.: Parametric integer programming. Operationnelle/Operations Research 22(3), 243–268 (1988)
9. Feautrier, P.: Dataflow analysis of array and scalar references. IJPP 20(1), 23–53 (1991)
10. Feautrier, P.: Some efficient solutions to the affine scheduling problem: I. one-dimensional time. IJPP 21(5), 313–348 (1992)
11. Feautrier, P.: Some efficient solutions to the affine scheduling problem. part II. multidimensional time. IJPP 21(6), 389–420 (1992)
12. Girbal, S., Vasilache, N., Bastoul, C., Cohen, A., Parello, D., Sigler, M., Temam, O.: Semi-automatic composition of loop transformations for deep parallelism and memory hierarchies. IJPP 34(3), 261–317 (2006)
13. Griebl, M.: Automatic Parallelization of Loop Programs for Distributed Memory Architectures. FMI, University of Passau, Habilitation Thesis (2004)
14. Irigoin, F., Triolet, R.: Supernode partitioning. In: POPL, pp. 319–329 (1988)
15. Kelly, W., Pugh, W.: A unifying framework for iteration reordering transformations. Technical Report CS-TR-3430, University of Maryland, College Park (1995)
16. Li, W., Pingali, K.: A singular loop transformation framework based on non-singular matrices. IJPP 22(2), 183–205 (1994)
17. Lim, A., Liao, S., Lam, M.: Blocking and array contraction across arbitrarily nested loops using affine partitioning. In: ACM SIGPLAN PPoPP, pp. 103–112 (2001)
18. Lim, A.W., Cheong, G.I., Lam, M.S.: An affine partitioning algorithm to maximize parallelism and minimize communication. In: ACM ICS, pp. 228–237 (1999)
19. Lim, A.W., Lam, M.S.: Maximizing parallelism and minimizing synchronization with affine partitions. Parallel Computing 24(3-4), 445–475 (1998)
20. LooPo - Loop parallelization in the polytope model,
    http://www.fmi.uni-passau.de/loopo
21. Penrose, R.: A generalized inverse for matrices. Proceedings of the Cambridge Philosophical Society 51, 406–413 (1955)
22. Pouchet, L.-N., Bastoul, C., Cohen, A., Vasilache, N.: Iterative optimization in the polyhedral model: Part I, one-dimensional time. In: ACM CGO (March 2007)
23. Quilleré, F., Rajopadhye, S.V., Wilde, D.: Generation of efficient nested loops from polyhedra. IJPP 28(5), 469–498 (2000)
24. Ramanujam, J., Sadayappan, P.: Tiling multidimensional iteration spaces for multicomputers. Journal of Parallel and Distributed Computing 16(2), 108–230 (1992)
25. Schreiber, R., Dongarra, J.: Automatic blocking of nested loops. Technical report, University of Tennessee, Knoxville, TN (August 1990)
26. Schrijver, A.: Theory of Linear and Integer Programming. Wiley, Chichester (1987)
27. Vasilache, N., Bastoul, C., Cohen, A.: Polyhedral code generation in the real world. In: Mycroft, A., Zeller, A. (eds.) CC 2006. LNCS, vol. 3923, pp. 185–201. Springer, Heidelberg (2006)
28. Vasilache, N., Bastoul, C., Girbal, S., Cohen, A.: Violated dependence analysis. In: ACM ICS (June 2006)
29. Wolf, M., Lam, M.S.: A data locality optimizing algorithm. In: PLDI, pp. 30–44 (1991)
30. Xue, J.: Communication-minimal tiling of uniform dependence loops. JPDC 42(1), 42–59 (1997)

# How to Do a Million Watchpoints: Efficient Debugging Using Dynamic Instrumentation

Qin Zhao[1], Rodric Rabbah[2], Saman Amarasinghe[3],
Larry Rudolph[4], and Weng-Fai Wong[1]

[1] National University of Singapore
[2] IBM Research
[3] Massachusetts Institute of Technology
[4] VMware, Inc.

**Abstract.** Application debugging is a tedious but inevitable chore in any software development project. An effective debugger can make programmers more productive by allowing them to pause execution and inspect the state of the process, or monitor writes to memory to detect data corruption. This paper introduces the new concept of *Efficient Debugging using Dynamic Instrumentation* (EDDI). The paper demonstrates for the first time the feasibility of using dynamic instrumentation on-demand to accelerate software debuggers, especially when the available hardware support is lacking or inadequate. As an example, EDDI can simultaneously monitor millions of memory locations without crippling the host processing platform. It does this in software and hence provides a portable debugging environment. It is also well suited for interactive debugging because of its low overhead. EDDI provides a scalable and extensible debugging framework that can substantially increase the feature set of current debuggers.

## 1 Introduction

Application debugging is an inevitable part of any software development cycle. It is increasingly important in modern day programming practices because of the growing complexity of software and hardware.

Software debuggers often run as separate processes that attach to user applications and trace through runtime events to detect execution anomalies. It is often that case that runtime errors arise because a program's memory is somehow corrupted. Common examples include out-of-bounds accesses and buffer overflow bugs which lead to null-pointer exceptions or the execution of illegal branch instructions. Other errors include the use of uninitialized variables, and data races in the case of shared-memory multi-threaded applications. All of these errors are notoriously difficult to discover and diagnose because it is often not clear when the memory corruption occurred, and which instructions were responsible.

A debugger allows the programmer to inspect the code at the site of an anomaly and trace back in the program stack to derive more clues about the

L. Hendren (Ed.): CC 2008, LNCS 4959, pp. 147–162, 2008.
© Springer-Verlag Berlin Heidelberg 2008

cause of the problem. A particularly useful debugging feature that helps with memory corruption bugs is the data breakpoint, also known as the *watchpoint*. A watchpoint pauses program execution when an update to a specific memory location is encountered. Watchpoints are similar to instruction breakpoints that allow the user to pause execution at specific instructions.

## 1.1    Challenges Faced by Current Approaches

Data breakpoints are very expensive to implement without architectural support because they require watching all updates to memory: every write (store) to memory triggers a lookup of the store's address in the *watchlist*. The watchlist consists of all "watched" memory locations that are of interest to user.

The GNU Debugger (GDB) [1] on x86 architectures uses four debugging registers to accelerate the watchpoint debugging feature. The hardware-assist leads to imperceptible or acceptable slowdowns. With hardware-assist forcibly disabled, we observed that even a simple program slows down by a factor of a thousand when a single watchpoint is set.

Hardware-assist has its limitations however. In case of GDB, when the watchlist consists of more than handful of addresses, GDB is forced into a single-step mode that scans a linked list of breakpoints and watchpoints following the execution of every instruction. The performance quickly deteriorates and the cost becomes prohibitively expensive for interactive debugging. As a result, a large number of watchpoints is generally not practical and their use, while potentially very helpful, remains quite limited in scope.

Furthermore, the feature sets offered by most existing standalone debuggers are either not sufficiently rich, or exhibit high overhead and poor scalability for practical and ubiquitous use. There are some advanced debuggers that can manage the performance penalties with static program analysis and advanced compilation [2,3,4], but they require additional compilation steps, and generally cannot apply to precompiled binaries or dynamically linked code. These factors may impede their adoption by programmers.

## 1.2    A New and Practical Alternative

This paper contributes a new approach to debugging, with a primary emphasis on debugging with watchpoints. We leverage advances in binary instrumentation and code manipulation tools [5,6,7,8] to provide an effective and efficient debugging framework that can substantially increase the feature set of standard off-the-shelf debuggers.

We present *Efficient Debugging using Dynamic Instrumentation* (EDDI). We demonstrate how to lower the cost and frequency of checking for runtime anomalies and breakpoint conditions using a unique combination of on-demand dynamic instrumentation and a set of simple and carefully engineered optimizations and heuristics. We believe this is the first paper to demonstrate the feasibility of using a dynamic binary instrumentor in an interactive debugging environment.

The paper describes our prototype implementation of EDDI using a state-of-the-art binary instrumentation infrastructure, and an off-the-shelf debugger, namely GDB. The prototype inherits the properties of the binary instrumentor to run on off-the-shelf IA32 processors. It can handle dynamically linked and stripped binaries without the need for application source code or recompilation.

In the context of debugging using watchpoints, we demonstrate that we can monitor more than a million data locations, with a slowdown of less than 3x compared to native execution. The low overhead makes EDDI practical for interactive debugging. This is in contrast to existing tools that use dynamic instrumentation for program analysis and bug discovery [9,10] but suffer from high overheads. For example, MemCheck [9] – which can detect uninitialized memory reads, writes to unallocated memory, and other memory use errors – can incur slowdowns between 10x and 30x compared to native execution. Such tools are better suited for regression testing than interactive debugging.

The ability to monitor a large number of memory locations significantly broadens the scope of debugging with watchpoints, and allows for a lot of versatility in defining a wide range of watchlists. For example, a user can choose to watch (1) objects of a specific size or type, (2) objects allocated from specific call sites, (3) entire data structures (e.g., arrays, records, graphs), and (4) reads from addresses written by specific instructions. This new ability leads to potential uses in constraint and consistency checks on heap data structures, data race detection in multi-threaded programs, taint analysis for security analysis, and many other scenarios. We highlight and evaluate a few practical debugging scenarios to concretely demonstrate some of the new debugging capabilities afforded by EDDI. Specifically, we dynamically watch the return addresses of all functions, and break if an instruction modifies a return address. This scenario is useful for detecting malicious attacks that attempt to hijack a program's execution. Second, we identify all static instructions that reference heap objects of a particular types. This particular use scenario can be useful for dynamic pointer analysis. Lastly, we use EDDI to discover all runtime read-accesses from uninitialized heap location, and similarly, we use watchpoints to detect buffer overflow errors.

The contributions of the paper are summarized as follows:

- We designed and engineered EDDI, the first on-demand accelerated debugger using binary instrumentation.
- We demonstrate that EDDI provides an efficient and scalable implementation of an important debugging facility, namely data breakpoints (watchpoints).
- We show that EDDI is practical for interactive debugging, and its ability to monitor millions of memory locations provides new debugging capabilities.

## 2   Interactive Debugging with EDDI

Our goal is to substantially reduce the overhead associated with application debugging so that it is possible to implement new debugging capabilities that can substantially ease the burden on users when they are tracking down programming errors. Our approach with EDDI is to use dynamic instrumentation with

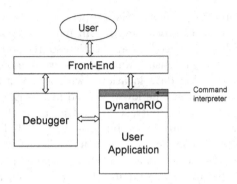

**Fig. 1.** The EDDI interactive debugging infrastructure

an off-the-shelf debugger to provide on-demand acceleration and efficient execution under a debugger. An interactive debugger with EDDI consists of four components as illustrated in Figure 1.

The first component is the user application that is interpreted using a binary instrumentation and code manipulation system. We use DynamoRIO [8], although Pin [6] or other systems can also be used. DynamoRIO is a transparent runtime code manipulation system that can execute and manipulate real world applications running on IA-32 hardware. It works under both Linux and Windows. When an application is running with DynamoRIO, it is copied into a thread-private code cache one basicblock at a time, and then runs directly from the code cache. When some basicblocks on a common path become "hot", they are stitched together to form a single-entry multiple-exits trace, and promoted to a trace cache. The basicblock and trace caches are collectively called the *code cache*. DynamoRIO uses thread-private code caches, and this allows for tailoring the instrumentation per thread when necessary. We modify the signal handler in DynamoRIO to intercept and process all runtime signals before relaying them to and from the user application.

The second component is the debugger. It runs as a separate process, and provides typical debugging functionality. We use GDB as-is for this purpose.

The third component is the front-end. It functions as the interface between the user, the debugger, and the instrumentation layer. Programmers use the front-end to relay commands to the debugger, and the debugger relays output back to the user through the front-end. Some commands are directly relayed to a command interpreter that translates the commands into actions for DynamoRIO. The front-end also consolidates the code manipulation carried out by EDDI against the code mapping assumed by the debugger.

The command interpreter is the fourth component. It receives commands from the front-end, and then collaborates with the debugger to instrument the user application to implement the appropriate commands. For example, to set a data breakpoint and then watch for updates to that memory location, EDDI instruments store instructions in the program to check if the address being written to matches the address being watched[1]. EDDI uses a set of optimizations and heuristics to reduce the instrumentation and runtime overhead of checking breakpoint conditions and predicates.

## 3  Efficient Debugging Using Dynamic Instrumentation: Software Watchpoint

We believe that binary instrumentation can significantly improve the performance of standard debuggers. In turn, this can lead to richer debugging features that can improve programmer productivity. In this paper, our goal is an efficient and scalable implementation of software watchpoints. We believe this work enables new and potentially very powerful debugging capabilities, with likely applicability in other use scenarios as well.

Watchpoints essentially require monitoring every memory read (load) and write (store), and comparing the addresses against a list of watched addresses. A basic monitoring approach using dynamic binary instrumentation adds new instructions before every memory reference to perform the following tasks: (1) determine the memory address referenced by the load or store, (2) check if address is watched, and (3) raise a trap if the address is watched. We refer to this scheme as *full instrumentation* (FI). A naïve implementation of this scheme adds more than 10 instructions per static memory reference, and can degrade performance by an average of 15x compared to native execution.

We refined this approach in two ways. First, we implemented a set of optimizations to substantially reduce the monitoring overhead as is detailed in Section 4. Second, we used a coarse-grained monitoring scheme that first operates at page granularity before switching to a more fine-grained monitoring mode that inspects individual memory references. We call this coarse-grained scheme *partial instrumentation* (PI).

The PI scheme is tuned for the common case: the majority of memory references do not access watched locations. It focuses primarily on instructions that may reference watched locations, and uses the page protection mechanisms in the operating system to help identify those instructions. In this scheme, pages that contain watched data are protected, and any instructions that try to access these pages trigger a signal. The signal handler checks if the referenced address is watched and takes appropriate action. The runtime overhead for PI is highly dependent on the number of references to the protected pages because signal handling involves expensive operating system mechanisms. As with the FI scheme, we lower the PI overhead by taking advantage of dynamic instrumentation as is described in Section 5.

In addition to the monitoring schemes, we pay particular attention to the design of the *watchlist*. The watchlist is the data structure that records the watchpoints. Since the watchlist is accessed on every memory reference, it is

---

[1] EDDI will first attempt to use any available hardware-assist resources before falling back on a more general software-only approach.

important to design an efficient watchpoint organization and to implement a fast and scalable query mechanism with reasonable space-time properties.

A linked-list watchlist organization is not practical since the time for a query scales linearly with the number of watchpoints. An alternate strategy is to use shadow tags [4,11,12,13] to represent each byte in memory. If a tag is set, then the corresponding byte in memory is watched. In this scenario, a watchpoint query requires loading the appropriate tag and checking its status. The query cost for this approach is constant and independent of the number of watchpoints.

In our work, we designed a new shadow tag based watchlists for efficient tag lookup and with good scalability. The basic idea is to use an on-demand watchlist. Each application memory page is associated with an equal sized shadow page when necessary. The status of a byte in an application page is indicated by the tag at the same offset in the associated shadow page (if the tag is zero, the byte is not watched). We use a byte-long tag for byte-addressable memory. The extra bits in each tag encode the status of adjacent bytes[2].

A *lookup table* maintains the mapping between the application pages and their shadow pages. On 64-bit architectures, a hierarchical lookup table is required, although an optimized one-level table is feasible via careful memory allocation for shadow tags.

## 4  Optimizations for Full Instrumentation (FI)

The full instrumentation scheme inserts instructions to check the watchlist before every memory reference. Figure 2 shows the necessary instrumentation for a single x86 store instruction mov esi -> [eax, ebx]. The instrumentation performs the following tasks before the store:

1. Save any registers that are used or side-effected by the watchlist query.
2. Calculate the reference address and lookup its associated tag.
3. Checks if the tag is set to "watched", and trap if it is.
4. Otherwise, restore the saved registers and continue execution.

In this example, the lookup table stores the displacement between the shadow page and the accessed data. There are 20 new instructions in total. Instructions 1–6 and 16–20 save and restore the execution context. Instruction 7 obtains the effective address in register ecx. Then the lookup table entry is identified and checked by instructions 8–10. Instructions 11–14 check the tag found in the shadow pages. If the lookup table entry is null, the tag check is skipped.

The naïve instrumentation described above suffers from a significant runtime overhead. We implemented and applied a series of optimizations to systematically and drastically reduce that overhead. We group the optimizations into three categories: previously published, watchlist-specific, and local analysis.

---

[2] Special care is required to handle two adjacent memory addresses that span two pages. Due to space limitations, we do not describe the encoding in any more detail.

```
01: mov   %ecx → [ECX_slot]        ! Steal registers
02: mov   %eax → [EAX_slot]
03: seto  [OF_slot + 3]            ! Save oflag
04: lahf                           ! Save eflags
05: mov   %eax → [AF_slot]
06: mov   [EAX_slot]   → %eax      ! Restore eax
07: lea   [%eax, %ebx] → %ecx      ! Get address
          ! Compute table index
08: shr   %ecx, $12 → %ecx         ! Shift right
09: cmp   table[%ecx, 4], $0       ! Check entry
10: je    SKIP_CHECK
          ! Check if tag is set to 'watched'
11: add   %eax, table[%ecx, 4] → %eax
12: testb $0xAA, [%eax, %ebx]
13: jz    AFTER_TRAP
14: trap                           ! Watchpoint trap
AFTER_TRAP:
15: sub   %eax, table[%ecx, 4] → %eax
          ! Restore all
SKIP_CHECK:
16: mov   [AF_slot] → %eax
17: add   [OF_slot], $0x7f000000 → [OF_slot]
18: sahf
19: mov   [EAX_slot] → %eax
20: mov   [ECX_slot] → %ecx
```

**Fig. 2.** Example instrumentation code

*1. Previously published optimizations.* We applied two optimizations published by Qin et al. [12].

- *Context Switch Reduction* (CSR) performs register liveness analysis in each basicblock to identify registers that can be safely used without requiring a register spill and restore.
- *Group Checks* (GC) consolidates two consecutive memory reference checks into a single check if there are no intervening instructions that affect the address calculation of the second memory reference.

*2. Watchlist-specific optimizations.* The following two optimizations take advantage of the watchlist design.

- *Merged Checks* (MC) aims to exploit the locality of memory references. For example, two instructions in the same basicblock may access different members of the same object (e.g., mov 0 -> [%eax + 4] followed by mov 0 -> [%eax + 8]). In this case, a single shadow tag lookup is initiated before the first reference. If the tag is zero, then neither location is watched. Otherwise, the tag lookup is carried out for each reference individually.
- *Stack Displacement* (STK) aims to reduce the watchlist query for stack accesses that use the stack pointer. This optimization elides the mapping step through the lookup table. This is achieved through a simple precomputation step. When a thread is initialized, we allocate a shadow memory for the application stack, and calculate the constant offset between the stack and its corresponding shadow memory. Subsequently, when an instruction that

accesses the stack via the stack pointer is encountered, the instrumentation code directly calculates the displacement to the shadow tag without going through the lookup table.

*3. Local optimizations.*

- *Local Variables Check Elimination* (LVE) eliminates tag checks on local scalar variables referenced via the stack pointer (e.g., `mov 0 -> [esp + 20]`) since they are amenable to static analysis.

There are many other optimization that can further reduce the monitoring overhead. Our purpose is not to be exhaustive but rather to demonstrate that online memory reference monitoring can be achieved with reasonable overhead.

## 5   Partial Instrumentation (PI)

In addition to the fine-grained instrumentation approach, we rely on a coarse grained partial instrumentation technique to further manage the runtime overhead associated with monitoring memory updates. With PI, we only instrument memory references that may reference watched locations. Partial instrumentation optimizes for the common cases where references do not access watched locations.

PI relies on the operating system page protection mechanism to switch between a coarse-grained mode and a fine-grained mode that checks memory instructions with greater scrutiny. When a watchpoint is set, we make a twin copy of the pages containing that watchpoint. The access rights of the original pages are then set to be protected. During the program execution, if an instruction $I$ references an address on the watched pages, a `SIGSEGV` signal is raised. Our signal handler catches that signal, and subsequently replaces the code fragments containing the instruction $I$ with a new code fragment that includes additional instrumentation. The instrumentation serves dual roles. First, it performs any necessary tag checks. Second, it performs *reference redirection* so that the instruction $I$ accesses the copied pages instead of the protected pages, hence avoiding future `SIGSEGV` signals from the same instruction.

PI is suitable for many situations, especially when monitoring data accesses to the heap. For example, consider the case where a user wants to monitor all references to objects allocated from a specific call site. With PI, we can (1) allocate memory from a special pool of protected pages, (2) update the lookup table, and (3) return the allocated address to the application. Meanwhile, we allocate the twin page from another pool such that the difference between the corresponding locations of a data object in both pools is a constant $D_p$. This simplifies the redirection code. Figure 5 shows an example of reference redirection for the x86 instruction `mov 0 --> [%eax + 0x10]`, where $D_p$ is 0x30000.

As is the case with full instrumentation, it is possible to apply more optimization to further reduce the overhead associated with partial instrumentation.

```
mov %ecx → [ECX_SLOT]           ! steal ecx
lea [%eax+0x10] → %ecx          ! calculate address
...                             ! save eflags
shr %ecx, 20 → %ecx             ! right shift
cmp table[%ecx], $0             ! check table entry
je  LABEL_ORIG
...                             ! check tag status
...                             ! restore eflags and ecx
mov 0 → [%eax + 0x030010]       ! redirected reference
jmp LABEL_NEXT
LABEL_ORIG:
...                             ! restore eflags and ecx
mov 0 → [%eax+0x10]             ! access original location
LABEL_NEXT:
...                             ! continue execution
```

**Fig. 3.** An example of reference redirection

# 6   Evaluation and Results

We measured the performance overhead associated with EDDI in the context of software watchpoints. We conducted a set of experiments to quantify the impact of our optimizations for full and partial instrumentation. We also designed some experiments to showcase various debugging scenarios that make use of the large number of watchpoints that can be monitored with EDDI.

We ran all of our experiments on a 2.66 GHz Intel Core 2 processor with 2 GBytes of RAM. The operating system is Linux Fedora Core 4. We used the full SPEC CPU2000 [14] benchmark suite and the reference input workloads. All benchmarks were compiled with GCC 4.0 using -O3. We used a shadow page lookup table with $2^{20}$ entries. We used shadow pages that are 4 KBytes in size to match the default Linux page size.

**Results for FI.** Figure 4 compares the native performance of each benchmark to the same benchmark run with DynamoRIO and the full instrumentation scheme (along with its accompanying optimizations). In this set of experiments, there are no user-defined watchpoints (i.e., all shadow tag bits are zero). We are simply measuring the instrumentation overhead attributed to the monitoring of memory accesses and watchlist queries.

We report the results for full instrumentation with common optimizations (CSR and GC), merged checks (MC), stack displacement (STK), and local variable check elimination (LVE). The performance results are normalized to native execution, and hence a value greater than one indicates a slowdown, with smaller numbers reflecting lower runtime overhead.

The common optimizations reduced the runtime overhead from an average slowdown of 15x in the unoptimized instrumentation scheme (data not shown), to an average of 5x. The addition of MC reduced the overhead further. MC is especially effective on benchmarks with good temporal and spatial locality (e.g., 252.eon). Performance improvement due to STK were mixed. This particular optimization reduces the opportunities for merged checks. The LVE optimization improved performance significantly because it removes all checks for scalar (i.e.,

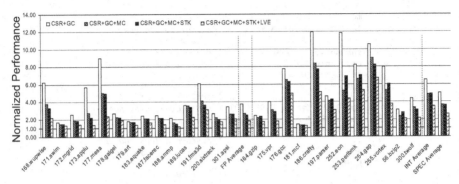

**Fig. 4.** Impact of optimizations on FI

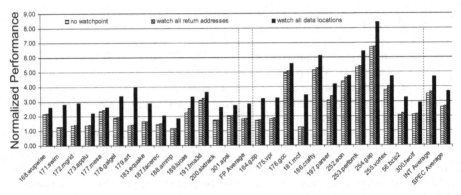

**Fig. 5.** Performance of FI with different watchlist configurations

non-array) local variables. Overall, FI with all of our optimizations incurs an average slowdown of 2.59x compared to native execution.

Next, we measured our system performance using three watchlist configurations: no watchpoints[3], watch all function return targets, and watch all data locations. In an actual debugging scenario, data breakpoints that are triggered alert the user and the debugger interrupts execution and waits for additional commands from the user. In our experiments, however, when a watchpoint was triggered, the instruction that accessed the watched location was merely marked and execution continued. Figure 5 shows the results normalized to native execution time. As expected, the runtime overhead increased as the number of watchpoints increased. The low additional overhead that is observed when watching all return targets is due to the efficacy of the STK optimization. In the worst case, the average overhead is 3.68x when all memory locations are watched.

**Results for PI.** We studied the performance implications of the partial instrumentation scheme using several SPEC INT benchmarks. Two benchmarks were

---

[3] This set of data point corresponds to the fourth bar in each set of bars from Figure 4.

**Table 1.** Runtime overhead using PI

| Benchmarks | Native (sec) | PI (sec) | Overhead PI / Native | No. of Redirects | Watched Objects | No. of SIGSEGV |
|---|---|---|---|---|---|---|
| 164.gzip | 24.379 | 26.189 | 1.074 | $1.45\times10^{8}$ | 20423 | 45 |
| 175.vpr | 48.346 | 50.605 | 1.047 | $1.04\times10^{6}$ | 10000 | 76 |
| 176.gcc | 7.980 | 10.026 | 1.256 | $1.51\times10^{6}$ | 1 | 22 |
| 181.mcf | 53.243 | 80.659 | 1.515 | $1.08\times10^{10}$ | 1 | 468 |
| 186.crafty | 58.777 | 249.777 | 4.250 | $2.77\times10^{8}$ | 37 | 443 |
| 252.eon | 35.961 | 41.470 | 1.153 | $3.50\times10^{1}$ | 1 | 8 |
| 253.perlbmk | 9.101 | 24.489 | 2.691 | $7.69\times10^{7}$ | 1 | 249 |
| 255.vortex | 29.940 | 47.582 | 1.589 | $1.65\times10^{9}$ | 10 | 219 |
| 256.bzip | 27.598 | 50.837 | 1.842 | $9.01\times10^{9}$ | 7 | 541 |
| 300.twolf | 155.725 | 161.442 | 1.037 | $2.78\times10^{5}$ | 1100 | 470 |

ignored: 197.parser allocates a large memory pool at the start of execution, and 254.gap requests a chunk of memory only to free it immediately without using it.

We selected watchpoints by intercepting allocation requests and randomly deciding to watch the allocated objects. Objects that are watched were allocated from a designated memory pool with protected pages. This approach allowed us to easily define watchpoints at runtime without any user intervention. The results are summarized in Table 1. The column labeled "Watched Objects" lists the number of watched heap objects. It is worthy to note that these objects are not necessarily uniform (i.e., they may vary in type and size).

The second column in Table 1 reports the native execution time, and the third column shows the execution time when using EDDI and partial instrumentation. The last column reports the number of SIGSEGV signals that were caught (due to accesses to watched regions), and the column labeled "No. of Redirects" reports the number of subsequent reference redirections that occurred. The overhead in PI is mainly due to the redirection mechanism. The benchmarks 181.mcf, 175.vpr, and 256.bzip have $10^{9}$ or more redirections with slowdowns ranging from 51% to 84%. The two benchmarks with the highest overhead, 186.crafty and 253.perlbmk, execute a large number of string operations that require a relatively more heavyweight redirection mechanism. The benchmarks 176.gcc and 252.eon incur a large DynamoRIO overhead (not shown). The added PI overhead is these two benchmarks and the remaining three is less than 7%.

In general, partial outperforms full instrumentation. The former optimizes for the common cases and only instruments a small number of static instructions.

**Space Overhead.** The size of the shadow memory depends on the number of watchpoints. Since we use a demand-driven watchlist, we expect the shadow memory footprint to be typically small. In the worst case when all memory locations are watched, FI doubles the total memory footprint since every application page requires a shadow page. The PI scheme needs additional memory since it also clones the application pages. Hence the total memory footprint grows three-fold when watching all heap data.

There is also some instruction memory overhead since the watchlist monitoring adds instrumentation code. In practice, this is usually small compared to the size of data memory. Note that these are virtual memory overheads, and our results show that the spatial footprints remain manageable. We do not expect the space overhead to be a serious concern on 64 bit processors.

**Debugging Scenarios.** We believe that EDDI can be a useful tool for understanding program behavior and discovering software bugs. Here we highlight several debugging scenarios that demonstrate how a user may use the large number of watchpoints afforded by EDDI.

- We used EDDI to discover all the instructions that access the return addresses of functions. To do this, a watchpoint is automatically set on the return address of a function when it is called. This watchpoint is cleared when the function returns. Note that such a task is nearly impossible to achieve in a standard debugger like GDB. The middle set of bars in Figure 5 show the expected performance for the SPEC benchmarks. Interestingly, we found that besides the return instructions, there are several functions such as setjmp that also read the return address.
- We also used EDDI to perform a kind of dynamic pointer analysis. In particular, using 181.mcf as an example, we watched all 33,112 instances of the node data type and identified the 468 static instructions that referenced these node objects $1.08 \times 10^{10}$ times during execution.
- A common programming error is the use of uninitialized variables. We used EDDI to detect such occurrences by replacing calls to calloc with malloc in 181.mcf. Unlike calloc, malloc does not initialize the allocated memory. We used EDDI to discover reads to uninitialized values by marking all allocated memory as watched. Once an object is initialized, it is removed from the watchlist. EDDI reported all reads to uninitialized memory locations correctly. As an example, the first uninitialized read in 181.mcf occurs 0.001 seconds from the start of execution. EDDI reports the error in 0.037 seconds, and overall, the instrumented execution is 83% slower using PI and 250% slower using FI.
- The last use scenario that we investigated was inspired by software security attacks. We used EDDI on a set of benchmarks for buffer overflow attacks [15]. By placing watchpoints on buffer boundaries, EDDI successfully identified all offending instructions. By setting watchpoints on key locations that include return addresses, stack frame pointers, and function pointers, many kinds of intrusion schemes can be detected. Furthermore, because EDDI monitors all instructions executed in user mode, it will discover any buffer overflows that occur in shared libraries as well.

The above use-cases are not exhaustive. The ability to watch large and variable sized regions of memory efficiently is very powerful. We believe that EDDI affords new capabilities and potentially new approaches for debugging.

# 7 Related Work

**Application Debugging.** There are many software, hardware and hybrid techniques for application debugging, especially for detecting memory bugs. Hardware schemes such as SafeMem [16], iWatcher [17], and MemTracker [18] are geared toward low overhead detection mechanisms of inappropriate memory uses. DISE [19] (Dynamic Instruction Steam Editing) is a general hardware mechanism for interactive debugging. HeapMon [20] is a hardware/software approach for detecting memory bugs with a helper thread. An important drawback of these techniques is that they require specialized hardware.

There are many software tools use dynamic instrumentation to discovery memory related bugs. For example, Purify [21] and MemCheck [9] are two widely used software tools for discovering memory problems. However, their significant overhead make them unsuitable for interactive debugging purposes. Tdb [22] is a tool that integrates dynamic instrumentation with GDB. However, the paper only describes how to handle the code mapping between the application code and the code cache, and uses code breakpoints as a demonstration vehicle. In contrast, EDDI encompasses instruction and data breakpoints and can monitor memory operations efficiently.

**Software Watchpoint.** Watchpoint is an important debugging facility that helps users identify data corruption bugs. Almost all state-of-the-art processors provide limited hardware watchpoints facilities. There has also been several proposals in the past on how to implement software watchpoints. They can be generally classified as three approaches: page protection, trap patching, and code patching. Wahbe [3] and Roberts [23] both compared the above implementation strategies, and made the same conclusion that code patching has the lowest overhead. Wahbe then proposed an efficient implementation of software watchpoints [4] using code patching and static analysis. However, that work could not be used on shared libraries. Copperman and Thomas [2] extended the work to use a post-loading technique to insert checks into an executable and solve the shared library issue. EDDI can monitor all memory accesses efficiently. In addition, EDDI's optimized page protection strategy outperforms the code patching approach in certain situations.

Another interesting approach proposed by Keppel [24] is to use checkpointing to discover data updates, but we did not find any implementation details or any results on this work. There is a published patch to MemCheck in Valgrind [25] to perform watchpointing. However, the watchpoints are organized in a linked-list and performance scales very poorly. This clearly was not designed to operate at the scale that we envision for EDDI.

**Shadow Memory.** Shadowing memory is important for efficient software watchpoints. Cheng et al. [11] suggested splitting the address space with half of it used for shadow memory. This approach simplifies the address calculation for locating the tag in the shadow memory to a single add. However, this is also the most space consuming proposal. Wahbe et al. [4] suggested a bit-map approach that associates a one-bit tag to every 4 bytes. On byte-addressable architectures like the x86, the required space overhead is 12.5%, or 512 MBytes for a 32-bit address space [12]. Unfortunately, on 64-bit architectures, this scheme requires $2^{61}$ contiguous bytes. MemCheck [13] use a two-level table to organize the shadow memory that is similar to our approach. However, our approach is more flexible, and allows for a more efficient tag lookup.

# 8   Conclusion

The state of debugging technology has largely remained unchanged for more than a decade, and many programmers still rely on the "debug by printing" approach to track down and resolve software bugs. As software becomes larger and more complex, new approaches are required to improve programmer productivity. We believe that the union of traditional debuggers and binary rewriting systems can bring about many new debugging features and techniques. Our contribution in this paper is to show the viability of such an approach.

We presented EDDI, a debugging framework that uses on-demand dynamic instrumentation and runtime optimizations to accelerate and extend features found in traditional debuggers. We showed how EDDI can be used to implement a data watchpoint facility that allows users to set orders of magnitude more watchpoints than is practical today. EDDI does not rely on any specialized hardware, and is evaluated in this paper using several SPEC2000 benchmarks running on an Intel Core 2 machine. The results show that the average overhead is 3x, which is low enough to make EDDI practical for interactive debugging. Besides a large number of variable sized watchpoints, EDDI also provides dynamic event handling capability and customized trigger actions. We highlighted several practical uses of EDDI in debugging, program analysis and security. Combined with the orthogonal effort of 'reversible' debugging [26], we believe EDDI can contribute to powerful new ways of debugging software.

# References

1. GNU/FSF GDB: The GNU Project Debugger
2. Copperman, M., Thomas, J.: Poor man's watchpoints. SIGPLAN Not. 30, 37–44 (1995)
3. Wahbe, R.: Efficient data breakpoints. In: Proceedings of the Fifth International Conference on Architectural Support for Programming Languages and Operating Systems, pp. 200–212 (1992)
4. Wahbe, R., Lucco, S., Graham, S.L.: Practical data breakpoints: design and implementation. In: Proceedings of the SIGPLAN 1993 Conference on Programming Language Design and Implementation, pp. 1–12 (1993)
5. Nethercote, N.: Dynamic Binary Analysis and Instrumentation. PhD thesis, University of Cambridge (2004), http://valgrind.org/
6. Luk, C.-K., Cohn, R., Muth, R., Patil, H., Klauser, A., Lowney, G., Wallace, S., Reddi, V.J., Hazelwood, K.: Pin: building customized program analysis tools with dynamic instrumentation. In: Proceedings of the SIGPLAN 2005 Conference on Programming Language Design and Implementation, pp. 190–200 (2005)

7. Bala, V., Duesterwald, E., Banerjia, S.: Dynamo: a transparent dynamic optimization system. In: Proceedings of the SIGPLAN 2000 Conference on Programming Language Design and Implementation, pp. 1–12 (2000)

8. Bruening, D.: Efficient, Transparent, and Comprehensive Runtime Code Manipulation. PhD thesis, Massachusetts Institute of Technology (2004), http://www.cag.csail.mit.edu/rio/

9. Seward, J., Nethercote, N.: Using Valgrind to detect undefined value errors with bit-precision. In: Proceedings of the 2005 USENIX Annual Technical Conference, pp. 17–30. USENIX Association, Berkeley, CA, USA (2005)

10. Zhang, X., Gupta, N., Gupta, R.: Locating faults through automated predicate switching. In: Proceeding of the 28th international conference on Software engineering, pp. 272–281 (2006)

11. Cheng, W., Zhao, Q., Yu, B., Hiroshige, S.: Tainttrace: Efficient flow tracing with dynamic binary rewriting. In: Proceedings of the 11th IEEE Symposium on Computers and Communications, Washington, pp. 749–754 (2006)

12. Qin, F., Wang, C., Li, Z., Kim, H.s., Zhou, Y., Wu, Y.: LIFT: A Low-Overhead Practical Information Flow Tracking System for Detecting Security Attacks. In: Proceedings of the 39th Annual International Symposium on Microarchitecture, Washington, pp. 135–148 (2006)

13. Nethercote, N., Seward, J.: How to shadow every byte of memory used by a program. In: Proceedings of the 3rd international conference on Virtual execution environments, pp. 65–74 (2007)

14. Standard Performance Evaluation Corporation. SPEC CPU 2000 Benchmark suite (2000), http://www.spec.org/osg/cpu2000/

15. Wilander, J., Kamkar, M.: A comparison of publicly available tools for dynamic buffer overflow prevention. In: Proceedings 10th Network and Distributed System Security Symposium, pp. 149–162 (2003)

16. Qin, F., Lu, S., Zhou, Y.: SafeMem: Exploiting ECC-Memory for Detecting Memory Leaks and Memory Corruption During Production Runs. In: Proceedings of the 2005 International Symposium on High Performance Computer Architecture, pp. 291–302 (2005)

17. Zhou, P., Qin, F., Liu, W., Zhou, Y., Torrellas, J.: iWatcher: Efficient Architectural Support for Software Debugging. In: Proceedings of the 31st International Symposium on Computer Architecture, pp. 224–237 (2004)

18. Venkataramani, G., Roemer, B., Prvulovic, M., Solihin, Y.: MemTracker: Efficient and Programmable Support for Memory Access Monitoring and Debugging. In: HPCA07, February 2007, pp. 273–284 (2007)

19. Corliss, M.L., Lewis, E.C., Roth, A.: Low-Overhead Interactive Debugging via Dynamic Instrumentation with DISE. In: Proceedings of the 2005 International Symposium on High Performance Computer Architecture, Washington, DC, USA, pp. 303–314. IEEE Computer Society Press, Los Alamitos (2005)

20. Shetty, R., Kharbutli, M., Solihin, Y., Prvulovic, M.: HeapMon: a helper-thread approach to programmable, automatic, and low-overhead memory bug detection. IBM Journal of Research and Development 50, 261–275 (2006)

21. Hastings, R., Joyce, B.: Purify: Fast detection of memory leaks and access errors. In: Proceedings of the Winter USENIX Conference 1992, pp. 125–136 (1992)

22. Kumar, N., Childers, B.R., Soffa, M.L.: Tdb: a source-level debugger for dynamically translated programs. In: Proceedings of the sixth international symposium on Automated analysis-driven debugging, pp. 123–132 (2005)

23. Roberts, P.E.: Implementation And Evaluation Of Data Breakpoint Scheme. In: An Interactive Debugger. Master's thesis, University of Utah (1996), http://www.cs.utah.edu/flux/papers/perobert_abstract.html
24. Keppel, D.: Fast Data Breakpoints. Technical Report TR-93-04-06, University of Washington (1993)
25. Walsh, R.: Patches for Valgrind (2005), http://valgrind.org/downloads/variants.html
26. The GNU GDB Project: GDB and Reversible Debugging (2006), http://sourceware.org/gdb/news/reversible.html

# Compiler-Guaranteed Safety in Code-Copying Virtual Machines

Gregory B. Prokopski and Clark Verbrugge

Sable Research Group
School of Computer Science, McGill University
Montreal, Quebec, Canada
{gproko,clump}@sable.mcgill.ca

**Abstract.** Virtual Machine authors face a difficult choice between low performance, cheap interpreters, or specialized and costly compilers. A method able to bridge this wide gap is the existing *code-copying* technique that reuses chunks of the VM's binary code to create a simple JIT. This technique is not reliable without a compiler guaranteeing that copied chunks are still functionally equivalent despite aggressive optimizations. We present a proof-of-concept, minimal-impact modification of a highly optimizing compiler, GCC. A VM programmer marks chunks of VM source code as *copyable*. The chunks of native code resulting from compilation of the marked source become addressable and self-contained. Chunks can be safely copied at VM runtime, concatenated and executed together. This allows code-copying VMs to safely achieve speedup up to 3 times, 1.67 on average, over the *direct* interpretation. This maintainable enhancement makes the code-copying technique reliable and thus practically usable.

## 1  Introduction

Virtual Machines (VMs) are used as a target compilation architecture by many languages. The most widely known example is Java, but the same is true of a host of languages with dynamic properties, including Python, PHP, Perl6, Forth and many others. The choice of the operations represented by the virtual assembly (bytecodes) and the construction of a Virtual Machine differ for each language but they all require a virtual machine, and thus also a translation mechanism involving either the use of a cheap but slower *interpreter* or the use of a more dynamic just-in-time or ahead-of-time compiler that generates better optimized code, at greater cost. For many environments efficiency remains important, but the development and maintenance costs of an optimizing compiler are outweighed by the simplicity and rapid development time of an interpreter-based VM.

*Code-copying* has been proposed as a VM interpreter implementation technique that improves performance, reducing the gap between interpreters and compilers [5,10]. In this work we address the main safety, practical implementation and maintenance problems inherent in such a technique that were left mostly unsolved by the previous works. Our design builds on the well-known GCC compiler to ensure semantic guarantees appropriate for code-copying in VM designs.

L. Hendren (Ed.): CC 2008, LNCS 4959, pp. 163–177, 2008.
© Springer-Verlag Berlin Heidelberg 2008

This allows dynamic code construction and interpretation with good efficiency versus maintenance tradeoffs. Supporting language enhancements in a continually evolving, optimizing compiler such as GCC can be complex; we thus further show how changes to the basic VM compiler itself can be minimally intrusive, requiring changes dependent mainly on core, stable internal compiler structures. Low maintenance and easily isolated changes are important practical requirements for a feasible system.

An attractive feature of supporting advanced interpreter execution designs is that a static compiler such as GCC can become an effective back-end for multiple VM architectures. This provides optimized execution at low cost for a number of interpreted languages. We provide experimental data from an implementation based on the SableVM Java Virtual Machine [5]. Our results show that our automatic and verified safe design is able to match, and sometimes exceed that of previous, labour-intensive, hand-done and unverified attempts. This demonstrates the viability of our approach in terms of performance and portability.

We make the following specific contributions:

- We develop safe and practical code-copying techniques appropriate for a high-performance interpreter using GCC as a back-end. This also allows us to provide previously elusive safety guarantees for the code-copying technique.
- Our approach ensures a maintainable design within the context of GCC itself and should also be applicable to other compilers. Ensuring safety in code-copying could be performed by large, invasive efforts at nearly all levels of compilation; instead our technique minimizes the impact on general GCC development to insertion of few well-separated phases: initial code alterations and insertion of copyable code areas markers (early phases), restoration of basic block order and other properties of copyable code areas (after most of optimizations), and final verification (after all optimizations).
- Our work provides an attractive, single-compiler solution with potential for use in a variety of different programming languages and virtual machines. This takes advantage of the ubiquity and continuous development of a major compiler framework such as GCC.

In the next section we give related work on code-copying and other interpreter optimization techniques. Section 3 then gives background on code-copying techniques and requirements. Our design and GCC modifications are detailed in Section 4, and Section 5 provides some experimental results from our implementation.

## 2   Related Work

In our work we are concerned with optimizing interpreter-based VMs by enabling them to practically and safely use the *code-copying* technique. This technique originates from *direct-threaded* interpretation and was first described by Rossi and Sivalingam [10]. Compilers used at that time did not use too many optimizations that would make code-copying impossible, but their solution also did not give safety guarantees.

Gagnon was the first to use the code-copying technique in a Java interpreter [5]. While this implementation solved some important problems specific to the interpretation of Java bytecode, its code-copying engine required manual tuning that could not give guarantees of safe execution and therefore could not be regarded as a production-ready solution. Interestingly, experiments done with a simple, non-optimizing portable JIT for SableVM (SableJIT [1]) showed that such a JIT was only barely able to achieve speeds comparable to the code-copying engine. This demonstrated once again that code-copying is a very attractive solution, save only for its lack of safety.

One of the important reasons why code-copying is significantly faster than other interpretation techniques is its positive influence on the success rate of branch predictors commonly used in today's hardware containing branch target buffers (BTB). As Ertl showed in his work on indirect branch prediction in interpreters [4] other solutions that improve branch prediction, like bytecode duplication, can also give significant performance improvement. Speedup due to branch prediction improvements much outweighs other negative effects such as increased instruction-cache misses.

A solution similar to a code copying engine is a JIT using code generated by a C compiler, as developed by Ertl [2]. In this solution, however, the pieces of code were actually modified (patched) on the fly, so as to contain immediate values and remove the need for the instruction counter. Due to the patching architecture-specific code was necessary. Ertl's solution did include automated tests to detect code chunks that were definitely not copyable, but it was not guaranteed to find all such chunks (see Figure 6 in [9] for an example) and thus did not ensure safety. Our solution can not only detect non-copyable code but actually change a formerly non-copyable code chunk into a copyable one.

Other solutions include systems like DyC [6] which dynamically recompiles programs during their execution to benefit from run-time values allowing for optimizations based on partial evaluation. There also exist portable JITs like GNU Lightning, but these often come with support for limited number of platforms and their own limited set of code primitives.

Specialized interpreters are another route to optimized performance. In Vmgen the VM system can be trained on a set of programs to detect the most often occurring small sequences of bytecodes and then modify the source of the interpreter to combine these sequences into superinstructions, optimized the next time the interpreter is recompiled [3]. While the speed benefits of this solution are indisputable, it still requires non-automated training, selection of the set of training programs and interpreter recompilation.

Another optimization based on exploitation of frequently occurring bytecode sequences were shown by Stephenson under the name of *multicode substitution* [11]. He showed that to limit the total number of instructions (including those created by the optimization itself) such an approach must be combined with careful selection of sequences based on how well a sequence of bytecodes can be optimized.

A completely different approach to execution of bytecode was taken by GCJ and LLVM. GCJ is a GCC-based Ahead-Of-Time compiler, including also a direct-threaded interpreter for dynamically loaded code. GCJ takes as its input either Java source or Java bytecode (class files) and compiles them to an architecture-specific executable. LLVM is a compilation framework created for lifelong program analysis that features its own code representation, own compiler and other tools that make it very extendable and reusable.

## 3   VM Execution and Code-Copying

Figure 3 shows a rough taxonomy of the different kinds of execution engines used by Virtual Machines; in general this is through an interpreter or compiler, though mixed designs are also possible [12]. On the right side of Figure 3 compiler approaches translate streams of bytecodes into native machine code, either Ahead-Of-Time, where the compiled code is stored and made ready for multiple, repeated execution, or Just-in-Time, compiling the code just prior to execution and (typically) discarding the result after the program is completed. Compilation is desirable for performance, but implies a very non-trivial resource commitment not always available to VM designers.

Interpreters have the advantage of simplicity, although improved performance is possible with different design approaches. We illustrate the main designs on the left side of Figure 3 to situate the code-copying approach; these include a basic *switch-threaded* interpreter, and a *direct-threaded* model.

A *switch-threaded* interpreter simulates a basic fetch, decode, execute cycle, reading the next bytecode to execute and using a large *switch-case*

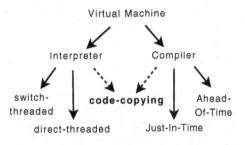

**Fig. 1.** The taxonomy of Virtual Machines execution engines

statement to branch to the actual VM code appropriate for that bytecode. This process is straightforward but if, such as in Java, bytecodes often encode only small operations the overhead of fetching and decoding an instruction is proportionally high, making the overall design quite inefficient.

A *direct-threaded* interpreter is a more advanced interpreter that minimizes decoding overhead. This kind of interpreter requires an extension offered by some compilers known as *labels-as-values*. Many operating systems, their tools and VMs are written in C or its close derivatives. Normally a C program can contain *goto*s only to labels. With the labels-as-values extension it is possible to take an address of a label and store it in a pointer type variable. Later this variable can be used as an argument of a goto. In a direct-threaded interpreter a stream of bytecodes is thus replaced by a stream of addresses of labels. The labels themselves are placed at the start of the code responsible for the execution of operations encoded by each bytecode. With this mechanism the interpreter can immediately execute a direct *goto* to the right chunk of code. Optimization is implied by reducing the repeated decoding of instructions, trading repeated test-and-branch sequences for a one-time preparatory action where a stream of bytecodes is translated into a stream of addresses.

It is important to notice that the speed advantage of a direct-threaded interpreter over a switch-threaded interpreter already comes with the requirement of additional, specialized support from the compiler used to compile the interpreter.

### 3.1   Code-Copying Technique

In some sense, and as indicated in Figure 3, code-copying[1] bridges interpreter and compiler-based VM implementation approaches. Code-copying is a further optimization to interpreter design, but one which makes relatively strong assumptions about compiler code generation. The basic idea of code-copying is to make use of the compiler applied to the VM to generate binary code for matching bytecodes. Parts or *chunks* of the VM code are used to implement the behaviour of each bytecode. Those chunks of code are marked with labels at their beginning and end. At runtime, the interpreter copies the binary chunks corresponding to an input stream of bytecodes and concatenates them into a new place in memory, as shown in Figure 2. Such a set of concatenated instructions is called a *superinstruction* and it can execute at a much greater speed than using any of the other two formerly described techniques. Depending on the application and other factors the code-copying technique can give from 1.2 to 3 times performance gain [5] over the direct-threaded technique.

### 3.2   Safety

As numerous studies have shown the performance gains from using code-copying technique are clear [4,5,10]. However one of the biggest problems the implementators of code-copying VMs face is ensuring that the fragments of the code chunks copied to construct superinstructions are still fully functional in their new locations and as parts of superinstructions.

Unfortunately, the C standard does not contain any semantics that would allow us to express and impose the necessary restrictions on selected parts of code. For instance the bracketing labels placed before and after source code of chunks and used to address them do not guarantee contiguity of the resulting binary code chunks, nor do they place restrictions on the use of relative addressing. Without ensured contiguity compiler optimizations will often relocate basic blocks of a chunk outside of the bracketing labels. At VM runtime this will result in incomplete copies of such a code chunk. The use of relative addressing of jump or call targets outside of a code chunk will make the copies of such chunk contain

---

[1]   Note that in the literature what we call code-copying is sometimes referred to as *inlining* or *inline-threading* [5]; these latter terms, however, we find, mislead most compiler developers and researchers to think of inlining of functions or methods.

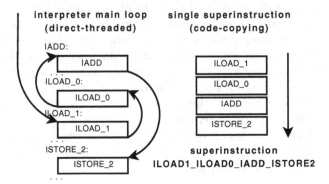

**Fig. 2.** A simplified comparison of direct-threaded and code-copying engines

jumps or calls to invalid addresses. These and other related serious issues have to be handled, otherwise virtual machine crashes or undefined behavior are to be expected. To the best of our knowledge there is no production-quality solution that would ensure creation of code chunks by an optimizing C compiler that can be safely copied and executed.

Without guaranteed safety of code-copying an interpreter cannot practically, reliably make use of this powerful technique. Previous results used hand-done examination, trial-and-error, and manual porting combined with specialized test suites [9] in attempt to ensure safety. The large effort required, and the lack of a fully verified result motivates our design in the next section.

## 4   Design

For VM designers our approach requires the additional use of simple identifiers bracketing copyable code. We make use of the well-known *#pragma* operator to surround and thus help identify copyable chunks. The bulk of our design effort is in ensuring safety for code copying, a result guaranteed by a small set of well-specified additional passes within GCC. Below we first detail requirements for code to be *relocatable* and thus suitable for code-copying, followed by a description of the GCC modifications, including the final verification phase.

### 4.1   Generation of Safely Copyable Code

There are specific requirements that a chunk of code has to meet so it could be copied to another location in memory, concatenated with other chunks and safely executed. A code chunk can only be safely copied if its copy is *functionally equivalent*, i.e. chunk of code $C_{baseaddr\alpha} \equiv C_{baseaddr\beta}$ where $\alpha \neq \beta$.

We thus define a chunk of code $C$ to be *copyable* if all of the following conditions ensuring functional equivalence are true:

- $C$ occupies a single contiguous space in memory that starts and ends with two distinct code labels specified by a programmer.

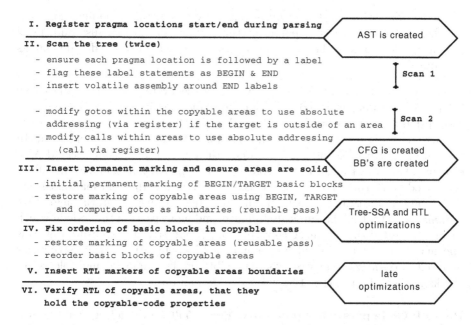

**Fig. 3.** To produce copyable code with minimal changes to the internal structure of the compiler we inserted several well isolated passes

- Natural control flow enters $C$ only at its "top" and exits only at its "bottom."
- Any jump from inside of $C$ to code outside of $C$ (e.g. to an exception handler) uses an absolute target address.
- Any jump from the inside of $C$ to another place inside $C$ uses a relative target address.
- Any function call from inside of $C$ uses an absolute target address.
- At $C$ boundaries registers must be used consistently with other code chunks boundaries (this is already ensured by GCC's computed goto extension).

### 4.2   GCC Modifications

Our goal was to modify a highly optimizing C compiler, such as GNU C Compiler 4.2, to selectively generate code that meets these requirements therefore ensuring functional equivalence of selected code chunks.

To compile a single function GCC executes several dozens of optimization passes. These passes modify the code in ways that are usually supposed to improve the speed of the resulting code, or its other parameters. It is not feasible to modify and maintain all of these passes to selectively generate code conforming to our requirements. Instead we modify the compiler to:

- preserve the information about which parts of the code have to be treated specially—from the moment the source code is parsed to the moment the final assembly is generated,

– allow (almost) all of the optimizations to execute without modifications and then at certain selected points of the compilation process use additional passes that modify the code in a manner that makes selected code chunks copyable.

The overall set of modifications is divided into separate passes that collectively track or restore information throughout the whole compilation process; a general description is shown in Figure 3. Depending on the representation of the code at each stage of compilation this information is tracked in a different form. In the source code it exists as *#pragma* lines, then as special flags of selected AST elements, later we attach it to basic blocks and *computed goto's,* and eventually it is inserted in a form of *notes* into the assembly. Tracking this information turned out to be the most difficult part of our work. It is because of all the aggressive optimizations that might duplicate, remove, and move parts of the code in which we are interested that ensuring copyable code is non-trivial. We ensure that this information is not lost, misplaced or mangled by separating it from structures accessed by optimization passes where possible and by employing multiple sanity checks in each of our passes that use this information.

**Phase I: Code parser pragma hook.** Figure 5 illustrates a fragment of interpreter source code for a single code chunk. The code of an instruction (bytecode) is surrounded by the special *copyable #pragma* statements that mark the beginning and end of the copyable chunk.

**Phase II: Scan the tree (1).** To ensure chunks are properly identified and separated an initial pass is performed to check starting and ending conditions. Each location of *#pragma copyable begin* and *end* registered during parsing is checked to ensure it is followed by a label. These *start* and *end* labels have then their special *start* and *end* flags set accordingly. Finally the code is modified by artificially inserting into the stream of statements two empty *volatile assembly* instructions around the *end* label.

The volatile assembly code acts as a barrier to code movement, and is used to ensure the basic blocks directly following areas, the *target* blocks, are preserved and act as the sole and unique exits of the natural control flow from a copyable area. Our tests showed that otherwise some optimizations would attempt to remove or merge *target* blocks.

**Phase II: Scan the tree (2).** In most architectures control flow jumps can be *relative* or *absolute*. Relative jumps have the advantage of being (usually) smaller instructions, but having a machine-specific limitations on the distance for which they are useful. Absolute jumps are often longer instruction sequences since the complete target address must be encoded, not just the relative displacement. As mentioned in Section 4.1 for control flow that goes outside of the copyable area *absolute* jumps are required to ensure the code behaves the same once copied. Similarly, jumps within a copyable region must use relative addressing to guarantee a copy will behave in an equivalent fashion.

Original code within a copyable area:

```
goto NullPointerException; /* label outside of the copyable area */
```

Is replaced with:

```
{ void *address = &&NullPointerException;
  /* this assembly prevents constant propagation    */
  __asm__ __volatile__ ("" : "=r" (address) : "0" (address) : "memory");
  goto *address; /* computed goto uses absolute addressing */ }
```

**Fig. 4.** To ensure absolute addressing a *goto* to outside of a copyable area is replaced with a specially crafted *computed goto*.

Our second phase thus includes a pass to convert control flow statements that go outside of a copyable area (and not to the *target block*) to use absolute addresses for their targets. There are two cases of such control flow: a *goto* and a function call, both complicated by the fact that GCC itself does *not* produce the final binary code, rather it uses an external, platform-specific assembler program. It is in fact the assembler's role to choose the addressing mode for each call or jump; typically the shortest addressing mode to reach the target is chosen, but there is no general and relatively platform-agnostic way to specify in the assembler input that a jump or a call is to use absolute addressing. Below we describe how we ensure absolute jumps are used through the use of *computed gotos*, and then how we process the code chunk to ensure control flow is safe for copying.

To force selected jumps and calls to use absolute addressing we modify the code of these instructions to make jumps and calls via a register. As shown in Figure 4, in C these instructions are represented respectively by a *computed goto* and a function call using a *function pointer*. A *computed goto* is a special feature of the *labels-as-values* extension of GCC used by direct-threaded engine. It is a *goto* whose argument is not a label but a variable containing the address of a label (or any other address). Using a register to hold the destination address may have a negative impact on the performance that will vary from platform to platform, or even CPU type. Here the benefits of maintainability and safety are paramount, and as we will show in Section 5 our solution is efficient in practice. Nevertheless, more portable ways of expressing absolute addressing could slightly improve performance.

Our current system assumes that code chunks are small enough that the compiler will use optimal, relative jumps within the code of instructions found in a region. While it does not attempt to ensure intra-area jumps are relative, an appropriate pass could easily be added. Violations to this assumption, however, will still be detected in our final verification phase.

**Phase III: Mark and ensure areas are solid.** Rather than modifying a large part of GCC to ensure properties of copyable code regions are preserved at all subsequent compilation stages, by all compilation passes, we instead inserted two additional passes. The first pass modifies the code in a way that ensures the minimal information about copyable code regions is always preserved. The second (reusable) pass uses this information and is capable of finding all the basic blocks belonging to copyable areas after arbitrary optimizations. Both passes include sanity checks mentioned earlier ensuring the additional information on code chunks is not lost or mangled.

After the source code is parsed into the stream of statements the compiler creates descriptions of basic blocks. Each such description contains pointers to the first and the last instruction that a basic block contains. We found that a basic block is a convenient unit to carry the additional information about the copyable code. It gives an easy access to smaller components of the code, like each particular instruction, while also being easily accessible via higher-level structures like the control flow graph. We extended the data structure describing a basic block to store the unique id of the

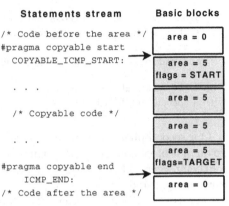

**Fig. 5.** Initial marking of basic blocks right after parsing

copyable area a block belongs to and to store a field of utility flags. The initial marking of basic blocks is straightforward. We scan the stream of statements for labels earlier marked as *start* and *end*, and mark basic blocks with corresponding flags.

In general optimizations can create new basic blocks, move or split existing ones. One of the possible results is that some basic blocks that functionally are part of a copyable area might no longer be placed between the *start* and *target* basic blocks of this area and might not carry the initial marking. To recover marking after optimizations we rely on the preservation of the *start* and *target* blocks, which in turn is ensured with sanity checks. Area marking restoration can then be done through simple propagation along the control flow graph, from the *start* block of each area until the *target* block and jumps via computed gotos. It is critical that the compiler had earlier modified all the jumps to outside of copyable areas to use computed gotos. This way it is possible to always find the limits of copyable areas.

Importantly, our approach *does not use a heuristic* and is guaranteed to properly restore the list of blocks belonging to each copyable area. We still included extensive sanity checks that in practice should never be triggered. This is because, for instance, we earlier inserted volatile assembly around chunks end labels and disabled *cross-jump* optimization (see below). With these measures in place previously executed optimizations should not have inserted or deleted *start* or *target* blocks or cause the control flow graphs of different code chunks to interfere.

For functions containing copyable code we disabled *cross-jump* optimization which attempts to find identical code chunks within a function and share a single instance of the code. This clearly conflicts with with the need of the code-copying engine to use self-contained code chunks.

**Phase IV: Fix basic blocks ordering.** The main reason for our basic block reordering pass is an optimization performed by GCC by default, *basic block partitioning*. This pass does two things. It divides the set of basic blocks of a function into those that are expected to be executed frequently (hot blocks) and those that are expected to be executed rarely (cold blocks). In the final assembly all the hot blocks of each function are located contiguously in the upper part of the code, and the cold blocks are located below the hot blocks. This optimization also reorders basic blocks to ensure that the fall-thru edges are used for the most often encountered control flow. These are heuristic techniques for improving instruction cache hit rate and simplifying control flow, and this optimization can in practice improve the performance of a virtual machine by several percent, therefore we want to allow for it.

For a chunk of code to be copyable the compiler has to restore the order of basic blocks so that the marked code is self-contained. In this case the goal is to move basic blocks to ensure that the *start* basic block of the copyable area is followed by all other blocks belonging to it, which are then followed by the *target* basic block of the same copyable area. After the marking of basic blocks belonging to all areas is restored (as described in the previous section) it is relatively easy to move all basic blocks belonging to an area into the wanted positions. Positions of other basic blocks, not belonging to copyable areas, are left unchanged.

### 4.3   Phase V and VI: RTL Markers and Final Verification

The additional passes described above modify the structure of the code based on up to date information about the boundaries of basic blocks, construction of the control flow graph, and other data. During the last compilation passes the GCC compiler discards some of this information or does not keep it up to date. In our tests we found that these last optimization passes do not change the structure of the code enough to invalidate the properties of copyable code. Nonetheless, this was not sufficient for the safety guarantees we required and another solution was needed. We therefore added two passes.

Not long before the information about basic blocks and control flow graph becomes unavailable an additional pass inserts into the program representation (*RTL* stream) special (untouchable by other passes) *notes* that mark the start and end of copyable areas, including the ID of an area. The second pass is then a simple verification pass that uses only a minimum of information. It is executed just before the final assembly is sent to the external assembler. With the *notes* inserted by our previous pass it is possible to verify all the necessary properties of copyable areas when the code is final. The verification algorithm takes each instruction from the instruction stream and ensures that:

- all copyable areas are present,
- copyable areas do not interleave with one another,

– jumps from a copyable area $A$ are either to a target within $A$ or to this area's target label (the label that begins the target basic block). Note that it is also necessary to ensure that all jumps within $A$ are also within the allowable range of a relative jump[2],
– jumps to the outside of an area are made via register and not a symbol (thus are absolute),
– all calls from within areas are made via register and not a symbol (thus are absolute).

A verification error at this point is uncorrectable and is treated as an internal compiler error. This guarantees that if source code compiles properly then the copyable chunks of binary code will be safe to copy and execute in a code-copying VM. Sanity checks in all the passes ensure proper flow of the information on code chunks which allows the final verification to function reliably. In our experience we have not yet encountered a case where the verification pass would fail when all the former passes executed properly.

## 5    Experimental Results

To examine practicality of our design we modified a Java Virtual Machine, SableVM [5], to use our enhanced GCC. In SableVM source we marked code chunks with our *copyable #pragma*. Code-copying was already supported in SableVM, but required globally disabling block reordering in GCC and did not provide safety guarantees. During preparations we used our enhanced GCC to verify the unsafe code formerly used by SableVM's code-copying engine and found several cases where execution of a less likely control flow path in a byte-code would result in a VM crash due to a function call using relative addressing.

The goal of our main experiments was thus to demonstrate that our new approach allows the code-copying strategy to be realistically and more reliably used while maintaining the performance. The results shown in Figure 6 have been gathered using a machine with Intel Pentium IV at 3GHz, 512MB RAM. The SPEC benchmarks, averaged over 10 runs, were executed with their default settings (-S 100), and performance is shown normalized to the speed of the direct-threaded engine as a baseline for comparison. SableCC and Soot are large, object-oriented, in-house benchmarks.

The benefits of code-copying are clear. We are able to achieve approximate parity with the unsafe code-copying approach. More surprising perhaps is that the performance of SableVM version 1.13 modified to use our GCC extensions actually improved over the manual code-copying design in most cases. We attribute the general improvement to the fact that previously SableVM had to globally disable basic block reordering for the code-copying engine to work at all. With the added GCC support for code-copying this useful optimization was enabled. We also note that the performance of two SPEC benchmarks that benefit the most from code-copying, as well as *Soot* slightly decreased, about 2-3%.

---

[2] This check has not been implemented in our current system.

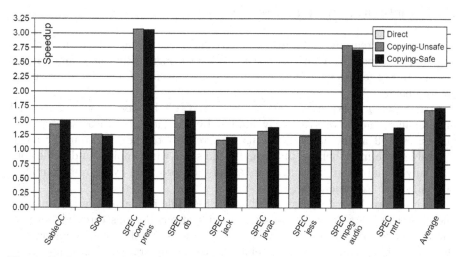

**Fig. 6.** Performance comparison of SableVM with standard direct-threaded engine, unsafe code-copying engine and safe code-copying engine using the GCC copyable-code enhancement

We suspect that this effect is caused by the memory barriers inserted into the code in places where the special *#pragma* is used. These barriers might be inhibiting some of the optimizations. Previously Gu et al. [8, 7], however, showed that changes to the executable code placement without actual changes to the functioning of a VM can cause a tremendous variance (up to almost 10%) in the VM performance. More detailed analysis of performance gains and losses is thus warranted, but certainly the magnitude of correlation in Figure 6 is sufficient to demonstrate the general success of our compiler-facilitated approach. Overall, the effect is clear: our modifications efficiently enable code-copying as a safe technique for VM interpreter design.

| Metric | # |
|---|---|
| Data structures modified | 4 |
| Fields added to data structures | 6 |
| Data structures added | 3 |
| Functions added to existing files | 4 |
| Function calls/hooks inserted | 8 |
| Code lines added or modified | 139 |
| Code lines in new files | 1500 |

**Fig. 7.** Metrics of code modified and added to GCC

One of our goals was to minimize the impact of our changes to GCC on GCC maintenance. Figure 7 shows the results of our impact measurements in terms of required changes to code and data structures. In a truly large project such as a GCC we see these numbers as indicators that our extension has minimal impact on the existing GCC code and its maintenance. We also report that a major upgrade of our enhanced GCC from 3.4 to 4.2 (about 2 years of GCC development) took only a few hours and consisted mostly of renaming and testing. We believe this validates our claim that a relatively simple compiler modification can help improve the performance of dynamic execution environments.

# 6    Conclusions and Future Work

For a variety of reasons, including simplicity and dynamic support, many modern languages are based on virtual machine (VM) designs. Efficiency and ease of design are key features for rapidly evolving languages and associated execution environments.

*Code-copying* interpreters offer a good trade-off between performance and maintenance, but were previously limited by the lack of critical safety guarantees, as well maintenance concerns with respect to the VM compiler itself. Copyable code must behave functionally the same when copied, and while conceptually trivial these guarantees are simply not provided by current compilers or C language extensions.

With our work we demonstrate that it is possible to make code-copying safe and practical. Our approach to GCC modifications demonstrates viability of our technique for ensuring the safety properties essential to code-copying. We show how this technique can be relatively easily integrated with a modern C compiler, while keeping the changes relatively isolated and making only limited assumptions about the inner workings of a compiler, thus ensuring long-term maintainability.

The implementation of a code-copying GCC extension on which we based this paper was focused on supporting the i386 architecture. On other architectures there might be additional issues with delay slots (e.g. MIPS), relative addressing of externs and globals (e.g. x86_64), or relative-jump span limitations (e.g. PowerPC). We are currently working on incorporating the necessary detection and correction mechanisms into our GCC extension leading to full support of more architectures.

As well as deeper performance analysis, further determining the source of our gains over hand-done code-copying, our immediate future work is in the application of our technique to other VM architectures and other hardware architectures. Simplified use of code-copying could improve performance for a variety of predominantly interpreted languages, and we hope to show greater generality of our design by replicating the code-copying technique in other environments.

This research was supported in part by NSERC and FQRNT. The authors would also like to thank Etienne M. Gagnon for his suggestion regarding compiler modification as a way of making code-copying practically usable. The source code of our modified GCC 4.2 is available at http://www.prokopski.com .

# References

1. Bélanger, D.: SableJIT: A retargetable just-in-time compiler. Master's thesis, McGill University (August 2004)
2. Ertl, M.A., Gregg, D.: Retargeting JIT compilers by using C-compiler generated executable code. In: Parallel Architecture and Compilation Techniques (PACT 2004), pp. 41–50 (2004)
3. Ertl, M.A., Gregg, D., Krall, A., Paysan, B.: Vmgen: a generator of efficient virtual machine interpreters. Softw. Pract. Exper. 32(3), 265–294 (2002)

4. Ertl, M.A., Thalinger, C., Krall, A.: Superinstructions and replication in the Cacao JVM interpreter. Journal of.NET Technologies 4, 25–32 (2006); Journal papers from .NET Technologies 2006 conference
5. Gagnon, E.M.: A Portable Research Framework for the Execution of Java Bytecode. PhD thesis, McGill University (2002)
6. Grant, B., Philipose, M., Mock, M., Chambers, C., Eggers, S.J.: A retrospective on: an evaluation of staged run-time optimizations in DyC. SIGPLAN Not. 39(4), 656–669 (2004)
7. Gu, D., Verbrugge, C., Gagnon, E.: Code layout as a source of noise in JVM performance. In: Component And Middleware Performance workshop, OOPSLA (2004)
8. Gu, D., Verbrugge, C., Gagnon, E.M.: Relative factors in performance analysis of Java virtual machines. In: VEE 2006: Proceedings of the 2nd international conference on Virtual execution environments, pp. 111–121. ACM Press, New York (2006)
9. Prokopski, G.B., Gagnon, E.M., Arcand, C.: Bytecode testing framework for SableVM code-copying engine. Technical Report SABLE-TR-2007-9, Sable Research Group, School of Computer Science, McGill University, Montréal, Québec, Canada (September 2007)
10. Rossi, M., Sivalingam, K.: A survey of instruction dispatch techniques for bytecode interpreters. Technical Report TKO-C79, Faculty of Information Technology, Helsinki Univeristy of Technology (May 1996)
11. Stephenson, B., Holst, W.: Multicodes: optimizing virtual machines using bytecode sequences. In: OOPSLA 2003: Companion of the 18th annual ACM SIGPLAN conference on Object-oriented programming, systems, languages, and applications, pp. 328–329. ACM Press, New York (2003)
12. Suganuma, T., Ogasawara, T., Takeuchi, M., Yasue, T., Kawahito, M., Ishizaki, K., Komatsu, H., Nakatani, T.: Overview of the IBM Java just-in-time compiler. IBM Syst. J. 39(1), 175–193 (2000)

# Hardware JIT Compilation for Off-the-Shelf Dynamically Reconfigurable FPGAs

Etienne Bergeron, Marc Feeley, and Jean Pierre David

DIRO, Université de Montréal
GRM, École Polytechnique de Montréal
{bergeret,feeley}@iro.umontreal.ca, jpdavid@polymtl.ca

**Abstract.** JIT compilation is a model of execution which translates at run time critical parts of the program to a low level representation. Typically a JIT compiler produces machine code from an intermediate bytecode representation. This paper considers a *hardware JIT compiler* targeting FPGAs, which are digital circuits configurable as needed to implement application specific circuits. Recent FPGAs in the Xilinx Virtex family are particularly attractive for hardware JIT because they are reconfigurable at run time, they contain both CPUs and reconfigurable logic, and their architecture strikes a balance of features.

In this paper we discuss the design of a hardware architecture and compiler able to dynamically enhance the instruction set with hardware specialized instructions. A prototype system based on the Xilinx Virtex family supporting hardware JIT compilation is described and evaluated.

## 1 Introduction

Software just-in-time (JIT) compilation is a well-known technique for improving the execution speed of virtual machine interpreters. The virtual machine identifies through run-time profiling which program parts are critical to its performance (so called *hot spots*) and compiles these parts into optimized machine code that is directly executed by the processor. Because the program's behavior evolves throughout its execution, the virtual machine continually monitors the program to find the new hot spots to compile. The compiled code is often stored in a limited size cache which contains the most recently compiled parts of the program. Speed-ups are obtained when the monitoring and compilation effort are more than compensated by the execution time savings of the compiled hot spots. For this reason, time-consuming complex optimizations are typically not performed by JIT compilers.

Hardware just-in-time compilation is an extension of this model to field-programmable gate arrays (FPGAs). Figure 1 contrasts the software and hardware JIT models. FPGAs are highly parallel configurable digital circuits whose behavior can be tailored to a specific application in the field through the process of *configuration*. Normally this configuration is performed at power-up, but some FPGA families, namely the Xilinx Virtex II [19] and above, can reconfigure sections of the device at run time. This FPGA family also supports up

L. Hendren (Ed.): CC 2008, LNCS 4959, pp. 178–192, 2008.
© Springer-Verlag Berlin Heidelberg 2008

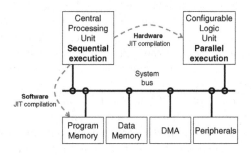

**Fig. 1.** Software and hardware JIT models

to two classical processors inside the reconfigurable logic, which can be used to implement a virtual machine interpreter in software. A hardware JIT compiler, embedded in the virtual machine interpreter, will compile program hot spots into the low-level description (*bitstream*) of a digital circuit performing the same computation. The circuit's layout and position in the reconfigurable logic as well as its interconnection with the processor running the virtual machine interpreter are determined dynamically.

Circuit synthesis, placement and routing are rather time-consuming tasks. It is not uncommon for standard synthesis tools to take several minutes on a high-performance workstation to produce the bitstream for a simple computation. This high cost of compilation must be amortized on abnormally long running hot spots to achieve any speed-up. In order for hardware JIT compilation to be useful for executing more typical programs, it is necessary to decrease the compilation time by a few orders of magnitude. This is the obstacle we tackle in this work.

Since the bitstream format of dynamically configurable FPGAs is not documented by the vendors, all the related work involving dynamical configuration are based on vendor-supplied proprietary compilation tools. Our recent work [1] has enabled us to extract enough information on the bitstream format to be able to generate partial bitstreams on-the-fly in a fraction of a second without any proprietary tool. We believe this is a key result on the road to general purpose reconfigurable computing.

This paper describes the fast synthesis technique we have designed for a hardware JIT compiler. Sections 2 and 3 report on related work and give some background information on FPGAs. We describe a prototype compiler in Section 4. An evaluation of its performance is given in Section 5. We specifically focus our attention on the synthesis times.

## 2   Related Work

Reconfigurable architectures such as PipeRench [8,16] and WASMII [15] gave birth to the concept of *virtual hardware*. The idea is analogous to virtual memory.

Since the hardware resources on a chip are limited, it may be interesting to "store hardware" out of the chip and "swap hardware" when required. Such hardware manipulations require a dedicated area of the chip that is configurable. This means that it is possible to alter the logic or the connections via software. The store and swap mechanisms thus actually access the configurations bits, which are also called *bitstream*.

Xilinx Virtex II and above FPGAs, which support dynamic reconfiguration, have also been used for virtual hardware implementation [4]. Two synthesis flows are proposed by Xilinx to handle the creation of dynamic modules using their tools [18]. Essentially, each possible global configuration of the FPGA must be pre-compiled using the standard synthesis process. Then, partial bitstreams are extracted from the complete bitstream for each module. The swapping from one configuration to another is achieved by sending a partial configuration to the FPGA. Standard tools were not originally developed for this type of compilation and their use imposes severe limitations on the design of virtual hardware. At present, it is still very difficult to develop, debug and guarantee the stability of dynamic applications.

The RTR-JVM (Reconfigurable Run-Time Java Virtual Machine) [9] proposes a different approach where the concept of dynamic configuration is integrated in the language and its virtual machine. This architecture allows the dynamic loading of hardware modules produced from Java source code and translated to VHDL code. By profiling the hot spots, the system is able to identify good candidates for hardware implementation. The main limitation of this system is that modules are produced statically (by the standard synthesis flow) and preliminary executions are required.

Warp processors [11] are another example of hardware virtualization. The authors propose to translate binary code to hardware [17] in order to make the production of dynamic modules transparent to the user. The advantage of this mode of execution is that it can be integrated to a conventional processor. That work is based on a custom FPGA [12] as well as custom tools, compilers and algorithms [13,14], which benefit from the regular structure of the custom FPGA. A drawback of custom FPGAs is that they lag commercial ones in terms of size, speed, and cost. The Warp project nevertheless demonstrated that JIT compilation is viable on modern FPGAs.

We believe that on-the-fly generation of dynamic modules is appealing and needs more investigation. In this paper, we demonstrate that these techniques are applicable to commercial FPGAs despite their limitations in terms of architecture and synthesis tools.

## 3   Target Architecture

Our methodology assumes a dynamically reconfigurable FPGA with an embedded processor as illustrated in Figure 2. The application and the compiler are stored in an external memory and run on the embedded processor. Some peripherals can be mapped inside the FPGA configurable logic, allowing the

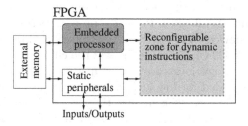

**Fig. 2.** Diagram of a system supporting dynamic reconfiguration on a FPGA

application to perform input/output. This zone is static, which means that it is configured at power-up and will not be modified later. The rest of the logic constitutes the *reconfigurable zone*, which will behave as a hardware cache for the dynamically generated specialized instructions. The compiler produces these instructions on-the-fly and configures the dynamic zone to make them available to the application through standard I/O instructions.

In practice, we use Xilinx Virtex-II Pro devices, which are one of the few commercial devices currently supporting dynamic and partial reconfiguration. Moreover, these devices (and later series) are the most dense FPGAs available on the market. Figure 3 shows the layout of a small Virtex-II Pro device with one embedded PowerPC processor.

A FPGA is mostly a grid of configurable blocks that can be interconnected in a configurable way. Input/Output Blocks (IOBs) are physically connected to the external pads. They are placed on the grid's periphery. Configurable Logic Blocks (CLBs) are the heart of the processing power of the FPGA. Basically, each CLB contains user-defined lookup tables (LUT), registers and a programmable routing matrix to manage the connections to other CLBs. Virtex-II Pro FPGAs also

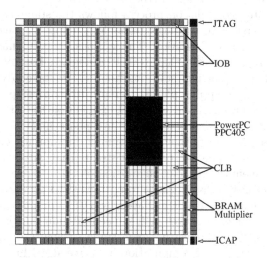

**Fig. 3.** Virtex-II Pro Device Grid

contain hard-wired cores to increase the design density. The densest FPGA (2VP 100) is equipped with 2 embedded PowerPC processors running at 400 MHz, 12 clock management devices, 444 18x18 bit multipliers, 444 block RAMs (18 kbits each) and almost 100000 CLBs spread all over the chip.

Some special blocks are located at the chip's periphery. The JTAG block is a serial interface provided for low level debugging. The Internal Configuration Access Port (ICAP) is used to configure the FPGA. In our architecture, it is connected statically to the PowerPC processor to enable dynamic configuration through standard I/O instructions.

Given this architecture, the challenge we face is to quickly generate the configuration of the dynamic zone to enable efficient JIT hardware. More precisely, we have to configure the blocks and their interconnection. This is addressed in the next section.

## 4    Compiler Architecture

The next step is to build an execution environment running on the processors. Instead of writing a whole system from scratch, we decided to port the Gambit [6] Scheme to C compiler to the embedded PowerPC. This way, we inherit all Scheme features and a dynamic execution model (dynamic software module loading, dynamic code interpretation, etc). Gambit uses a fast interpretation technique [7] and gives access to the AST representation of the running program which the JIT compiler uses.

Many languages can benefit from this kind of execution and we believe they can use a common back-end. High-level language synthesis, which consists in choosing how high-level concepts are mapped to hardware, is the most language-dependent phase but the running time of this phase is not a bottleneck. We have already addressed this issue in a previous work in the context of a static hardware compiler [2].

The hardware JIT compilation process follows the standard phases used to produce a FPGA bitstream: synthesis, technology mapping, place and route, bitstream generation and configuration. The synthesis phase translates a Scheme expression into a representation that explicitly indicates how high-level concepts are implemented (e.g. pipeline, state-machine,...) to take advantage of hardware. The technology mapping phase attempts to map components generated by the synthesis to patterns and resources existing on the FPGA (multipliers, block RAMs, slices,...). The place and route phase finds a location for each of the resources and connects them by assigning appropriate wires. Finally, the bitstream generation produces a partial bitstream that will be downloaded into the configuration memory in the configuration phase.

In a static compiler, these phases are optimized to produce a high-density, fast and low-power design. Problems faced by a JIT compiler are not the same and new techniques must be developed; the compilation time is one of the most important aspects. To minimize it, some trade-offs must be made. Thus, we prefer greedy algorithms over computation-intensive algorithms that could yield a more optimized design.

In the following sections, we describe the algorithms and design choices made at each phase of the compilation.

## 4.1  Source Language and High-Level Synthesis

High-level synthesis of digital systems consists in transforming a behavioral (algorithmic) description of a design into a RTL (register transfer level) description of the design. This phase determines how the high-level concepts of the programming language are translated to low-level primitives.

Decisions must be taken on how high-level concepts can be implemented in hardware. For example: should a function be implemented as a pipeline able to handle parallel calls, or as a state machine, much more compact but unable to handle parallelism? Other decisions must be taken such as which communication protocol to use between software and hardware.

We chose to use Scheme [10] because it is a dynamic language quite easy to use and learn. Scheme provides a small set of primitive constructs with which most high-level features can be implemented. This simplifies the structure of the compiler.

To elegantly provide dynamic compilation to hardware, our compiler is made available as a user-callable **synthesize** primitive. This primitive maps a function object, possibly a closure, onto the reconfigurable hardware. The sole parameter is a function and it returns a function which performs the same computation in hardware (i.e. semantically **synthesize** is the identity function). If the compilation fails, the primitive returns the argument unchanged. Thus, the complexity of hardware synthesis is hidden behind a single function.

This approach meshes nicely with *function closures* which remember their environment of definition. For people versed in functional programming languages dynamic hardware synthesis with this extension is very natural. Hardware specialization is simply viewed as the partial evaluation of the function body given the binding of variables in the definition environment (i.e. the closure's free variables).

Figure 4 shows a use of the **synthesize** primitive. The call (adder 4) returns the closure which is an instance of the lambda-expression at line 3. This closure is a specialized version of an adder which always adds 4 to its argument.

```
1  (define adder
2    (lambda (x)
3      (lambda (y)
4        (+ x y))))
5
6  (pretty-print
7    (map (synthesize (adder 4))
8         '(1 2 3 4 5 6 7 8 9 10)))
```

**Fig. 4.** Hardware synthesize/invocation of a specialized instruction

By passing this closure to the `synthesize` primitive, the system dynamically compiles the closure, configures the dynamic zone and returns another closure able to communicate with the dynamic instruction. When `map` calls that closure, the argument is sent to the hardware's input and the result is obtained from the hardware's output.

High-level synthesis is complex because many issues must be taken into account (e.g. memory access, global variables, continuations, threads...). In our current prototype, we only support simple expressions containing arithmetic and logic operators. Much work remains to be done to determine how to perform high-level synthesis on general purpose languages.

### 4.2   Technology Mapping

Technology mapping consists in transforming technology-independent logical circuits into a technology-dependent mapping on a given technology. Typically, this phase is driven by a set of technology patterns defined in a library. Mapping is constrained by characteristics such as available physical gates, delays, available power and area.

Compiler back-ends solve a similar problem when generating code. Two approaches are typically used: top-down and bottom-up. The top-down approach, often called Maximal Munch, consists in finding, in the library, a pattern that matches as much as possible from the root of the tree. Parts that were not matched are processed in the same way. Another approach is to use dynamic programming to find a way to cover the tree with a set of patterns.

Our pattern library is designed to be a bridge between a high-level language and the low-level requirements imposed by the FPGA fabric. A typical operator has a height of 4 CLBs and uses one slice column (i.e. half of a CLB column). The use of a column of slices can be justified by the way fast carry chain logic works. We decided to use 4 CLBs (and 16-bit operators) because the configuration process works with 32-bit words and a CLB is 3 bytes wide. Thus, we obtain operators representable by a sequence of three 32-bit words. In addition, embedded multipliers are 18x18-bit and can implement 16-bit multiplication directly. Figure 5 shows typical operator patterns of our library.

In our prototype, we decided to use a fast top-down approach. This phase takes less than a millisecond to perform mapping of a specialized instruction. It does not require much memory and is far from being the bottleneck of synthesis.

### 4.3   Place and Route

Placement consists in finding a location for each component of the design. Locations are chosen to minimize the distance between dependent components and to maximize the probability of success of the routing phase. Sometimes, other criteria such as power consumption must also be taken into account. Routing consists in finding a path through static wires for each net.

Placement and routing are the slowest phases of synthesis on FPGA. Running times of several minutes are common for these phases. Although phases are

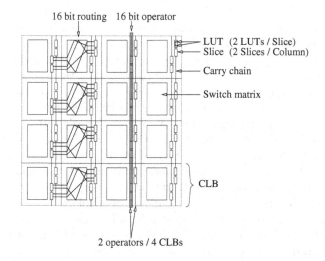

16 bit routing    16 bit operator

LUT  (2 LUTs / Slice)
Slice  (2 Slices / Column)

Carry chain

Switch matrix

CLB

2 operators / 4 CLBs

**Fig. 5.** Mapping of operators onto the FPGA fabric

run separately, they are interdependent. A good placement facilitates routing, whereas a bad placement makes routing extremely complex. Because of the complexity of these phases, their algorithms are crucial to be optimized if we want to attain short compilation times. To understand current fast techniques, we briefly explain the VPR and the ROCR tools which are the fastest available algorithms for FPGA compilation. We then describe algorithms accelerating these phases.

The VPR (Versatile Place and Route) [3] tool uses the simulated annealing algorithm for placement. The basic idea is to perform a random initial placement of all components. At each iteration, components are randomly swapped with a probability function of temperature and cost. The temperature gradually decreases until a threshold is reached. The VPR routing algorithm is an improvement over the Pathfinder negotiated algorithm [5]. Initially, it routes all nets with the shortest path regardless of the availability of resources. Dijkstra's algorithm is used to find the shortest path. At each iteration, every route is sequentially re-routed by the lowest cost path. The cost of using a resource is a function of the overuse of that resource. At the end of the iteration, the costs of routing resources are adjusted accordingly to the amount of overuse in the previous iteration. By gradually increasing the cost of oversubscribed routing resources, the algorithm forces nets to avoid them and to use alternative routes. Although VPR is quite fast, it is not fast enough for JIT place and route.

ROCR (Riverside On-Chip Router) [13] is designed for hardware JIT compilation. It uses the basic cost model of VPR. To perform routing, it uses a global and detailed routing algorithm. The design of the fabric allows the algorithm to represent routing between CLBs as routing between switch matrices to which CLBs are connected. The global routing algorithm works like the VPR algorithm. Nets are initially routed with a greedy algorithm. Instead of un-routing all nets, only illegal nets are re-routed in an iteration. While using the same routing cost model as the VPR router, ROCR incorporates a small routing adjustment cost to all routing resources used by an illegal route. The routing adjustment cost discourages the greedy routing algorithm from selecting the same initial path in subsequent iterations. Once global routing is done, ROCR performs detailed routing which consists in assigning the channels (path in the switch matrix) used for each route. Two routes present a conflict when both routes pass through a given switch matrix and are assigned the same channel. This problem can be solved by a graph-coloring algorithm. The use of Brelaz's vertex coloring algorithm allows a linear time approximation which is good enough for solving the routing problem. ROCR takes advantage of the regular and basic structure of the switch matrix of a custom made fabric. It is an order of magnitude faster than VPR and uses an order of magnitude less memory.

To obtain a faster place and route algorithm, we explored several approaches. As JIT systems are typically used for high-level languages, we chose to restrict ourselves to fixed-width operators. We reduced the size of the problem by increasing the granularity of the operators, which operate on 16-bit integers. We also allowed algorithms to fail when problems are too complex, with a fallback invoking the more expensive algorithms.

**Placement.** To simplify the placement algorithm, all operators are placed on a horizontal line whose height equals 4 CLB. Thus, the placement problem has only one dimension.

We implemented a classical simulated annealing algorithm. It takes about 120 ms for a circuit of 30 operators and 300 nets. This algorithm gives quite good results and routing always succeeded in our tests.

In our search for a faster algorithm, we attempted to implement a simpler algorithm which worked surprisingly well on our tests. We performed initial placement by flattening the expression tree in the topological order of the data dependencies. Then we performed a peep-hole optimization by trying every possible permutation of operators in a sliding window and kept the result with the lowest cost. This algorithm is greedy because it always keeps a better candidate when it finds one and never goes back to a worse solution. The algorithm loops until a stable state is reached. It usually needs about 3 iterations to find the best candidate, which takes less than 2 ms. The sliding window is illustrated in Figure 6. Notice that a CLB can have two overlapping operators (one for each column of slices) and the routing matrix is shared by the two operators (Figure 5).

This algorithm only requires a few kilobytes of memory. The results are not as good as the ones obtained by the simulated annealing algorithm but this does not affect the performance of the final circuit.

**Routing.** Routing is more complex than placement. Figure 7 shows routing resources used in our algorithm. FPGA routing resources consist of switch matrices connected by external wires. There are various kinds of external wires: simple, double and hex. Simple wires connect direct neighbors, double wires connect the first and second neighbors, and hex wires connect third and sixth

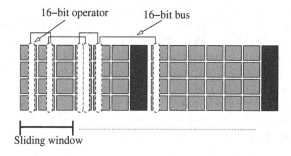

**Fig. 6.** Fast placement with peephole minimisation

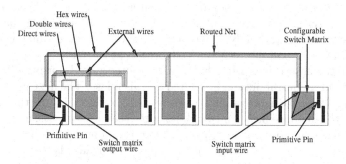

**Fig. 7.** Routing resources and a typical route

neighbors. Longer paths are routed through multiple switch matrices using multiple external wires.

A typical route starts from a primitive pin, passes through a switch matrix, uses a wire to another switch matrix and ends at another primitive pin. All programmable interconnect points (PIP) are in the switch matrix and nothing is configurable outside the CLB.

The routing algorithm is split into two levels: *external* and *internal* routing. The algorithm applies a sequence of greedy external routers that call different internal routers to manage the routing inside the switch matrices. By carefully pairing external and internal routers and by applying greedy and efficient algorithms first, it is possible to minimize the routing time and obtain an efficient routing.

**Internal Router.** Paths inside a switch matrix and their corresponding Programmable Interconnects Points (PIP) are determined by the internal router. Internal routing is hard to achieve because the switch matrix is irregular, not fully connected and paths may be of various depths. This router finds the shortest path in the switch matrix from an input wire to an output wire. It takes into consideration all used resources and may fail if there is no path or if the routing is too complex.

The first internal router is implemented using a lookup table. The shortest paths from all inputs to all outputs of a switch matrix are pre-computed. Therefore, if a resource in the shortest path is already used, the routing simply fails.

The second internal router uses depth-first traversal. This algorithm is faster than Dijkstra's algorithm because paths are usually very short. The depth-first search was implemented by a set of mutually recursive functions that represent the connectivity of the switch matrix. Thus, there is no data manipulation, only fast code execution. We ordered the recursive calls to maximize the likelihood of reaching an output point.

**External Router.** The external router drives the algorithm to determine where the next switch matrix is and which external wire is taken between switch matrices. As stated above, it uses an internal router as a helper to solve connections inside the switch matrix. External phases are sorted in such a way that most of the nets will be routed rapidly at the beginning while the remaining nets will be routed by a slower and more complex algorithm at the end.

The *direct* phase routes nets that can be routed only by using direct wires. Thus, only direct neighbors can be routed by this phase. The next phase, *general routing*, tries to route nets that only use one double or hex wire. As the placement minimizes the distance between neighbors, after these two phases, almost all nets are routed except those passing through more than one switch matrix or larger than 6 CLBs. So, the next phase is *greedy routing*. The idea is to find recursively the best path through switch matrices by jumping as close as possible to the target. The last phase uses *dynamic programming* to find a valid path and is able to route any net unless resource conflicts make it impossible.

Figure 8 shows examples of nets routed by each phase. As we see with the direct and general phases, only one external wire connecting two switch matrices is used. Greedy and dynamic routing use multiple external wires. We see the difference between greedy routing and dynamic programming routing: the greedy routing always jumps as close as possible. In the example, it jumps the longest

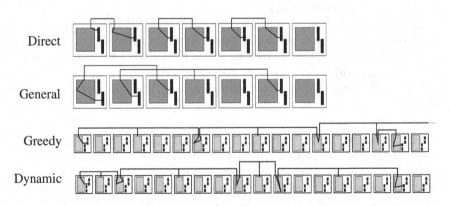

**Fig. 8.** Typical routes obtained with the 4 external routers

possible path (6 CLBs) twice. The dynamic routing is able to find an alternative route but it is slower. It is used when conflicts occur with the greedy algorithm.

**Nets cache.** Each external router keeps a cache of routed nets to determine if another net can be routed the same way by applying a translation. There are many cache hits because we use fixed-width operators and all the bits of a given operator are often routed in the same way.

## 5    Results

We synthesized the design on the ML310 demo board made by Xilinx. This system board has a Virtex-II Pro FPGA (2VP30) and 256 MB of external memory. The board has more components (e.g. PCI Bus, VGA, Ethernet connector...) but they were not used in our basic design; we only used the external memory, the FPGA and the serial link. The program is running on the processor and communicates through a console attached to the serial link.

Figure 9 shows a FPGA editor screenshot of a specialized intruction dynamically generated by our compiler. We observe the horizontal placement of 4 CLB high operators.

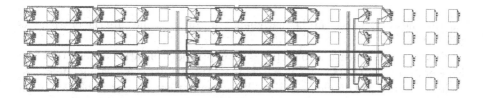

**Fig. 9.** Specialized instruction dynamically produced by the JIT compiler

To achieve high processing rates it is important to have a close coupling of the processor and the dynamic instructions to minimize the communication costs. It is also important for the dynamic instructions to exploit parallelism, for example with a pipelined circuit. Because these aspects are orthogonal to the placement and routing problems tackled in this paper we have used a less efficient interface adequate for testing the correctness of the synthesized circuits. In our prototype the input and output of the dynamic instructions are not interfaced to the processor bus. The parameters and results are communicated through the Internal Configuration Access Port (ICAP). The parameters become constant values and the result is read back from the state of the output register. Given the relatively slow speed of the ICAP interface, application speed-ups are not possible. To solve this issue we must work-around Xilinx design flow limitations; this work is still in progress. Given our goal to show that compilation time can be low enough to support hardware JIT compilation, we focus our attention on the synthesis phases. Therefore, instead of benchmarking applications, we evaluate

**Table 1.** Place and route times for specialized intructions

| slices | nets | Place (ms) | | Route (ms) | | | |
|---|---|---|---|---|---|---|---|
| | | S.A. | fast-place | dynamic | no-table | no-cache | fast-route |
| 48 | 80 | 3 | 0 | 3 | 2 | 4 | 2 |
| 64 | 112 | 8 | 0 | 5 | 3 | 5 | 3 |
| 80 | 144 | 7 | 0 | 4 | 3 | 3 | 3 |
| 144 | 272 | 47 | 2 | 12 | 5 | 4 | 4 |
| 224 | 432 | 166 | 6 | 227 | 143 | 19 | 14 |
| 440 | 864 | 763 | 46 | 1161 | 385 | 101 | 50 |

**Table 2.** Number of nets routed by each internal phase

| nets | pre-computed tables | | | | depth-first traversal | | | |
|---|---|---|---|---|---|---|---|---|
| | direct | general | greedy | dynamic | direct | general | greedy | dynamic |
| 80 | 56 | 16 | 0 | 0 | 8 | 0 | 0 | 0 |
| 112 | 68 | 32 | 0 | 0 | 12 | 0 | 0 | 0 |
| 144 | 56 | 80 | 0 | 0 | 8 | 0 | 0 | 0 |
| 272 | 140 | 120 | 0 | 0 | 12 | 0 | 0 | 0 |
| 432 | 136 | 252 | 35 | 0 | 8 | 0 | 0 | 0 |
| 864 | 224 | 532 | 88 | 0 | 0 | 0 | 0 | 0 |

the time needed to perform the placement and routing which are the bottlenecks of synthesis.

Table 1 shows place and route times for expressions of various sizes (from 6 to 55 operators). For the placement, we compare the simulated annealing implementation with our fast implementation. We observe that our fast implementation is about 20 times faster. It is important to note that our simulated annealing implementation is already faster than current hardware synthesis tools because it also performs one-dimensional placement of fixed-width operators.

The last set of columns shows the routing time of expressions. By disabling the cache, we observe that the routing speed is halved. We also observe the speed-up obtained by using pre-computed tables for switch matrices by comparing the *fast-route* and the *no-table* columns. The *dynamic* column shows the worst case of our algorithm when all nets are routed with the dynamic programming router.

Typical routing tools use the Pathfinder and Dijkstra's algorithm. At each iteration, they re-route wires. Our algorithm is not iterative and routes each wire only once. Dijkstra's algorithm's speed should be similar to the dynamic router speed. As VPR uses an iterative algorithm with Dijkstra's algorithm, its speed should be of the same order. Our algorithm does not iterate and only applies a sequence of greedy routers. Speed-ups come from the fact that most nets are routed by a faster router. Table 2 shows how many nets are routed by each internal and external router. Almost all nets are routed by the direct and general routers and a few nets really need a depth-first traversal to find a path. This explains why our algorithm is efficient.

# 6    Conclusion

We have described a hardware JIT compiler for dynamically reconfigurable FP-GAs. At run time, the JIT compiles function closures to a hardware circuit which is downloaded to the reconfigurable zone of the FPGA. The JIT performs all the normal phases of hardware synthesis including placement and routing. To achieve good compilation speed we use a set of routing algorithms of increasing complexity which are tried in a cascade. Most if not all of the work is usually performed by the cheaper algorithms. The prototype we have built for the Xilinx Virtex II Pro FPGA demonstrates that modest sized functions can be compiled to hardware in a few milliseconds. Our experiments show that naive algorithms and lookup tables significantly speed-up placement and routing.

Various heuristics and naive fast algorithms may be adapted to FPGAs depending on their specific characteristics. We do not claim to have the best set of algorithms. Our claim is that compilation times compatible with JIT compilation are attainable on current reconfigurable FPGAs. We hope that our work will spur further research on hardware JIT compilation for general-purpose languages.

# References

1. Bergeron, E., Feeley, M., David, J.P.: Toward On-Chip JIT Synthesis on Xilinx Virtex-II Pro FPGAs. In: 50th International Midwest Symposium on Circuits and Systems/5th International Northeast Workshop on Circuits (MWCAS/NEWCAS), Montreal, Canada (August 2007)
2. Bergeron, E., Saint-Mleux, X., Feeley, M., David, J.P.: High-level synthesis for data-driven applications. In: IEEE International Workshop on Rapid System Prototyping, pp. 54–60 (2005)
3. Betz, V., Rose, J.: VPR: A new packing, placement and routing tool for FPGA research. In: Glesner, M., Luk, W. (eds.) FPL 1997. LNCS, vol. 1304, pp. 213–222. Springer, Heidelberg (1997)
4. Brebner, G.: The swappable logic unit: a paradigm for virtual hardware. In: FCCM 1997: Proceedings of the 5th IEEE Symposium on FPGA-Based Custom Computing Machines, Washington, DC, USA (1997)
5. Ebeling, C., McMurchie, L., Hauck, S.A., Burns, S.: Placement and routing tools for the Triptych FPGA. IEEE Trans. Very Large Scale Integr. Syst. 3(4), 473–482 (1995)
6. Feeley, M.: Gambit-C, http://www.iro.umontreal.ca/~gambit
7. Feeley, M., Lapalme, G.: Using closures for code generation. Computer Languages 12(1), 47–66 (1987)
8. Goldstein, S.C., Schmit, H., Budiu, M., Cadambi, S., Moe, M., Taylor, R.R.: PipeRench: A reconfigurable architecture and compiler. Computer 33(4), 70–77 (2000)
9. Greskamp, B., Sass, R.: A Virtual Machine for Merit-Based Runtime Reconfiguration. In: IEEE Symposium on Field-Programmable Custom Computing Machines (April 2005)
10. Kelsey, R., Clinger, W., Rees, J. (eds.): Revised[5] Report on the Algorithmic Language Scheme. ACM SIGPLAN Notices 33(9), 26–76 (1998)

11. Lysecky, R., Stitt, G., Vahid, F.: Warp processors. ACM Transactions on Design Automation of Electronic Systems, 659–681 (July 2006)
12. Lysecky, R., Vahid, F.: A configurable logic architecture for dynamic hardware/-software partitioning. In: Design Automation and Test in Europe Conference (2004)
13. Lysecky, R., Vahid, F., Tan, S.X.-D.: Dynamic FPGA routing for just-in-time FPGA compilation. In: Design Automation Conference, pp. 954–959 (2004)
14. Lysecky, R., Vahid, F., Tan, S.X.-D.: A study of the scalability of on-chip routing for just-in-time FPGA compilation. In: IEEE Symposium on Field-Programmable Custom Computing Machines, pp. 57–62 (2005)
15. Ling, X.-p., Amano, H.: Performance evaluation of WASMII: a data driven computer on a virtual hardware. In: Reeve, M., Bode, A., Wolf, G. (eds.) PARLE 1993. LNCS, vol. 694, pp. 610–621. Springer, Heidelberg (1993)
16. Schmit, H., Whelihan, D., Tsai, A., Moe, M., Levine, B., Taylor, R.R.: PipeRench: A virtualized programmable datapath. In: Proceedings of the IEEE 2002 Custom Integrated Circuits Conference, pp. 63–66 (2002)
17. Stitt, G., Vahid, F.: Binary Synthesis. ACM Transactions on Design Automation of Electronic Systems 12(3), 34 (2007)
18. Xilinx. XAPP290: Two Flows for Partial Reconfigurable Core Based on Small Bit Manipulations. Technical report, Xilinx (September 2002)
19. Xilinx. Virtex-II Pro and Virtex-II Pro X Platform FPGAs: Complete Data Sheet. Technical report, Xilinx (June 2005)

# Visualization of Program Dependence Graphs*

Thomas Würthinger, Christian Wimmer, and Hanspeter Mössenböck

Institute for System Software
Christian Doppler Laboratory for Automated Software Engineering
Johannes Kepler University Linz
Linz, Austria
{wuerthinger,wimmer,moessenboeck}@ssw.jku.at

**Abstract.** The analysis of a compiler's intermediate data structures helps at debugging complex optimizations. We present a graphical tool for analyzing the program dependence graph of Sun Microsystems' Java HotSpot$^{TM}$ server compiler. The tool saves snapshots of the graph during the compilation. It displays the graphs and provides filtering mechanisms based on customizable JavaScript code and regular expressions. High performance and sophisticated navigation possibilities enable the tool to handle large graphs with thousands of nodes.

## 1 Introduction

The Java HotSpot$^{TM}$ server compiler [5] of Sun Microsystems uses a program dependence graph [2] as the intermediate data structure when compiling Java bytecodes to machine code. It applies optimizations such as global value numbering, conditional constant propagation, and loop transformations to produce faster code. When debugging the compiler, only a textual output of the graph is currently available.

We present a tool that facilitates analyzing the compiler by providing a graphical representation of the program dependence graph. The tool captures snapshots of the graph during the compilation of a method, so the user can reconstruct the transformations applied to the graph by compiler optimizations. The tool applies filters based on regular expressions to make the appearance of the graph customizable and enables the user to quickly focus on specific parts of the graph, which is especially helpful for the analysis of large graphs.

While the main focus of the tool is currently the visualization of the data structures of the server compiler, it can easily be adapted for other programs that work on directed graphs. A more detailed description of the tool and the program dependence graph can be found in [8].

## 2 Architecture

The program dependence graph of the Java HotSpot$^{TM}$ server compiler combines control, data, and memory dependencies into a single graph. A node has ordered

---

* This work was supported by Sun Microsystems, Inc.

L. Hendren (Ed.): CC 2008, LNCS 4959, pp. 193–196, 2008.
© Springer-Verlag Berlin Heidelberg 2008

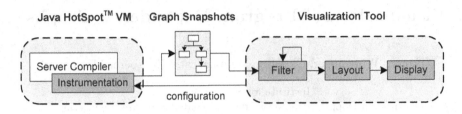

**Fig. 1.** Interaction between the compiler and the visualization tool

input slots and produces a single output value. Projection nodes are used when a node produces a tuple. Figure 1 shows the interaction between the visualization tool and the server compiler.

We instrument the compiler to take snapshots of the graph. The snapshots are either stored in an intermediate file or directly sent to the visualization tool via a network connection, which additionally allows configuration data to be sent back to the compiler. The user can select a set of filters to be applied to the graph. After the graph is transformed by the filters, the layout algorithm calculates node positions and interpolation points for the edges. Then the graph is displayed on the screen.

**Data Model.** The graphs are stored in an XML based format. They can be exported to a file to allow subsequent analysis. The snapshot of a graph is serialized as the difference to the previous snapshot. This reduces the storage requirements when snapshots of the graph are taken frequently.

Properties of nodes are stored as textual key-value pairs to improve extensibility. New properties can be introduced without changing the tool. Filters select nodes based on regular expressions on the value of a property with a certain name, and custom filters for arbitrary properties can be defined. This way, the tool can be used to visualize directed graphs whose nodes have other properties than the nodes of the server compiler.

The data transmitted from the server compiler to the visualization tool contains a clustering of the nodes into basic blocks when this information is already available in the compiler. Otherwise the tool calculates an approximate scheduling of the nodes. The basic data model does not contain any display information. Before the filters are applied, the transmitted graph is converted into a graph with display information such as node positions and node colors. A node can have multiple output slots in this model, e.g. if a filter merges several nodes.

**Graph Layout.** We use a hierarchical layout algorithm based on the approach of Sugiyama [6] and the GraphViz tool *dot* [3]. The main focus of our implementation is performance, because the graph of large methods can have a few thousand nodes and more than ten thousand edges. Long edges are cut so that only the beginnings and endings are drawn. This improves the overview as well as the performance. A special routing for backward edges ensures that they also start at the bottom of their start node and end at the top of their destination node.

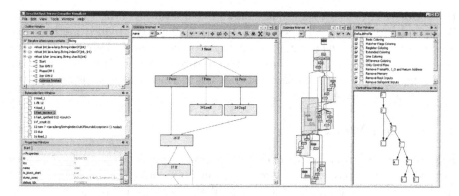

**Fig. 2.** Screenshot of the visualization tool showing two graphs

# 3  Usage

Figure 2 shows the tool when displaying an extract of a graph in normal view and a whole graph in satellite view. The methods retrieved from the server compiler are listed in the top left window. Double-clicking on the graph snapshot of a certain method opens the graph in the middle area. The top right window contains the available filters; checkboxes activate them. The list of filters can be edited, and the selected set of filters can be saved as a profile. The bottom right window corresponds to the control flow graph approximation of the active program dependence graph. The bottom left window displays the textual key-value properties of the selected nodes. The middle left window contains the bytecodes of the compiled method.

**Filtering.** Before layouting and displaying the graph, filters are applied that can remove, add, merge, split, and color nodes and edges. The filters can be specified by predefined JavaScript functions, which use regular expression based rules on the node properties. The following JavaScript statement assigns a red background color to all nodes whose name starts with the letter "I". Semantically, this highlights all integer instructions: `colorize("name", "I.*", red);`

**Difference.** The tool can display the difference between snapshots graphically. It is also capable of calculating the approximate difference between two arbitrary graphs, e.g. snapshots before and after a compiler change. The difference is made visible using color filters. This helps identifying the effects of modifications in the compiler.

**Navigation.** Despite standard graph navigation techniques like showing and hiding nodes or going to pre- and successors of a node, the tool provides a way to navigate in the graph by only double clicks on nodes. The tool maintains the set S of fully shown nodes. It draws all nodes that are immediate pre- or successors of a node of the set S as semi-transparent. The user can add one of those semi-transparent nodes to the set S by a double click on it. Performing this action on a node of the set S removes it from the set.

**Bytecodes.** The bytecodes window shows the input data of the server compiler. If methods are inlined, this is a tree structure where the inlined methods are shown as children of the method call. Navigation between the bytecodes and the graph is available for instructions that may throw an exception. For all other instructions, the server compiler does not track which instructions are created for a certain bytecode.

## 4    Related Work

Balmas presents a tool that displays the program dependence graph for C source code with focus on creating hierarchical groups of nodes [1]. Krinke developed a similar tool that additionally gives a textual representation of program slices [4]. The main differences to our application are that they do not have built-in filtering mechanisms and they are not designed to visualize a program dependence graph structure that changes during compilation of a method as compiler optimizations are applied.

## 5    Conclusions

We presented a tool for displaying the program dependence graph of the Java HotSpot$^{TM}$ server compiler at various stages during compilation. It helps at debugging the server compiler and analyze its built-in compiler optimizations. A property-based filter system makes the tool flexible and also usable for the analysis of other directed graph structures. The HotSpot$^{TM}$ compiler team at Sun Microsystems is currently evaluating the tool and integrating the server compiler instrumentation into the upcoming JDK 7 [7]. They are planning to include the visualization tool in the OpenJDK project.

## References

1. Balmas, F.: Displaying dependence graphs: A hierarchical approach. In: Proceedings of the Working Conference on Reverse Engineering, pp. 261–270 (2001)
2. Ferrante, J., Ottenstein, K.J., Warren, J.D.: The program dependence graph and its use in optimization. ACM Transactions on Programming Languages and Systems 9(3), 319–349 (1987)
3. Gansner, E.R., Koutsofios, E., North, S.C., Vo, K.P.: A technique for drawing directed graphs. IEEE Transactions on Software Engineering 19(3), 214–230 (1993)
4. Krinke, J.: Visualization of program dependence and slices. In: Proceedings of the IEEE International Conference on Software Maintenance, pp. 168–177 (2004)
5. Paleczny, M., Vick, C., Click, C.: The Java HotSpot$^{TM}$ server compiler. In: Proceedings of the Java Virtual Machine Res. and Techn. Symposium, pp. 1–12 (2001)
6. Sugiyama, K., Tagawa, S., Toda, M.: Methods for visual understanding of hierarchical system structures. IEEE Transactions on Systems, Man, and Cybernetics 11(2), 109–125 (1981)
7. Sun Microsystems, Inc.: JDK 7 Project (2007), https://jdk7.dev.java.net/
8. Würthinger, T.: Visualization of program dependence graphs. Master's thesis, Johannes Kepler University Linz (2007)

# On the Relative Completeness of Bytecode Analysis Versus Source Code Analysis

Francesco Logozzo and Manuel Fähndrich

Microsoft Research
{logozzo,maf}@microsoft.com

**Abstract.** We discuss the challenges faced by bytecode analyzers designed for code verification compared to similar analyzers for source code. While a bytecode-level analysis brings many simplifications, *e.g.*, fewer cases, independence from source syntax, name resolution, etc., it also introduces precision loss that must be recovered either via preprocessing, more precise abstract domains, more precise transfer functions, or a combination thereof.

The paper studies the *relative* completeness of a static analysis for bytecode compared to the analysis of the program source. We illustrate it through examples originating from the design and the implementation of Clousot, a generic static analyzer based on Abstract Interpretation for the analysis of MSIL.

## 1 Introduction

We are interested in static program analysis for program verification, where the goal is to infer *invariants* that are sufficient to discharge assertions which appear in the program either explicitly (specified by the user through assertions) or implicitly (*e.g.*, array bound checks, null dereferences, division by zero, etc.). Such analyses need to be precise enough to validate the assertions. In this paper, we will focus our attention on static analyses for program verification and we call these PSA, *Precise enough Static Analyses*.

PSA are often designed to work at the program source level, *e.g.*, [5,17,18,6,26]). There are many reasons for that. The program source provides a uniform view which abstracts machine details. Source code analysis is also able to directly exploit program structure, such as loops, to increase the precision via techniques such as reductive iterations [12], and the narrowing application by re-execution from a post-fixpoint [8].

As we will see in this paper, the most immediate benefit of source analysis however is that it provides the analysis designer with a *large code window*, allowing him/her to specialize transfer functions for extra precision.

The analysis of low level code provides different advantages: 1) it is more faithful, as it analyzes the code that is actually executed (or closer to), 2) it enables the analysis of libraries when source code is not available, 3) the analyzer avoids redundant work that the compiler performed, such as name resolution, type checking, template/generics instantiation, 4) the semantics of high-level

L. Hendren (Ed.): CC 2008, LNCS 4959, pp. 197–212, 2008.
© Springer-Verlag Berlin Heidelberg 2008

constructs that are expanded by the compiler, such as try...catch...finally, delegates, partial classes in C#, or generics in C# and Java, need not be duplicated. As a consequence a low-level code analyzer needs to deal with many fewer constructs than a source analyzer, reducing its complexity. Finally, 5) the analyzer can be language independent; e.g., analyzing the common target language MSIL of the .NET platform provides analysis of C#, VB, Managed C++, F#.

Because of these advantages, plenty of static analyses have been developed for low-level code. Most of them address non-relational properties like type checking [14,16,25], non-cyclicity [27], nullness [10], etc. Others target numerical properties, e.g., to check buffer overruns [3] or array accesses [20].

Our observation is that while writing a static analyzer for a low-level language or bytecode is simpler than writing one for source code due to the above advantages, it is non-trivial to match the precision of a similar analysis performed at source level, due to the missing high-level structure and the reduced size of the *code window* used by transfer functions. The rest of this paper elucidates this observation with examples and general principles.

*Example 1 (Motivating Example).* Suppose we analyze a program containing the high level statement $S \equiv$ assume $x - y \leq 7$, using the difference bounds abstract domain [22]. At source level, the constraint $x - y \leq 7$ is a difference constraint, and it can be represented faithfully by the abstract state. Now consider the compilation of $S$ into three address code:

$$0 : t_1 \leftarrow x - y$$
$$1 : t_2 \leftarrow t_1 \leq 7$$
$$2 : \text{assume } t_2$$

Analyzing this code sequence with the same domain used at the source level raises immediate problems:

**Expression complexity.** The assignment at line 0 involves three variables, which cannot be captured precisely by the difference bounds domain. As a consequence, the abstract value for $t_1$ is $\top$.

**Type complexity.** At line 1, $t_2$ is assigned the result of a boolean expression[1]. At the source level there was no such boolean assignment, and in fact, the domain used at source level cannot encode the relation between $t_1$ and $t_2$.

As a result, the analysis of the code sequence using the same domain as at the source level produces an abstract state that contains no information about the relation of $x$ and $y$. Several solutions are possible to mitigate the above problems.

- Use a more precise numerical abstract domain for the low-level analysis that handles relations among more than two variables, such as Octahedra [7], or Polyhedra [9,2]. This approach however leads to scaling problems, as these domains exhibit exponential complexity. No polynomial domains are known that can handle more than two variables [23].

---

[1] Please note that this case is orthogonal to the previous one, *i.e.*, the problem shows up even if the assignment was $t_2 \leftarrow (x - y \leq 7)$.

- Split the current abstract domain in two at the boolean assignment: one where $t_2 ==$ `true` and one where $t_2 ==$ `false`. This method has two main drawbacks: (i) it may lead to exponential explosion by doubling the abstract states at each conditional branch; and (ii) it still introduces loss of precision, because the relation to be assumed at line 2 is lost.
- A more general solution which addresses both of the problems and all others related to the limited code window, is to use a lightweight symbolic abstract domain to compute available expressions at each program point.

Let us briefly sketch how the use of a symbolic domain to recover expressions works on the example. At line 2, the analysis *first* asks the symbolic domain to refine variable $t_2$. This refinement, using line 1, produces $t_2 \equiv t_1 \leq 7$, which can be further refined, using line 0, to produce $t_2 \equiv x - y \leq 7$. The analysis *then* passes the refined expression $x - y \leq 7$ to the difference bounds domain, which handles it exactly as the source analysis does.                                    □

As the example shows, PSA of low-level code requires more than just reusing the domains suitable for high-level code, otherwise, precision is lost. In this paper, we investigate the *relative* completeness of low-level code analysis versus source code analysis, i.e., what is required for bytecode analysis to be as precise as source code analysis, without requiring the use of domains with worse complexity.

We present representative issues that crop up when designing precise and scalable bytecode analyses. We faced those issues during the design and implementation of Clousot [19], a PSA for .NET based on abstract interpretation. The issues described are not specific to .NET, but arise for all low-level analyses. They manifest in (i) the precise handling of assignments, tests and branches, and (ii) the fixpoint iteration strategy, in particular for narrowing and reductive iterations. We discuss how to overcome these issues, and the solutions we have adopted in Clousot. In general, quantifing the impact of such issues is hard. We tried a rough (under-)estimation by switching off some precision refinements discussed in this paper (not all of them could be switched off, as many are buried deep in the architecture of Clousot). We obtained a loss of precision of 10% in the analysis of the array accesses of mscorlib.dll, the main library in the .NET framework. Such loss of precision is enough to generate more than 1400 false positives, *i.e.*, to make the analysis *de facto* unuseful.

## 2   Languages

We use a while-language as a representative for high-level languages, and a three address code instruction set as a representative of low-level code.

### 2.1   While-Language

Our high level language is a simple while-language with no dynamic memory allocation, shown in Fig. 1. The semantics is standard. We use a single type, integers. Following widespread convention, we assume that 0 stands for `false`

```
Stm ::= skip; | Var := Exp; | Stm Stm | while(BExp) {Stm}; | if(BExp) {Stm }else {Stm }; |
        assume BExp; | assert BExp;
Exp ::= Lit | Exp op Exp
BExp ::= Lit | Exp relop Exp | !(BExp) | BExp && BExp | BExp || BExp
Lit ::= Var | int          Var ::= ··· | x | y | ...      int ::= ··· | −1 | 0 | 1 | ...
op ::= + | − | * | /        relop ::=<|≤|==
```

**Fig. 1.** The while-language: a high-level language

```
IstrStream ::= Label : Istr | Label : Istr '\n' IstrStream | ε
     Label ::= 0 | ... | 2^{32}
      Istr ::= Var ← ExpTwoOps |
               jmp Label | jmpIf Var Label | assert Lit | assume Lit | nop
ExpTwoOps ::= Lit | Lit op Lit | Lit relop Lit | Lit && Lit | Lit || Lit
```

**Fig. 2.** Three address code: a low-level language

and all the other integers for **true**. Boolean expressions *shortcut* evaluation. We also consider assert and assume statements, which enable assume/ guarantee reasoning, *e.g.*, to (abstract) method calls. The statement **assert e**; checks if the expression e holds. If it does not, then the program fails. The statement **assume e**; acts as an execution guard for the following statements. If the condition does not hold, execution gets stuck.

## 2.2   Three Address Code

Our low-level language is a three address code instruction set shown in Fig. 2. This language is higher level than MSIL, Java bytecode, or assembly, but it simplifies our presentation and is sufficient to exhibit the problems of interest.

An instruction stream is a sequence of labeled instructions. An assignment instruction $x \leftarrow e_{2ops}$ updates the value of the variable x with the result of the evaluation of the expression $e_{2ops}$ which contains *at most* two operands. As a consequence the expressions that can be atomically evaluated and assigned at low level are a subset of those at higher level, *i.e.*, ExpTwoOps ⊆ Exp ∪ BExp. In the next sections, we will see how this impacts the precision and performances of PSA.

## 2.3   Compilation

We assume two compilation functions: $\mathcal{C} \in [\text{Stm} \rightarrow \text{IstrStream}]$ compiles a program expressed in the high-level language into a low-level instruction stream one, and $\mathcal{C}_e \in [(\text{Exp} \cup \text{BExp}) \rightarrow \text{IstrStream}]$ compiles expressions into a sequence of instructions for evaluating them. The result of the evaluation is in a (reserved) variable **res**. We expect the functions $\mathcal{C}$ and $\mathcal{C}_e$ to perform naive compilation, *i.e.*, a straightforward translation without any program optimization [1].

# 3 Abstract Interpretation

Abstract interpretation is a theory of approximations [8]. It formalizes the intuition that semantics are more or less precise depending on the observation level. The more precise the abstract semantics, the more precise the properties about the execution of the program it captures. A static analysis is an abstract semantics which is rough enough to be computable. A precise static analysis is a static analysis which is precise *enough* to capture the properties of interests, *e.g.*, those needed to prove the absence of certain runtime errors.

## 3.1 Abstract Domains

An abstract domain $\bar{D}$ is the complete lattice $\langle E, \sqsubseteq, \bot, \top, \sqcup, \sqcap \rangle$, where $E$ is the set of abstract elements, ordered according to the relation $\sqsubseteq$. The smallest abstract element is $\bot$, the largest is $\top$. The join $\sqcup$, and the meet $\sqcap$, are also defined. With a slight abuse of notation, we will confuse an abstract domain $\bar{D}$ with the set of its elements $E$.

The elements of an abstract domain are related to the concrete domain $D$ (also a complete lattice), by means of a monotonic concretization function $\gamma \in [\bar{D} \to D]$. In this paper we assume the concrete domain to be the complete boolean lattice $\mathcal{P}(\Sigma)$, where $\Sigma = [\text{Var} \to \mathbb{Z}]$.

Given two abstract domains, $\bar{D}_1$ and $\bar{D}_2$, their reduced cartesian product is $\bar{D}_1 \otimes \bar{D}_2$, whose elements are pairs which satisfy the reduction condition:

$$\forall \langle \bar{d}_1, \bar{d}_2 \rangle \in \bar{D}_1 \otimes \bar{D}_2.\ \gamma_{\bar{D}_1 \otimes \bar{D}_2}(\langle \bar{d}_1, \bar{d}_2 \rangle) \subseteq \gamma_{\bar{D}_1}(\bar{d}_1) \cap \gamma_{\bar{D}_2}(\bar{d}_2)\ .$$

An abstract domain is said to be *relational* if it keeps relations between program variables. Otherwise it is said to be *non-relational*.

The elements of the abstract domain of intervals, Intv, are $\{[i, s] \mid i, s \in \mathbb{Z} \cup \{-\infty, +\infty\}\}$. The concretization function, $\gamma_{\text{Intv}} \in [\text{Intv} \to \mathcal{P}(\mathbb{Z})]$ is defined as $\gamma_{\text{Intv}}([i, s]) = \{z \in \mathbb{Z} \mid i \le z \le s\}$. The abstract domain of boxes, Boxes, is the functional lifting of Intv, *i.e.*, Boxes $= [\text{Vars} \to \text{Intv}]$. The concretization of a box, $\gamma_{\text{Boxes}} \in [\text{Boxes} \to \mathcal{P}(\Sigma)]$ is defined as $\gamma_{\text{Boxes}}(f) = \{\sigma \in \Sigma \mid \forall \text{x}.\text{x} \in \text{dom}(f) \implies \sigma(\text{x}) \in \gamma_{\text{Intv}}(f(\text{x}))\}$. From the definition of $\gamma_{\text{Boxes}}$, it follows that the meaning of a variables in Boxes is independent from all the others, which implies that Boxes is a non-relational abstract domain. The time and space complexity of the operations on Boxes is $\mathcal{O}(n)$, where $n$ is the number of variables.

The abstract domain of Polyhedra, Poly [9], captures linear constraints between program variables: $\sum_{i=0}^{i<n} a_i * \text{x}_i \le z$, with $a_i, z \in \mathbb{Z}$. The concretization function $\gamma_{\text{Poly}} \in [\text{Poly} \to \mathcal{P}(\Sigma)]$ is defined as the intersection of all the constraints : $\gamma_{\text{Poly}}(P) = \bigcap_{\sum_{i=0}^{i<n} a_i * \text{x}_i \le z \in P} \{\sigma \in \Sigma \mid \sum_{i=0}^{i<n} a_i * \sigma(\text{x}_i) \le z\}$. From the concretization function, it follows that Poly can capture properties between an arbitrary number of variables, thus it is a relational domain. The complexity of Poly is $\mathcal{O}(2^n)$ both in space and time.

## 3.2   Transfer Functions

Abstract interpreters implement an upper approximation $\bar{\tau}$ of the best abstract transformer $\bar{\tau}^*$, *i.e.* $\forall \bar{d} \in \bar{D}.\ \bar{\tau}^*(\bar{d}) \sqsubseteq \bar{\tau}(\bar{d})$. An abstract transfer function $\bar{\tau}$ is (i) usually hand-crafted, and (ii) tuned to maximize the precision/cost trade-off.

It is common practice for the implementation of an abstract domain $\bar{D}$ to provide two abstract transfer functions: one for the assignment and one for the handling of tests [5,18,28]. The assignment abstract transfer function, $\bar{D}.\mathsf{assign}$, is an over-approximation of the states reached with the concrete assignment:

$$\forall x, e.\forall \bar{d}.\ \{\sigma[x \mapsto v] \mid \sigma \in \gamma(\bar{d}), [\![e]\!](\sigma) = v\} \subseteq \gamma(\bar{D}.\mathsf{assign}(\bar{d}, x, e)).$$

The test abstract transfer function, $\bar{D}.\mathsf{test}$, acts as a kind of filter to the input states:

$$\forall e.\forall \bar{d}.\ \{\sigma \in \gamma(\bar{d}) \mid [\![e]\!](\sigma) \neq 0\} \subseteq \gamma(\bar{D}.\mathsf{test}(\bar{d}, e)).$$

It is vital for a PSA to provide a precise approximation of $\mathsf{test}$.

# 4   Relative Completeness of Precise Analysis of Bytecode

In this section, we define a generic abstract semantics for the high level language, $\bar{\mathbb{H}}[\![\cdot]\!] \in [\mathtt{Stm} \to \bar{D} \to \bar{D}]$, by structural induction. In parallel, we define the abstract semantics for the low level language, $\bar{\mathbb{L}}[\![\cdot]\!] \in [\mathtt{IstrStream} \to \bar{D} \to \bar{D}]$. For each kind of statement and expression, we (i) express whether and under what conditions $\bar{\mathbb{L}}[\![\cdot]\!]$ is complete w.r.t. $\bar{\mathbb{H}}[\![\cdot]\!]$, *i.e.*, when $\bar{\mathbb{L}}[\![\cdot]\!]$ is as precise as $\bar{\mathbb{H}}[\![\cdot]\!]$, and (ii) show how best to overcome precision problems, *e.g.*, by refining the abstract domain or the transfer functions.

## 4.1   Notions of Relative Completeness

We distinguish two notions of relative completeness: strong and weak. Strong relative completeness requires the low-level analysis not to lose information when using the *same* abstract domain. Weak relative completeness allows the low-level analysis to use a *refinement* of the abstract domain used at source level.

**Definition 1 (Strong Relative Completeness).** *Given statement* Stm, *abstract domain* $\bar{D}$, *and projection function* $\pi \in [\bar{D} \to \bar{D}]$, *which removes all the temporary variables introduced by compilation, if*

$$\forall \bar{d} \in \bar{D}.\ \pi(\bar{\mathbb{L}}[\![\mathcal{C}(\mathtt{Stm})]\!](\bar{d})) \sqsubseteq \bar{\mathbb{H}}[\![\mathtt{Stm}]\!](\bar{d}), \qquad (1)$$

*then* $\bar{\mathbb{L}}[\![\cdot]\!]$ *is strong-relatively complete w.r.t. to* $\bar{\mathbb{H}}[\![\cdot]\!]$ *for statement* Stm.

Note that the definition above does not require equality of precision, only subsumption. It may be the case that the analysis at the bytecode level is more precise in some cases.

**Definition 2 (Weak Relative Completeness).** *Given statement* Stm, *two abstract domains* $\bar{D}$ *and* $\bar{D}^+$ *such that* $\bar{D}^+$ *is more precise than* $\bar{D}$ : $\bar{D}^+ \xrightarrow[\alpha]{\gamma} \bar{D}$, *and projection function* $\pi \in [\bar{D}^+ \to \bar{D}^+]$, *which removes all the temporary variables introduced by compilation, if*

$$\forall \bar{d} \in \bar{D}.\ \alpha(\pi(\bar{\mathbb{L}}[\![\mathcal{C}(\mathtt{Stm})]\!](\gamma(\bar{d})))) \sqsubseteq \bar{\mathbb{H}}[\![\mathtt{Stm}]\!](\bar{d}), \tag{2}$$

*then* $\bar{\mathbb{L}}[\![\cdot]\!]$ *is weak-relatively complete w.r.t. to* $\bar{\mathbb{H}}[\![\cdot]\!]$ *for statement* Stm *up to the refined domain* $\bar{D}^+$.

Weak relative completeness relaxes the previous definition by enabling the use of a more precise abstract domain for the analysis of the bytecode. It is evident that strong relative completeness implies weak relative completeness.

## 4.2  Skip

Handling of skip is straightforward: $\bar{\mathbb{H}}[\![\mathtt{skip}]\!] = \lambda\bar{d}.\bar{d}$. The skip statement is compiled with a nop: $\mathcal{C}(\mathtt{skip}) = n : \mathtt{nop}$, and $\bar{\mathbb{L}}[\![n : \mathtt{nop}]\!] = \lambda\bar{d}.\bar{d}$. As a consequence, in this case the bytecode analysis is trivially strongly complete.

## 4.3  Sequence

The analysis of a sequence of statements is usually just the composition of the analyses:

$$\bar{\mathbb{H}}[\![\mathtt{Stm_1 Stm_2}]\!] = \bar{\mathbb{H}}[\![\mathtt{Stm_2}]\!] \circ \bar{\mathbb{H}}[\![\mathtt{Stm_1}]\!]. \tag{3}$$

The compilation is the juxtaposition of two sequences of instructions:

$$\mathcal{C}(\mathtt{Stm_1 Stm_2}) = \begin{bmatrix} \mathcal{C}(\mathtt{Stm_1}) \\ \mathcal{C}(\mathtt{Stm_2}) \end{bmatrix}.$$

The abstract semantics of a sequence of instructions is the compositions of the analyses:

$$\bar{\mathbb{L}}[\![k : \mathtt{Istr} \ '\backslash n' \ \mathtt{IstrStream}]\!] = \bar{\mathbb{L}}[\![\mathtt{IstrStream}]\!] \circ \bar{\mathbb{L}}[\![k : \mathtt{Istr}]\!]. \tag{4}$$

Assuming that low-level analysis is complete (resp. weakly complete) for the subsequences, from (i) the fact that projection is an abstraction; and (ii) the monotonicity of the abstract functions, it follows that the low-level analysis of the sequence is complete (resp. weakly complete) w.r.t. the high-level analysis.

Note that in general, sequencing may cause loss of precision for both high- and low-level analysis w.r.t. the concrete semantics.

## 4.4  Assignments

A source language analysis just passes the assignment to the underlying abstract domain $\bar{D}$:

$$\bar{\mathbb{H}}[\![\mathtt{x} := \mathtt{e};]\!] = \lambda\bar{d}.\bar{D}.\mathtt{assign}(\bar{d}, \mathtt{x}, \mathtt{e}). \tag{5}$$

The compilation of the assignment generates a sequence of instructions to evaluate e, and an assignment of the result to x:

$$\mathcal{C}(x := e; ) = \begin{bmatrix} \mathcal{C}_e(e) \\ k : x \leftarrow \mathbf{res} \end{bmatrix} \quad . \tag{6}$$

Without loss of generality, we will assume in the sequel that the last instruction of $\mathcal{C}_e(e)$ assigns directly to the target variable x instead of $\mathbf{res}$. Thus, the final assignment is similarly passed to underlying abstract domain:

$$\bar{\mathbb{L}}[\![k : x \leftarrow e2op]\!] = \lambda\sigma.\bar{\mathsf{D}}.\mathsf{assign}(\sigma, x, e2op). \tag{7}$$

If the source expression e is such that $e \equiv 1$ or $e \equiv 1_1 op\, 1_2$, where $1, 1_1, 1_2 \in \mathsf{Lit}$, and op is as in Fig. 1, then (5), (6) and (7) imply the strong relative completeness of $\bar{\mathbb{L}}[\![k : x \leftarrow e2op]\!]$. However, this is not the case for more complex expressions, as the next (counter-) examples show.

*Example 2 (Precision Loss using Interval Arithmetic).* Suppose we use the Boxes domain to analyze the assignment $\mathcal{A} \equiv z := (x+y)*y$. Let $\bar{b}_0 = [x \mapsto [2,3], y \mapsto [-1,1]]$ be the abstract input state. Then

$$\bar{\mathbb{H}}[\![z := (x+y)*y;]\!](\bar{b}_0) = \bar{b}_0[z \mapsto [-2,4]],$$

using a specialized source transfer function. On the other hand, the compilation of $\mathcal{A}$ is

$$\mathcal{C}(z := (x+y)*y; ) = \begin{bmatrix} 0 : t \leftarrow x + y \\ 1 : z \leftarrow t * y \end{bmatrix}, \tag{8}$$

so that the abstract state after the program point 0 is $\bar{b}_0[t \mapsto [1,4]]$, and hence the abstract post-state is $\bar{\mathbb{L}}[\![\mathcal{C}(z := (x+y)*y; )]\!](\bar{b}_0) = \bar{b}_0[t \mapsto [1,4], z \mapsto [-4,4]]$.                                         □

The example shows that the analysis of the compiled code introduces a loss of precision w.r.t. to a specialized source level transfer function. Intuitively, it is caused by the fact that the domain Boxes is non-relational, and hence at program point 1 it has lost the information that t depends on y, so that two spurious cases are introduced.

As the incompleteness originates from the use of a non-relational numerical domain, one may advocate the usage of a relational domain. If we chose to analyze (8) with Oct, the problem, unfortunately, does not go away. At program point 0, we have an assignment that involves *three* variables. The domain cannot track the relation between t, x and y. As a consequence, no improvement is obtained at 1 using Octagons.

If we chose instead to analyze (8) with Poly, then the assignment at 0 can be precisely captured by this domain. So the abstract post-state is $\bar{p} = \{2 \leq x \leq 3, -1 \leq x \leq 1, t - x - y = 0\}$. The instruction at 1 involves a quadratic expression (the multiplication of two variables), which a naive implementation of Poly.assign may simply decide to ignore. However, it is easy to see how a more refined implementation can figure out that, because of $\bar{p}$, $t = x + y$ it can use this equality to simplify the multiplication and infer the tightest lower bound $-2 \leq z$, and hence satisfy (2).

*Example 3 (Precision Loss using Octagons).* Let us analyze the assignment $\mathcal{B} \equiv$ $z := 2*x - y$; with the Oct domain. Let the initial abstract state be $\bar{o}_0 = \{x - y \leq 1, y - x \leq -1\}$. Even if the source expression is not in the octagonal form, the designer of the domain can refine Oct.assign (i) to replace $x$ in the right hand side of the $\mathcal{B}$ by $y - 1$, and (ii) to perform the basic algebraic simplifications, so that

$$\bar{\mathbb{H}}[\![z := 2*x - y;]\!](\bar{o}_0) = \bar{o}_0 \cup \{z - y \leq 2, y - z \leq -2\}.$$

On the other hand, the compilation of $\mathcal{B}$ is

$$\mathcal{C}(z := 2*x - y;) = \begin{bmatrix} 0 : t \leftarrow 2*x \\ 1 : z \leftarrow t - y \end{bmatrix}. \tag{9}$$

At program point 0, there is no way one can refine Oct.assign to provide an octagonal constraint for $t$. For instance, the substitution of $x$ by $y - 1$ produces $t \leftarrow 2*y - 2$, which cannot be represented by an octagon constraint, too. As a consequence, no constraint can be inferred on $t$ and hence $z$: $\bar{\mathbb{L}}[\![\mathcal{C}(z := 2*x - y;)]\!](\bar{o}_0) = \bar{o}_0$. □

Intuitively, the precision loss in the previous example is caused by splitting "large" expressions into smaller chunks, thereby reducing the expression window seen by the atomic operations in the abstract domain, and hence limiting their ability to infer relations.

If we chose instead to analyze (9) with Poly, then both assignments at program points 0 and 1 are linear constraints that are represented exactly by this abstract domain. As a consequence, the low-level analysis, when performed on a more precise abstract domain is (weak-relatively) complete.

**Discussion: Choosing the Right Abstract Domain.** The previous examples suggest that we can obtain weak completeness by systematically using Poly. This is the direction taken by some analyzers for low-level code, *e.g.*, [11,20,4]. We do not advocate this approach, as Poly exhibits an exponential complexity in practice (in the number of variables). In order to overcome this issue in Clousot, we have chosen to not refine directly the numerical domain $\bar{D}$, but to combine it with a symbolic domain Symb to propagate expressions, [1,24]. In other words the analysis is done on the refined abstract domain $Symb \otimes \bar{D}$. The analysis of $k : z \leftarrow e2op$ with an abstract element $\langle \bar{s}, \bar{d} \rangle$, first uses $\bar{s}$ to refine e2op to an expression $e2op^+$, then it performs the assignment over the basic numerical domain: $\bar{D}.assign(\bar{d}, z, e2op^+)$.

## 4.5  Assumptions and Assertions

We consider just the **assume** statement, the case for **assert** being similar. At source level, the PSA just passes the expression to be assumed to the underlying domain:

$$\bar{\mathbb{H}}[\![\text{assume } e;]\!] = \lambda \bar{d}.\bar{D}.test(\bar{d}, e).$$

The compilation generates code to evaluate the condition $e$, and it assumes the result:

$$\mathcal{C}(\texttt{assume e; }) = \begin{bmatrix} \mathcal{C}_e(\texttt{e}) \\ k : \texttt{assume res} \end{bmatrix} . \tag{10}$$

The bytecode semantics passes the literal to the underlying abstract domain:

$$\bar{\mathbb{L}}[\![k : \texttt{assume 1}]\!] = \lambda\bar{\texttt{d}} \in \bar{\texttt{D}}.\texttt{test}(\bar{\texttt{d}}, 1).$$

The compilation schema (10), which is common to *e.g.*, the C# and Java compilers, introduces severe imprecision in analyses, as illustrated by Ex. 1 and by:

*Example 4 (Precision Loss in Tests).* Consider the statement $\mathcal{D} \equiv \texttt{assume } 0 \leq$ x; to be analyzed with Oct, in the initial state $\top_{\text{Oct}} = \emptyset$. Then, $\bar{\mathbb{H}}[\![\texttt{assume } 0 \leq \texttt{x;}]\!](\top_{\text{Oct}}) = \{-\texttt{x} \leq 0\}$. The compilation of $\mathcal{D}$ is

$$\mathcal{C}(\texttt{assume } 0 \leq \texttt{x; }) = \begin{bmatrix} 0 : \texttt{res} \leftarrow 0 \leq \texttt{x} \\ 1 : \texttt{assume res} \end{bmatrix} . \tag{11}$$

At program point 0, res is assigned the result of evaluating the boolean condition. Since nothing is known in the input state about x, nothing can be concluded about the truth of $0 \leq \texttt{x}$, and hence res is unconstrained. As a consequence, $\bar{\mathbb{L}}[\![\mathcal{C}(\texttt{assume } 0 \leq \texttt{x; })]\!](\top_{\text{Oct}}) = \top_{\text{Oct}}$. □

The previous example shows that strong relative completeness does not hold. If we analyze (11) with Poly, the situation does not change, because even Poly cannot capture the relation between a variable and the truth value of an expression. Thus, if we seek weak relative completeness, we need to refine the abstract domain with either an abstract domain for tracking boolean expressions, or more generally use the symbolic abstract domain Symb introduced in Sect 4.4 to "reconstruct" larger expressions, that can then be passed to the underlying numerical abstract domain.

Whereas in Sect 4.4 the use of Symb was just an alternative w.r.t. the use of a more precise numerical domain, it becomes a *necessity* for handling boolean expressions. The use of the symbolic domain during low-level analysis requires a refinement of the transfer functions, as shown by the next example.

*Example 5 (Precision Loss Induced by Compilation).* Consider a slight modification of the previous example: $\mathcal{F} \equiv \texttt{assume !}(0 \leq \texttt{x})$; to be analyzed with Oct, in the entry state $\top_{\text{Oct}}$. $\bar{\mathbb{H}}[\![\texttt{assume !}(0 \leq \texttt{x});]\!](\top_{\text{Oct}}) = \{\texttt{x} \leq -1\}$. The compilation of $\mathcal{F}$ (*e.g.*, by C#) is

$$\mathcal{C}(\texttt{assume !}(0 \leq \texttt{x}); ) = \begin{bmatrix} 0 : \texttt{t} \leftarrow 0 \leq \texttt{x} \\ 1 : \texttt{res} \leftarrow \texttt{t} == 0 \\ 2 : \texttt{assume res} \end{bmatrix} . \tag{12}$$

At program point 2, the analysis of the compiled code, using the refined domain Symb $\otimes$ Oct infers the abstract state $\bar{r} = \langle [\texttt{t} \mapsto 0 \leq \texttt{x}, \texttt{res} \mapsto \texttt{t} == 0], \top_{\text{Oct}} \rangle$. Then, res is refined to the expression $\texttt{res}^+ \equiv (0 \leq \texttt{x}) == 0$, which cannot be generated by the syntax in Fig. 1. As a consequence, Oct.assign,

designed for the high level, does not understand $\mathtt{res}^+$, and hence ignores it:
$$\bar{\mathbb{L}}[\![\mathcal{C}(\mathtt{assume}\ !(0 \leq \mathtt{x});)]\!](\langle \top_{\mathsf{Symb}}, \top_{\mathsf{Oct}} \rangle) = \bar{r}. \qquad \square$$

**Discussion: Refining the Transfer Functions, and Program Transformations.** The example above underlines the fact that, in order to obtain weak completeness, one must also refine the transfer functions. For instance, in the example Oct.assign must be refined to perform the semantic preserving rewritings $(0 \leq \mathtt{x}) == 0 \rightsquigarrow !(0 \leq \mathtt{x}) \rightsquigarrow \mathtt{x} < 0$.

In practice, a PSA designer has two choices: perform the rewriting phase online or offline. In the first case, a transfer function first rewrites the boolean expressions, *e.g.*, by applying the De Morgan laws, by rewriting $\mathtt{e} == 0$ as $!(\mathtt{e})$, etc., and then proceeds. In the second case, in a pre-processing step, a program $\mathcal{S}$ is analyzed with just Symb, all the expressions in $\mathcal{S}$ are first refined and then simplified as above, to obtain a refined program $\mathcal{S}^+$. Then, $\mathcal{S}^+$ is analyzed using $\bar{\mathsf{D}}$. In Clousot, we have adopted the first approach.

### 4.6  Conditionals

The analysis of conditional statements (i) refines the input abstract state with the guard, (ii) analyzes the two branches in the refined state, and (iii) joins the results at the exit point. Precise handling of guards is essential for a PSA.

$$\bar{\mathbb{H}}[\![\mathtt{if}(\mathtt{e})\ \{\mathtt{Stm}_1\}\mathtt{else}\ \{\mathtt{Stm}_2\};]\!] = \\ \lambda \bar{d}.\bar{\mathbb{H}}[\![\mathtt{Stm}_1]\!](\bar{\mathsf{D}}.\mathtt{test}(\bar{d}, \mathtt{e})) \sqcup \bar{\mathbb{H}}[\![\mathtt{Stm}_2]\!](\bar{\mathsf{D}}.\mathtt{test}(\bar{d}, !(\mathtt{e}))). \tag{13}$$

One possible compilation is:

$$\mathcal{C}(\mathtt{if}(\mathtt{e})\ \{\mathtt{Stm}_1\}\mathtt{else}\ \{\mathtt{Stm}_2\};) = \begin{bmatrix} \mathcal{C}_e(\mathtt{e}) \\ k : \mathtt{b} \leftarrow \mathtt{res} == 0 \\ k+1 : \mathtt{jmpIf}\ \mathtt{b}\ t \\ \mathcal{C}(\mathtt{Stm}_1) \\ \mathtt{jmp}\ out \\ t : \mathcal{C}(\mathtt{Stm}_2) \\ out : \mathtt{nop} \end{bmatrix}. \tag{14}$$

The low level analysis of (14) can be made very similar to (13), provided that some preprocessing of the bytecode is performed. The first step is to construct the control flow graph from (14), as in Fig. 3. However, that is not enough, because one wants to know that $!(\mathtt{b})$ (resp. $\mathtt{b}$) holds at program point $k+2$ (resp. $t$). Propagating such an information during a dataflow analysis is non-trivial.

A better approach is to provide another view of the code (14), in which the guard of the conditional is made explicit in the true-branch and the false-branch as assume statements. This is the direction we have taken in Clousot. In general, let $\boxed{\mathtt{B}}$ the block which computes the truth value of the guard $\mathtt{e}$, $\boxed{\mathtt{T}(\mathtt{e})}$ and $\boxed{\mathtt{F}(\mathtt{e})}$ the (compilation of the) two branches of the conditional dominated by (resp.)

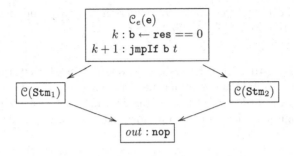

**Fig. 3.** The control flow graph constructed from $\mathcal{C}(\texttt{if(e)}\ \{\texttt{Stm}_1\}\texttt{else}\ \{\texttt{Stm}_2\};)$

`assume b` and `assume !(b)`, and $\boxed{0}$ be the exit block. Then the low level semantics can be defined as:

$$
\overline{\mathbb{L}}\left[\!\!\left[\ \begin{array}{c} \boxed{\text{B}} \\ \swarrow \quad \searrow \\ \boxed{\text{T(e)}} \qquad \boxed{\text{F(e)}} \\ \searrow \quad \swarrow \\ \boxed{0} \end{array}\ \right]\!\!\right] = 
\begin{array}{l}
\lambda \bar{r} \in \bar{\mathsf{D}} \otimes \mathsf{Symb}. \\
\text{let } \bar{r}_1 = \bar{\mathbb{L}}[\![\mathrm{B}]\!](\bar{r}) \text{ in} \\
\text{let } \bar{r}_t = \bar{\mathbb{L}}[\![\mathrm{T(e)}]\!]((\bar{\mathsf{D}} \otimes \mathsf{Symb}).\mathrm{test}(\bar{r}_1, \mathrm{e})) \text{ in} \\
\text{let } \bar{r}_f = \bar{\mathbb{L}}[\![\mathrm{F(e)}]\!]((\bar{\mathsf{D}} \otimes \mathsf{Symb}).\mathrm{test}(\bar{r}_1, !(\mathrm{e}))) \text{ in} \\
\text{in } \bar{r}_t \sqcup \bar{r}_f\ .
\end{array}
$$

$$(15)$$

However, incompleteness can still show up if the compilation scheme is different from (14), in particular for the handling of expressions. The next example is inspired by the way the C# compiler [21], generates code for shortcutting boolean expressions.

*Example 6 (Loss of Precision Induced by Compilation of Shortcut Expressions).* Let $\mathcal{G}$ be the code snippet `if(0 ≤ i && i < len) {Stm₁} else {Stm₂}`. The $C\#2.0$ compiler generates code that looks like the one in Fig. 4. Briefly, if one of the operands of `&&` is false, then it jumps to line 8, which sets `res` to 0 . Otherwise, it sets `res` to 1. The two flows are then merged at program point 9, which implies that `res == 0` and `res == 1` are joined, *i.e.*, the information about the truth of the guard, `res == 0 ⟺ !(0 ≤ i && i < len)` and `res == 1 ⟺ (0 ≤ i && i < len)` is lost. So it cannot be further propagated in the two branches of the conditional. □

The incompleteness in the previous example can be resolved either by precisely modeling the relation between boolean variables and boolean expressions with BDDs as in [15], or by approximating the double implication with a simple implication, *e.g.*, using trace partitioning, [13]. As a consequence, the underlying abstract domain must be refined to the reduced cardinal power $\mathcal{P}(\texttt{Lit}) \rightarrow (\bar{\mathsf{D}} \otimes \mathsf{Symb})$, so as to obtain the weak relative completeness for shortcut conditionals.

$$\mathcal{C}(\texttt{if}(0 \leq \texttt{i \&\& i} < \texttt{len}) \{\texttt{Stm}_1\}\texttt{else}\{\texttt{Stm}_2\}) =$$

$$
\begin{array}{lll}
0 : \texttt{t}_1 \leftarrow 0 \leq \texttt{i} & & 9 : \texttt{jmpIf res } k+1 \\
1 : \texttt{b}_1 \leftarrow \texttt{t}_1 == 0 & 5 : \texttt{jmpIf b}_2\ 8 & 10 : \mathcal{C}(\texttt{Stm}_2) \\
2 : \texttt{jmpIf b}_1\ 8 & 6 : \texttt{res} \leftarrow 1 & k : \texttt{jmp } out \\
3 : \texttt{t}_2 \leftarrow \texttt{i} < \texttt{len} & 7 : \texttt{jmp } 9 & k+1 : \mathcal{C}(\texttt{Stm}_1) \\
4 : \texttt{b}_2 \leftarrow \texttt{t}_2 == 0 & 8 : \texttt{res} \leftarrow 0 & out : \texttt{nop}
\end{array}
$$

**Fig. 4.** The (simplified version of the) code generated by the $C\#2.0$ compiler for the statement $\texttt{if}(0 \leq \texttt{i \&\& i} < \texttt{len}) \{\texttt{Stm}_1\}\texttt{else}\{\texttt{Stm}_2\}$

### 4.7 Loops

The semantics of a loop is given as a least fixpoint over a suitable partial order:

$$\bar{\mathbb{H}}[\![\texttt{while(e) \{ Stm \};}]\!] = \lambda\bar{\texttt{d}}.\ \text{let } \bar{\texttt{inv}} = \textsf{lfp}_{\bar{\perp}}^{\sqsubseteq}\lambda X.\ \bar{\texttt{d}} \sqcup \bar{\mathbb{H}}[\![\texttt{Stm}]\!](\bar{\texttt{D}}.\text{test}(X, \texttt{e}))$$
$$\text{in } \bar{\texttt{D}}.\text{test}(\bar{\texttt{inv}}, !(\texttt{e})).$$

The least fixpoint equals the limit of the increasing iterations starting from $\perp$. In general the iterations may not converge, so that a widening operator [8] is used to force convergence to a post-fixpoint. Then, a narrowing operator [8] is applied to recover some precision. An easy yet generic and useful form of narrowing is given by doing one more iteration starting from the post-fixpoint, as shown by the next example.

*Example 7 (Narrowing by Re-Execution).* Let $\mathcal{W} \equiv \texttt{z} := 0;\ \texttt{while(z} < 100)\ \{\ \texttt{z} := \texttt{z} + 1;\};\texttt{assert z} == 100;$ and let us analyze it with the Intv abstract domain. The fixpoint iterations produce the increasing chain of intervals $[0,0] \sqsubseteq [0,1] \sqsubseteq [0,2] \ldots \sqsubseteq [0,n]$, which is extrapolated by the standard widening on intervals to $[0,+\infty]$, so that $\texttt{inv}^\nabla = [\texttt{z} \mapsto [0,+\infty]]$ is an invariant for the loop. On the other hand, it is not precise enough to prove the assertion after the loop. By *first* re-executing the body starting from the fixpoint, one gets $[0,0] \sqcup [1,100] = [0,100]$, so that $\texttt{inv}^\Delta = [\texttt{z} \mapsto [0,100]]$. *Then,* $\texttt{inv}^\Delta$ intersected with the negation of the loop guard is enough to prove the assertion. $\square$

The compilation of a while statement looks like

$$
\mathcal{C}(\texttt{while(e) \{ Stm \}; }) =
\left[
\begin{array}{l}
b : \mathcal{C}_e(\texttt{e}) \\
k : \texttt{b} \leftarrow \texttt{res} == 0 \\
\phantom{k :}\ \texttt{jmpIf b } out \\
\phantom{k :}\ \mathcal{C}(\texttt{Stm}) \\
\phantom{k :}\ \texttt{jmp } b \\
out : \texttt{nop}
\end{array}
\right]. \tag{16}
$$

A typical analysis of the unstructured code above first detects the back edges, in order to find the program points where widening is needed. However, back edges detection is not enough to ensure relative completeness when extrapolating operators are used, as shown by the next example.

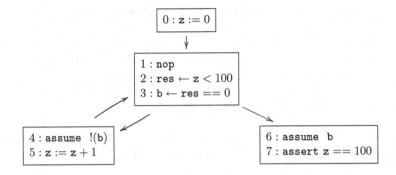

**Fig. 5.** The enhanced CFG graph for the three addresses compilation for the code in Ex. 7. Exact narrowing requires the knowledge that the left branch leads to a cycle.

*Example 8 (Narrowing by Re-Execution, continued).* The CFG graph for $\mathcal{W}$ is in Fig. 5. A standard back-edges analysis detects that the block starting at 1 is the target of a back edge, and hence the widening point. Then, we analyze the program on the domain $\mathsf{Intv} \otimes \mathsf{Symb}$, and we infer the invariant $z \mapsto [0, +\infty]$ at program point 1. Now we want to refine it using the re-execution based narrowing. In the source level case, we just proceeded by induction on the structure. At the low-level, we don't know which edge leads into the loop, and which edge leads out of the loop. If we push the invariant *first* onto the left branch (*i.e.*, on program point 4), then we obtain the desired refined $z \mapsto [0, 100]$, which is then pushed onto the right branch, where it is enough to prove the assertion is not violated. On the other hand, if we push the invariant *first* onto the right branch (*i.e.*, on program point 6), we obtain no invariant refinement.     □

The example shows that applying standard narrowing techniques from source level analysis is tricky on low-level code, as the necessary high-level loop structures are not apparent. Symbolic expression recovery is not sufficient, as control flow is involved. Thus, to obtain relative completeness for loops, some form of loop recovery must be performed.

## 5   Conclusions

We have presented a series of issues faced by low-level code analyzers if their precision is to match the precision typically achieved by a source analysis. We have formalized the relation between the low-level and high-level analyses via the concepts of strong and weak relative completeness. By analysis on the program constructs, we have shown: (i) how strong relative completeness can be obtained only for trivial cases, and (ii) how weak relative completeness can be obtained by refining the underlying domain for the analysis, the transfer functions, and by pre-processing of the program. However, it turns out that the refinement step must be handled with care by the designer of the precise static analysis, in order to avoid transforming a polynomial problem (*e.g.*, the analysis of the source program with Octagons) into an exponential one.

# References

1. Aho, A.V., Sethi, R., Ullman, J.D.: Compilers: Principles, Techniques, and Tools. Addison Wesley, Reading (1986)
2. Bagnara, R., Hill, P.M., Zaffanella, E.: The Parma Polyhedra Library., http://www.cs.unipr.it/ppl/
3. Balakrishnan, G., Reps, T.W.: Analyzing memory accesses in x86 executables. In: Duesterwald, E. (ed.) CC 2004. LNCS, vol. 2985, Springer, Heidelberg (2004)
4. Barnett, M., Chang, B.-Y.E., DeLine, R., Jacobs, B., Leino, K.R.M.: Boogie: A modular reusable verifier for Object-Oriented programs. In: de Boer, F.S., Bonsangue, M.M., Graf, S., de Roever, W.-P. (eds.) FMCO 2005. LNCS, vol. 4111, Springer, Heidelberg (2006)
5. Blanchet, B., Cousot, P., Cousot, R., Feret, J., Mauborgne, L., Miné, A., Monniaux, D., Rival, X.: A static analyzer for large safety-critical software. In: PLDI 2003, ACM Press, New York (2003)
6. Bourdoncle, F.: Abstract debugging of higher-order imperative languages. In: PLDI 2003, ACM Press, New York (1993)
7. Clarisó, R., Cortadella, J.: The octahedron abstract domain. In: Giacobazzi, R. (ed.) SAS 2004. LNCS, vol. 3148, Springer, Heidelberg (2004)
8. Cousot, P., Cousot, R.: Abstract interpretation: a unified lattice model for static analysis of programs by construction or approximation of fixpoints. In: POPL 1977, ACM Press, New York (1977)
9. Cousot, P., Halbwachs, N.: Automatic discovery of linear restraints among variables of a program. In: POPL 1978, ACM Press, New York (1978)
10. Fähndrich, M.A., Leino, K.R.M.: Declaring and checking non-null types in an Object-Oriented language. In: OOPSLA 2003, pp. 302–312. ACM Press, New York (2003)
11. Gopan, D., Reps, T.W.: Lookahead widening. In: Ball, T., Jones, R.B. (eds.) CAV 2006. LNCS, vol. 4144, Springer, Heidelberg (2006)
12. Granger, P.: Improving the results of static analyses programs by local decreasing iteration. In: FSTTCS, pp. 68–79. Springer, Heidelberg (1992)
13. Handjieva, M., Tzolovski, S.: Refining static analyses by trace-based partitioning using control flow. In: Levi, G. (ed.) SAS 1998. LNCS, vol. 1503, Springer, Heidelberg (1998)
14. ECMA Int. Standard ECMA-355, common language infrastructure (June 2006)
15. Jeannet, B.: Representing and approximating transfer functions in abstract interpretation of hetereogeneous datatypes. In: Hermenegildo, M.V., Puebla, G. (eds.) SAS 2002. LNCS, vol. 2477, Springer, Heidelberg (2002)
16. Leroy, X.: Bytecode verification on Java smart cards. Software - Practice and Experience (SPE) 32(4) (2002)
17. Lev-Ami, T., Manevich, R., Sagiv, S.: TVLA: A system for generating abstract interpreters. In: 18th IFIP Congress Topical Sessions, August 2004, Kluwer, Dordrecht (2004)
18. Logozzo, F.: Cibai: An abstract interpretation-based static analyzer for modular analysis and verification of Java classes. In: Cook, B., Podelski, A. (eds.) VMCAI 2007. LNCS, vol. 4349, Springer, Heidelberg (2007)

19. Logozzo, F., Fähndrich, M.A.: Pentagons: A weakly relational abstract domain for the efficient validation of array accesses. In: ACM SAC 2008 - OOPS, ACM Press, New York (2008)

20. Hermenegildo, M.V., Mendez, M., Navas, J.: An efficient, parametric fixpoint algorithm for analysis of Java bytecode. In: Bytecode 2007, Elsevier, Amsterdam (2007)

21. Microsoft Inc. Visual C#. http://msdn2.microsoft.com/-us/vcsharp/

22. Miné, A.: A new numerical abstract domain based on difference-bounds matrices. In: Danvy, O., Filinski, A. (eds.) PADO 2001. LNCS, vol. 2053, Springer, Heidelberg (2001)

23. Miné, A.: Weakly Relational Numerical Abstract Domains. PhD thesis, École Polytechnique (2004)

24. Miné, A.: Symbolic methods to enhance the precision of numerical abstract domains. In: Emerson, E.A., Namjoshi, K.S. (eds.) VMCAI 2006. LNCS, vol. 3855, Springer, Heidelberg (2005)

25. Palacz, K., Baker, J., Flack, C., Grothoff, C., Yamauchi, J., Vitek, H.: Engineering a common intermediate representation for Ovm framework. The Science of Computer Programming 57(3), 357–378 (2005)

26. RopasWork, Inc. Airac5, http://ropas.snu.ac.kr/airac5/

27. Rossignoli, S., Spoto, F.: Detecting non-cyclicity by abstract compilation into boolean functions. In: Emerson, E.A., Namjoshi, K.S. (eds.) VMCAI 2006. LNCS, vol. 3855, Springer, Heidelberg (2005)

28. Venet, A., Brat, G.P.: Precise and efficient static array bound checking for large embedded c programs. In: PLDI 2004, ACM Press, New York (2004)

# Efficiency, Precision, Simplicity, and Generality in Interprocedural Data Flow Analysis: Resurrecting the Classical Call Strings Method

Uday P. Khedker and Bageshri Karkare

Indian Institute of Technology, Bombay

**Abstract.** The full call strings method is the most general, simplest, and most precise method of performing context sensitive interprocedural data flow analysis. It remembers contexts using call strings. For full precision, all call strings up to a prescribed length must be constructed. Two limitations of this method are (a) it cannot be used for frameworks with infinite lattices, and (b) the prescribed length is quadratic in the size of the lattice resulting in an impractically large number of call strings. These limitations have resulted in a proliferation of ad hoc methods which compromise on generality, precision, or simplicity.

We propose a variant of the classical full call strings method which reduces the number of call strings, and hence the analysis time, by orders of magnitude as corroborated by our empirical measurements. It reduces the worst case call string length from quadratic in the size of the lattice to linear. Further, unlike the classical method, this worst case length need not be reached. Our approach retains the precision, generality, and simplicity of call strings method without imposing any additional constraints. It can accommodate demand-driven approximations and hence can be used for frameworks with infinite lattices.

## 1 Introduction

Interprocedural data flow analysis extends the scope of analysis across procedure boundaries. A *context insensitive* interprocedural analysis does not distinguish between different calling contexts of a procedure and merges the data flow information across all contexts. *Context sensitive* analysis maintains separate data flow information for distinct contexts for each procedure call and hence typically computes a more precise solution.

The full call strings method [22] is the most general, simplest, and most precise method of performing context sensitive interprocedural data flow analysis. It represents context information in the form of a call string. For full precision, all call strings up to a prescribed length have to be constructed. Two limitations of this method are (a) it cannot be used for frameworks with infinite lattices, and (b) the prescribed length is quadratic in the size of the lattice resulting in an impractically large number of call strings. These limitations have resulted in a proliferation of ad hoc methods which compromise on generality, precision, or simplicity.

We modify the full call string method by identifying contexts which need not be explicitly maintained. This reduces the number of contexts dramatically without compromising on the precision, generality, and simplicity of the method. The worst case

L. Hendren (Ed.): CC 2008, LNCS 4959, pp. 213–228, 2008.
© Springer-Verlag Berlin Heidelberg 2008

call string length is reduced from quadratic in the size of the lattice to linear. Further, unlike the original method, our variant does not need to construct all call strings up to the worst case length. Since it can accommodate demand-driven approximations, it can be used for frameworks with infinite lattices also. Our empirical measurements show a dramatic reduction in the number of call strings and analysis time.

Interestingly, we achieve all of the above by a very simple change in the original method without affecting the essential principles of the method: In our variant, the termination of call string construction is based on the equivalence of data flow values instead of prescribed lengths. This allows us to discard call strings where they are redundant, and regenerate them when required. For cyclic call strings, regeneration facilitates iterative computation of data flow values without explicitly constructing most of the call strings. This is based on interesting insights which are explained intuitively and proved formally in this paper.

The rest of the paper is organized as follows: Section 2 provides the background, Section 3 investigates the reasons of inefficiency in call strings method and sets the stage for Section 4 which proposes our variant. Section 5 compares our work with other approaches to interprocedural analysis. Section 6 presents the empirical data and Section 7 concludes the paper.

## 2   Background

This section discusses safety, precision, and efficiency in the interprocedural analysis and reviews the original call strings method.

***Safety, Precision, and Efficiency in Data Flow Analysis.***   Data flow analysis examines static representations of programs. Some paths in these representations may not correspond to valid execution paths. Some path may be valid execution paths but may be irrelevant because their analysis may not result in new information. Safety of analysis can be ensured by covering all valid paths; excluding a valid path may result in an unsafe solution. Precision can be ensured by restricting the analysis only to valid paths; including invalid paths may result in an imprecise solution. Efficiency can be ensured by restricting the analysis to relevant paths.

A *flow sensitive* intraprocedural analysis honours the control flow and computes possibly different data flow information for each program point. A *flow insensitive* analysis does not consider the control flow and hence computes imprecise (but safe) solution. A flow sensitive method excludes spurious paths and hence computes more precise solutions. A flow insensitive analysis merely accumulates the information and hence requires a single pass over a control flow graph.

Interprocedural data flow analysis is usually performed on a *supergraph* which connects control flow graphs of different procedures with call and return edges. It contains control flow paths which violate nestings of matching call return pairs. An interprocedurally valid path is a feasible execution path containing a legal sequence of call and return edges. A *context sensitive* interprocedural analysis retains distinct calling contexts to ensure propagation of information from the callee to appropriate callers. This involves restricting the analysis to interprocedurally valid paths. A *context insensitive*

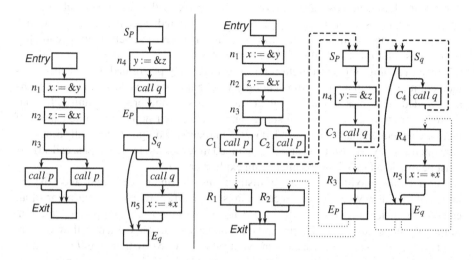

**Fig. 1.** Control flow graphs of recursive procedures and the corresponding supergraph

analysis does not distinguish between valid and invalid paths and computes safe, but imprecise solution compared to a context sensitive analysis. For maximum statically achievable precision, context sensitive analysis must also be flow sensitive at the intraprocedural level. Efficiency of context sensitive interprocedural analysis requires restricting the number of contexts without merging information across distinct contexts. Context insensitive analysis effectively restricts the number of contexts to one and thus is much more efficient than context sensitive analysis.

***The Call Strings Approach.*** The full call strings method embeds context information in the data flow information. It treats procedure calls and returns similar to the intraprocedural control transfers and ensures the validity of interprocedural paths by maintaining a history of calls in terms of call strings. A *call string* at a program point $u$ is a sequence $c_1 c_2 \ldots c_k$ of call sites corresponding to unfinished calls at $u$ and can be viewed as a snapshot of the call stack at $u$; $\lambda$ denotes an empty call string. Figure 1 shows a program and its supergraph. $S_p$ and $E_p$ denote the start and end of procedure $p$ while those for the main program are *Entry* and *Exit*. A call site $c_i$ is split into a call node $C_i$ and the corresponding return node $R_i$ and appropriate call and return edges are added. Some call strings for this program are $\lambda$, $c_1$, $c_1 c_3$, $c_1 c_3 c_4$, $c_1 c_3 c_4 c_4$ etc.

Call string construction is governed by the interprocedural edges in a supergraph. Let $\sigma$ be a call string reaching node $m$ in procedure $p$. For an intraprocedural edge $m \to n$, $\sigma$ reaches $n$ unmodified. For a call edge $m \to n$ where $m$ is $C_i$ and $n$ is $S_q$, call string $\sigma \cdot c_i$ reaches $S_q$. For a return edge $m \to n$ where $m$ is $E_p$ and $n$ is $R_i$, if the last call site in $\sigma$ is $c_i$ then the call string remaining after removing $c_i$ from $\sigma$ reaches $R_i$. This ensures that the data flow information is propagated to the correct caller.

The augmented data flow information is a pair $\langle \sigma, d \rangle$ where $d$ is the data flow value propagated along call string $\sigma$. Note that $d$ is modified by an intraprocedural edge only.

A work list based iterative algorithm is used to perform the data flow analysis. The process terminates when no new pair $\langle \sigma, d \rangle$ is computed; merging data flow values propagated along all call strings reaching $u$ results in a meet-over-all-interprocedurally-valid-paths solution at $u$ for distributive frameworks.

Since matching of call and return nodes is inherently performed in the call strings method, it ensures that all interprocedurally valid paths are traversed and invalid paths are avoided. Thus use of call strings guarantees a safe and precise solution. In non-recursive programs, since the call strings are acyclic, their number is finite and all of them are generated during analysis. However, in recursive program, new call strings are generated with every visit to a call node involved in recursion. In such cases, call strings must be restricted to a finite number using explicit criteria.

Let $K$ be the maximum number of distinct call sites in any call chain and $L$ be the lattice of data flow values. The full call strings method [22] requires construction of all call strings of length up to $K \times (|L| + 1)^2$ for computing a safe and precise solution. Intuitively, the argument by Sharir can be explained as follows: Let a data flow value at call node $C_i$ be $v_i$ and the corresponding value at $R_i$ be $v_i'$. Since there are $|L| + 1$ values for $v_i$ and $v_i'$ (due to presence of a fictitious value $\Omega$), $(|L| + 1)^2$ distinct combinations are possible, for which $(|L| + 1)^2$ distinct call strings are required. If $c_i$ is in recursion, $(|L| + 1)^2$ occurrences of $c_i$ guarantee that all these call strings are generated and hence guarantee all possible computations. Since there can be $K$ distinct call sites, call strings of length $K \times (|L| + 1)^2$ ensure that all possible data flow values are computed. For separable frameworks, the prescribed length reduces to $K \times (|\widehat{L}| + 1)^2$ where $\widehat{L}$ is the component lattice for an entity. For bit-vector frameworks, this length is $3 \times K$.

## 3    Efficiency of Call Strings Approach

This section discusses the factors affecting the efficiency of the classical full call strings method.

*Orthogonality of Call Strings and Data Flow Values.* Analysis of non-recursive programs constructs a finite number of call strings and the termination of analysis is governed solely by the convergence of data flow values. In recursive programs, termination of call string construction needs to be ensured explicitly. Once the termination of call strings is ensured, the usual fixed point criterion can be applied to data flow values to ensure the termination of analysis exactly as in iterative intraprocedural analysis.

In the classical full call strings method, call string construction is terminated by truncating call strings at a prescribed length. We ask the following question: Is it possible to use data flow values instead of a prescribed length to bound the cyclic call strings? Intuitively, a criterion can be devised to stop the construction of new call strings when the old values repeat along cyclic call strings. But this further raises questions regarding safety and precision: Do the call strings thus terminated ensure traversing all interprocedurally valid paths and avoiding all invalid paths? We answer these questions by characterizing the minimal set of call strings required for recursive procedures.

Let the cyclic call sequence be $c_x \cdot c_{x+1} \cdots c_{x+y} \cdots \equiv \sigma_c$. Let the flow function along the cyclic call sequence be $f$, along cyclic return sequence be $g$, and that along the recursion ending path be $h$. The prescribed length is $m$.

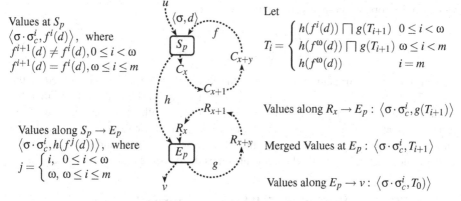

Values at $S_p$
$\langle \sigma \cdot \sigma_c^i, f^i(d) \rangle$, where
$f^{i+1}(d) \neq f^i(d), 0 \leq i < \omega$
$f^{i+1}(d) = f^i(d), \omega \leq i \leq m$

Let
$$T_i = \begin{cases} h(f^i(d)) \sqcap g(T_{i+1}) & 0 \leq i < \omega \\ h(f^\omega(d)) \sqcap g(T_{i+1}) & \omega \leq i < m \\ h(f^\omega(d)) & i = m \end{cases}$$

Values along $R_x \to E_p$ : $\langle \sigma \cdot \sigma_c^i, g(T_{i+1}) \rangle$

Values along $S_p \to E_p$
$\langle \sigma \cdot \sigma_c^i, h(f^j(d)) \rangle$, where
$j = \begin{cases} i, & 0 \leq i < \omega \\ \omega, & \omega \leq i \leq m \end{cases}$

Merged Values at $E_p$ : $\langle \sigma \cdot \sigma_c^i, T_{i+1} \rangle$

Values along $E_p \to v$ : $\langle \sigma \cdot \sigma_c^i, T_0 \rangle$

**Fig. 2.** Modeling recursion for call strings. $\sigma_c$ may have multiple occurrence of a call node and hence can be any arbitrary recursive call sequence. Though the recursion ending path has been shown in procedure $p$ it may not exist in $p$ but in some other procedure in recursion.

***Issues in Terminating Call String Construction for Recursive Programs.*** The prescribed length defined in the classical method is based on a crude estimate to ensure complete analysis in both call and return sequences as explained below. Hence many cyclic call strings generated using the prescribed length are redundant in that they carry the same data flow information as some shorter call strings.

Consider the situation in Figure 2 which models a recursive call. The strongly connected component consisting of call nodes $(C_x, C_{x+1}, \ldots, C_{x+y})$ is a *cyclic call sequence* and is denoted by $\sigma_c$. The corresponding *cyclic return sequence* $(R_{x+y}, \ldots, R_{x+1}, R_x)$ forms another strongly connected component which we denote by $\sigma_r$. The dashed line from $S_p$ to $E_p$ represents the recursion ending control flow path. In a valid interprocedural path involving $\sigma_c$ and $\sigma_r$, $\sigma_c$ is traversed at least as many times as $\sigma_r$. Observe that we do not require the call sites along a cyclic call sequence to be distinct. Thus this figure models a general recursive path. We have shown the recursion ending path in procedure $p$ but as Corollary 1 shows, it does not matter if this path exists in some other procedure in recursive call chain.

Each application of $g$ requires traversing the cyclic return sequence once. In the process, the last occurrence of $\sigma_c$ is removed from every call string. Thus, $g$ can be applied only as many times as the maximum number of $\sigma_c$ in any call string reaching the entry of $E_p$. Note that the application of $f$ does not have such a requirement because the call strings are constructed rather than consumed while applying $f$. Achieving safety and precision in call strings method requires the following:

*Precision.* In any path from $S_p$ to $E_p$, the number of applications of $g$ should not exceed that of $f$. This is ensured by the call string construction algorithm implying that only interprocedurally valid paths are considered.

*Safety.* In order to guarantee safety, the call strings should be long enough to allow computation of all possible data flow values in both cyclic call and return sequences. In a cyclic call sequence this is guaranteed by constructing call strings $\sigma \cdot \sigma_c^i$, $0 \leq i \leq \omega$. If we select $m$ that is large enough to allow for computation of all possible values of the following recurrence then these call strings also guarantee convergence of data flow values in the corresponding cyclic return sequence.

$$T_i = \begin{cases} h(f^\omega(d)) \sqcap g(T_{i+1}) & \omega \leq i < m \\ h(f^\omega(d)) & i = m \end{cases} \tag{1}$$

Note that the computation starts from the last call string and is performed in the order: $T_m, T_{m-1}, \ldots, T_{m-\omega+1}, T_{m-\omega}$. The convergence lemma (Lemma 3) shows that this sequence follows a strictly descending chain. Let the length of this chain be $\eta$. Then $m$ should be at least $\omega + \eta$. If $m < \omega + \eta$, then some data flow values corresponding to unbounded recursion may not be computed. Since the values of $\omega$ and $\eta$ are not known a priori, the classical prescribed length subsumes the possible worst case scenarios.

## 4   An Efficient Variant of Call Strings Approach

This section presents the proposed variant of call strings method.

### 4.1   Concepts and Notations

A program point $v$ is *context dependent* on program point $u$ if (a) there is a path from $u$ to $v$ which is a subpath of an interprocedurally valid path from *Entry* to $v$, and (b) on every such path from $u$ to $v$, every occurrence of an $E_p$ is matched by a corresponding occurrence of $S_p$. For a procedure $p$, all program points within $p$ and all program points within all callees in every call chain starting in $p$, are context dependent on $S_p$.

We view call and return nodes as being *significant* nodes. When $v$ is context dependent on $u$, a *context defining path* from $u$ to $v$ is a sequence of significant nodes appearing in a path from $u$ to $v$ such that this path is a subpath of a valid interprocedural path from *Entry* to $v$. Observe that each adjacent pair of nodes in a context defining path may correspond to many intraprocedural paths. Let $Cd(u)$ denote the set of program points which are context dependent on program point $u$. Then, $Cdp(u,v)$ denotes the set of context defining paths from $u$ to $v \in Cd(u)$. $Cs(u,v)$ denotes the set of call strings corresponding to paths in $Cdp(u,v)$.

The concept of context defining path can be seen as a more general abstraction of the concept of the same-level-valid-paths [19] which are interprocedural paths which start and end in the same procedure and have matching call return pairs.

Let $\mathcal{V}(\sigma, u)$ denote the value associated with call string $\sigma$ at program point $u$. We define the equivalence of call strings at a given program point $u$ as follows:

$$\sigma_1 \overset{u}{=} \sigma_2 \overset{def}{=} \{\sigma_1, \sigma_2\} \subseteq Cs(Entry, u) \wedge \mathcal{V}(\sigma_1, u) = \mathcal{V}(\sigma_2, u) \tag{2}$$

Equivalence of contexts in terms of data flow values has been observed by [14,24] and has been used for non-recursive portions of programs.

We assume that the work list based analysis is *intraprocedurally eager* i.e. it processes intraprocedural paths completely before propagating data flow information from a significant node to another significant node. This requires two separate work lists: One for intraprocedural nodes and the other for significant nodes. A significant node is selected for processing only when the work list of intraprocedural nodes is empty.

## 4.2  Call String Invariants

This section presents the following results: The *context invariance* lemma (Lemma 1) guarantees that the same set of call strings reaches all program points in a procedure. Hence, if a mechanism is devised to ignore some call strings in a procedure, it would be possible to reconstruct them wherever they are required. The *call strings equivalence* lemma (Lemma 2) guarantees that if call strings are partitioned on the basis of data flow values, the equivalence classes remain unchanged in a procedure although the values associated with them may change. The *convergence* lemma (Lemma 3), and the *sufficiency* theorem (Theorem 1) guarantee that if there is a way of computing the correct value of $\sigma \cdot \sigma_c^{\omega}$ at $E_p$, call strings $\sigma \cdot \sigma^i$, $\omega < i \leq m$ need not be constructed (Figure 2).

**Lemma 1.** *(Context Invariance). The calling contexts of all intraprocedural program points in a procedure are identical.*
INTUITION:  Calling contexts of a procedure depend on the callers so they cannot be different for different program points within the procedure.
PROOF:  Omitted.                                                          ∎

**Lemma 2.** *(Call String Equivalence). Consider $v \in \mathrm{Cd}(u)$. Assume that the recursive paths in $\mathrm{Cdp}(u,v)$ are unbounded. When the work list of intraprocedural nodes is empty in an intraprocedurally eager call strings based method,*

$$\sigma_1 \overset{u}{=} \sigma_2 \Rightarrow \forall \sigma \in \mathrm{Cs}(u,v),\ (\sigma_1 \cdot \sigma) \overset{v}{=} (\sigma_2 \cdot \sigma)$$

INTUITION:  Since $\sigma_1$ and $\sigma_2$ are transformed in the same manner by following the same set of paths, the values associated with them will also be transformed in the same manner and will continue to remain equal.
PROOF:  Omitted.                                                          ∎

This lemma assumes unbounded recursion. However, practical call strings method uses a prescribed length. Hence as illustrated in Figure 2, last $\eta$ call strings do not have the same value at $E_p$ in spite of the fact that they have the same value at $S_p$. If the call strings had unbounded occurrences of $\sigma_c$, then this exception would not arise. However, this exception does not matter because the associated values follow a strictly descending chain and converge on the least value as shown by the following lemma. It refers to Section 3 and Figure 2.

**Lemma 3.** *(Convergence). Assume that the call strings method constructs call strings long enough so that all call strings $\sigma \cdot \sigma_c^i$, $0 \leq i \leq m$ are constructed where $m \geq \omega + \eta$ for all possible values of $\omega$ and $\eta$. Then,*

$$\forall \eta,\ \mathcal{V}(\sigma \cdot \sigma_c^{m-\eta}, E_p) \sqsubseteq \mathcal{V}(\sigma \cdot \sigma_c^i, E_p),\ m - \eta \leq i \leq m$$

INTUITION:  When a data flow value is repeatedly computed using the same function and is merged with the same value at each step, the resulting values must follow a strictly descending chain until convergence.

PROOF: Since call strings $\sigma \cdot \sigma_c^i, \omega \leq i \leq m$ have the same data flow value at $S_p$, from Lemma 2, they have the same value, say $d'$, just before $E_p$ along the recursion ending path. Since $\omega \leq m - \eta$, the value associated with call strings $\sigma \cdot \sigma_c^i, m - \eta \leq i \leq m$ at $E_p$ along the recursion ending path will also be $d'$. From Figure 2 and equation (1),

$$\mathcal{V}(\sigma \cdot \sigma_c^i, E_p) = T_i = \begin{cases} d' \sqcap g(T_{i+1}) & m - \eta \leq i < m \\ d' & i = m \end{cases}$$

Then the proof obligation reduces to showing $T_{m-\eta} \sqsubseteq T_i$, $m - \eta \leq i \leq m$. We prove this by inducting on the distance of $i$ from $m$ by rewriting $T_i$ as $T_{m-j}, 0 \leq j \leq \eta$ and by showing that $T_{m-(j+1)} \sqsubseteq T_{m-j}, 0 \leq j < \eta$. The basis of induction is $j = 0$. Since $T_m = d'$ and $T_{m-1} = d' \sqcap (\ldots)$, it follows that $T_{m-1} \sqsubseteq T_m$. For the inductive step, assume that $T_{m-(j+1)} \sqsubseteq T_{m-j}$. We need to show that $T_{m-(j+2)} \sqsubseteq T_{m-(j+1)}$. From (1),

$$T_{m-(j+2)} = d' \sqcap g(T_{m-(j+1)}) \tag{3}$$

$$T_{m-(j+1)} = d' \sqcap g(T_{m-j}) \tag{4}$$

From the inductive hypothesis and monotonicity of functions,

$$T_{m-(j+1)} \sqsubseteq T_{m-j} \Rightarrow g(T_{m-(j+1)}) \sqsubseteq g(T_{m-j})$$

The inductive step follows by substituting this in the right hand sides of (3) and (4) and comparing them.                                                                                                      ∎

If the recursion ending path is not within procedure $p$ but is in some other procedure, then $T_i$ at $E_p$ will simply be $g^{i-m}(d')$.

**Lemma 4. (Convergence in a Cycle).** *When the computation of a data flow value converges at a program point in a cycle, it must converge at each program point in the cycle. Further, due to monotonicity, all values must converge in the same direction.*

**Corollary 1.** $T_i$ *of the form* $g^{i-m}(d')$ *at* $E_q$ *must converge.*

**Theorem 1. (Sufficiency of Cyclic Call Strings).**

$$\prod_{i=0}^{m} \mathcal{V}(\sigma \cdot \sigma_c^i, E_p) = \prod_{i=0}^{\omega} \mathcal{V}(\sigma \cdot \sigma_c^i, E_p)$$

INTUITION: When the data flow values along call strings in a cyclic return sequence follow a descending chain, only the last value matters in the overall merge.

PROOF:    Since the data flow value computation converges for the value associated with $\sigma \cdot \sigma_c^{m-\eta}$, from Lemma 3, $\mathcal{V}(\sigma \cdot \sigma_c^i, E_p) = \mathcal{V}(\sigma \cdot \sigma_c^{i+1}, E_p)$, $\omega \leq i < m - \eta$. As consequence, $\mathcal{V}(\sigma \cdot \sigma_c^\omega, E_p) \sqsubseteq \mathcal{V}(\sigma \cdot \sigma_c^i, E_p)$, $\omega \leq i < m$ which proves the theorem.    ∎

### 4.3   Modifying Call Strings Method

The basic principle of our approach is to maintain a single representative call string for an equivalence class within the scope of a maximal context dependent region. For procedure $p$, the decision of representation is taken at $S_p$ and remains valid at all program

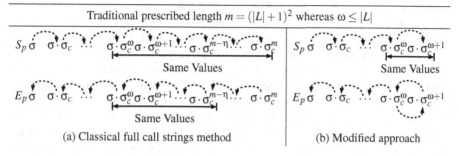

Traditional prescribed length $m = (|L|+1)^2$ whereas $\omega \leq |L|$

(a) Classical full call strings method    (b) Modified approach

**Fig. 3.** Modifying the call strings method for representing and regenerating cyclic call strings

points which are context dependent on $S_p$. $E_p$ is the last such point and the call strings must be regenerated so that appropriate data flow values can be propagated to different callers of $p$. Similar to the scope of variables in a program, this representation may be "shadowed" by other context dependent regions created by procedure calls.

Let $shortest(\sigma, u)$ denote the shortest call string which has the same value as $\sigma$ at $u$. Then, representation at $S_p$ and regeneration at $E_p$ is performed as follows:

$$represent(\langle \sigma, d \rangle, S_p) = \langle shortest(\sigma, S_p), d \rangle \tag{5}$$

$$regenerate(\langle \sigma, d \rangle, E_p) = \{\langle \sigma', d \rangle \mid \mathcal{V}(\sigma, S_p) = \mathcal{V}(\sigma', S_p)\} \tag{6}$$

This change obviates the need to construct all call strings up to a prescribed length. For finite lattices, the termination of call strings automatically follows. Effectively, this facilitates fixed point computation of contexts and avoids merging contexts.

Our method constructs call strings $\sigma \cdot \sigma_c^i, 0 \leq i \leq \omega$ for the recursive contexts. Call string $\sigma \cdot \sigma_c^{\omega+1}$ is represented by $\sigma \cdot \sigma_c^{\omega}$ at $S_p$ and no subsequent call string is created. Thus, call strings $\sigma \cdot \sigma_c^i, \omega+1 < i \leq m$ are not regenerated at $E_p$ as illustrated in Figure 3. All other call strings are regenerated completely.

Observe that the actual value of $\omega$ governs the construction of call strings (without the need of knowing $\omega$) in our method. However, the value of $\eta$ does not play any role in construction of call strings. This is because the computation of $f^i(d)$ in a cyclic call sequence (Figure 2) begins with the first call string whereas the computation of $T_i$ in the corresponding cyclic return sequence begins with the last call string.

### 4.4 Safety, Precision, Efficiency, and Complexity

**Theorem 2.** *(Safety and Precision). The final data flow values computed by representing and regenerating call strings using (5) and (6) are identical to the values computed by the original call strings method with length bound.*

INTUITION: Representation and regeneration discards only those call strings which contain redundant values and performs the desired computation iteratively.

PROOF: For the non-recursive contexts, the theorem is obvious. For recursive contexts we show that our method computes the same data flow value for call string $\sigma \cdot \sigma_c^{\omega}$ at $E_p$ as would be computed by the original method.

At $E_p$, $\sigma \cdot \sigma_c^{\omega+1}$ is regenerated and the data flow value (say $d'$) associated with $\sigma \cdot \sigma_c^{\omega}$ is propagated to it. The analysis propagates the pair $\langle \sigma \cdot \sigma_c^{\omega+1}, d' \rangle$ along the cyclic return sequence. This traversal removes the last occurrence of $\sigma_c$ from $\sigma \cdot \sigma_c^{\omega+1}$, computes $g(d')$, which is merged with the value of $\sigma \cdot \sigma_c^{\omega}$ along the recursion ending path. Thus $\mathcal{V}(\sigma \cdot \sigma_c^{\omega}, E_p) = d' \sqcap g(d')$ after one traversal. This is same as the value associated with call string $\sigma \cdot \sigma_c^{m-1}$ in the original method. At $E_p$, this is again copied to the call string $\sigma \cdot \sigma_c^{\omega+1}$ overwriting the previous value and the pair $\langle \sigma \cdot \sigma_c^{\omega+1}, d' \sqcap g(d') \rangle$ is propagated along the cyclic return sequence. The process repeats as long as new values are computed for $\sigma \cdot \sigma_c^{\omega}$; effectively, traversal $i$ over the cyclic return sequence computes the value $T_{m-i}$ for $\sigma \cdot \sigma_c^{\omega}$. The process terminates after $\eta$ traversals. This computes the desired value for $\sigma \cdot \sigma_c^{\omega}$.                                                    ∎

Effectively, our method computes the correct value for $\sigma \cdot \sigma_c^{\omega}$ by iterating over the cyclic return sequence $\eta$ times, rather than constructing all call strings up to $\sigma \cdot \sigma_c^{m}$. Traditional prescribed length $m$ is orders of magnitude larger than $\omega$, hence terminating the call strings construction at $\sigma \cdot \sigma_c^{\omega}$ results in a dramatic reduction in the number of call strings. Further improvements in efficiency arise because the reduction in the number of call strings is exponential—at each call site, much fewer call strings are passed on to callees along a call chain. The iterative computation does not entail any additional cost because these computations are anyway performed by the original method.

The elegance of our method lies in the fact that not only does it reduce space and time dramatically in practice, it also brings down the worst case complexity of call string length from quadratic to linear in the size of the lattice.

**Theorem 3.** *(Complexity). Using the value based termination of call strings, the maximum length of a call string is $K \times (|L| + 1)$.*

INTUITION: At the start of each procedure, the call strings are partitioned by the data flow values associated with them.

PROOF: The lemma trivially holds for call strings in non-recursive contexts. For recursive contexts, we maintain the call strings $\sigma \cdot \sigma_c^{\omega}$ at the exit of $S_p$. Since all call strings which have the same value are represented by a single call string, at most $|L|$ distinct call strings will be maintained at $S_p$. Thus, $\omega \leq |L|$ and no call site needs to appear more than $|L|$ times in a call string. We may have an additional call string at the entry of $S_p$ which gets represented at exit of $S_p$. Hence the theorem.                                    ∎

Even in the worst case, our method would construct much fewer call strings. Further, in practice, our method does not construct all call strings up to the worst case length. This is different from the original method which requires construction of all call strings of length up to $K \times (|L| + 1)^2$.

**Corollary 2.** *For separable frameworks, the bound reduces to $K \times (|\widehat{L}| + 1)$ where $\widehat{L}$ is the component lattice representing the data flow values of one entity. For bit vector frameworks, it further reduces to $K \times 3$ since $|\widehat{L}| = 2$.*

## 4.5   An Example of Points-To Analysis

Consider the supergraph in Figure 1 for interprocedural May Points-to analysis [5,11]. Figure 4 shows some important steps in the analysis using our method; $In_n$ and $Out_n$

denote entry and exit points of $n$. The data flow information is stored as $\langle \sigma, d \rangle$ where $d$ is the May points-to information which is a set of elements $x \rightarrow S$ indicating that $x$ points to the variables contained in set $S$.

Observe the computation of representative call strings at node $S_p$ as shown in rows 5 and 6. Since both call strings $c_1$ and $c_2$ reaching the entry of procedure $p$ carry the same data flow value, they are represented by a single call strings $c_1$. Note that $c_2$ is also eligible as the representative call string. Further, the *represent* function is applied at $S_q$ (see rows 10, 11) where two call strings $c_1 c_3$ and $c_1 c_3 c_4$ carry the same data flow value and hence are represented by the shortest call string $c_1 c_3$.

The regeneration takes place at the exit of procedure $q$ (see rows 12, 13). The regenerated call string $c_1 c_3 c_4$ reaches $R_4$. Effect of statement $x = *x$ in node $n_4$ is observed on the data flow value associated with call string $c_1 c_3$. At $In_{E_q}$, values associated with $c_1 c_3$ are merged (row 16) and function *regenerate* is applied once again (row 17). In the subsequent visit to node $n_4$ (not shown in the table), statement $x = *x$ modifies the points-to information of $x$ again and merging of information and regeneration of call strings is performed once again at $E_q$.

Eventually, call string $c_1 c_3$ reaches $R_3$ and is transformed into $c_1$. This call string reaches $E_p$ and function *regenerate* is applied to reconstruct call strings $c_1$ and $c_2$ at the exit of $E_p$ as shown in rows 18, 19 of Figure 4. Effectively, we perform safe and precise May points-to analysis using only acyclic call strings. We construct 5 call strings for the same. The overall lattice of May points-to framework for this example contains 512 elements. Considering $K = 3$ (the total number of distinct call sites in a call chain), the classical method would construct all call strings with lengths up to 7,89,507. Clearly, it would require millions of call strings.

## 4.6  An Approximate Version

It is possible to increase the efficiency of the proposed method by using an approximate version which can adjust the approximation on demand. The approximation is quantified in terms of the number of occurrences of a call site in any call string. Let this number be $\delta$. When a call string $\sigma$ containing $\delta - 1$ occurrences of call site $c_i$ reaches call node $C_i$, $\sigma \cdot c_i$ is created. If some other call string $\sigma'$ containing $\delta - 1$ occurrences of $c_i$ reaches $C_i$, instead of constructing $\sigma' \cdot c_i$ the value of $\sigma'$ is merged with $\sigma \cdot c_i$. In other words, the first call string that grows to contain $\delta$ occurrences of $c_i$ becomes the representative call string for all call strings containing $\delta$ or more occurrences of $c_i$. When a call string with the prefix $\sigma \cdot c_i$ reaches $C_i$, it is represented by $\sigma \cdot c_i$ (which is the representative call string) instead of suffixing another $c_i$ to it and its modified value is merged with the earlier value of $\sigma \cdot c_i$ at $C_i$. The process is repeated iteratively until the merged value converges. This converged value is then propagated back to each represented call string during regeneration at $R_i$. Since no context is missed out, this is safe but since values are merged across contexts, this is possibly imprecise. The degree of imprecision depends on the choice of $\delta$. The existing methods which merge the values in recursive contexts can be seen as a special case of our approximate method with $\delta = 1$.

Apart from increasing efficiency, demand driven summarization facilitates application of call strings method to data flow frameworks with infinite lattices which have finite heights (eg. constant propagation [1]).

| | Point i | New information at $i$ | | Point i | New information at $i$ |
|---|---|---|---|---|---|
| 1 | $In_{Entry}$ | $\langle \lambda, \{x \mapsto \emptyset, y \mapsto \emptyset, z \mapsto \emptyset\}\rangle$ | 11 | $Out_{S_q}$ | $\langle c_1 c_3, \{x \mapsto \{y\}, y \mapsto \{z\}, z \mapsto \{x\}\}\rangle$ |
| ... | | | ... | | |
| 2 | $Out_{n_2}$ | $\langle \lambda, \{x \mapsto \{y\}, y \mapsto \emptyset, z \mapsto \{x\}\}\rangle$ | 12 | $In_{E_q}$ | $\langle c_1 c_3, \{x \mapsto \{y\}, y \mapsto \{z\}, z \mapsto \{x\}\}\rangle$ |
| ... | | | 13 | $Out_{E_q}$ | $\langle c_1 c_3, \{x \mapsto \{y\}, y \mapsto \{z\}, z \mapsto \{x\}\}\rangle,$ |
| 3 | $Out_{C_1}$ | $\langle c_1, \{x \mapsto \{y\}, y \mapsto \emptyset, z \mapsto \{x\}\}\rangle$ | | | $\langle c_1 c_3 c_4, \{x \mapsto \{y\}, y \mapsto \{z\}, z \mapsto \{x\}\}\rangle$ |
| 4 | $Out_{C_2}$ | $\langle c_2, \{x \mapsto \{y\}, y \mapsto \emptyset, z \mapsto \{x\}\}\rangle$ | 14 | $In_{R_4}$ | $\langle c_1 c_3 c_4, \{x \mapsto \{y\}, y \mapsto \{z\}, z \mapsto \{x\}\}\rangle$ |
| 5 | $In_{S_p}$ | $\langle c_1, \{x \mapsto \{y\}, y \mapsto \emptyset, z \mapsto \{x\}\}\rangle,$ | ... | | |
| | | $\langle c_2, \{x \mapsto \{y\}, y \mapsto \emptyset, z \mapsto \{x\}\}\rangle$ | 15 | $Out_{n_5}$ | $\langle c_1 c_3, \{x \mapsto \{z\}, y \mapsto \{z\}, z \mapsto \{x\}\}\rangle$ |
| 6 | $Out_{S_p}$ | $\langle c_1, \{x \mapsto \{y\}, y \mapsto \emptyset, z \mapsto \{x\}\}\rangle$ | 16 | $In_{E_q}$ | $\langle c_1 c_3, \{x \mapsto \{y,z\}, y \mapsto \{z\}, z \mapsto \{x\}\}\rangle$ |
| ... | | | 17 | $Out_{E_q}$ | $\langle c_1 c_3, \{x \mapsto \{y,z\}, y \mapsto \{z\}, z \mapsto \{x\}\}\rangle,$ |
| 7 | $Out_{C_3}$ | $\langle c_1 c_3, \{x \mapsto \{y\}, y \mapsto \{z\}, z \mapsto \{x\}\}\rangle$ | | | $\langle c_1 c_3 c_4, \{x \mapsto \{y,z\}, y \mapsto \{z\}, z \mapsto \{x\}\}\rangle$ |
| ... | | | ... | | |
| 8 | $In_{S_q}$ | $\langle c_1 c_3, \{x \mapsto \{y\}, y \mapsto \{z\}, z \mapsto \{x\}\}\rangle$ | 18 | $In_{E_p}$ | $\langle c_1, \{x \mapsto \{x,y,z\}, y \mapsto \{z\}, z \mapsto \{x\}\}\rangle$ |
| ... | | | 19 | $Out_{E_p}$ | $\langle c_1, \{x \mapsto \{x,y,z\}, y \mapsto \{z\}, z \mapsto \{x\}\}\rangle,$ |
| 9 | $Out_{C_4}$ | $\langle c_1 c_3 c_4, \{x \mapsto \{y\}, y \mapsto \{z\}, z \mapsto \{x\}\}\rangle$ | | | $\langle c_2, \{x \mapsto \{x,y,z\}, y \mapsto \{z\}, z \mapsto \{x\}\}\rangle$ |
| ... | | | ... | | |
| 10 | $In_{S_q}$ | $\langle c_1 c_3, \{x \mapsto \{y\}, y \mapsto \{z\}, z \mapsto \{x\}\}\rangle,$ | | | |
| | | $\langle c_1 c_3 c_4, \{x \mapsto \{y\}, y \mapsto \{z\}, z \mapsto \{x\}\}\rangle$ | | | |

**Fig. 4.** Some important steps in intraprocedurally eager work list algorithm for interprocedural May points-to analysis using value based termination of call strings for supergraph in Figure 1

## 5 Related Work

We compare our work with other methods on the basis of precision, efficiency, generality and simplicity. The approximate call strings method [22] which retains fixed length suffixes is a popular variant of call strings method. Although it is efficient and flexible, it compromises on precision in recursive as well as non-recursive programs and the degree of precision varies with the length of suffixes.

Functional approach [22] involves computing flow functions in a context independent manner and applying them in a context sensitive manner. Although this approach guarantees precision, it is known to be inefficient due to high time and space complexity resulting from function computations [1]. Tabulation method [22] is an efficient implementation of functional approach, which uses memoization to store input and output data flow values at each program point, instead of storing the functions. Similar to our approach, this approach also uses the basic principle of restricting the reanalysis of procedures only for distinct inputs. However, unlike our method, tabulation method merges the newly computed data flow values with the old values at each program point to guarantee termination. Further, since contexts are not remembered separately, meaningful approximation is not possible and hence cannot be used for frameworks with infinite lattices. The method of computing partial transfer functions (PTF) [24,18] looks very similar to tabulation. However, PTFs involve summarization of input in recursive contexts whereas our method and tabulation do not do so and hence are more precise. The graph reachability method [19,21,10] is a variant of tabulation based functional approach which requires computation of an exploded supergraph. It is applicable only to finite distributive frameworks.

Many approaches have been developed specifically for context-sensitive points-to analysis. BDD-based approaches [23,25,26] construct all acyclic contexts but merge values along recursive portions resulting in loss of precision. Since BDDs have efficient implementations and they exploit the commonality across contexts carrying equivalent values [14], these approaches are scalable. Many approaches [4,13,15,7,16] achieve efficiency by using flow-insensitive algorithms for intraprocedural analysis thereby causing additional imprecision. The context-sensitive points-to analysis using invocation graph [5] requires construction of separate invocation graph and is reported not to be scalable [23]. This method computes conservative solution along recursive portions. Summary-based points-to analysis approaches [24] are reported to be the precise, but they do not guarantee full precision along recursive portions. As observed in a comparison of context sensitive points-to analyses [14], treating recursive portions in a context insensitive manner leads to significant imprecision in practical programs.

Some context sensitive methods (eg. automata based methods [6,20,3], generic assertion based method [8], linear algebra based method [17]) have approached interprocedural data flow analysis from a view point of building theoretical underpinnings and their precision-efficiency trade off or generality (eg. applicability to frameworks such as points-to analysis) is not clear.

We feel that context-insensitivity along recursive paths is being looked upon as an unavoidable compromise for efficiency and is being accepted as a regular practice [9]. This may be because the orthogonality of bounding contexts and computing data flow values makes it impossible to identify and eliminate all redundant contexts. To ensure precision, the only available option is to use functional approaches or to use the worst case bounds for call strings. Both these approaches are extremely inefficient.

The occurrence based bound for call strings for bit-vector frameworks [12] is an improvement over the classical length bound [22]. It constructs call strings with any call site occurring at most 3 times instead of all call strings with lengths up to $3K$. However, it still allows many redundant call strings since the termination of call strings is orthogonal to the convergence of data flow values.

## 6  Empirical Measurements

We have implemented interprocedural Reaching Definitions analysis using the proposed algorithm in gcc 4.0 as an additional pass that constructs supergraph and performs the call strings based analysis on the Gimple IR. We have measured the performance of the algorithm on the following programs: Hanoi[1], sim[2], bit_gray[3], 181.mcf and 256.bzip2 from SPEC-2000, analyzer, distray, mason and fourinarow from FreeBench v1.03 suite. Among these programs, analyzer, distray and 256.bzip2 are non-recursive whereas all other programs are recur-

---

[1] http://www.ece.cmu.edu/~ece548/hw/lab1/hanoi.c

[2] http://gd.tuwien.ac.at/perf/benchmark/aburto/sim/sim.c

[3] http://paul.rutgers.edu/~rhoads/Code/bit_gray.c

| Program | LoC | #F | #C | 3K length bound | | | | | Proposed Approach | | | |
| | | | | K | #CS | MaxL | #CSPN | Time | #CS | MaxL | #CSPN | Time |
|---|---|---|---|---|---|---|---|---|---|---|---|---|
| hanoi | 33 | 2 | 4 | 4 | 100000+ | 12 | 99922 | $3973 \times 10^3$ | 8 | 3 | 7 | 2.37 |
| bit_gray | 53 | 5 | 11 | 7 | 100000+ | 21 | 31374 | $2705 \times 10^3$ | 17 | 4 | 6 | 3.83 |
| analyzer | 288 | 14 | 20 | 2 | 21 | 2 | 4 | 20.33 | 21 | 2 | 4 | 1.39 |
| distray | 331 | 9 | 21 | 6 | 96 | 6 | 28 | 322.41 | 22 | 3 | 4 | 1.11 |
| mason | 350 | 9 | 13 | 8 | 100000+ | 11 | 22143 | $432 \times 10^3$ | 14 | 3 | 4 | 0.43 |
| fourinarow | 676 | 17 | 45 | 5 | 510 | 15 | 158 | 397.76 | 46 | 3 | 7 | 1.86 |
| sim | 1146 | 13 | 45 | 8 | 100000+ | 14 | 33546 | $1427 \times 10^3$ | 211 | 13 | 105 | 234.16 |
| 181_mcf | 1299 | 17 | 24 | 6 | 32789 | 18 | 32767 | $484 \times 10^3$ | 41 | 9 | 11 | 5.15 |
| 256_bzip2 | 3320 | 63 | 198 | 7 | 492 | 7 | 63 | 258.33 | 406 | 7 | 34 | 200.19 |

LoC is the number of lines of code, #F is the number of procedures, #C is the number of call sites, #CS is the number of call strings (100000+ indicates that call strings construction was aborted after 100000 call strings), #CSPN denotes the maximum number of call strings reaching any node. MaxL denotes the maximum length of any call strings. The analysis time is in milliseconds.

**Fig. 5.** Empirical measurements

sive. These experiments were carried out on a P4 (3.06 GHz) machine with 1GB RAM running Fedora Core 6.

Figure 5 gives the details of the benchmark programs and the call string related measurements for the $3 \times K$ length [22] and the proposed method. For the purpose of experimentation we had to restrict the number of call strings to $10^5$ for $3 \times K$ bound. This was done primarily due to the compiler running out of space. The table clearly shows that our approach of terminating call strings construction using data flow values reduces the number of call strings and hence the analysis time by orders of magnitude.

## 7   Conclusions and Future Work

The classical full call strings method is context sensitive and computes as precise solution as is statically possible. However, it suffers from terrible inefficiency and hence has been relegated to the set of classical methods which are of academic interest only. This paper resurrects and rejuvenates the call strings method by observing some subtle insights and proposing minimal changes to the method. These changes are simple, do not impose any additional constraints, and faithfully retain the essential principles of the method and the consequent properties: precision, simplicity, and generality. These changes discard call strings where they are not required, regenerate them where they are required and iteratively compute data flow values in cyclic call strings in return sequences as summarized in Figure 3. This results in dramatic improvements in efficiency.

Our investigations deviate from the current trends along the following two aspects:

- Most contemporary investigations seem to assume that compromising precision (at least in recursive contexts) is essential for achieving efficiency. We believe that any trade-off between precision and efficiency without making a clear distinction between relevant contexts and irrelevant contexts is undesirable. We have shown that this distinction can be very easily and efficiently made by using the convergence of data flow values for convergence of contexts without compromising on precision.

- A majority of contemporary investigations involve specialized algorithms in order to achieve efficiency. They may be specialized in terms of a very sophisticated representation of the programs or in terms of using insights from the specific analyses for which they are implemented. We believe that it is important to seek efficiency in a general method which is applicable to all data flow frameworks (including those with infinite lattices) and which can be implemented very easily. Simplicity and generality are essential for exploring the possibility of automatic construction of interprocedural data flow analyzers. We find this direction to be promising because the scalability of our method depends on the convergence of data flow values rather than merely on program structure. When programs are written in modular fashion with loose coupling between different modules, the convergence of data flow values does not scale with program size as much as the number of contexts.

We have implemented this method for Reaching Definitions analysis and the results are very promising. We are in the process of implementing this method for points-to analysis and would like to test the method on large programs. Note that point-to analysis is non-distributive and the classical call string method would also suffer from imprecision. Our variant does not create any additional imprecision because the results presented in this paper do not assume distributivity property.

Our quick and dirty implementation was aimed at the first level measurements. We would like to improve the implementation by engineering better data structures and algorithms and observe their impact on the efficiency. We would also like to measure the precision vs. efficiency trade-off using the approximate version of our method.

## Acknowledgments

Implementation of these analyses was carried out by Seema Ravandale. Divya Krishan was involved in the implementation of earlier versions of call strings methods.

## References

1. Aho, A.V., Lam, M.S., Sethi, R., Ullman, J.D.: Compilers: Principles, Techniques, and Tools, 2nd edn. Addison-Wesley Longman Publishing Co., Inc. (2006)
2. Alt, M., Martin, F.: Generation of efficient interprocedural analyzers with PAG. In: Static Analysis Symposium, pp. 33–50 (September 1995)
3. Amiranoff, P., Cohen, A., Feautrier, P.: Beyond iteration vectors: Instancewise relational abstract domains. In: Static Analysis Symposium, pp. 161–180 (2006)
4. Burke, M., Carini, P., Choi, J., Hind, M.: Flow-insensitive interprocedural alias analysis in the pressence of pointers. In: Pingali, K.K., Gelernter, D., Padua, D.A., Banerjee, U., Nicolau, A. (eds.) LCPC 1994. LNCS, vol. 892, Springer, Heidelberg (1995)
5. Emami, M., Ghiya, R., Hendren, L.J.: Context-sensitive interprocedural points-to analysis in the presence of function pointers. In: Proc. of the ACM SIGPLAN Conference on Programming Language Design and Implementation, pp. 242–256 (1994)
6. Esparza, J., Knoop, J.: An automata-theoretic approach to interprocedural data-flow analysis. In: Foundations of Software Science and Computation Structure, pp. 14–30 (1999)
7. Fahndrich, M., Rehof, J., Das, M.: Scalable context-sensitive flow analysis using instantiation constraints. In: Proc. of the ACM SIGPLAN Conference on Programming Language Design and Implementation, pp. 253–263 (2000)

8. Gulwani, S., Tiwari, A.: Computing procedure summaries for interprocedural analysis. In: De Nicola, R. (ed.) ESOP 2007. LNCS, vol. 4421, pp. 253–267. Springer, Heidelberg (2007)

9. Hardekopf, B., Lin, C.: The ant and the grasshopper: fast and accurate pointer analysis for millions of lines of code. In: Proc. of the ACM SIGPLAN Conference on Programming Language Design and Implementation, pp. 290–299 (2007)

10. Horwitz, S., Reps, T., Sagiv, M.: Demand interprocedural dataflow analysis. In: 3rd ACM Symposium on Foundations of Software Engineering, pp. 104–115 (1995)

11. Kanade, A., Khedker, U.P., Sanyal, A.: Heterogeneous fixed points with application to points-to analysis. In: Proc. of the Asian Symposium on Programming Languages and Systems, pp. 298–314 (2005)

12. Karkare, B., Khedker, U.P.: An improved bound for call-strings based interprocedural analysis of bit vector frameworks. ACM Trans. Program. Lang. Syst. 29(6), 38 (2007)

13. Lattner, C., Lenharth, A., Adve, V.: Making context-sensitive points-to analysis with heap cloning practical for the real world. In: Proc. of the ACM SIGPLAN Conference on Programming Language Design and Implementation (June 2007)

14. Lhoták, O., Hendren, L.J.: Context-sensitive points-to analysis: is it worth it? In: Mycroft, A., Zeller, A. (eds.) CC 2006. LNCS, vol. 3923, pp. 47–64. Springer, Heidelberg (2006)

15. Liang, D., Harrold, M.J.: Efficient points-to analysis for whole-program analysis. SIGSOFT Software Engineering Notes 24(6), 199–215 (1999)

16. Milanova, A.: Light context-sensitive points-to analysis for java. In: Proc. of ACM SIGPLAN-SIGSOFT Workshop on Program Analysis for Software Tools and Engineering (June 2007)

17. Müller-Olm, M., Seidl, H.: Precise interprocedural analysis through linear algebra. In: Proc. of the ACM SIGPLAN-SIGACT Symposium on Principles of Programming Languages, New York, NY, USA, pp. 330–341 (2004)

18. Murphy, B.R., Lam, M.S.: Program analysis with partial transfer functions. In: Proc. of the 2000 ACM SIGPLAN Workshop on Partial Evaluation and Semantics-based Program Manipulation, pp. 94–103 (2000)

19. Reps, T., Horwitz, S., Sagiv, M.: Precise interprocedural dataflow analysis via graph reachability. In: Proc. of the ACM SIGPLAN-SIGACT Symposium on Principles of Programming Languages, pp. 49–61 (1995)

20. Reps, T., Schwoon, S., Jha, S., Melski, D.: Weighted pushdown systems and their application to interprocedural dataflow analysis. Science of Computer Programming 58(1-2), 206–263 (2005)

21. Sagiv, M., Reps, T., Horwitz, S.: Precise interprocedural dataflow analysis with applications to constant propagation. Theoretical Computer Science 167(1–2), 131–170 (1996)

22. Sharir, M., Pnueli, A.: Two approaches to interprocedural data flow analysis. In: Muchnick, S.S., Jones, N.D. (eds.) Program Flow Analysis: Theory and Applications, Prentice-Hall Inc., Englewood Cliffs (1981)

23. Whaley, J., Lam, M.S.: Cloning-based context-sensitive pointer alias analysis using binary decision diagrams. In: Proc. of the ACM SIGPLAN Conference on Programming language design and implementation (June 2004)

24. Wilson, R.P., Lam, M.S.: Efficient context-sensitive pointer analysis for C programs. In: Proc. of the ACM SIGPLAN Conference on Programming Language Design and Implementation (1995)

25. Zhu, J.: Towards scalable flow and context sensitive pointer analysis. In: Proc. of the 42nd Annual Conference on Design Automation, pp. 831–836 (2005)

26. Zhu, J., Calman, S.: Symbolic pointer analysis revisited. In: Proc. of the ACM SIGPLAN Conference on Programming Language Design and Implementation, pp. 145–157 (2004)

# Java Bytecode Verification for @NonNull Types

Chris Male, David J. Pearce, Alex Potanin, and Constantine Dymnikov

Victoria University of Wellington, NZ
{malechri,djp,alex,dymnikkost}@mcs.vuw.ac.nz

**Abstract.** Java's annotation mechanism allows us to extend its type system with non-null types. However, checking such types cannot be done using the existing bytecode verification algorithm. We extend this algorithm to verify non-null types using a novel technique that identifies aliasing relationships between local variables and stack locations in the JVM. We formalise this for a subset of Java Bytecode and report on experiences using our implementation.

## 1 Introduction

`NullPointerExceptions` are a common error arising in Java programs when references holding `null` are dereferenced. Java 1.5 allows us to annotate types and, hence, to extend the type system with @NonNull types. An important step in the enforcement of such types is the bytecode verifier which must efficiently determine whether or not non-null types are used soundly. The standard bytecode verifier uses a dataflow analysis which is insufficient for this task. To address this, we present a novel, lightweight dataflow analysis ideally suited to the problem of verifying non-null types.

Java Bytecodes have access to a fixed size local variable array and stack [19]. These act much like machine registers in that they have no fixed type associated with them; rather, they can have different types at different program points. To address this, the standard bytecode verifier automatically infers the types of local variables and stack locations at each point within the program. The following illustrates a simple program, and the inferred types that hold immediately before each instruction:

```
static int f(Integer);     locals      stack
   0:   aload_0            [Integer]   []
   1:   ifnull 8           [Integer]   [Integer]
   4:   aload_0            [Integer]   []
   5:   invokevirtual ...  [Integer]   [Integer]
   8:   return             [Integer]   []
```

Here, there is one local variable at index 0. On method entry, this is initialised with the `Integer` parameter. The `aload_0` instruction loads the local variable at index 0 onto the stack, and the `Integer` type is inferred for that stack location as a result.

A bytecode verifier for non-null types must infer that the value loaded onto the stack immediately before the `invokevirtual` method call cannot be `null`, as this is the call's receiver. The challenge here is that `ifnull` compares the top of the stack against `null`, but then discards this value. Thus, the bytecode verifier must be aware that, at

L. Hendren (Ed.): CC 2008, LNCS 4959, pp. 229–244, 2008.
© Springer-Verlag Berlin Heidelberg 2008

that exact moment, the top of the stack and local 0 are aliases. The algorithm used by the standard bytecode verifier is unable to do this. Therefore, we extend this algorithm to maintain information about such aliases, and we refer to this technique as *type aliasing*. More specifically, this paper makes the following contributions:

- We formalise our non-null bytecode verifier for a subset of Java Bytecode.
- We detail an implementation of our system for Java Bytecode.
- We report on our experiences with using our system on real-world programs.

While there has already been considerable work on non-null types (e.g. [25,10,16,3,8]), none has directly addressed the problem of bytecode verification. While these existing techniques could be used for this purpose, they operate on higher-level program representations and must first translate bytecode into their representation. This introduces unnecessary overhead that is undesirable for the (performance critical) bytecode verifier. Our technique operates on bytecode directly, thus eliminating this inefficiency.

## 2   Preliminaries

We extend Java types to allow references to be declared as non-null and for arrays to hold non-null elements (in §5 we extend this to Java Generics). For example:

```
Vector v1;
@NonNull Vector v2;
@NonNull Integer @NonNull [] a1;
```

Here, v1 is a *nullable* reference (one which may be null), while v2 is a non-null reference (one which may not be null); similarly, a1 is a non-null reference to an array holding non-null elements. When annotating arrays, the leftmost annotation associates with the element type, whilst that just before the braces associates with the array reference type. We formalise a cut-down version of the non-null types supported by our system using the following grammar:

$$\alpha \quad ::= \quad \texttt{@NonNull} \mid \epsilon$$
$$T \quad ::= \quad T \, \alpha \, [\,] \mid \alpha \, C \mid null \mid \perp$$

Here, the special *null* type is given to the null value, $\epsilon$ denotes the absence of a @NonNull annotation, $C$ denotes a class name (e.g. Integer) and $\perp$ is given to locations which hold no value (e.g. they are uninitialised, in deadcode, etc).

An important question is how our system deals with subtyping. For example, we require all array element types be identical between subtypes[1]. A formal definition of the subtype relation for our simplified non-null type language is given in Figure 1. An important property of our subtype relation is that it forms a *complete lattice* (i.e. that every pair of types $T_1, T_2$ has a unique least upper bound, $T_1 \sqcup T_2$, and a unique greatest lower bound, $T_1 \sqcap T_2$). This helps ensure termination of our non-null verification algorithm.

---

[1] While this contrasts slightly with Java's treatment of arrays, we cannot do better without adding runtime non-null type information to arrays.

$$\frac{}{\texttt{@NonNull} \leq \epsilon}$$

$$\frac{\alpha_1 \leq \alpha_2}{T_1 \, \alpha_1 \, [\,] \leq T_1 \, \alpha_2 \, [\,]}$$

$$\frac{\alpha_1 \leq \alpha_2 \quad C \text{ extends } B}{\alpha_1 \, C \, \leq \alpha_2 \, B}$$

$$\frac{}{T_1 \, \alpha \, [\,] \leq \alpha \, \texttt{java.lang.Object}}$$

$$\frac{}{\bot \leq T \, \alpha \, [\,]} \quad \frac{}{\bot \leq \alpha \, C} \quad \frac{}{\bot \leq null}$$

$$\frac{}{null \leq T_1 \, [\,]} \quad \frac{}{null \leq C}$$

**Fig. 1.** Subtyping rules for non-null Java types. We assume reflexivity and transitivity, that java.lang.Object is the root of the class hierarchy and, hence, is also ⊤.

A well-known problem, however, is that Java's subtype relation does not form a complete lattice [17]. This arises because two classes can share the same super-class and implement the same interfaces; thus, they may not have a unique least upper bound. To resolve this, we adopt the standard solution of ignoring interfaces entirely and, instead, treating interfaces as type java.lang.Object. This works because Java supports only single inheritance between classes. This is the approach taken in Sun's Java Bytecode verifier and, hence, our system is no less general than it.

## 3 Non-null Type Verification

Our non-null type verification algorithm infers the nullness of local variables at each point within a method. We assume method parameters, return types and fields are already annotated with @NonNull. Our algorithm is intraprocedural; that is, it concentrates on verifying each method in isolation, rather than the whole program together. The algorithm constructs an abstract representation of each method's execution; if this is possible, the method is type safe and cannot throw a NullPointerException. The abstract representation of a method mirrors the control-flow graph (CFG); its nodes contain an abstract representation of the program store, called an *abstract store*, giving the types of local variables and stack locations at that point.

We now formalise this construction process for methods. Constructors are ignored for simplicity and discussed informally in §5. Also, while the full Java Bytecode instruction set is supported, only a subset is considered here for brevity.

### 3.1 Abstract Store

In the Java Virtual Machine (JVM), each method has a fixed-size local variable array (for storing local variables) and a stack of known maximum depth (for storing temporary values). Our system models this using an abstract store, which we formalise as $(\Sigma, \Gamma, \kappa)$, where $\Sigma$ is the *abstract meta-heap*, $\Gamma$ is the *abstract location array* and $\kappa$ is the *stack pointer* which identifies the first free location on the stack. Here, $\Gamma$ maps *abstract locations* to *type references*. These abstract locations are labelled $0, \ldots, n-1$, with the first $m$ locations representing the local variable array, and the remainder representing the stack (hence, $n-m$ is the maximum stack size and $\kappa \leq n$ ). A type reference is a reference to a *type object* which, in turn, can be thought of as a non-null type with identity. Thus, we can have two distinct type objects representing the same non-null type. Crucially, this types-as-references approach allows two abstract locations to be *type aliases*; that is, refer to the same type object. For example, in the following abstract store, locations 0 and 2 are type aliases:

$$\Sigma = \{r_1 \mapsto \texttt{@NonNull Integer}, r_2 \mapsto \texttt{String}\}, \Gamma = \{0 \mapsto r_1, 1 \mapsto r_2, 2 \mapsto r_1\}, \kappa = 3$$

Here, the abstract meta-heap, $\Sigma$, maps type references to non-null types. It's called a *meta-heap* as $\Sigma$ does not abstract the program heap; rather it is an internal structure used only to enable type aliasing.

**Definition 1.** *An abstract store* $(\Sigma, \Gamma, \kappa)$ *is well-formed iff* $dom(\Gamma) = \{0, \ldots, n-1\}$ *for some* $n$, $ran(\Gamma) \subseteq dom(\Sigma)$ *and* $0 \leq \kappa \leq n$.

### 3.2   Abstract Semantics

The effect of a bytecode instruction is given by its *abstract semantics*, which we describe using transition rules. These summarise the abstract store immediately after the instruction in terms of the abstract store immediately before it; any necessary constraints on the abstract store immediately before the instruction are also identified.

The abstract semantics for the bytecode instructions considered in our formalism are given in Figure 2. Here, $\Gamma[r_1/r_2]$ generates an abstract store from $\Gamma$ where all abstract locations holding $r_1$ now hold $r_2$. Several helper functions are used: **fieldT**$(0, N)$, returns the type of field $N$ in class $0$; **methodT**$(0, M)$ returns the type of method $M$ in class $0$; **thisMethT**$()$ gives the current method's type; finally, **validNewT**$(T_1)$ holds if $T_1 \neq$ @NonNull $T_2$ $\alpha$ [] for any $T_2$. The latter prevents creation of arrays holding @NonNull elements, as Java always initialises array elements with null (see §5).

A useful illustration of our abstract semantics is the arrayload bytecode. This requires the array index on top of the stack, followed by the array reference itself; these are popped off the stack and the indexed element is loaded back on. Looking at the arrayload rule, we see $\kappa$ decreases by one, indicating the net effect is one less element on the stack. The notation $\Gamma[\kappa - 2 \mapsto r]$ indicates the abstract store is updated so that abstract location $\kappa - 2$ now holds type reference $r$; thus, $r$ has been pushed onto the stack and represents the loaded array element. The reference on top of the stack is ignored since this represents the actual index value, and is of no concern. The constraint $r \notin \Sigma$ ensures $r$ references a *fresh* type object; such constraints are used to ensure an abstract location is not type aliased with any other. Another constraint ensures the array reference is non-null, thus protecting against a NullPointerException.

Considering the remaining rules from Figure 2, the main interest lies with ifceq. There is one rule for each of the true/false branches. The true branch uses the greatest lower bound operator, $T_1 \sqcap T_2$ (recall §2). This creates a single type object which is substituted for both operands to create a type aliasing relationship. For the false branch, a special *difference* operator, $T_1 - T_2$, is employed which is similar to set difference. For example, the set of possible values for a variable o of type Object includes all instances of Object (and its subtypes), as well as null; after a comparison o!=null, null is removed from this set. Thus, it is defined as follows:

$$\texttt{store } i : \Sigma, \Gamma, \kappa \longrightarrow \Sigma, \Gamma[i \mapsto \Gamma(\kappa-1)], \kappa-1 \quad \texttt{load } i : \Sigma, \Gamma, \kappa \longrightarrow \Sigma, \Gamma[\kappa \mapsto \Gamma(i)], \kappa+1$$

$$\frac{r \notin \Sigma \quad \Sigma' = \Sigma \cup \{r \mapsto null\}}{\texttt{loadnull} : \Sigma, \Gamma, \kappa \longrightarrow \Sigma', \Gamma[\kappa \mapsto r], \kappa+1} \qquad \frac{\text{validNewT}(T)}{\frac{r \notin \Sigma \quad \Sigma' = \Sigma \cup \{r \mapsto \texttt{@NonNull } T\}}{\texttt{new } T : \Sigma, \Gamma, \kappa \longrightarrow \Sigma', \Gamma[\kappa \mapsto r], \kappa+1}}$$

$$\frac{\Sigma(\Gamma(\kappa-2)) = T \texttt{ @NonNull [ ]}}{\frac{r \notin \Sigma \quad \Sigma' = \Sigma \cup \{r \mapsto T\}}{\texttt{arrayload} : \Sigma, \Gamma, \kappa \longrightarrow \Sigma', \Gamma[\kappa-2 \mapsto r], \kappa-1}} \qquad \frac{\Sigma(\Gamma(\kappa-1)) = T_1 \quad T_1 \leq T_2}{\frac{\Sigma(\Gamma(\kappa-3)) = T_2 \texttt{ @NonNull [ ]}}{\texttt{arraystore} : \Sigma, \Gamma, \kappa \longrightarrow \Sigma, \Gamma, \kappa-3}}$$

$$\frac{\Sigma(\Gamma(\kappa-1)) = \texttt{@NonNull } C}{\frac{T = \text{fieldT}(\texttt{0, N})}{\frac{r \notin \Sigma \quad \Sigma' = \Sigma \cup \{r \mapsto T\}}{\texttt{getfield 0.N} : \Sigma, \Gamma, \kappa \longrightarrow \Sigma', \Gamma[\kappa-1 \mapsto r], \kappa}}} \qquad \frac{\Sigma(\Gamma(\kappa-1)) = T_1}{\frac{\Sigma(\Gamma(\kappa-2)) = \texttt{@NonNull } C}{\frac{T_2 = \text{fieldT}(\texttt{0, N}) \quad T_1 \leq T_2}{\texttt{putfield 0.N} : \Sigma, \Gamma, \kappa \longrightarrow \Sigma, \Gamma, \kappa-2}}}$$

$$\frac{(P_1, \ldots, P_n) \to T_r = \text{methodT}(\texttt{0, M})}{\frac{\Sigma(\Gamma(\kappa-n)), \ldots, \Sigma(\Gamma(\kappa-1)) = T_1, \ldots, T_n}{\frac{\Sigma(\Gamma(\kappa-(n+1))) = \texttt{@NonNull } C}{\frac{T_1 \leq P_1, \ldots, T_n \leq P_n}{\frac{r \notin \Sigma \quad \Sigma' = \Sigma \cup \{r \mapsto T_r\} \quad \kappa' = \kappa-n}{\texttt{invoke 0.M} : \Sigma, \Gamma, \kappa \longrightarrow \Sigma', \Gamma[\kappa'-1 \mapsto r], \kappa'}}}}} \qquad \frac{(P_1, \ldots, P_n) \to T_r = \text{thisMethT}()}{\frac{\Sigma(\Gamma(\kappa-1)) = T \quad T \leq T_r}{\texttt{return} : \Sigma, \Gamma, \kappa \longrightarrow \emptyset, \emptyset, 0}}$$

$$\frac{r_1 = \Gamma(\kappa-2) \quad r_2 = \Gamma(\kappa-1)}{\frac{\Sigma(r_1) = T_1 \quad \Sigma(r_2) = T_2 \quad r_3 \notin \Sigma}{\frac{\Sigma' = \Sigma \cup \{r_3 \mapsto T_1 \sqcap T_2\} \quad \kappa' = \kappa-2}{\texttt{ifceq} : \Sigma, \Gamma, \kappa \overset{true}{\longrightarrow} \Sigma', \Gamma[r_1/r_3, r_2/r_3], \kappa'}}} \qquad \frac{r_1 = \Gamma(\kappa-2) \quad r_2 = \Gamma(\kappa-1)}{\frac{\Sigma(r_1) = T_1 \quad \Sigma(r_2) = T_2 \quad r_3, r_4 \notin \Sigma}{\frac{\Sigma' = \Sigma \cup \{r_3 \mapsto T_1 - T_2, r_4 \mapsto T_2 - T_1\}}{\texttt{ifceq} : \Sigma, \Gamma, \kappa \overset{false}{\longrightarrow} \Sigma', \Gamma[r_1/r_3, r_2/r_4], \kappa-2}}}$$

**Fig. 2.** Abstract semantics for Java Bytecodes considered. Note, $\texttt{ifceq}$ stands for $\texttt{if\_cmpeq}$.

**Definition 2.** $T_1 - T_2$ is @NonNull $T$, if $T_1 = \alpha\, T \wedge T_2 = null$, and $T_1$ otherwise.

The semantics for the $\texttt{return}$ bytecode indicate that: firstly, we always expect a return value (for simplicity); and, secondly, no bytecode can follow it in the CFG.

Finally, the Java Bytecodes not considered in Figure 2 include all arithmetic operations (e.g. $\texttt{iadd}$, $\texttt{imul}$, etc), stack manipulators (e.g. $\texttt{pop}$, $\texttt{dup}$, etc), other branching primitives (e.g. $\texttt{ifnonnull}$, $\texttt{tableswitch}$, etc), synchronisation primitives (e.g. $\texttt{monitorenter}$, etc) and other miscellaneous ones (e.g. $\texttt{instanceof}$, $\texttt{check cast}$, $\texttt{athrow}$ and $\texttt{arraylength}$). It is easy enough to see how our abstract semantics extends to these and our implementation (see §5) supports them all.

### 3.3 An Example

Figure 3 illustrates the bytecode instructions for a simple method and its corresponding abstract representation. When a method is called, the local variable array is initialised with the values of the incoming parameters, starting from 0 and using as many as necessary; for instance methods, the first parameter is always the $\texttt{this}$ reference. Thus, the first abstract location of the first store in Figure 3 has type $\texttt{Test}$; the remainder have

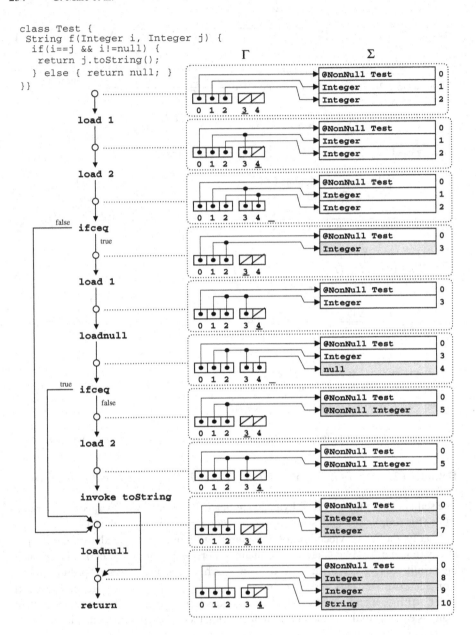

**Fig. 3.** Bytecode representation of a simple Java Method (source given above) and the state of the abstract store, $(\Sigma, \Gamma, \kappa)$, going into each instruction. The value of $\kappa$ is indicated by the underlined abstract location; when the stack is full, this points past the last location. The type objects in $\Sigma$ are given a unique identifier to help distinguish new objects from old ones; we assume unreferenced type objects are immediately garbage collected, which is reflected in the identifiers becoming non-contiguous. Type aliases are indicated by references which are "joined". For example, the second abstract store reflects the state immediately after the load 1 instruction, where locations 1 and 3 are type aliases.

nullable type `Integer`, with each referring to a unique type object (since we must conservatively assume parameters are not aliased on entry).

In Figure 3, the effect of each instruction is reflected in the changes between the abstract stores before and after it. Of note are the two `ifceq` instructions: the first establishes a type aliasing relationship between locations 1 and 2 (on the true branch); the second causes a retyping of location 1 to `@NonNull Integer` (on the false branch) which also retypes location 2 through type aliasing. Thus, at the `invoke` instruction, the top of the stack (which represents the receiver reference) holds `@NonNull Integer`, indicating it will not throw a `NullPointerException`.

We now consider what happens at join points in the CFG. The `return` instruction in Figure 3 is a good illustration, since two distinct paths reach it and each has its own abstract store. These must be combined to summarise all possible program stores at that point. In Figure 3, the store coming out of the `invoke` instruction has a type aliasing relationship, whereas that coming out of the `loadnull` instruction does not; also, in the former, location 2 has type `@NonNull Integer`, whilst the latter gives it nullable type `Integer`. This information must be combined conservatively. Since location 2 can hold `null` on at least one incoming path, it can clearly hold `null` at the join point. Hence, the least conservative type for location 2 is `Integer`. Likewise, if a type alias relationship does not hold on all incoming paths, we cannot assume it holds at the join. We formalise this notion of conservatism as a subtype relation:

**Definition 3.** *Let* $S_1 = (\Sigma_1, \Gamma_1, \kappa)$, $S_2 = (\Sigma_2, \Gamma_2, \kappa)$ *be well-formed abstract stores. Then* $S_1 \leq S_2$ *iff* $\forall x, y \in \{0 \ldots \kappa\} [\Sigma_1(\Gamma_1(x)) \leq \Sigma_2(\Gamma_2(x)) \wedge (\Gamma_2(x) = \Gamma_2(y) \implies \Gamma_1(x) = \Gamma_1(y))]$.

Note, Definition 3 requires $\kappa$ be identical on each incoming store; this reflects a standard requirement of Java Bytecode. Now, to construct the abstract store at a join point, our verification system finds the least upper bound, $\sqcup$, of incoming abstract stores — this is the least conservative information obtainable. We formalise this as follows:

**Definition 4.** *Let* $G = (V, E)$ *be the control-flow graph for a method* $M$. *Then, the dataflow equations for* $M$ *are given by* $S_M(y) = \bigsqcup_{x \xrightarrow{l} y \in E} f(I(x), S_M(x), l)$.

Here, the *transfer function*, $f$, is defined by the abstract semantics of Figure 2, $I(x)$ gives the bytecode at node $x$, and the edge label, $l$, distinguishes the true/false branches for `ifceq`. Thus, $S_M(y)$ gives the abstract store going into $y$. Finally, the dataflow equations can be solved as usual by iterating to a fixed point using a *worklist algorithm*.

## 4   Soundness

We now demonstrate that our algorithm *terminates* and is *correct*; that is, if a method passes our verification process, then it cannot throw a `NullPointerException`.

Several previous works have formalised Java Bytecode and shown the standard verification algorithm is correct (e.g. [14,17]). Our system essentially operates in an identical fashion to the standard verifier, except that it additionally maintains type aliases and propagates `@NonNull` annotations. Indeed, our abstract semantics of Figure 2 would be identical to previous work (e.g. [17]) if we removed the requirement for `@NonNull` types at dereference sites and prohibited type aliasing relationships. Thus, we leverage upon these existing works to simplify our proof by restricting attention to those details particular to our system.

An important issue regarding our formalism is that it applies only to *methods*, not *constructors*. The reason for this is detailed in §5. Therefore, in the following, we assume all fields annotated with @NonNull are correctly initialised.

### 4.1 Termination

Demonstrating termination amounts to showing the dataflow equations always have a *least fixed-point*. This requires the transfer function, $f$, is monotonic and that our subtyping relation is a *join-semilattice* (i.e. any two abstract stores always have a unique least upper bound). These are addressed by Lemmas 1 and 2.

Strictly speaking, Definition 3 does not define a join-semilattice over abstract stores, since two stores may not have a unique least upper bound. For example, consider:

$$S_1 = (\{r_1 \mapsto \text{Integer}, r_2 \mapsto \text{Float}\}, \{0 \mapsto r_1, 1 \mapsto r_1, 2 \mapsto r_2\}, 3)$$
$$S_2 = (\{r_1 \mapsto \text{Integer}, r_2 \mapsto \text{Float}\}, \{0 \mapsto r_2, 1 \mapsto r_2, 2 \mapsto r_1\}, 3)$$

Then, the following are minimal upper bounds of $S_1$ and $S_2$:

$$S_3 = (\{r_1 \mapsto \text{Number}, r_2 \mapsto \text{Number}\}, \{0 \mapsto r_1, 1 \mapsto r_1, 2 \mapsto r_2\}, 3)$$
$$S_4 = (\{r_1 \mapsto \text{Number}, r_2 \mapsto \text{Number}\}, \{0 \mapsto r_2, 1 \mapsto r_2, 2 \mapsto r_1\}, 3)$$

Here, $S_3 \leq S_4$, $S_4 \leq S_3$, $\{S_1, S_2\} \leq \{S_3, S_4\}$ and $\neg \exists S.[\{S_1, S_2\} \leq S \leq \{S_3, S_4\}]$. Hence, there is no unique least upper bound of $S_1$ and $S_2$. Such situations arise in our implementation as type objects are Java Objects and, hence, $r_1 \neq r_2$ simply means different object addresses. Now, while $S_3$ and $S_4$ are distinct, they are also *equivalent*:

**Definition 5.** *Let* $S_1 = (\Sigma_1, \Gamma_1, \kappa)$, $S_2 = (\Sigma_2, \Gamma_2, \kappa)$, *then* $S_1$ *and* $S_2$ *are equivalent, written* $S_1 \equiv S_2$, *iff* $S_1 \leq S_2$ *and* $S_1 \geq S_2$.

**Lemma 1.** *Let* $S_1 = (\Sigma_1, \Gamma_1, \kappa)$, $S_2 = (\Sigma_2, \Gamma_2, \kappa)$ *with* $dom(\Gamma_1) = dom(\Gamma_2)$. *If* $U$ *is the set of minimal upper bounds of* $S_1$ *and* $S_2$, *then* $U \neq \emptyset$ *and* $\forall x, y \in U.[x \equiv y]$.

*Proof.* See companion Technical Report [20].

**Lemma 2.** *The dataflow equations from Definition 4 are monotonic.*

*Proof.* By case analysis on the instructions of Figure 2. See companion Technical Report [20].

### 4.2 Correctness

We now show the type aliasing information maintained is correct (Lemma 3), and that any location with @NonNull type cannot hold null (Lemma 4). This yields an overall correctness result for the subset of Java Bytecode we have formalised (Theorem 1).

**Definition 6.** *A Java method is considered to be valid if it passes the standard JVM verification process [19].*

The consequences of Definition 6 include: all conventional types (i.e. ignoring non-null types) are used safely; stack sizes are always the same at the meet points; method and field lookups always resolve; etc.

**Lemma 3.** *Let $S_M = (\Sigma, \Gamma, \kappa)$ be the abstract store for an instruction in a valid method $M$. If $\{l_1 \mapsto r, l_2 \mapsto r\} \subseteq \Gamma$, then the local array/stack locations represented by $l_1$, $l_2$ refer to the same object or array immediately before that instruction in any execution trace of $M$.*

*Proof.* By case analysis on the different instruction types of Figure 2 and the notion of conservatism from Definition 3. See companion Technical Report [20]. □

**Lemma 4.** *Let $S_M = (\Sigma, \Gamma, \kappa)$ be the abstract store for an instruction in a valid method $M$. Assume the parameters of $M$, the fields accessed by $M$ and the return value of all methods invoked by $M$ respect their declared non-null type. Then, if $\{l \mapsto r\} \subseteq \Gamma \wedge \{r \mapsto$ @NonNull $T\} \subseteq \Sigma$, the local array/stack location represented by $l$ does not hold null immediately before that instruction in any execution trace of $M$.*

*Proof.* Again, by case analysis on the different instruction types of Figure 2, the notion of conservatism from Definition 3 and Lemma 3. See companion Technical Report [20].
□

**Theorem 1.** *If our abstract representation can be correctly constructed for all methods in a Java Bytecode program, then no method will throw a* NullPointerException, *assuming all fields are correctly initialised.*

*Proof.* By induction on the call sequence, starting from main(String[]). Using Lemma 4, we formulate an inductive hypothesis stating, for a method $M$, that if the arguments to $M$ respect their non-null types, so do the return value of $M$, the arguments to any calls made by $M$, and any assignments to fields / array elements made by $M$. See companion Technical Report [20]. □

## 5  Implementation

We have implemented our system on top of Java Bytecode and we now discuss many aspects not covered by our discussion so far.

**Constructors.** In Java, a field is assigned null before it is initialised in a constructor [10]. Thus, a field with non-null type will temporarily hold null inside a constructor. Figure 4 highlights the problem. We must ensure such fields are properly initialised, and must restrict access prior to this occurring. Two mechanisms are used to do this:

1. A simple dataflow analysis is used to ensure that all non-null (instance) fields in a class declaration are initialised by that class's constructor.
2. Following [10], we use a secondary type annotation, @Raw, for references to indicate the object referred to may not be initialised. Reads from fields through these return nullable types. The this reference in a constructor is implicitly typed @Raw and @Raw is strictly a supertype of a normal reference.

**Inheritance.** When a method overrides another via inheritance our tool checks that @NonNull types are properly preserved. As usual, types in the parameter position are *contravariant* with inheritance, whilst those in the return position are *covariant*.

```
class Parent {
  Parent() { doBadStuff(); } // error #1, f1 not initialised yet!
  int doBadStuff() { return 0; }
}
class Child extends Parent {
  @NonNull String f1; @NonNull String f2;
  Child() {
    doBadStuff();      // error #2, f1 not initialised before call!
    f1 = "Hello World";
  }                    // error #3, f2 not initialised yet!
  int doBadStuff() { return f1.length(); }
}}
```

**Fig. 4.** Illustrating three distinct problems with constructors and default values. Error #3 arises as all @NonNull fields must be initialised! Error #2 arises as a method is called on this before all @NonNull fields are initialised. Error #1 arises as, when the Child's constructor is called, it calls the Parent's constructor. This, in turn, calls doBadStuff() which dynamically dispatches to the Child's implementation. However, field f1 has not yet been initialised!

**Field Retyping.** Consider this method and its bytecode (recall local 0 holds this):

```
class Test {              0.  load 0
  Integer field;          2.  getfield Test.field
  void f() {              5.  ifnull 16
    if(field != null) {   8.  load 0
      field.toString()    10. getfield Test.field
}}}                       13. invoke Integer.toString
                          16. return
```

The above is not type safe in our system as the non-nullness of the field is lost when it is reloaded. This is strictly correct, since the field's value may have been changed between loads (e.g. by another thread). We require this is resolved manually by adjusting the source to first store the field in a local variable (which is strictly thread local).

**Generics.** Our implementation supports Java Generics. For example, we denote a Vector containing non-null Strings with Vector<@NonNull String>. Extending the subtype relation of Figure 1 is straightforward and follows the conventions of Java Generics (i.e. prohibiting variance on generic parameters). Verifying methods which accept generic parameters is more challenging. To deal with this, we introduce a special type, $T_i$, for each (distinct) generic type used in the method; here, $T_i \leq$ java.lang.Object and $T_i \not\leq T_j$, for $i \neq j$. When checking a method f(T x), the abstract location representing x is initialised to the type $T_i$ used exclusively for representing the generic type T. The subtyping constraints ensure $T_i$ can only flow into variables/return types declared with the same generic type T. However, an interesting problem arises with some existing library classes. For example:

```
class Hashtable<K,V> ... { ...
  V get(K key) { ...; return null; } }
```

Clearly, this class assumes null is a subtype of every type; unfortunately, this is not true in our case, since e.g. null $\not\leq$ @NonNull String. To resolve this, we prohibit instances of Hashtable/HashMap from having a non-null type in V's position.

**Casting + Arrays.** We explicitly prevent the creation of arrays with non-null elements (e.g. `new @NonNull Integer[10]`), as Java always initialises array elements of reference type with `null`. Instead, we require an explicit *cast* to `@NonNull Integer[]` when the programmer knows the array has been fully initialised. Casts from nullable to non-null types are implemented as runtime checks which fail by throwing `ClassCastExceptions`. Their use weakens Theorem 1, since we are essentially trading `NullPointerExceptions` for `ClassCastExceptions`. While this is undesirable, it is analogous to the issue of downcasts in Object-Oriented Languages.

**Instanceof.** Our implementation extends the type aliasing technique to support retyping via `instanceof`. For example:

```
if(x instanceof String) { String y = (String) x; .. }
```

Here, our system retypes x to type `@NonNull String` on the true branch, rending the cast redundant (note, an `instanceof` test never passes on `null`).

**Type Annotations.** The Java Classfile format doesn't allow annotations on generic parameters or in the array type reference position. Therefore, we use a simple mechanism for encoding this information into a classfile. We expect future versions of Java will support such types directly and, indeed, work is already underway in this regard [9].

## 6   Case Studies

We have manually annotated and checked several real-world programs using our non-null type verifier. The largest practical hurdle was annotating Java's standard libraries. This task is enormous and we are far from completion. Indeed, finishing it by hand does not seem feasible; instead, we plan to develop (semi-)automatic procedures to help.

We now consider four real-world code bases which we have successfully annotated: the `java/lang` and `java/io` packages, the `jakarta-oro` text processing library and `javacc`, a well-known parser generator. Table 1 details these. Table 2 gives a breakdown of the annotations added, and the modifications needed for the program to type check. The most frequent modification, "Field Load Fix", was for the field retyping issue identified in §5. To resolve this, we manually added a local variable into which the field was loaded before the null check. Many of these fixes may represent real concurrency bugs, although a deeper analysis of each situation is needed to ascertain this. The next most common modification, "Context Fixes", were for situations where the programmer knew a reference could not hold `null`, but our system was unable to determine this. These were resolved by adding dummy null checks. Examples include:

**Table 1.** Details of our four benchmarks. Note, `java/lang` does not include subpackages.

| benchmark | version | LOC | source |
| --- | --- | --- | --- |
| `java/lang` package | 1.5.0 | 14K | `java.sun.com` |
| `java/io` package | 1.5.0 | 10.6K | `java.sun.com` |
| `jakarta-oro` | 2.0.8 | 8K | `jakarta.apache.org/oro` |
| `javacc` | 3.2 | 28K | `javacc.dev.java.net` |

**Table 2.** Breakdown of annotations added and related metrics. "Annotated Types" gives the total number of annotated parameter, return and field types against the total number of reference / array types in those positions. A breakdown according to position (i.e. parameter, return type or field) is also given. "Field Load Fixes" counts occurrences of the field retyping problem outlined in §5. "Context Fixes" counts the number of dummy null checks which had to be added. "Required Null Checks" counts the number of required null checks, versus the total number of dereference sites. Finally, "Required Casts" counts the number of required casts, versus the total number of casts.

| | Annotated Types | Parameter Annotations | Return Annotations | Field Annotations |
|---|---|---|---|---|
| java/lang | 931 / 1599 | 363 / 748 | 327 / 513 | 241 / 338 |
| java/io | 515 / 1056 | 322 / 672 | 96 / 200 | 97 / 184 |
| jakarta-oro | 413 / 539 | 273 / 320 | 85 / 108 | 55 / 111 |
| javacc | 420 / 576 | 199 / 278 | 53 / 65 | 168 / 233 |

| | Field Load Fixes | Context Fixes | Other Fixes | Required Null Checks | Required Casts |
|---|---|---|---|---|---|
| java/lang | 65 | 61 | 36 | 281 / 2550 | 51 / 96 |
| java/io | 59 | 82 | 21 | 207 / 2254 | 54 / 110 |
| jakarta-oro | 53 | 327 | 29 | 73 / 2014 | 29 / 33 |
| javacc | 109 | 137 (28) | 74 | 287 / 5700 | 141 / 431 |

- `Thread.getThreadGroup()` returns `null` when the thread in question has stopped. But, `Thread.currentThread().getThreadGroup()` will return a non-null value, since the current thread cannot complete `getThreadGroup()` if it has stopped! This assumption was encountered in several places.
- Another difficult situation for our tool is when the nullness of a method's return value depends either on its parameters, or on the object's state. A typical example is illustrated in Figure 5. More complex scenarios were also encountered where, for example, an array was known to hold non-null values up to a given index.
- As outlined in §5, `Hashtable.get(K)` returns `null` if no item exists for the key. A programmer may know that, for specific keys, `get()` cannot return `null` and so can avoid unnecessary `null` check(s). The `javacc` benchmark used many `hashtables` and many context fixes were needed as a result. In Table 2, the number of "Context Fixes" for this particular problem are shown in brackets.

The "Other Fixes" category in Table 2 covers other miscellaneous modifications needed for the code to check. Figure 6 illustrates one such example. Most relate to the initialisation of fields. In particular, helper methods called from constructors which initialise fields are a problem. This is because our system checks each constructor initialises its fields, but does not account for those initialised in helper methods. To resolve this, we either inlined helper methods or initialised fields with dummy values before they were called.

The "Required Null Checks" counts the number of explicit null checks (as present in the original program's source), against the total number of dereference sites. Since, in the normal case, the JVM must check every dereference site, this ratio indicates the potential for speedup resulting from non-null types. Likewise, "Required Casts" counts

```
public void actionPerformed(@NonNull ActionEvent ae) { ...
  JFileChooser jfc = new JFileChooser(); ...
  int rval = jfc.showOpenDialog(null);
  if(rval == JFileChooser.APPROVE_OPTION) {
    File f = jfc.getSelectedFile();
    filePath.setText(f.getCanonicalPath());
  ...
```

**Fig. 5.** A common scenario where the nullness of a method's return type depends upon its context; in this case, if `rval==APPROVE_OPTION`, then `getSelectedFile()` won't return `null`. To resolve this, we must add a "dummy" check that `f!=null` before the method call.

```
public ThreadGroup(String name) {
  this(Thread.currentThread().getThreadGroup(), name);
  ...
```

**Fig. 6.** An interesting example from `java.lang.ThreadGroup`. The constructor invoked via the `this` call requires a non-null argument (and this is part of its Javadoc specification). Although `getThreadGroup()` can return `null`, it cannot here (as discussed previously). Our tool reports an error for this which cannot be resolved by inserting a dummy `null` check, since the `this` call must be the first statement of the constructor. Therefore, we either inline the constructor being called, or construct a helper method which can accept a `null` parameter.

the number of casts actually required, versus the total number present (recall from §5 that our tool automatically retypes local variables after `instanceof` tests, making numerous casts redundant.)

We were also interested in whether or not our system could help documentation. In fact, it turns out that of the 1101 public methods in `java/lang`, 83 were misdocumented. That is, the Javadoc failed to specify that a parameter must not be `null` when, according to our system, it needed to be. We believe this is actually pretty good, all things considered, and reflects the quality of documentation for `java/lang`. Interestingly, many of the problem cases were found in `java/lang/String`.

Finally, a comment regarding performance seems prudent, since we have elided performance results for brevity. In fact, the performance of our system is very competitive with the standard bytecode verifier. This is not surprising, since our system uses a very similar algorithm to the standard bytecode verifier, albeit extended with type aliasing.

## 7   Related Work

Several works have considered the problem of checking non-null types. Fähndrich and Leino investigated the constructor problem (see §5) and outlined a solution using raw types [10]. However, no mechanism for actually checking non-null types was presented. The FindBugs tool checks @NonNull annotations using a dataflow analysis that accounts for comparisons against `null` [16,15]. Their approach does not employ type aliasing and provides no guarantee that all potential errors will be reported. While this is reasonable for a lightweight software quality tool, it is not suitable for bytecode verification. ESC/Java also checks non-null types and accounts for the effect of conditionals [11]. The tool supports type aliasing (to some extent), can check very subtle pieces of code and is strictly more precise than our system. However, it relies upon a theorem prover which employs numerous transformations and optimisations on the intermediate representation, as well as a complex back-tracking search procedure. This makes it rather unsuitable for bytecode verification, where efficiency is paramount.

Ekman *et al.* implemented a non-null checker within the JustAdd compiler [8]. This accounts for the effect of conditionals, but does not consider type aliasing as there is little need in their setting where a full AST is available. To apply their technique to Java Bytecode would require first reconstructing the AST to eliminate type aliasing between stack and local variable locations. This would add additional overhead to the bytecode verification process, compared to our more streamlined approach. Pominville *et al.* also discuss a non-null analysis that accounts for conditionals, but again does not consider type aliasing [25]. They present empirical data suggesting many internal null checks can be eliminated, and that this leads to a useful improvement in program performance.

Chalin *et al.* empirically studied the ratio of parameter, return and field declarations which are intended to be non-null, concluding that $2/3$ are [3]. To do this, they manually annotated existing code bases, and checked for correctness by testing and with ESC/-Java. JavaCOP provides an expressive language for writing type system extensions, such as non-null types [2]. This system cannot account for the effects of conditionals; however, as a work around, the tool allows assignment from a nullable variable x to a non-null variable if this is the first statement after a `x!=null` conditional.

CQual is a flow-sensitive qualifier inference algorithm which supports numerous type qualifiers, but does not account for conditionals at all [12,13]. Building on this is the work of Chin *et al.* which also supports numerous qualifiers, including `nonzero`, `unique` and `nonnull` [5,6]. Again, conditionals cannot be accounted for, which severely restricts the use of `nonnull`. The Java Modelling Language (JML) adds formal specifications to Java and supports non-null types [7]. However, JML is strictly a specification language, and requires separate tools (such as ESC/Java) for checking.

Related work also exists on type inference for Object-Oriented languages (e.g. [21,24,28]). These, almost exclusively, assume the original program is completely untyped and employ set constraints (see [1]) for inferring types. This proceeds across method calls, necessitating knowledge of the program's call graph (which must be approximated in languages with dynamic dispatch). Typically, a constraint graph representing the entire program is held in memory at once, making these approaches somewhat unsuited to separate compilation [21]. Such systems share a strong relationship with other constraint-based program analyses, such as *points-to* analysis (e.g. [18,26,22,23]).

Several works also use techniques similar to type aliasing, albeit in different settings. Smith *et al.* capture aliasing constraints between locations in the program store to provide safe object deallocation and imperative updates [27]; for example, when an object is deallocated the supplied reference and any aliases are retyped to *junk*. Chang *et al.* maintain a graph, called the *e-graph*, of aliasing relationships between elements from different abstract domains [4]; their least upper bound operator maintains a very similar invariant to ours. Zhang *et al.* consider aliasing of constraint variables in the context of set-constraint solvers [29].

## 8  Conclusion

We have presented a novel approach to the bytecode verification of non-null types. A key feature is that our system infers two kinds of information from conditionals: nullness information and type aliases. We have formalised this system for a subset of Java Bytecode, and proved soundness. Finally, we have detailed an implementation of our system and reported our experiences gained from using it. The tool itself is freely available from http://www.mcs.vuw.ac.nz/~djp/JACK/.

**Acknowledgements.** Thanks to Lindsay Groves, James Noble, Paul H.J. Kelly, Stephen Nelson, and Neil Leslie for many excellent comments on earlier drafts. This work is supported by the University Research Fund of Victoria University of Wellington.

## References

1. Aiken, A.: Introduction to set constraint-based program analysis. Science of Computer Programming 35(2–3), 79–111 (1999)
2. Andreae, C., Noble, J., Markstrum, S., Millstein, T.: A framework for implementing pluggable type systems. In: OOPSLA, pp. 57–74. ACM Press, New York (2006)
3. Chalin, P., James, P.R.: Non-null references by default in Java: Alleviating the nullity annotation burden. In: Ernst, E. (ed.) ECOOP 2007. LNCS, vol. 4609, pp. 227–247. Springer, Heidelberg (2007)
4. Chang, B.-Y.E., Leino, K.R.M.: Abstract interpretation with alien expressions and heap structures. In: Cousot, R. (ed.) VMCAI 2005. LNCS, vol. 3385, pp. 147–163. Springer, Heidelberg (2005)
5. Chin, B., Markstrum, S., Millstein, T.: Semantic type qualifiers. In: PLDI, pp. 85–95. ACM Press, New York (2005)
6. Chin, B., Markstrum, S., Millstein, T., Palsberg, J.: Inference of user-defined type qualifiers and qualifier rules. In: Sestoft, P. (ed.) ESOP 2006. LNCS, vol. 3924, pp. 264–278. Springer, Heidelberg (2006)
7. Cielecki, M., Fulara, J., Jakubczyk, K., Jancewicz, L.: Propagation of JML non-null annotations in Java programs. In: PPPJ, pp. 135–140. ACM Press, New York (2006)
8. Ekman, T., Hedin, G.: Pluggable checking and inferencing of non-null types for Java. Journal of Object Technology 6(9), 455–475 (2007)
9. Ernst, M.: Annotations on Java types. Java Specification Request (JSR) 308 (2007)
10. Fähndrich, M., Leino, K.R.M.: Declaring and checking non-null types in an object-oriented language. In: OOPSLA, pp. 302–312. ACM Press, New York (2003)
11. Flanagan, C., Leino, K.R.M., Lillibridge, M., Nelson, G., Saxe, J.B., Stata, R.: Extended static checking for Java. In: Proc. PLDI, pp. 234–245. ACM Press, New York (2002)
12. Foster, J.S., Fähndrich, M., Aiken, A.: A theory of type qualifiers. In: Proc. PLDI, pp. 192–203. ACM Press, New York (1999)
13. Foster, J.S., Terauchi, T., Aiken, A.: Flow-sensitive type qualifiers. In: Proc. PLDI, pp. 1–12. ACM Press, New York (2002)
14. Goldberg, A.: A Specification of Java Loading and Bytecode Verification. In: Conference on Computer & Communications Security, pp. 49–58. ACM Press, New York (1998)

15. Hovemeyer, D., Pugh, W.: Finding more null pointer bugs, but not too many. In: Proc. PASTE, pp. 9–14. ACM Press, New York (2007)
16. Hovemeyer, D., Spacco, J., Pugh, W.: Evaluating and tuning a static analysis to find null pointer bugs. In: Proc. PASTE, pp. 13–19. ACM Press, New York (2005)
17. Leroy, X.: Java bytecode verification: algorithms and formalizations. Journal of Automated Reasoning 30(3/4), 235–269 (2003)
18. Lhoták, O., Hendren, L.J.: Context-sensitive points-to analysis: Is it worth it? In: Mycroft, A., Zeller, A. (eds.) CC 2006. LNCS, vol. 3923, pp. 47–64. Springer, Heidelberg (2006)
19. Lindholm, T., Yellin, F.: The Java Virtual Machine Specification, 2nd edn. The Java Series. Addison Wesley Longman, Inc., Amsterdam (1999)
20. Male, C., Pearce, D.J., Potanin, A., Dymnikov, C.: Java bytecode verification for @NonNull types. Technical report, Victoria University of Wellington (2007)
21. Palsberg, J., Schwartzbach, M.I.: Object-oriented type inference. In: Proc. OOPSLA, pp. 146–161. ACM Press, New York (1991)
22. Pearce, D.J., Kelly, P.H.J., Hankin, C.: Online cycle detection and difference propagation: Applications to pointer analysis. Software Quality Journal 12(4), 309–335 (2004)
23. Pearce, D.J., Kelly, P.H.J., Hankin, C.: Efficient field-sensitive pointer analysis for C. Transactions on Programming Languages and Systems 30(1) (2008)
24. Plevyak, J., Chien, A.A.: Precise concrete type inference for object-oriented languages. In: Proc. OOPSLA, pp. 324–340. ACM Press, New York (1994)
25. Pominville, P., Qian, F., Vallée-Rai, R., Hendren, L., Verbrugge, C.: A framework for optimizing Java using attributes. In: Wilhelm, R. (ed.) CC 2001. LNCS, vol. 2027, pp. 334–554. Springer, Heidelberg (2001)
26. Rountev, A., Milanova, A., Ryder, B.G.: Points-to analysis for Java using annotated constraints. In: Proc. OOPSLA, pp. 43–55. ACM Press, New York (2001)
27. Smith, F., Walker, D., Morrisett, G.: Alias types. In: Smolka, G. (ed.) ESOP 2000. LNCS, vol. 1782, pp. 366–381. Springer, Heidelberg (2000)
28. Wang, T., Smith, S.F.: Precise constraint-based type inference for Java. In: Knudsen, J.L. (ed.) ECOOP 2001. LNCS, vol. 2072, pp. 99–117. Springer, Heidelberg (2001)
29. Zhang, Y., Nielson, F.: A scalable inclusion constraint solver using unification. In: King, A. (ed.) LOPSTR 2007. LNCS, vol. 4915, Springer, Heidelberg (2007)

# Efficient Context-Sensitive Shape Analysis
# with Graph Based Heap Models

Mark Marron[1], Manuel Hermenegildo[1,2], Deepak Kapur[1], and Darko Stefanovic[1]

[1]University of New Mexico
{marron,kapur,darko}@cs.unm.edu
[2] Technical University of Madrid and IMDEA-Software
herme@fi.upm.es

**Abstract.** The performance of heap analysis techniques has a significant impact on their utility in an optimizing compiler. Most shape analysis techniques perform interprocedural dataflow analysis in a context-sensitive manner, which can result in analyzing each procedure body many times (causing significant increases in runtime even if the analysis results are memoized). To improve the effectiveness of memoization (and thus speed up the analysis) *project/extend* operations are used to remove portions of the heap model that cannot be affected by the called procedure (effectively reducing the number of different contexts that a procedure needs to be analyzed with). This paper introduces *project/extend* operations that are capable of accurately modeling properties that are important when analyzing non-trivial programs (sharing, nullity information, destructive recursive functions, and composite data structures). The techniques we introduce are able to handle these features while significantly improving the effectiveness of memoizing analysis results (and thus improving analysis performance). Using a range of well known benchmarks (many of which have not been successfully analyzed using other existing shape analysis methods) we demonstrate that our approach results in significant improvements in both accuracy and efficiency over a baseline analysis.

## 1  Introduction

Recent work on shape analysis techniques [25,28,1,14,15,9,8] has resulted in a number of techniques that are capable of accurately representing the properties (connectivity, interference, and shape) that are needed for a range of optimization and parallelization applications. However, the computational cost of performing these analyses has limited their applicability. A significant component of the analysis runtime is due to the need to perform a context-sensitive interprocedural analysis, where each procedure body may be analyzed multiple times (once for each different calling context).

The practice of using a memo-table to avoid recomputing analysis results and the use of a *project* operation to remove portions of the heap that cannot affect or be affected by the called procedure are standard techniques for minimizing the number of times each function needs to be analyzed during interprocedural dataflow analysis [2,17,16,19]. The two major goals of the *project* operation are improving the effectiveness of memoizing analysis results by removing portions of the heap that could cause spurious inequalities

L. Hendren (Ed.): CC 2008, LNCS 4959, pp. 245–259, 2008.
© Springer-Verlag Berlin Heidelberg 2008

between calling contexts and preventing the loss of precision that occurs when recursive procedures use a summary representation for multiple out-of-scope references (e.g. local reference variables with the same name but that exist in different call frames).

The *project* operation for heap models and the utility of locality axioms have been analyzed in a number of papers [22,21,7,12,4]. These techniques use variations on the notion of a *frame rule* as presented in [11,20] and identify a number of features of the *project* operation that are of particular importance for interprocedural analysis using heap domains. A major distinction is made between the projection operation in *cutpoint-free* cases, where there are no pointers that cross from a section of the heap that is *unreachable* from the procedure arguments into a section of the heap that is *reachable* from the procedure arguments, and cases where such pointers may exist.

This paper presents a method for using cutpoints to support interprocedural heap analysis. We then use the technique to quickly analyze (10's of seconds) programs that are larger (by a factor of 2-4) and more varied (in terms of data structures and algorithms) than any other analysis technique to date. Our first contribution is the reformulation of the project/extend operations in [21] so that they can be used in a graph based (as opposed to an access path based) heap model which allows us to use a very compact and efficient representation of heap connectivity. Our second contribution is the extension of the original approach to handle two classes of programatic events that are critical to analyzing real world programs, analyzing programs that involve non-trivial sharing and composite data structures [1,15] and propagating nullity test information from callee to caller scope. Finally we use the results of the heap analysis to drive the parallelization of a range of benchmarks (several of which have not been successfully analyzed/parallelized using shape information) achieving an average parallel speedup of 1.69 on a dual-core machine.

## 2   Example Code

To develop intuition about the mechanism and purpose of *project/extend* operations we look at a simple function (Figure 1) that illustrates the basic functioning of the *project/extend* operations and the propagation of nullity information from the callee to the caller scope. Our lists are made of objects of *type* LNode, each LNode object has two fields, a nx field which refers to the next element in the list and a field f which stores a boolean.

```
LNode LInit(LNode l)
  if(l == null)
    return;

  tin = l.nx;
  LInit(tin);
  l.f = true;
```

**Fig. 1.** Recursive List Initialize

Accurately analyzing the initialization method (LInit) requires the analysis to propagate information inferred about cutpoints in the callee scope back into the caller scope. If the analysis is unable to use the `l == null` test in the callee scope to infer that `l.nx` is `null` in the caller scope then the analysis will not be able to infer that after the method returns the argument list is either `null` or must have the `true` value in all the `f` fields.

## 3   Heap Model

We model the concrete heap as a labeled, directed multi-graph $(V, E)$ where each vertex $v \in V$ is an object in the store or a variable in the environment, and each labeled directed edge $e \in E$ represents a pointer between objects or a reference from a variable to an object. Each edge is given a label that is an identifier from the program, an edge $(a, b) \in E$ labeled with $p$, we use the notation $a \xrightarrow{p} b$ to indicate that $a$ points to the object $b$ via the field name (or identifier) $p$.

A *region* of memory $\mathfrak{R}$ is a subset of the objects in memory, with all the pointers that connect these objects and all the cross-region pointers that start or end at an object in this region. Formally, let $C \subseteq V$ be a subset of objects, and let $P_i = \{p \mid \exists a, b \in C, a \xrightarrow{p} b\}$ and $P_c = \{p \mid \exists a \in C, x \notin C, a \xrightarrow{p} x \lor x \xrightarrow{p} a\}$ be respectively the set of internal and cross-region pointers for $C$. Then a region is the tuple $(C, P_i, P_c)$. For a region $\mathfrak{R} = (C, P_i, P_c)$ and objects $a, b \in C$, we say $a$ and $b$ are *connected* in $\mathfrak{R}$ if they are in the same weakly-connected component of the graph $(C, P_i)$. Objects $a$ and $b$ are *disjoint* in $\mathfrak{R}$ if they are in different weakly-connected components of the graph $(C, P_i)$.

### 3.1   Abstract Heap Model

The underlying abstract heap domain is a graph where each node represents a region of the heap or a variable and each edge represents a set of pointers or a variable target. The nodes and edges are augmented with additional instrumentation predicates. The abstract domain evaluates the predicates using a *3-valued* semantics: predicates are either definitely true, definitely false, or unknown [25]. Our analysis tracks the following set of instrumentation predicates. Our choice of predicates is influenced by common predicates tracked in previous papers on shape analysis [5,24,28,20].

*Types.* For each type $t$ in the program, there is an instrumentation predicate (also written $t$) that is true at a concrete heap node if any concrete object represented by the node may have type $t$.

*Linearity.* Each abstract node has a *linearity* that represents whether it represents at most one concrete node (linearity 1) or any set of 0 or more concrete nodes (written #).

*Abstract Layout.* To track the connectivity and shape of the region a node abstracts, the analysis uses *abstract layout* predicates *Singleton*, *List*, *Tree*, *MultiPath*, or *Cycle*. The *Singleton* predicate states that there are no pointers between any of the objects represented by an abstract node. The *List* predicate is similar to the inductive *List* predicate in separation logic [20]. The other predicates correspond to the definitions for Trees, Dags, and Cycles in the literature, for the formal definitions see [14].

*Interference.* The heap model uses two properties to track the potential that two references can reach the same memory location in the region that a node represents.

The first property is for references that are represented by different edges in the heap model. Given the concretization function $\gamma$ and two edges $e_1, e_2$ that are incoming edges to the node $n$, the predicate that defines *inConnected* in the abstract domain is: $e_1, e_2$ are *inConnected* with respect to $n$ if it is possible that $\exists r_1 \in \gamma(e_1) \wedge \exists r_2 \in \gamma(e_2) \wedge \exists a, b \in \gamma(n)$ s.t. $(r_1$ refers to $a) \wedge (r_2$ refers to $b) \wedge (a, b$ connected$)$. For improved precision we also track *may* and *must* aliasing ($e_1, e_2$ are *inConnected* and $a = b$) between the references the edges abstract (*must* aliasing is only meaningful if the edge represents a single references, see [15] for an approach that generalizes *must-aliasing* to sets of references).

The second property is for the case where the references are represented by the same edge. To model this the *interfere* property is introduced. An edge $e$ represents interfering references if there may exist references $r_1, r_2 \in \gamma(e)$ such that the objects that $r_1, r_2$ refer to are connected/aliased. A three-element lattice, $np < ip < ap$, $np$ for edges with all non-interfering references and $ip$ for potentially interfering references and $ap$ for potentially aliasing references, is used to represent the interference property.

*The Heap Graph.* Each node in the graph either represents a region of the heap or a variable. The variable nodes are labeled with the variable that they represent. Nodes representing the concrete heap regions contain a record that tracks the types of the concrete objects that the node represents (*types*), the number of objects (either 1 or #) that may be in the region (*count*), and the abstract layout of a node (*layout*). Each node also tracks the connectivity relation between pairs of incoming edges. A binary relation *connR* is used to track the *inConnected* relation. Although the connectivity relation is a property of the nodes, for readability in the figures we associate the information with the edges. Thus, each node is represented as a record of the form [types layout count].

As in the case of the nodes, each edge contains a record that tracks additional information about the edge. The *offset* component indicates the offsets (labels) of the references that are abstracted by the edge. The number of references that the edge may represent is tracked with the *maxCut* property. The *interfere* property tracks the possibility that the edge represents references that interfere. Finally, we have a field *connto* which is a list of all the other edges/variables that the edge may be connected to according to the *connR* relation (we add a ( ! ) for the edges in the list that represent references which *may* alias and a ($\sim$) if the edges represent single references that *must* alias). To simplify the figures if the *connto* field is empty we omit it entirely from the record in the figure. Since the variable edges always represent single references and the offset label is implicitly the name of the variable the record simply contains the *connR* information or is omitted entirely if the *connR* relation is empty. To simplify the discussion of the examples each edge also has a unique label. The pointer edges in the figures are represented as records {label offset maxCut interfere connto}.

The abstract heap domain is restricted via a normal form [14,15]. The normal form ensures that the heap graph remains finite, and that equality comparisons are efficient. The local data flow analysis is performed using a *Hoare (Partially Disjunctive) Power Domain* [13,26] over these graphs. Interprocedural analysis is performed in a context-sensitive manner and the procedure analysis results are memoized. At each call/return site the portion of the heap graphs passed to the call are joined into a single graph. The design of the join operation is such that, in general, information lost in the join can be recovered when needed later in the program. The decision to perform joins at call sites (programs tend to have uniform expectations of the portion of the heap passed to and returned from calls) and to perform the join only on the portion of the heap passed to the called method results in very little loss of precision while ensuring the abstract model remains compact.

*Abstract Call Stack.* Our concrete model for the *call stack* is a function $S_m : (LV \times \mathbb{N}) \mapsto O$, where $LV$ is the set of local variable names and $\mathbb{N}$ represents the depth in the call sequence (main is at depth 1) and $O$ is the set of all live objects. Thus, the pair $(v, 4)$ refers to the value of the variable $v$ in the scope of the $4^{th}$ call frame.

To represent the concrete call stack we introduce *stack variables* which represent the values of local variables on the stack (for a variation on this approach see [22]). In our extension each *stack variable* summarizes all the possible targets (in a given graph) for a given variable name on the stack. Given a variable name $v$ and a heap graph $G$ we define a variable name $v'$ for use in the abstract domain (we will select a better naming scheme in Section 4) where: $v'$ is the abstraction of all the variables in the call stack, $\exists i \in \mathbb{N}$, node $n \in G$, object $o_n$ s.t. $o_n \in \gamma(n) \wedge S_m(v, i) = o_n$.

By associating the set of stack locations that are abstracted with the set of targets in a given abstract heap graph, we can naturally partition the *stack variables* along with the heap graphs. Since each *stack variable* is associated with only the values on the stack that point into a region of the heap represented by the given heap graph, it is straightforward to partition and join them when partitioning the heap graphs.

Thus, during the local analysis the heap graph represents the portion of the program heap that is visible from the local variables and is augmented with some number of *stack variables* and *cutpoint variables* which relate variable values and the heap in the caller scope to the portions of the heap reachable from callee scope local variables.

For efficiency and in order to ensure analysis termination the naming scheme we choose will result in situations where multiple cutpoint (or stack) edges are given the same name. This may result in some amount of information loss (particularly with respect to reachability and aliasing). To minimize the loss that occurs we introduce an instrumentation domain for the stack/cutpoint variable edges, *nameColl* = {*pdj*, *pua*, *pa*}. Where *pdj* indicates a cutpoint/stack name representing (a single edge) or edges where the edges do not represent any pairwise *connected* references, *pua* indicates a name representing multiple edges where there are no pairwise *aliases*, while *pa* is the indicates the name represents edges that they may have pairwise *aliasing*. Thus, the cutpoint variable edges are represented with records {maxCut interfere connto nameColl} (stack variables are not used in this example).

## 4    Stack Variables, Cutpoint Labels

When performing the project operation in heaps with cutpoints we need to name the *stack variables* as well as the *cutpoint* edges. We use a simple technique for the stack variables: given a variable name v defined in the caller function fcaller we use the name $fcaller*v to represent this variable in the callee scope. This naming scheme can create false dependencies on the local scope names unless the variable information is normalized during the comparisons of entries in the memo-table.

Naming edges that cross the cutpoints is more complex since we need to balance the accuracy of the analysis with the potential of introducing spurious differences resulting from isomorphic (or nearly so) cutpoint edges being given different names. For the renaming of the cutpoint edges we assume that special names for the arguments to the function have been introduced. The first pointer parameter is referred to by the special variable name p1 and the $i^{th}$ pointer argument is referred to by the variable pi.

Figure 2(c) shows a recursive call to LInit where the special argument name p1 has been added to represent the value of the first argument to the function. In this figure the edge *e1* is a cutpoint edge since it starts in the portion of the heap that is unreachable from the argument variables and ends in a portion of the heap that is reachable from the argument variables (this differs slightly from the definition for cutpoints in [21] but allows us to handle edges uniformly).

For each cutpoint edge we generate a pair of names: one is used in the unreachable section of the heap graph and one in the reachable section, which allows an abstract heap model to represent both incoming and outgoing cutpoint edges that are isomorphic and exist in the same abstract heap component without loss of precision.

If we are adding a cutpoint for the method call fcaller and the edge $e$, which is a cutpoint, starting at $n$ and ending at $n'$, and has edge label fe. We can find the shortest path (f1 ... fk) from any of the pi variables to $n'$ (using lexographic comparison on the path names to break ties). Using the pi argument variable and the path (f1 ... fk) we derive the cutpoint basename = fcaller*pi*f1*...*fk*fe We compute a pair of static names (*unreachN*, *reachN*) where *unreachN* = $basename- and *reachN* = $basename+. In Figure 2(d) the cutpoint name $p1+ (for brevity we simply label the cutpoint with the pi variable) is used to represent the endpoint of the cutpoint edge in the reachable component of the heap and $p1- to track a dummy node associated with the cutpoint edge in the unreachable component of the heap.

## 5    Example

The example program, Figure 1, recursively initializes the f fields in a linked list to the value true. Figure 2(a) shows the abstract heap model at the entry of the first call to the procedure (for simplicity we ignore any caller scope variables).

In Figure 2(a), variable 1 refers to a node that represents LNode objects (*types* = {LNode}, abbreviated to LN), that represents a region with no internal connections (*Layout* = S), which contains a single object (*count* = 1), and where all the incoming edges represent disjoint pointers (the connto lists on the edges are omitted). In this figure we also have that the elements in the list have unknown truth values in the f

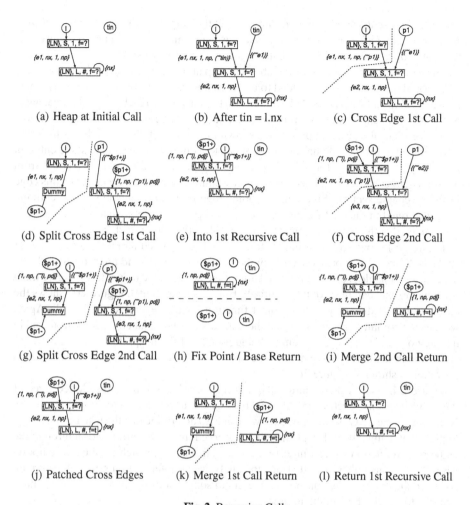

**Fig. 2.** Recursive Calls

fields (f=?). There is a single edge out of this node representing pointers stored in the nx field of the object represented by the node. This edge represents a single pointer (*maxCut* = 1) and all the pointers are non-interfering (*interfere* = *np*). Finally, this edge refers to a node that also represents LNode objects but may represent many of these objects (*count* = #) and, since the *Layout* value is *List*, we know that the objects may be connected in a list-like shape. Since there is a single incoming edge and it represents a single pointer, we can safely assume that this edge refers to the head of the list structure.

Figure 2(b) shows the abstract heap model just after executing the statement tin = 1.nx. Since we know that *e1* refers to the head element of the list from Figure 2(a) we replaced the single *List*-shaped node with a node representing the unique head element and a node representing the tail of the list. Since the head element is unique we set the *count* of this new node to 1. Additionally, the only possible layout for a node of *count* 1 is *Singleton*. Finally, if a node represents a single object then all the outgoing field edges can each represent a single pointer. Thus, we set the outgoing edge to have a *maxCut* = 1. Also note that after the load the analysis has determined that tin and e1 must alias (indicated by the ∼e1 and ∼tin entries in the connectivity lists).

Figure 2(c) shows the state of the abstract heap at the entry of the *project* procedure. The special name *p1* has been added to represent the value of the first pointer argument to the function and we have added a dotted line to indicate the reachable and unreachable portions of the heap. Note that the edge *e1* is a cutpoint edge according to our definition.

The result of the project operation is shown in Figure 2(d). The *e1* edge, which was a cutpoint edge for the call, has been remapped to a dummy node and the static cutpoint names $p1− and $p1+ (for brevity we omit the procedure name and edge labels from the static names) have been introduced at the dummy node and at the target of this edge in the reachable section. Since this cutpoint edge only represents the single cutpoint edge generated in this call frame nameColl = pdj. Also note that the analysis has determined that the formal parameter p1 must alias the cutpoint edge $p1+.

Figure 2(e) shows the resulting abstract heap that is passed into the callee scope for analysis. Since all the local variables in the caller scope either did not refer to nodes in the callee reachable section or are dead after the call return we do not have to give them stack names and can remove them entirely from the heap model. Figure 2(f) shows the abstract heap at the entry to the project function for the second recursive call. Again we have a cutpoint edge *e2*. Note that the reachable cutpoint label, $p1+ introduced in the previous call is now in the unreachable portion of the heap, thus ($p1+) does not conflict with the unreachable name added in this call ($p1−). The result of the project operation is shown in Figure 2(g).

Figure 2(h) shows the eventual fixpoint approximation (above the dotted line) of the analysis of this function and also the base case return value (below the dotted line). Notice in the base case return value we were able to determine that the test l == null implies that l must be null and since we preserved must alias information through the cutpoint introduction we can infer that l must alias $p1+, which implies the cutpoint edge ($p1+) must also be null. Thus, the analysis can infer that on return the cutpoint edge is either null or is non-null and refers to some list in which all the f fields have been set to true (f=t in the figure).

In Figure 2(i) we show how the fixpoint approximation for the reachable section of the heap is recombined with the unreachable section of the heap using the *extend* operation. After the recombination we get the abstract heap model shown in Figure 2(j). In Figure 2(i) we have unioned the graphs and are ready to patch up the cutpoint cross edge information. The static name $p1+ in the reachable portion of the heap has been used to compute the associated unreachable name ($p1−). Then the algorithm identifies the edge associated with the dummy node referred to by $p1− (*e2*) and remapped this edge to end at the target of $p1+ (tin has been nullified since it is dead).

Figure 2(k) shows the *extend* operation at the return from the first recursive call which is similar to the situation in the second recursive call. The resulting abstract heap is shown in Figure 2(l) which can be joined with the result of the base case test and then completes the analysis of the method. As desired, the analysis has determined that the recursive list initialize procedure preserves the list shape of the argument list and that all of the f fields in the list have been set to true (f=t in the figures).

## 6    Project and Extend Algorithms

*Project.* We assume that before the *projectHeap* function is invoked all of the special argument variable names have been added to the heap model. This allows *projectHeap* (Algorithm 1 below) to easily compute the section of the heap model that is reachable in the callee procedure and then compute the set of nodes that comprise the unreachable portion of the heap model.

---

**Algorithm 1.** projectHeap

---

**input**  : $h$: the heap model to be partitioned
**output**: $h_r$, $h_u$: the reachable and unreachable partitions, *snu*, *ncs*: the static names used and
    newly created
*reachNodes* ← set of nodes reachable from args;
*unreachNodes* ← set of nodes unreachable from args;
*crossEdges* ← set of edges that start in *unreachNodes* and end in *reachNodes*;
*snu* ← ∅;
*ncs* ← ∅;
**foreach** edge $e$ in *crossEdges* **do**
    *(sn, isnew)* ← procCrossEdge($h$, $e$, *reachNodes*);
    *snu*.add(*sn*);
    **if** *isnew* **then** *ncs*.add(*sn*);

$h_u$ ← subgraph of $h$ on the nodes *unreachNodes* ∪ {dummy nodes from procCrossEdge};
$h_r$ ← subgraph of $h$ on the nodes *reachNodes*;
**return** *($h_r$, $h_u$, snu, ncs)*;

---

For each edge that crosses from the unreachable section into the reachable section we add a pair of static names to represent the edge (Algorithm 2). Since the heap model stores a number of domain properties in each edge, we create a dummy node and remap the edge to end at this node. Then, the *unreachN* static name is set to refer to this dummy node. In the reachable portion of the heap graph we simply set the *reachN* static name to refer to the target of the cross edge.

When adding the *reachN* static name to the reachable section of the heap graph the name may or may not already be present in the heap graph. If the name is not present then we add it to the static name map and for later use we note that this is the call where the name is introduced. Otherwise a name collision has occurred and we must mark the edges representing the possible cutpoints appropriately (for simplicity we mark all the edges). If there may be aliasing we note that the cutpoints from different frames may have aliasing targets (*pa*) and similarly if the new cutpoint edge may be connected with an existing cutpoint edge we mark them as being pairwise connected (*pua*). The functions *makeEdgeForUnreachCutpoint* and *makeEdgeForReachCutpoint* are used to produce edges to represent the cutpoint (based on the static name and the cutpoint edge properties) in the unreachable and reachable portions of the heap.

Once all of the cutpoint edges have been replaced by the required static names, the heap can be transformed into the unreachable version (where all the nodes in the reachable section and all the variables/static names that only refer to reachable nodes have been removed) and the reachable version (where the nodes in the unreachable section and the associated names have been removed).

---

**Algorithm 2.** procCrossEdge

---

**input**  : $h$: the heap, $e$: the cross edge, *reachNodes*: set of reachable nodes
**output**: *rsn*: the name used, *isnew*: true if *rsn* a new name
$n_e \leftarrow$ the node $e$ ends at;
$n_i \leftarrow$ new dummy node;
*(ursn, rsn)* $\leftarrow$ genStaticNamePairForEdge($h, e$);
$e_u \leftarrow$ makeEdgeForUnreachCutpoint($e$, *ursn*);
set endpoint of $e_u$ to $n_i$;
add $e_u$ as an edge for *ursn*;
$e_r \leftarrow$ makeEdgeForReachCutpoint($e$, *rsn*);
set endpoint of $e_r$ to $n_e$;
remap the endpoint of $e$ to $n_i$;
**if** the name *rsn* exists and has edges pointing to a node in *reachNodes* **then**
    *rsnes* $\leftarrow \{e'|e'$ is an edge for the cutpoint var *rsn*$\}$;
    add $e_r$ as an edge for *rsn*;
    **if** $e_r$ *is inConnected with an edge in* rsnes **then** set edges in *rsnes* and $e_r$ to *pua*;
    **if** $e_r$ *may alias with an edge in* rsnes **then** set edges in *rsnes* and $e_r$ to *pa*;
    **return** *(rsn, false)*;
**else**
    add the name *rsn* to $h$;
    add $e_r$ as an edge for *rsn*;
    **return** *(rsn, true)*;

---

*Extend.* After the call return we need to rejoin the unreachable portion of the heap that we extracted before the procedure call entry with the result we obtained from analyzing the callee procedure. This is done by looking at each of the static names that was used to represent a cutpoint edge and reconnecting as required. Then, each of the newly introduced cutpoint names can be removed from the heap model. The pseudo-code to do this is shown in Algorithm 3.

This algorithm merges all edges with the same reachable cutpoint name so that there is at most one target edge for a given cutpoint name in the reachable heap $h_r$ (this simplifies the algorithm and is in our experience is quite accurate). The algorithm then pairs up the two cutpoint names and remaps the edge we saved in the unreachable section to the target node in the reachable section subject to a number of tests to propagate sharing information (the nullity information is propagated due to the fact that the dummy node and all incoming edges are always removed but the foreach loop on the targets of *ursn* does not execute since the target set is empty). The $e_r.nameColl = pua$ test is true if this edge represents sets of pointers that do not have pairwise aliases. Thus, we mark the newly remapped edge and $e_r$ as pairwise unaliased. Similarly, the $e_r.nameColl = pdj$ test is true if this edge represents cutpoint/stack edges that are pairwise disjoint. Thus, we mark the newly remapped edge and $e_r$ as pairwise disjoint.

**Algorithm 3.** extendHeap

---

**input** : $h_r$, $h_u$: the reachable and unreachable partitions, *snu*, *ncs*: the static names used and
      newly created
**output**: $h$: the joined heap model
$h \leftarrow$ new *heap*();
$h$.heapGraph $\leftarrow$ mergeGraphs($h_r$.heapGraph, $h_u$.heapGraph);
**foreach** static name *sn* in *snu* **do**
    $ursn \leftarrow$ reachNameToUnreachName(*sn*);
    $n_r \leftarrow$ the target of *sn* in $h_r$.nameMap;
    **foreach** node $n_u$ that is a target of *ursn* in $h_u$.*nameMap* **do**
        $e_r \leftarrow$ the single incoming edge to $n_u$;
        remap $e_r$ to end at the target of $n_r$;
        $e_r$.interfere = $e_r$.interfere $\sqcup$ $n_r$.interfere;
        **if** $e_r$.nameColl = *pua* **then** set $e_r$ and $n_r$ as unaliased;
        **if** $e_r$.nameColl = *pdj* **then** set $e_r$ and $n_r$ as disjoint;

    $h_u$.removeNodeAllEdges(target of *ursn*);
    $h_u$.unmapStaticName(*ursn*);
    **if** sn *in* ncs **then** $h_r$.unmapStaticName(*sn*);

$h$.nameMap $\leftarrow$ mergeNameMaps($h_r$.nameMap, $h_u$.nameMap);
**return** $h$

---

The major components of this algorithm are the separation of the *mergeGraphs* action from the *mergeNameMaps* action and the elimination of the static cutpoint edge names that were introduced for this call.

The *mergeGraphs* function computes the union of the graph structures that represent the abstract heap objects, while the *mergeNameMaps* function computes the union of the name maps (which are maps from the stack/variable/cutpoint names to the nodes in the graph structure that represent them). This separation allows the algorithm to nullify the names created for this call which prevents the propagation of unneeded cutpoint edge targets to the caller scope. The function *unmapStaticName* is used to eliminate a given static name from the abstract heap model name map.

*Example Name Collision.* The introduction of the *nameColl* domain minimizes the precision loss that occurs when a cutpoint or stack variable name collision occurs. Figure 3 shows an example of such a situation. In this figure we show part of a heap where the edges *e2* and *e3* are both cutpoint edges and they do not represent any pairwise aliasing pointers (no ! in the *connTo* lists) although they each represent sets of pointers that may alias, *interfere = ap*.

In this example our naming scheme will result in *e2* and *e3* being represented with the same cutpoint name. However, our method will mark this cutpoint edge as *nameColl = pua* (Figure 3(b)). This means that on return the *extend* algorithm will set the edges that are mapped to this cutpoint as being pairwise unaliased (Figure 3(c)) as desired. Thus, even though there was a name collision for the cutpoints we avoided (in this case completely) the loss of sharing information about the heap.

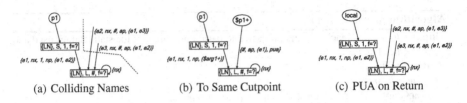

(a) Colliding Names        (b) To Same Cutpoint        (c) PUA on Return

**Fig. 3.** Name Collision

## 7   Experimental Results

The proposed approach has been implemented and the effectiveness and efficiency of the analysis have been evaluated on the source code for programs from a variation of the Jolden [3,18] suite and several programs from SPEC JVM98 [27] (raytrace, modified to be single threaded, db and compress). The analysis algorithm is written in C++ and was compiled using MSVC 8.0. The parallelization benchmarks were run using the Sun 1.6 JVM. All runs are from our 2.8 GHz PentiumD machine with 1 GB of RAM.

We ran the analysis with the project/extend operations enabled (the *Project* column) and disabled (the *No-Project* column) and recorded the analysis time, the average number of times a method needed to be analyzed, and used the resulting shape information to parallelize the programs, shown in Figure 4. The results indicate that the project/extend operations have a significant impact on the performance of the analysis, reducing the number of contexts that each function needs to be analyzed in (on average reducing the number of contexts by a factor of 4.3) which results in a substantial decrease in analysis times (by a factor of 18.4). As expected this reduction becomes more pronounced as the size and complexity of the benchmarks increases, in the case of raytrace the analysis time without the project/extend operation is impractically large (772.6 seconds) but when we use the project/extend operations the analysis time is reduced to 35.11 seconds.

We used the shape information from the analysis to drive the parallelization of the benchmarks by using multiple threads in loops and calls, resulting in the speedup columns in Figure 4. Given the shape information produced by the analysis it is straight forward to compute what parts of the heap are read and written by a loop body or method call and thus which loops and calls can be executed in parallel (in raytrace we treated the memoization of intersect computations as spurious dependencies). Once the analysis identified locations that could be parallelized we inserted calls to a simple thread pool (since our current work is focused on the analysis this is done by hand but can be fully automated [6,23,10]). In 8 of 9 benchmarks that are suitable for shape driven parallelization (compress, db and mst do not have any data structure operations that are amenable to shape driven parallelization) we achieve a promising speedup, averaging a factor of 1.69 over the benchmarks.

Our experimental results show that the information provided by the analysis can be effectively used (in conjunction with existing techniques) to drive the parallelization of programs. To the best of our knowledge this analysis is the only shape analysis that is able to provide the information required to perform shape driven parallelization for five of these benchmarks (em3d, health, voronoi, bh and raytrace). Given the speed with

| Benchmark Info | | | No-Project | | | Project | | |
|---|---|---|---|---|---|---|---|---|
| Benchmark | Stmt | Method | Time | Avg Cont. | Speedup | Time | Avg Cont. | Speedup |
| bisort | 260 | 13 | 0.86s | 10.6 | 1.00 | 0.28s | 1.9 | 1.72 |
| em3d | 333 | 13 | 0.12s | 2.5 | 1.75 | 0.08s | 1.8 | 1.75 |
| mst | 457 | 22 | 0.06s | 3.2 | NA | 0.04s | 3.0 | NA |
| tsp | 510 | 13 | 1.51s | 22.4 | 1.84 | 0.17s | 7.0 | 1.84 |
| perimeter | 621 | 36 | 54.57s | 105.9 | 1.00 | 2.97s | 50.2 | 1.00 |
| health | 643 | 16 | 3.24s | 12.9 | 1.00 | 2.26s | 4.2 | 1.76 |
| voronoi | 981 | 63 | 20.89s | 61.4 | 1.00 | 2.67s | 37.2 | 1.68 |
| power | 1352 | 29 | 5.71s | 26.8 | 1.93 | 0.17s | 1.3 | 1.93 |
| bh | 1616 | 51 | 8.64s | 32.8 | 1.75 | 2.68s | 7.3 | 1.75 |
| compress | 1102 | 41 | 0.29s | 2.9 | NA | 0.18s | 2.2 | NA |
| db | 1214 | 30 | 0.94s | 3.7 | NA | 0.68s | 2.8 | NA |
| raytrace | 3705 | 173 | 772.60s | 293.1 | 1.00 | 35.11s | 15.6 | 1.76 |
| Overall | 12794 | 523 | 869.43s | 48.2 | 1.36 | 47.29s | 11.2 | 1.69 |

**Fig. 4.** The Stmt and Method columns list the number of statements and methods for each benchmark. The columns for the No-Project and Project variations of the analysis list: the analysis time in seconds, the average number of times each method was analyzed and parallel speedup achieved on a 2 core 2.8 GHz PentiumD processor.

which the analysis is able to produce the information needed for the parallelization and the consistent parallel speedup that is obtained in the benchmarks (1.69 over all of the benchmarks and 1.77 if we exclude the benchmark mst), we find the results encouraging.

Of particular interest is the raytrace benchmark. This program is 2-4 times larger than any benchmarks used in the related work, builds and traverses several heap structures that have significant sharing between components. It also makes heavy use of virtual methods and recursion. This benchmark presents significant challenges in terms of the complexity and size of the program as well as in terms of the range of heap structures that need to be represented in order to accurately and efficiently analyze the program. Our analysis is able to manage all of these aspects and is able to produce a precise model of the heap (allowing us to obtain a speedup of 1.76 using heap based parallelization techniques). Further, the analysis is able to produce this result while maintaining a tractable analysis runtime.

## 8   Conclusion

We presented and benchmarked project/extend operations for a store-based heap model that is capable of precisely representing a range of shape, connectivity and sharing properties. The project and extend operations we introduced are designed to minimize the analysis time by reducing the number of unique calling contexts for each function and to minimize the imprecision introduced by the collisions that occur between stack/cutpoint names.

Our experimental results using the project/extend operations are very positive. The analysis was able to efficiently analyze benchmarks that build and manipulate a variety of data structures. Our benchmark set includes a number of kernels that were originally designed as challenge problems for automatic parallelization (the Jolden suite) and several benchmarks from the SPEC JVM98 suite (including a single threaded version of raytrace). Our experimental results demonstrate that the project/extend operations are effective in minimizing the number of contexts that need to be analyzed (on average a factor of 4.3 reduction), improving analysis accuracy (seen as improved parallelization results, in 4 out of 12 benchmarks) and substantially reducing the analysis runtime (by a factor of nearly 20). Our heap analysis was also able to provide sufficient information to successfully parallelize the majority of benchmarks we examined, including several that cannot be successfully analyzed/parallelized using other proposed shape analysis methods.

## Acknowledgments

This work is supported under subcontract R7A824-79200004 from the Los Alamos Computer Science Institute and Rice University and by the National Science Foundation (grant 0540600). Manuel Hermenegildo is also supported by the Prince of Asturias Chair at UNM, and projects MEC-MERIT, CAM-PROMESAS, and EU-MOBIUS.

## References

1. Berdine, J., Calcagno, C., Cook, B., Distefano, D., O'Hearn, P., Wies, T., Yang, H.: Shape analysis for composite data structures. In: Damm, W., Hermanns, H. (eds.) CAV 2007. LNCS, vol. 4590, pp. 178–192. Springer, Heidelberg (2007)
2. Bruynooghe, M.: A Practical Framework for the Abstract Interpretation of Logic Programs. J. Log. Program 10, 91–124 (1991)
3. Cahoon, B., McKinley, K.S.: Data flow analysis for software prefetching linked data structures in Java. In: PACT (2001)
4. Chong, S., Rugina, R.: Static analysis of accessed regions in recursive data structures. In: Cousot, R. (ed.) SAS 2003. LNCS, vol. 2694, pp. 463–482. Springer, Heidelberg (2003)
5. Ghiya, R., Hendren, L.J.: Is it a tree, a dag, or a cyclic graph? A shape analysis for heap-directed pointers in C. In: POPL (1996)
6. Ghiya, R., Hendren, L.J., Zhu, Y.: Detecting parallelism in C programs with recursive data structures. In: Koskimies, K. (ed.) CC 1998. LNCS, vol. 1383, pp. 159–173. Springer, Heidelberg (1998)
7. Gotsman, A., Berdine, J., Cook, B.: Interprocedural shape analysis with separated heap abstractions. In: Yi, K. (ed.) SAS 2006. LNCS, vol. 4134, pp. 240–260. Springer, Heidelberg (2006)
8. Gulwani, S., Tiwari, A.: An abstract domain for analyzing heap-manipulating low-level software. In: Damm, W., Hermanns, H. (eds.) CAV 2007. LNCS, vol. 4590, pp. 379–392. Springer, Heidelberg (2007)
9. Guo, B., Vachharajani, N., August, D.: Shape analysis with inductive recursion synthesis. In: PLDI (2007)
10. Hendren, L.J., Nicolau, A.: Parallelizing programs with recursive data structures. IEEE TPDS 1(1) (1990)
11. Ishtiaq, S.S., O'Hearn, P.W.: BI as an assertion language for mutable data structures. In: POPL (2001)

12. Jeannet, B., Loginov, A., Reps, T.W., Sagiv, S.: A relational approach to interprocedural shape analysis. In: Giacobazzi, R. (ed.) SAS 2004. LNCS, vol. 3148, pp. 246–264. Springer, Heidelberg (2004)

13. Manevich, R., Sagiv, S., Ramalingam, G., Field, J.: Partially disjunctive heap abstraction. In: Giacobazzi, R. (ed.) SAS 2004. LNCS, vol. 3148, pp. 265–279. Springer, Heidelberg (2004)

14. Marron, M., Kapur, D., Stefanovic, D., Hermenegildo, M.: A static heap analysis for shape and connectivity. In: Almási, G.S., Caşcaval, C., Wu, P. (eds.) KSEM 2006. LNCS, vol. 4382, pp. 345–363. Springer, Heidelberg (2007)

15. Marron, M., Majumdar, R., Stefanovic, D., Kapur, D.: Dominance: Modeling heap structures with sharing. Tech. report, CS Dept., Univ. of New Mexico (August 2007)

16. Müller-Olm, M., Seidl, H.: Precise interprocedural analysis through linear algebra. In: POPL (2004)

17. Muthukumar, K., Hermenegildo, M.V.: Compile-time derivation of variable dependency using abstract interpretation. J. Log. Program (1992)

18. Modified Jolden Benchmarks (August 2007), http://www.cs.unm.edu/~marron

19. Nielson, F., Nielson, H.R., Hankin, C.: Principles of Program Analysis. Springer, Heidelberg (1999)

20. Reynolds, J.: Separation logic: a logic for shared mutable data structures. In: LICS (2002)

21. Rinetzky, N., Bauer, J., Reps, T.W., Sagiv, S., Wilhelm, R.: A semantics for procedure local heaps and its abstractions. In: POPL (2005)

22. Rinetzky, N., Sagiv, S.: Interprocedural shape analysis for recursive programs. In: Wilhelm, R. (ed.) CC 2001. LNCS, vol. 2027, pp. 133–149. Springer, Heidelberg (2001)

23. Rugina, R., Rinard, M.C.: Automatic parallelization of divide and conquer algorithms. In: PPOPP (1999)

24. Sagiv, S., Reps, T.W., Wilhelm, R.: Solving shape-analysis problems in languages with destructive updating. In: POPL (1996)

25. Sagiv, S., Reps, T.W., Wilhelm, R.: Parametric shape analysis via 3-valued logic. In: POPL (1999)

26. Smyth, M.B.: Power domains and predicate transformers: A topological view. In: Díaz, J. (ed.) ICALP 1983. LNCS, vol. 154, pp. 662–675. Springer, Heidelberg (1983)

27. Standard Performance Evaluation Corporation. JVM98 Version 1.04 (August 1998), http://www.spec.org/osg/jvm98/jvm98/doc/index.html

28. Wilhelm, R., Sagiv, S., Reps, T.W.: Shape analysis. In: Watt, D.A. (ed.) CC 2000. LNCS, vol. 1781, pp. 1–17. Springer, Heidelberg (2000)

# Coqa: Concurrent Objects with Quantized Atomicity

Yu David Liu, Xiaoqi Lu, and Scott F. Smith

Department of Computer Science
The Johns Hopkins University
{yliu,xiaoqilu,scott}@cs.jhu.edu

**Abstract.** This paper introduces a new language model, *Coqa*, for deeply embedding concurrent programming into objects. Every program written in our language has the desirable behaviors of atomicity, mutual exclusion, and race freedom automatically built in. A key property of our model is the notion of *quantized atomicity*: every concurrent program execution can be viewed as being divided into quantum regions of atomic execution, greatly reducing the number of interleavings to consider. Rather than building atomicity locally, *i.e.* declaring some code blocks as atomic blocks and leaving other code segments with no guarantee of any atomicity property, we build it in globally, so that a form of atomicity, quantized atomicity, ubiquitously exists at all program points. We justify our approach both from a theoretical basis by showing that a formal representation, Kernel-Coqa, has provable quantized atomicity properties, and by implementing CoqaJava, a Java extension incorporating all of the Coqa features.

## 1 Introduction

*Coqa* (for *C*oncurrent *o*bjects with *q*uantized *a*tomicity) is a new object-oriented language aimed at facilitating programming in a multi-core CPU environment. Programming multi-core CPUs requires much greater programmer skill, and is one of the most significant new demands programmers will face in the coming decade. The design goal of Coqa is to build a language in which it is easier to naturally write concurrent programs with good concurrency properties. Unlike Java where good properties such as race freedom can only be achieved if the programmer *explicitly* declares it by using synchronized, the "default" mode in Coqa is inverted: good properties of race freedom, mutual exclusion, and atomicity are preserved unless programmers explicitly declare otherwise.

Existing concurrent object language designs are numerous and include for example [Agh90,Arm96,Mil,BST00]. What makes our work novel is the intrinsic properties Coqa preserves. Most important is atomicity, *i.e.* the property that a block of code can always be viewed as occurring atomically no matter what interleaving it is involved in. With tightly coupled computation running on multi-core CPUs, data sharing between threads is very common and the patterns are more complex than on a single-core CPU due to random variations in scheduling. To support atomicity, Coqa takes the route of "atomicity-by-design" for each

L. Hendren (Ed.): CC 2008, LNCS 4959, pp. 260–275, 2008.
© Springer-Verlag Berlin Heidelberg 2008

method: atomicity is *ubiquitous* because by default each complete method execution is observably atomic. Note this is much stronger than the `synchronized` methods of Java: the Coqa method *and all methods it invokes* are viewed as happening atomically. The `synchronized` methods in Java only provide a shallow notion of mutual exclusion.

One particular challenge of whole-method atomicity is that it can be overly strong, and the resulting executions will not be efficient, or may even deadlock if there is significant contention across methods. For this reason, Coqa allows programmers to relax whole-method atomicity by dividing a method into a small number of discrete zones of atomicity (called *quanta* in Coqa), and each quantum is serializable regardless of the interleaving of the actual execution. This property, called *quantized atomicity*, is preserved for all Coqa programs. The main appeal is to significantly reduce the number of interleavings possible in concurrent program runs, and thus to ease the debugging burden. If two pieces of code each have 100 execution steps, reasoning tools would have to consider $C_{200}^{100}$ (*i.e.*, around $10^{58}$) interleaving scenarios; however, if the aforementioned 100 steps can be split into 3 atomic quanta, there are only $C_6^3 = 20$ possibilities to consider. With quantized atomicity, next-generation verification tools can potentially enumerate all interleaving scenarios, a strategy largely impractical today. Actors [Agh90,AMST97] were in some sense the starting point for the design of Coqa: atomicity is preserved for each Actor method because its execution once initiated does not depend on the state of other actors and each method is therefore trivially serializable. Actors' ubiquitous atomicity arises from the fact that the model supports only asynchronous messaging, and so methods once initiated cannot receive outside inputs.

Another design goal of Coqa is to make a concurrent language design that naturally meshes well with object-oriented language features. This stands in contrast to the non-object-based syntax and semantics commonly used in existing languages for concurrent programming. Language abstractions such as library class `Thread`, thread spawning via its `start` method and `synchronized` blocks in Java, and the `atomic` blocks in various Software Transactional Memory (STM) systems that have been adopted into OO languages [CMC+06], are not that different from what was used three decades ago in non-object-oriented languages [Lom77].

Existing language models fall short of achieving the goals of both ubiquitous atomicity and easy OO-style concurrent programming. Ubiquitous atomicity is a global property of all programs; Java does not have a notion of atomicity built into the language and the form of atomicity in STM systems is only local atomicity. STM systems also require rollbacks to deal with atomicity-breaking contentions and are known to be inapplicable to I/O-intensive applications, such as GUI and network systems, so they can never be ubiquitous. Out of the desire of pervasiveness, we take a blocking and not a rollback approach to achieve atomicity. The Actor model achieves ubiquitous atomicity, but programming in Actors is very different from what programmers are used to, since with pure asynchronous messaging any processing of a message reply must be handled by

| messaging | what it is | why you should use it |
|---|---|---|
| o . m(v) | intra-task messaging | promotes mutual exclusion and atomicity |
| o -> m(v) | task creation | promotes parallelism by starting up a new task |
| o ⇒ m(v) | sub-tasking | promotes parallelism by encouraging early free |

**Fig. 1.** The Three Messaging Mechanisms and Their Relative Strengths

a completely new message, necessarily chopping up methods into many small pieces. So, Coqa shares the spirit of ubiquitous atomicity of Actors, but allows more familiar synchronous messaging syntax to be used which avoids the need to break up methods.

In this paper, we formalize Coqa in a formal system called KernelCoqa, in which we prove the properties of quantized atomicity, mutual exclusion and race freedom. We have also implemented a prototype language CoqaJava as a Java extension which simply replaces Java threads with our new forms of object messaging.

## 2    Informal Overview

The concurrency unit in our language is a *task*. A task is a unit of execution that can potentially be interleaved with other units. Tasks are closely related to (logical) threads, but come with inherent atomicity properties not found in threads, and we coin a new term to reflect this distinction. Coqa has a very simple syntax: the only difference from the Java object model is a richer syntax to support object messaging, as summarized in Fig. 1. Beyond the familiar o . m(v) message sending expression, o -> m(v) and o ⇒ m(v) are additionally provided for *task creation* (a form of thread spawning) and *subtasking* (a form of thread open nesting), respectively.

*The Running Example.* Throughout the section, we will use a simple example of basic banking operations, including account opening and balance transfer operations, as shown in Fig. 2. Bank accounts are stored in a hash table, implemented in a standard manner with bucket lists.

### 2.1    Task Creation

Tasks are created by simply sending asynchronous messages to objects, using the o -> m(v) expression. This is a more "object-based" thread creation than the current practice in Java, where a special `Thread` class is used. This notion is more aligned with Actor languages, where all message passings can be viewed as thread creations. In Fig. 2, the top-level `main` method starts up three concurrent tasks, two balance transfers and one account opening, by the invocations of lines M1, M2 and M3. Syntax `bk -> transfer("Alice", "Bob", 3)` indicates an asynchronous

```
class BankMain {
  public static void main (String [] args)  {
    Bank bk = new Bank();
    bk.open("Alice", 10); bk.open("Bob", 20); bk.open("Cathy", 30);
    bk -> transfer("Alice", "Bob", 3);              //(M1)
    bk -> transfer("Cathy", "Alice", 5);            //(M2)
    bk -> open("Dan", 40);                          //(M3)
  }
}
class Bank {
  void transfer (String from, String to, int bal) {
    Status status = new Status();                   //(A1)
    status.log();
    Account afrom = (Account)htable.get(from, status);  //(A2)
    afrom.withdraw(bal);                            //(A3)
    Account ato = (Account)htable.get(to, status);  //(A4)
    ato.deposit(bal);                               //(A5)
  }
  void open(String n, int b) { htable.put(n, new Account(n, b));}
  private HashTable htable = new HashTable();
}
class Account  {
  Account(String n, int b) {name = n; bal = b; }
  void deposit(int b) { bal += b; }
  void withdraw(int b) {bal -= b; }
  private String name;
  private int bal;
}
class Status  {
  void log() {
    String sysinfo = ... //prepare system info
    info.append(sysinfo);
  }
  private StringBuffer info = new StringBuffer();
}
```

**Fig. 2.** A Banking Program

message **transfer** sent to object bk with indicated arguments. Asynchronous message sending returns immediately, so the sender can continue, and a new task is created to execute the invoked method. This new task terminates when its method is finished. To keep the language simple, asynchronous invocations in Coqa do not return values.

## 2.2   Intra-task Messaging

Message sending o . m(v) is the same syntax as Java, but has different semantics giving stronger atomicity properties: when invoked, object o will be *captured* by the invoking task and cannot be used by other tasks until the current task is complete. Capturing is a blocking mechanism, but unlike Java where programmers need to explicitly specify what to lock and when to lock, the capture and blocking of objects is built into Coqa.

This intuitive definition for o . m(v) is the programmer view, but is not an efficient implementation strategy: only mutation affects the preservation of atomicity, and so we actually only need to capture objects "lazily" when their fields are read and written. Our notion of "capture" is a standard two-phase non-exclusive read lock and exclusive write lock [Gra78]. When an object's field is read, the object is said to be *read captured*; when the field is written, the object is said to be *write captured*. The same object can be read captured by multiple tasks at the same time, but to be write captured, the object has to be exclusively owned, *i.e.* not read captured or write captured by another task. Two-phase locking optimizes our model since reads are overwhelmingly more common than writes in most programs. Many other optimizations are also possible by static analysis, a topic we leave to future work.

The preservation of atomicity can be seen in the invocation of the **transfer** method of Fig. 2: the **HashTable** object referenced by **htable** is captured by a task, say the task created in line **M1**, and will not be released until the end of the method (and hence, the task). Therefore it is not possible for one **transfer** task to be reading from the **HashTable** object while at the same time a different **transfer** task is writing to it.

## 2.3   Subtasking

The model we have presented thus far admits significant parallelism if most object accesses are read accesses. Blocking is possible, however, when frequent writes are needed. For instance, consider the parallel execution of the two tasks spawned by (M1) and (M3). One of them will be blocked as (M1) reads from the **HashTable** object, while (M3) attempts to write.[1] And the task being blocked cannot make any progress until the other task completes and releases its captured object. Intuitively, the task of adding **Dan** as a new account, (M3), is totally unrelated to the task of transferring money from **Alice** to **Bob**, (M1), except for their shared access to the **HashTable** object. There should be at least some parallelism possible between the two tasks.

Coqa achieves this by allowing programmers to spawn off the access of the **HashTable** object (and all objects it indirectly accesses) as a new *subtask*. The high-level meaning behind a subtask is that it achieves a relatively independent goal; its completion signals a partial victory so that the captured objects used

---

[1] Strictly speaking, the read-write conflict happens on the object representing the bucket list inside the **HashTable**, but we omit this detail since we do not have space to give the source code for the internals of the **HashTable**.

to achieve this subtask can be "freed", *i.e.* no longer considered captured. In terms of syntax, the only change to the source code of transfer in Fig. 2 is to change the dot (.) messagings at (A2) and (A4) to ⇒ for subtask creation messaging. In this case, the task $t$ created at (M1) spawns a subtask $t'$ at (A2) via ⇒. The HashTable object will be captured by $t'$ but not $t$. More parallelism is achieved by such subtasking: other tasks waiting to capture the HashTable object would have to block for the duration of $t$ instead of the much shorter span of $t'$ if (.) was used. Subtasking is a synchronous invocation, *i.e.*, the task executing transfer waits until its subtask executing get returns a result. But the subtask has a *distinct* capture set of its own. And like a task, a subtask frees objects in its capture set when it finishes.

A subtask is also a task, so it prevents arbitrary interleaving. The change in line (A2) from (.) to ⇒ admits interleaving between task (M1) and (M3) that was not allowed before, but it does not mean that arbitrary interleaving can occur; for example, if M1 were in the middle of a key lookup M3 still *cannot* add a new bucket. We will discuss such concurrency properties in the presence of subtasking later in this section.

Subtasking is related to open nesting in STM systems [NMAT+07,CMC+06]. Open nesting is used to nest a transaction inside another transaction, where the nested transaction can commit before the enclosing transaction runs to completion. While the mechanism of open nesting of transactions can be summarized as early commit, subtasking can be summarized as early release.

*Capture set inheritance.* One contentious issue for open nesting is the case where a nested transaction and the transactions enclosing it both need the same object. For instance in Atomos [CMC+06], the issue is circumvented by restricting the read/write sets to be disjoint between the main and nested transaction. When the same issue manifests itself in the scenario of subtasking, the question is, "Can a subtask access objects already captured by its enclosing task(s)?"

We could in theory follow Atomos' approach. This however would significantly reduce programmability. Let us consider the example of the Status object in the transfer method. From the programmer's view, this object keeps track of the system status throughout the execution of the transfer method. However, if the Atomos's approach were taken, a subtask spawned by the transfer task for accessing the HashTable would not be able access the Status object because this object has already been captured by the transfer task. Even worse, a deadlock would be introduced in this case.

We believe the essence of having a subtasking relationship between a parent and a child is that the parent should generously share its resources with the child. Therefore accessing the Status in the subtask is perfectly legal in Coqa. Observe that the relationship between a task and its subtask is synchronous, so there is no concern of interleaving between a task and its subtask.

## 2.4   Properties

*Quantized Atomicity* Some tasks simply *should not* be considered wholly atomic because they are fundamentally needing to share data with other tasks, and for this case it is simply impossible to have full atomicity over the whole task. The main reason why a programmer wants to declare a subtask is to open a communication channel with other tasks for such sharing, as was illustrated in the subtasking example above. With subtasking, objects captured by the subtask can serve as communication points between different tasks. This is because the objects freed at the end of one subtask might be recaptured later, and the object may have been mutated by the original subtask.

Quantized atomicity is the property that for any task, its execution sequence can be viewed as a sequence of atomic regions, the *atomic quanta*, demarcated by task and subtask creation points. This atomicity property is weaker than a whole task being atomic, but as long as full task atomicity is broken only when it is really necessary (that is, a minimal number of ⇒ and → messagings are used), the atomic quanta will each be large, and significant reduction of interleaving can be achieved. In reality, what matters is not that the entire method must be atomic, but that the method admits a drastically limited number of interleaving scenarios. Quantized atomicity aims to strikes a balance between what is realistic and what is reasonable.

*Mutual Exclusion.* For objects accessed by synchronous messaging, the property of mutual exclusion over mutation spans the lifetime of the current task, even *across the boundaries of quanta*. For instance, over the entire duration of any task executing `transfer` in Fig. 2, the `Status` object is guaranteed not to be mutated by any other task before the current `transfer` ends, even if other tasks have reference to `Status`. Our notion of object mutual exclusion is much stronger than what Java's `synchronized` provides: Java only guarantees the object with the method is itself not mutated by other threads, while we are guaranteeing the property for *all* objects which are directly or indirectly sent synchronous messages to at run time by the method, many of which may be unknown to the caller.

*Race Freedom.* In Coqa, we show that two tasks cannot race to access any object field, except in the case where both may only read from the same object field.

*A Simple Memory Model.* With these concurrency properties, Coqa eliminates the need for the overly complex memory model of Java [MPA05].

## 3   Formalization

In this section we present KernelCoqa, a small formal kernel language of Coqa.

We first define some basic notation used in our formalization. We write $\overline{x_n}$ as shorthand for a set $\{x_1, \ldots, x_n\}$, with $\emptyset$ as empty set. $\overrightarrow{x_n \mapsto y_n}$ denotes a mapping $\{x_1 \mapsto y_1, \ldots, x_n \mapsto y_n\}$, where $\{x_1, \ldots x_n\}$ is the domain of the mapping, dom($H$). We also write $H(x_1) = y_1, \ldots, H(x_n) = y_n$. When no confusion arises, we drop the subscript $n$ for sets and mapping sequences. We write $H\{x \mapsto y\}$ as a mapping update: if $x \in$ dom($H$), $H$ and $H\{x \mapsto y\}$ are identical except that

$$P ::= \overrightarrow{cn \mapsto \langle l;\, Fd;\, Md\rangle}$$
$$Fd ::= \overrightarrow{fn}$$
$$Md ::= \overrightarrow{mn \mapsto \lambda x.e}$$
$$e ::= \textbf{null} \mid x \mid cst \mid \textbf{this}$$
$$\mid \textbf{new } cn$$
$$\mid fn \mid fn = e$$
$$\mid e.mn(e)$$
$$\mid e \rightarrow mn(e)$$
$$\mid e \Rightarrow mn(e)$$
$$\mid \textbf{let } x = e \textbf{ in } e$$
$$l ::= \textbf{exclusive} \mid \epsilon$$

| | |
|---|---|
| $cst$ | $constant$ |
| $cn$ | $class\ name$ |
| $mn$ | $method\ name$ |
| $fn$ | $field\ name$ |
| $x$ | $variable\ name$ |

$$H ::= \overrightarrow{o \mapsto \langle cn;\, R;\, W;\, F\rangle}$$
$$F ::= \overrightarrow{fn \mapsto v}$$
$$T ::= \langle t;\gamma;e\rangle \mid T \parallel T'$$
$$N ::= t \mapsto t'$$
$$R, W ::= \bar{t}$$
$$\gamma ::= o \mid \textbf{null}$$
$$v ::= cst \mid o \mid \textbf{null}$$
$$e ::= v \mid \textbf{wait } t$$
$$\mid e \uparrow e \mid \ldots$$
$$E ::= \bullet \mid fn = E$$
$$\mid E.m(e) \mid v.m(E)$$
$$\mid E \rightarrow m(e) \mid v \rightarrow m(E)$$
$$\mid E \Rightarrow m(e) \mid v \Rightarrow m(E)$$
$$\mid \textbf{let } x = E \textbf{ in } e$$

| | |
|---|---|
| $o$ | $object\ ID$ |
| $t$ | $task\ ID$ |

$$\textbf{anc}(N, t) = \begin{cases} \{t\}, & \text{if } N(t) = \textbf{null} \\ \{t\} \cup \textbf{anc}(N, t'), & \text{if } N(t) = t' \end{cases}$$

**Fig. 3.** Language Abstract Syntax and Dynamic Data Structure

$H\{x \mapsto y\}$ maps $x$ to $y$; if $x \notin \mathsf{dom}(H)$, $H\{x \mapsto y\} = H, x \mapsto y$. $H\backslash x$ removes the mapping $x \mapsto H(x)$ from $H$ if $x \in \mathsf{dom}(H)$, otherwise the operation has no effect.

KernelCoqa is an idealized object-based language with objects, messaging, and fields. Its abstract syntax is shown on the left of Fig. 3. A program $P$ is a set of classes. Each class has a unique name $cn$ and its definition consists of sequences of field ($Fd$) and method ($Md$) declarations. To make the formalization feasible, many features are left out, including types and constructors. Besides local method invocations via dot (.) notation, synchronous and asynchronous messages are sent to objects using $\Rightarrow$ and $\rightarrow$, respectively. A class declared exclusive will have its objects write captured upon any access. This label is useful for eliminating deadlocks inherent in a two-phase locking strategy, such as when two tasks first read capture an object, then both try to write capture the same object and thus deadlock.

*Operational Semantics.* Our operational semantics is defined as a contextual rewriting system over states $S \Rightarrow S$, where each state is a triple $S = (H, N, T)$ for $H$ the object heap, $N$ a task ancestry mapping, and $T$ a set of parallel tasks. Every task has a local evaluation context $E$. The relevant definitions are given in Fig. 3. $H$ is a mapping from objects $o$ to field records tagged with their class name $cn$. In addition, each $o$ has capture sets, $R$ and $W$, for recording tasks that have read or write captured this object. A task is a triple consisting of the task ID $t$, the object $\gamma$ this task currently operates on, and an expression $e$ to be evaluated.

SET
$$H(\gamma) = \langle cn; R; W; F \rangle$$
$$H' = H\{\gamma \mapsto \langle cn; R; W \cup \{t\}; F\{fn \mapsto v\}\rangle\} \text{ if } R \subseteq \mathbf{anc}(N, t), W \subseteq \mathbf{anc}(N, t)$$
$$\overline{H, N, \langle t; \gamma; \mathbf{E}[\, fn = v\,]\rangle \Rightarrow H', N, \langle t; \gamma; \mathbf{E}[\, v\,]\rangle}$$

GET
$$H(\gamma) = \langle cn; R; W; F \rangle \qquad P(cn) = \langle l; Md; Fd \rangle \qquad F(fn) = v$$
$$H' = \begin{cases} H\{\gamma \mapsto \langle cn; R; W \cup \{t\}; F \rangle\}, \text{ if } l = \mathtt{exclusive}, R \subseteq \mathbf{anc}(N, t), W \subseteq \mathbf{anc}(N, t) \\ H\{\gamma \mapsto \langle cn; R \cup \{t\}; W; F \rangle\}, \text{ if } l = \epsilon, W \subseteq \mathbf{anc}(N, t) \end{cases}$$
$$\overline{H, N, \langle t; \gamma; \mathbf{E}[\, fn\,]\rangle \Rightarrow H, N, \langle t; \gamma; \mathbf{E}[\, v\,]\rangle}$$

INVOKE
$$H(o) = \langle cn; R; W; F \rangle \qquad P(cn) = \langle l; Fd; Md \rangle \qquad Md(mn) = \lambda x.e$$
$$\overline{H, N, \langle t; \gamma; \mathbf{E}[\, o.mn(v)\,]\rangle \Rightarrow H, N, \langle t; o; \mathbf{E}[\, e\{v/x\}\!\uparrow\!\gamma\,]\rangle}$$

TASK$(t, \gamma, mn, v, o, t')$
$$t' \text{ fresh}$$
$$\overline{H, N, \langle t; \gamma; \mathbf{E}[\, o \rightarrow mn(v)\,]\rangle \Rightarrow H, N, \langle t; \gamma; \mathbf{E}[\, \mathbf{null}\,]\rangle \parallel \langle t'; o; \mathbf{this}.mn(v)\rangle}$$

SUBTASK$(t, \gamma, mn, v, \gamma, t')$
$$N' = N\{t' \mapsto t\} \qquad t' \text{ fresh}$$
$$\overline{H, N, \langle t; \gamma; \mathbf{E}[\, o \Rightarrow mn(v)\,]\rangle \Rightarrow H, N', \langle t; \gamma; \mathbf{E}[\, \mathbf{wait}\ t'\,]\rangle \parallel \langle t'; o; \mathbf{this}.mn(v)\rangle}$$

TEND$(t)$
$$H' = \biguplus_{H(o)=\langle cn; R; W; F \rangle} (o \mapsto \langle cn; R \backslash t; W \backslash t; F \rangle) \qquad N(t) = \mathbf{null}$$
$$\overline{H, N, \langle t; \gamma; v \rangle \Rightarrow H', N, \epsilon}$$

STEND$(t, v, t')$
$$H' = \biguplus_{H(o)=\langle cn; R; W; F \rangle} (o \mapsto \langle cn; R \backslash t; W \backslash t; F \rangle) \qquad N(t) = t'$$
$$\overline{H, N, \langle t; \gamma; v \rangle \parallel \langle t'; \gamma'; \mathbf{E}[\, \mathbf{wait}\ t\,]\rangle \Rightarrow H', N \backslash t, \langle t'; \gamma'; \mathbf{E}[\, v\,]\rangle}$$

**Fig. 4.** KernelCoqa Core Operational Semantics Rules

The core single-step evaluation rules are presented in Fig. 4. The rules for LET, RETURN and other standard constructs are omitted here; see [Lu07]. The rules implicitly operate over some fixed program $P$. The INVOKE rule for intra-task messaging is interpreted as a standard function application. The TASK rule creates a new task via asynchronous messaging. The SUBTASK rule creates a subtask of the current task via synchronous messaging, and the parent task enters a **wait** state until the subtask returns. When a task finishes, all objects it has captured are freed; the TEND and STEND are rules for ending a task and a subtask, respectively. The two-phase locking capture policy is implemented in the SET and the GET rules. The optional `exclusive` modifier requires an object to be write captured in both rules. When a task cannot capture an object it needs, it is implicitly *object-blocked* on the object until it is entitled to capture it—the SET/GET rule cannot progress.

*Atomicity Theorems.* Here we formally establish the informal claims about KernelCoqa: quantized atomicity, mutual exclusion of tasks, and race freedom. Proofs are provided in [Lu07]. The key Lemma is the Bubble-Down Lemma, Lemma 1, which shows that consecutive steps of a certain form in a computation path can be swapped to give an equivalent path. Then, by a series of bubblings, each quantum of steps can be bubbled to all be consecutive in an equivalent computation path, showing that the quanta are serializable: Theorem 1. The technical notion of a quantum is the *pmsp* below, a *pointed maximal subpath*. These are a series of local steps of one task with a nonlocal step at the end, which may be embedded in a larger concurrent computation path. We prove in Theorem 1 that any computation path can be viewed as a collection of *pmsp*'s, and all *pmsp*'s in the path are serializable and thus the whole path is.

**Definition 1 (Object State).** *Recall the global state is a triple $S = (H, N, T)$. The object state for $o$, written $s_o$, is defined as $H(o)$, the value of the object $o$ in the current heap $H$, or **null** if $o \notin dom(H)$.*

**Definition 2 (Local and Nonlocal Step).** *A step $st_r = (S, r, S')$ denotes a transition $S \Rightarrow S'$ by rule $r$ of Figure 4. $st_r$ is a local step if $r$ is one of the local rules: either GET, SET, THIS, LET, RETURN, INST or INVOKE. $st_r$ is a nonlocal step if $r$ is one of nonlocal rules: either TASK, SUBTASK, TEND or STEND.*

Every nonlocal rule has a label given in Fig 4, used as the observable.

**Definition 3 (Computation Path).** *A computation path $p$ is a finite sequence of steps $st_{r_1} \ldots st_{r_i}$ such that $st_{r_1} st_{r_2} \ldots st_{r_{i-1}} st_{r_i} = (S_0, r_1, S_1)\ (S_1, r_2, S_2) \ldots (S_{i-2}, r_{i-1}, S_{i-1})\ (S_{i-1}, r_i, S_i)$.*

When no confusion arises, we simply call it a path.

**Definition 4 (Observable Behavior).** *The observable behavior of a path $p$, $ob(p)$, is the sequence of labels for the nonlocal steps in $p$.*

Note that this definition encompasses I/O behavior elegantly since I/O in KernelCoqa can be viewed as a fixed object which is sent nonlocal and thus observable messages.

**Definition 5 (Observable Equivalence).** *Two paths $p_1$ and $p_2$ are observably equivalent, written $p_1 \equiv p_2$, iff $ob(p_1) = ob(p_2)$.*

**Definition 6 (Object-blocked).** *A task $t$ is in an object-blocked state $S$ at some point in a path $p$ if it would be enabled for a next step $st_r = (S, r, S')$ for which $r$ is a GET or SET step on object $o$, except for the fact that there is a capture violation on $o$: one of preconditions of the GET/SET fails to hold in $S$ and so $st_r$ cannot in fact be the next step at that point.*

**Definition 7 (Sub-path and Maximal Sub-path).** *Given a path $p$, for some $t$ a sub-path $sp_t$ of $p$ is a sequence of steps in $p$ which are all local steps of task $t$. A maximal sub-path is a $sp_t$ in $p$ which is longest: no local $t$ steps in $p$ can be added to the beginning or the end of $sp_t$ to obtain a longer sub-path.*

**Definition 8 (Pointed Maximal Sub-path).** *For a given path, a* pointed maximal sub-path *for $t$ ($pmsp_t$) is a maximal sub-path $sp_t$ with either 1) it has one nonlocal step appended to its end or 2) there are no more $t$ steps ever in the path.*

The second case is the technical case of when the (finite) path has ended but the task $t$ is still running. The last step of a $pmsp_t$ is called its *point*.

The *pmsp*'s are the units which we need to serialize: they are all spread out in the initial path $p$, and we need to show there is an equivalent path where each *pmsp* runs in turn as an atomic unit.

**Definition 9 (Task Indexed *pmsp*).** *For some fixed path $p$, define $pmsp_{t,i}$ to be the $i^{th}$ pointed maximal sub-path of task $t$ in $p$, where all the steps of the $pmsp_{t,i}$ occur after any of $pmsp_{t,i+1}$ and before any of $pmsp_{t,i-1}$.*

**Definition 10 (Waits-for and Deadlocking Path).** *For some path $p$, $pmsp_{t_1,i}$* waits-for *$pmsp_{t_2,j}$ if $t_1$ goes into a object-blocked state in $pmsp_{t_1,i}$ on an object captured by $t_2$ in the blocked state. A deadlocking path $p$ is a path where this waits-for relation has a cycle: $pmsp_{t_1,i}$ waits-for $pmsp_{t_2,j}$ while $pmsp_{t_2,i'}$ waits-for $pmsp_{t_1,j'}$.*

From now on we assume in this theoretical development that there are no such cycles. In Coqa deadlock is an error that should have not been programmed to begin with, and so deadlocking programs are not ones we want to prove facts about.

**Definition 11 (Quantized Sub-path and Quantized Path).** *A* quantized sub-path *contained in $p$ is a $pmsp_t$ of $p$ where all steps of $pmsp_t$ are consecutive in $p$. A* quantized path *$p$ is a path consisting of a sequence of quantized sub-paths.*

The main technical Lemma is the following Bubble-Down Lemma, which shows how local steps can be pushed down in a path. Use of such a Lemma is the standard technique to show atomicity properties. Lipton [Lip75] first described such a theory, called *reduction*; his theory was later refined by [LS89].

**Definition 12 (Equivalent Step Swap).** *For two consecutive steps $st_{r_1} st_{r_2}$ in a path $p$, where $st_{r_1} \in pmsp_{t_1}$, $st_{r_2} \in pmsp_{t_2}$, $t_1 \neq t_2$ and $st_{r_1} st_{r_2} = (S, r_1, S')(S', r_2, S'')$, if the step swap of $st_{r_1} st_{r_2}$, written as $st'_{r_2} st'_{r_1}$, gives a new path $p'$ such that $p \equiv p'$ and $st'_{r_2} st'_{r_1} = (S, r_2, S^*)(S^*, r_1, S'')$, then it is an equivalent step swap.*

**Lemma 1 (Bubble-down Lemma).** *For any path $p$ with any two consecutive steps $st_{r_1} st_{r_2}$ where $st_{r_1} \in pmsp_{t_1}$, $st_{r_2} \in pmsp_{t_2}$ and $t_1 \neq t_2$, if it is not the case that $pmsp_{t_1}$ waits-for $pmsp_{t_2}$ and if $st_{r_1}$ is a local step, then a step swap of $st_{r_1} st_{r_2}$ is an equivalent step swap.*

**Theorem 1 (Quantized Atomicity)** *For all paths p there exists an observably equivalent quantized path p'.*

**Theorem 2 (Data Race Freedom)** *For all paths, no two different tasks can access a field of an object in consecutive steps, where at least one of the two accesses changes the value of the field.*

**Theorem 3 (Mutual Exclusion over Tasks)** *It can never be the case that two tasks $t_1$ and $t_2$ overlap execution in a consecutive sequence of steps $st_{r_1} \ldots st_{r_n}$ in a path, and in those steps both $t_1$ and $t_2$ write the same object $o$, or one reads while the other writes the same object.*

# 4  Discussion and Related Work

*Implementation* We have implemented a prototype of Coqa, called CoqaJava. Polyglot [NCM03] was used to construct a translator from CoqaJava to Java. All language features introduced in Fig. 3 are included in the prototype. The implementation dynamically enforces the object capture, freeing, and mutual exclusion semantics of Coqa. Refer to [Lu07] for more details about CoqaJava. The compiler translates CoqaJava to Java. This approach serves as a proof of concept; it unavoidably suffers additional overhead because it is implemented directly on top of Java. For example, every object capture operation in CoqaJava requires a method invocation to realize it in the translated code. The overhead brought by those method invocations can be huge when a large number of capture operations are involved. Even with this highly inefficient implementation, preliminary benchmark results in [Lu07] show that CoqaJava programs on single-core CPUs have slowdowns of "only" 20% - 60% compared with a Java implementation of the same problem, a result we consider good given the opportunities available for improving it. Making our language more expressive and its implementation more efficient is an important future goal. For instance, we can build a more efficient CoqaJava by building object capture into the lower level Virtual Machine. It will also be interesting to add more concurrency-related language features, such as futures and synchronization constraints. Optimization techniques should also be able to minimize the amount of capture information that needs to be retained at runtime since many objects are completely local.

*Deadlocks.* Deadlock will be a more common occurrence in Coqa: accessing shared objects without using subtasking can potentially produce deadlocks. A primary task of writing and debugging Coqa programs will be refactoring code into the correct quanta to both minimize sharing and avoid deadlock. While these extra deadlocks may make it sound like a step backward has been taken, there is reason to be optimistic: Coqa programs will inherently have fewer semantically distinct interleavings, and thus the probability of catching deadlocks before deployment will be significantly greater since there will a much greater likelihood of exercising the different interleaving cases during program testing.

There are two forms of deadlock arising in Coqa. The first is inherent in two-phase locking, when an object is read captured by two tasks but neither task can further write capture it. The second form is cyclically dependent deadlock. The first form of deadlock can be avoided by declaring the class to be `exclusive` (see Sec. 3). Programmers can also explicitly introduce interleaving via ⇒ to break deadlock. There are also many static and dynamic analysis techniques and tools to ensure deadlock freedom; for an overview, see [Sin89]. Deadlock detection is an important topic of future work for Coqa. We are interested in applying some Java-based analysis tools such Java PathFinder [PF] directly to the target Java code generated by the compiler. The precision of static techniques are reduced due to the combinatorial explosion of interleaving, but Coqa code inherently has many fewer interleavings to consider and so stronger analysis results will *de facto* be obtained. We are also investigating language design approaches to write deadlock-free programs. It is known that by organizing objects into run-time hierarchies [BLR02], deadlock can be effectively avoided; one system we are considering adapting for this purpose is our *Pedigree Types* [Liu07].

*Blocking vs. Rollback.* Rollback is a suitable solution in an open database system where the inputs are arbitrary and unknown at the start, and thus a general purpose lock-based deadlock avoidance technique is not possible. Software applications on the other hand are largely closed systems in the sense that the code of an application is often entirely available at deployment time, and so all the code in all the potentially contending threads is known. Therefore, analyzing applications for deadlocks is a more realistic approach in a programming language than in a database system.

Atomicity is commonly addressed in STM systems via rollbacks; example approaches include Harris and Fraser [HF03], Transactional Monitors [WJH04] for Java, and Atomos [CMC+06]. Compared with blocking systems like ours, STM systems have the appeal of not introducing deadlocks. However, there is a counterpart to deadlock in STM systems, *livelock*, where rollbacks resulting from contention might result in further contentions and further rollbacks, *etc.* How frequently livelocks occur is typically gauged by experimental methods. In addition, rollback also may not be as easy as simply discarding the read/write set and retrying (see `AbortHandler`, *etc.* in [CMC+06] and `onAbort` *etc.* methods in [NMAT+07]). In terms of performance there have been no detailed studies that we know of comparing locking and rollback. A good overview of the pros and cons of blocking and rollback appears in [WHJ06].

Another reason why Coqa does not take a rollback approach is a desire for ubiquitous atomicity, even for I/O-intensive applications. Existing STM systems provide atomicity guarantees only for code explicitly specified by programmers, say, by declaring a block to be `atomic`; I/O cannot occur in these regions since it cannot generally be undone. In order to make sure that the system can roll back to the state before an abandoned transaction, a STM system needs to perform bookkeeping on the initial state of every transaction. So programmers have to be stingy in the number of atomic blocks declared, to avoid the overhead of such bookkeeping growing unexpectedly large with increasing number of threads and transaction sizes. As a result, in a large number of STM systems [HF03,WJH04,Cra05], code by default runs in a mode with no atomicity guarantees, and the interleaving of this code with atomicity-preserving code in fact can break the atomicity of the latter, an unfortunate consequence known as weak atomicity [CMC⁺06].

*Atomicity in Actors and Other Languages.* Our work is most related to Actor languages. Actors [Agh90,AMST97] provide a simple concurrent model where each actor is a concurrent unit. Inter-actor communication is only via asynchronous messaging. Ubiquitous atomicity is preserved in the Actor model because executing each actor method does not depend on the state of other actors and so each method execution is trivially serializable. However, the Actor model's per-method atomicity is only a *local* property in the sense that it neither includes more than one actor nor other methods invoked by the current method. So, Coqa is a significant extension to the Actor notion of atomicity. Morevoer, Actors are a model more suited to loosely-coupled distributed programming: for tightly-coupled message sequences, programming them in the pure Actor model means breaking off each method after each send and wrapping up the continuation as a new actor method. Typically when Actor languages are implemented [Arm96,Mil,HO06,YBS86], additional language constructs (such as futures, and explicit continuation capture) are included to ease programmability, but there is still a gap in that the most natural mode of programming, synchronous messaging, is not fully supported, only limited forms thereof. We elect to support full synchronous messaging so that Coqa coding style can be extremely close to standard programming practice.

Argus [Lis88] pioneered the study of atomicity in object-oriented languages. Like actors it is focused on loosely coupled computations in a distributed context, so it is quite remote in purpose from Coqa but there is still overlap in some dimensions. Argus allows nested transactions, called *subactions*. Unlike our subtasking, when a subaction ends, all its objects are merged with the parent action, instead of being released early to promote parallelism as a subtask does. Guava [BST00] was designed with the same philosophy as Coqa: code is concurrency-aware by default. The property Guava enforces is race freedom, which is a weaker and more low-level property than the quantized atomicity of Coqa.

## 5  Conclusion and Future Work

Coqa is a foundational study of how concurrency can be built deeply into object models; our particular target is tightly coupled computations running concurrently on multi-core CPUs. Coqa has a very simple and sound foundation – it is defined via only three forms of messaging, which account for (normal) local message send, thread spawning via asynchronous message send, and atomic subtasking via synchronous nonlocal send. We formalized Coqa as the language KernelCoqa, and proved that it observes a wide range of good concurrency properties, in particular *quantized atomicity*. We justify our approach by implementing CoqaJava, a Java extension incorporating all of the Coqa features.

# References

[Agh90]    Agha, G.: ACTORS: A model of Concurrent computations in Distributed
           Systems. MITP, Cambridge, Mass (1990)
[AMST97]   Agha, G., Mason, I.A., Smith, S.F., Talcott, C.L.: A foundation for actor
           computation. Journal of Functional Programming 7(1), 1–72 (1997)
[Arm96]    Armstrong, J.: Erlang — a Survey of the Language and its Industrial
           Applications. In: INAP 1996 — The 9th Exhibitions and Symposium on
           Industrial Applications of Prolog, Hino, Tokyo, Japan, pp. 16–18 (1996)
[BLR02]    Boyapati, C., Lee, R., Rinard, M.: Ownership types for safe programming:
           preventing data races and deadlocks. In: OOPSLA 2002, Seattle, Wash-
           ington, USA, pp. 211–230. ACM Press, New York, NY, USA (2002)
[BST00]    Bacon, D.F., Strom, R.E., Tarafdar, A.: Guava: a dialect of java without
           data races. In: OOPSLA 2000, pp. 382–400. ACM Press, New York (2000)
[CMC⁺06]   CarlStrom, B., McDonald, A., Chafi, H., Chung, J., Minh, C., Kozyrakis,
           C., Olukotun, K.: The atomos transactional programming language. In:
           PLDI 2006, Ottawa, Ontario, Canada (June 2006)
[Cra05]    Cray Inc. Chapel Specification (2005)
[Gra78]    Gray, J.: Notes on data base operating systems. In: Flynn, M.J., Jones,
           A.K., Opderbeck, H., Randell, B., Wiehle, H.R., Gray, J.N., Lagally, K.,
           Popek, G.J., Saltzer, J.H. (eds.) Operating Systems. LNCS, vol. 60, pp.
           393–481. Springer, Heidelberg (1978)
[HF03]     Harris, T., Fraser, K.: Language support for lightweight transactions. In:
           OOPSLA 2003, pp. 388–402 (2003)
[HO06]     Haller, P., Odersky, M.: Event-based programming without inversion of
           control. In: Dumke, R.R., Abran, A. (eds.) IWSM 2000. LNCS, vol. 2006,
           Springer, Heidelberg (2001)
[Lip75]    Lipton, R.J.: Reduction: a method of proving properties of parallel pro-
           grams. Commun. ACM 18(12), 717–721 (1975)
[Lis88]    Liskov, B.: Distributed programming in argus. Commun. ACM 31(3), 300–
           312 (1988)
[Liu07]    Liu, Y.D.: Interaction-Oriented Programming, PhD thesis, Johns Hop-
           kins University, Baltimore, MD, USA, (2007), electronic copy available at
           http://www.cs.jhu.edu/~yliu/thesis/
[Lom77]    Lomet, D.B.: Process structuring, synchronization, and recovery using
           atomic actions. SIGOPS Oper. Syst. Rev. 11(2), 128–137 (1977)
[LS89]     Lamport, L., Schneider, F.B.: Pretending atomicity. Technical Report
           TR89-1005, Digital Equipment Corporation (1989)
[Lu07]     Lu, X.: Coqa: A Concurrent Programming Model with Ubiquitous Atomic-
           ity. PhD thesis, Johns Hopkins University, Baltimore, MD, USA (Novem-
           ber 2007), electronic copy available at
           http://www.cs.jhu.edu/~xiaoqilu/thesis/
[Mil]      Miller, M.: The E Language, http://www.erights.org
[MPA05]    Manson, J., Pugh, W., Adve, S.V.: The java memory model. In: POPL
           2005, pp. 378–391. ACM Press, New York (2005)
[NCM03]    Nystrom, N., Clarkson, M.R., Myers, A.C.: Polyglot: An extensible com-
           piler framework for java. In: Hedin, G. (ed.) CC 2003. LNCS, vol. 2622,
           pp. 138–152. Springer, Heidelberg (2003)

[NMAT+07] Ni, Y., Menon, V., Adl-Tabatabai, A.-R., Hosking, A.L., Hudson, R.L., Moss, J.E.B., Saha, B., Shpeisman, T.: Open nesting in software transactional memory. In: ACM SIGPLAN 2007 Symposium on Principles and Practice of Parallel Programming (March 2007)

[PF]      Java PathFinder at, http://javapathfinder.sourceforge.net/

[Sin89]   Singhal, M.: Deadlock detection in distributed systems. IEEE Computer 22(11), 37–48 (1989)

[WHJ06]   Welc, A., Hosking, A.L., Jagannathan, S.: Transparently reconciling transactions with locking for java synchronization. In: Thomas, D. (ed.) ECOOP 2006. LNCS, vol. 4067, pp. 148–173. Springer, Heidelberg (2006)

[WJH04]   Welc, A., Jagannathan, S., Hosking, A.L.: Transactional monitors for concurrent objects. In: Odersky, M. (ed.) ECOOP 2004. LNCS, vol. 3086, pp. 519–542. Springer, Heidelberg (2004)

[YBS86]   Yonezawa, A., Briot, J.-P., Shibayama, E.: Object-oriented concurrent programming abcl/1. In: OOPLSA 1986: Conference proceedings on Object-oriented programming systems, languages and applications, pp. 258–268. ACM Press, New York (1986)

# Keep Off the Grass:
# Locking the Right Path for Atomicity

Dave Cunningham, Khilan Gudka, and Susan Eisenbach

Imperial College London
{dc04,khilan,sue}@doc.ic.ac.uk

**Abstract.** Atomicity provides strong guarantees against errors caused by unanticipated thread interactions, but is difficult for programmers to implement with low-level concurrency primitives. With the introduction of multicore processors, the problems are compounded. Atomic sections are a high level language feature that programmers can use to designate the blocks of code that need to be free from unanticipated thread interactions, letting the language implementation handle the low-level details such as deadlock. From a language designer's point of view, the challenge is to implement atomic sections without compromising performance.

We propose an implementation of atomic sections that inserts locks transparently into object-oriented programs. The main advantages of our approach are: (1) We infer *path* expressions (that at run-time resolve to actual objects) for many more accesses in the atomic section than previous work could infer. (2) We use multi-granularity locking for guarding iterative traversals. (3) We ensure freedom from deadlock by rolling back the lock acquisition phase. (4) We release locks as early as possible. In summary, our approach uses a finer-grained locking discipline than previous lock inference techniques.

## 1 Introduction

In shared memory concurrent software, to prevent erroneous behaviour due to unanticipated thread interactions, programmers ensure that appropriate blocks of code are *atomic* [18]. Atomicity is a stronger property than race-freedom [6], guaranteeing against high-level concurrency bugs such as stale values. A programmer can reason about atomic blocks with sequential intuition.

In an object-oriented language with locks, a block of code can be made atomic through the following process: A guarding discipline must be chosen (and obeyed) that specifies a lock for each shared memory object. For each block of atomic code and for each object accessed by the block, the appropriate locks must be acquired. Thus the developer must be aware of accesses internal to any invoked functions (breaking encapsulation). Furthermore, for correctness, the lock acquisitions and releases follow a two-phase discipline [5], i.e. the acquisitions must precede all releases in the block. Finally, locks must be acquired according to the same partial order to avoid deadlocks. In time, it will become necessary to maintain the code, where care must be taken to keep the lock acquisitions in sync with

L. Hendren (Ed.): CC 2008, LNCS 4959, pp. 276–290, 2008.
© Springer-Verlag Berlin Heidelberg 2008

newly introduced accesses in the code. The process is unforgiving. Any error introduces a possible bug (e.g. deadlock, stale value, race condition), which is hard to reproduce, and troublesome to trace to an underlying cause.

While atomicity allows us to more confidently assert the absence of concurrency errors, it cannot be reliably enforced by programmers. The problem of enforcement would be better solved by the programming language implementation, and the primitive that sets out to achieve this goal is the *atomic section*. By simply marking a block of code as atomic, the programmer can be assured that the implementation will execute as if all other threads were suspended, without having to implement any extra machinery.

Although atomic sections allow the programmer to pretend a block is executed sequentially, such an implementation would have poor performance. A transparent optimisation is for non-interfering threads to be allowed to execute in parallel with atomic sections. There are a number of proposed methods for efficient atomic section implementations, which can be divided into two categories: Optimistic approaches, in the form of Software or Hardware Transactional Memory [2,11,12,14,17,20,21,22,23], rely on being able to detect thread interference at runtime and rollback the state to the beginning of the atomic section where it is known to be uncorrupted. Pessimistic approaches statically attempt to infer locks sufficient for preventing interference [4,7,15,19,25]. The more efficient implementations of transactions and all lock inference implementations, including ours, prohibit the access of shared objects outside of atomic sections.

The optimistic approach can detect interference, whereas the nature of static inference means that only a conservative approximation can be made, reducing parallelism by taking more locks than required for a particular execution of an atomic section. On the other hand, the pessimistic approach does not require any runtime machinery for recording accesses, which if implemented in software can reduce performance. Additionally, no cycles will be wasted contributing towards a state which gets rolled back. If contention is high, transactional systems may spend more time rolling back than making useful progress. Finally, only internal invisible actions such as memory reads and writes can be rolled back; if an optimistic approach is to be used, external actions such as IO must not be allowed in an atomic section. This means that the compiler either has to reject such programs or transparently move the IO out of the atomic section. Pessimistic techniques have no such restriction.

We chose to implement atomic sections pessimistically using lock inference. We face the same challenges as programmers: Taking enough locks at the right time, striving for fine-grained locking while also trying to minimise the overhead of locking code, and avoiding deadlocks. We have strived to make our implementation transparent to the programmer, requiring no additional type or other annotations.

In Sect. 2, we summarise our approach and describe how we handle an example. In Sect. 3, we describe our program analysis in detail. In Sect. 4, we describe how we use the result of our program analysis to generate locking code, without deadlocking. In Sect. 5, we report on the use of our approach with part of a real program. In Sect. 6, we discuss how our approach differs to that of the related work. We conclude with Sect. 7.

## 2    General Approach and Features

We use a data-flow analysis, at link or JIT time, to infer the object accesses performed by each atomic section. This analysis needs to traverse any code that might be invoked by the block in question, so the whole program is needed. When the analysis terminates, we know, at each program point, the set of objects that are accessed from that point until the end of the atomic section. The inferred accesses then need to be translated into locks. We believe our representation of accesses is novel, and the most precise to date. As a simplification all objects after construction are shared. Detecting thread-local heap objects would benefit many systems like ours, and we do not discuss it here.

We try and use one lock per object, or *instance* locks, where possible, so that the parallelism can scale with the data. Sometimes code can access a statically unbounded number of objects. This happens during iterations over objects, and when we approximate an array index expression. In such cases, we use the type of the accessed objects to take a *multilock* which guards all instances of that type and subtypes. The semantics of multilocks require that if one thread has taken the multilock on an object, any other threads attempting to lock a subordinate instance of that multilock will be blocked until the multilock is released. We also distinguish between read/write accesses, and we use read/write locks to allow multiple parallel reads. We need re-entrant locks in case objects happen to be aliased at runtime, causing the same lock to be taken twice.

The code in Figure 1 is for an instant messaging system, where a client can send a stream of messages to another client, by name, through a central server. The Client constructor registers a new client in a centralised hashtable of clients. This must be an atomic operation in order that the uninitialised value of the hash entry e.val is not visible to other threads. Our system infers two locks – the hashtable itself (for reading), and the array of buckets inside the hashtable (for writing). Although the hash entry is modified, it is a newly constructed object and thus cannot be seen by other threads. We give the inferred locks as comments in the code, where ! denotes a write lock.

The atomic section starting on line (53) iterates (HashEntry.findKey is recursive) through a list of hash entries, and thus the analysis has to lock (for reading) the multilock that subsumes every hash entry. Atomic sections starting on lines (59) and (63) simply access a pair of clients and a single client object, and the locking reflects this. The atomic section starting on line (45) is only ever called from within another atomic section starting on line (59), so does not have any locking code inserted into it. If it were also called from a *pre-emptive* context (i.e. from outside an atomic section), we would have a problem inserting locking code into it, because this code would also be executed by the atomic section starting on line (59). We solve this problem by duplicating functions if they are called from both atomic and pre-emptive contexts.

```
1   class HashEntry {
2       string key;  Object val;  HashEntry next;
3       HashEntry (string key) { this.key = key; }
4       HashEntry findKey (string key) {
5           if (this.key==key) {
6               return this;
7           } else {
8               if (next==null) { return null; }
9               else { return next.findKey(key); }
10  }   }   }
11
12  class HashTable {
13      HashEntry[] buckets;
14      HashTable() { buckets = new HashEntry[100]; }
15      int index(string key) {
16          int hash = key.hash % buckets.length;
17          if (hash<0) { hash = hash + buckets.length; }
18          return hash;
19      }
20      HashEntry createHashEntry(string key) {
21          HashEntry entry = new HashEntry(key);
22          int index = index(key);
23          entry.next = buckets[index];
24          buckets[index] = entry;
25          return entry;
26      }
27      HashEntry findHashEntry(string key) {
28          HashEntry entry = buckets[index(key)];
29          if (entry==null) { return null; }
30          return entry.findKey(key);
31  }   }
32
33  class Client {
34      string name;  HashTable allClients;   Client interlocutor;
35      Client (HashTable allClients, string name) {
36          this.allClients = allClients;  this.name = name;
37          atomic {  //locks: {allClients, !allClients.buckets}
38              HashEntry e = allClients.createHashEntry(name);
39              e.val = this;
40          }
41          run();
42      }
43      string read() { return ""; }
44      void accept(Client source, string msg) {
45          atomic {  //omitted
46              print "<"+source.name+"> ----> <"+name+"> "+msg;
47      }   }
48      void run() {
49          while (true) {
50              string msg = read();
51              if (msg=="connect") {
52                  string name = read();
53                  atomic {  //locks: {HashEntry}
54                      HashEntry e = allClients.findHashEntry(name);
55                      interlocutor = (Client) e.val;
56              }   }
57              if (msg=="send") {
58                  string cargo = read();
59                  atomic {  //locks: {this, interlocutor}
60                      interlocutor.accept(this, cargo);
61              }   }
62              if (msg=="disconnect") {
63                  atomic {  //locks: {!this}
64                      interlocutor = null;
65  }   }   }   }   }
```

**Fig. 1.** Example source program using atomic sections

**Table 1.** Example of path graphs inferred at the top of two atomic sections from Fig. 1

| Line | Path set | Path graph |
|------|----------|------------|
| 37 | `allClients`<br>`allClients.buckets` | |
| 53 | `this`<br>`this.allClients`<br>`this.allClients.buckets`<br>`this.allClients.buckets[*]`<br>`this.allClients.buckets[*].next`<br>`this.allClients.buckets[*].next.next`<br>... | |

Our program analysis gives us information about what locks should be held at every program point in the atomic section. This means we have enough information to release locks straight after the last access of any objects they guard. Releasing locks early reduces contention, at no extra cost.

## 3    Path Graphs Inference

The keystone of our approach is an analysis that infers the object accesses in a given block of code. We assume that a control flow graph (CFG) is set up, with five types of node: **Copies** e.g. x=y (including assignment of **new** objects or **null**), **stores** e.g. x.f=y, **loads** e.g. x=y.f, **array stores** e.g. x[i]=y, and **array loads** e.g. x=y[i]. Our analysis is a backwards 'may' analysis. Each edge initially has no accesses, and we don't introduce accesses at the exit of the atomic section. Instead, accesses are *generated* by the CFG nodes (except for copy nodes), which also *transform* accesses. When the analysis terminates, the complete set of object accesses for the atomic section is left at its entry node.

The state at each edge is a *path graph*, which we use to represent a possibly-infinite set of *paths*. A path is a sequence of field or array accesses starting from a local variable, and can be used to statically characterise an object access. When statically analysing an iteration over an object structure, we do not know how many times the loop will repeat, and thus how many objects will be touched. Although the analysis can infer an infinite number of paths, the path graph representation is finite. Table 1 gives an example of two path graphs as produced by our analysis, and their corresponding path sets. The path sets are prefix-complete since we cannot access an object unless it is either bound to a variable before the atomic section began, or can be retrieved through another object.

In general, it will be impractical to record which element of an array was accessed, e.g. if the index was calculated using a complicated algorithm. The syntax [*] in the paths represents this. For brevity, in this presentation we immediately widen array element accesses to [*]. A system which already has some understanding of integer arithmetic could be more precise.

Path graphs are deterministic finite automata (DFA). The hollow node is the initial state, and all the other nodes are possible exit states, thus the set of paths is represented by the path graph. The atomic section starting on line (53), which

$$a[x = y]^n = \emptyset$$
$$a[x = \texttt{null}]^n = \emptyset$$
$$a[x = \texttt{new}]^n = \emptyset$$
$$a[x = y.f]^n = \{y \to n\}$$
$$a[x.f = y]^n = \{x \to n\}$$
$$a[x = y[i]]^n = \{y \to n\}$$
$$a[x[i] = y]^n = \{x \to n\}$$

$$t[x = y]^n(G) = G \setminus \{x \to n' | x \to n' \in G\} \cup \{y \to n' | x \to n' \in G\}$$
$$t[x = \texttt{null}]^n(G) = G \setminus \{x \to n' | x \to n' \in G\}$$
$$t[x = \texttt{new}]^n(G) = G \setminus \{x \to n' | x \to n' \in G\}$$
$$t[x = y.f]^n(G) = G \setminus \{x \to n' | x \to n' \in G\} \cup \{n \xrightarrow{f} n' | x \to n' \in G\}$$
$$t[x.f = y]^n(G) = G \setminus \{n' \xrightarrow{f} \_ | x \to n' \in G, (\nexists z \neq x : z \to n' \in G), (\nexists n''' : n''' \xrightarrow{} n' \in G)\}$$
$$\cup \{y \to n' | \_ \xrightarrow{f} n' \in G\}$$
$$t[x = y[\_]]^n(G) = G \setminus \{x \to n' | x \to n' \in G\} \cup \{n \xrightarrow{[*]} n' | x \to n' \in G\}$$
$$t[x[\_] = y]^n(G) = G \cup \{y \to n' | \_ \xrightarrow{[*]} n' \in G\}$$

**Fig. 2.** Data flow transfer functions

through iteration can access an unbounded number of objects, requires a cycle in the path graph in order to keep the representation finite. We represent the path graph as a set of edges, which are either labelled between a pair of nodes, or unlabelled between a variable and a node, e.g. the second path graph in Table 1 could be represented with the set:

$$\{this \to 1, 1 \xrightarrow{allClients} 2, 2 \xrightarrow{buckets} 3, 3 \xrightarrow{[*]} 4, 4 \xrightarrow{next} 4\}$$

As this representation allows multiple identically-named arrows from a state, it is actually a nondeterministic finite automaton (NFA). Our analysis computes NFAs but for locking purposes we convert them to minimised DFAs [16]. The numbered nodes in this representation correspond to the index of the CFG node where the access occurred. Because there are finitely many CFG nodes, variables, and fields, the set of edges and therefore the state of the analysis is also finite. It remains to give the transfer functions that compute, at each CFG node, the entry set from its exit set.

Figure 2 gives two functions, where ($\setminus$) binds tighter than ($\cup$), $x, y, z$ range over variables, $f, g$ range over fields, $G$ ranges over path graphs, and $\_$ represents an unbound variable. Function $a$ gives a path graph representing accesses generated by the given CFG node with index $n$. This path graph has meaning only in the state where the access occurred. Since we intend to lock the objects represented by this path graph at the top of the atomic section, and the state is mutated by assignments between these two points, the function $t$ will transform a path graph to compensate for the side-effect of a given CFG node. At each CFG node, we compute the entry path graph by applying $t$ to the exit path graph, and also include the result of $a$. Translating allows us to handle code like atomic {x=y ; x.f=42} without requiring that x and y are guarded by the same lock. Our analysis returns the path y.

When translating path graphs through copy nodes, paths starting with the lvalue are renamed so they start with the rvalue, except where the rvalue is a **new** object or **null**, where the accesses are simply killed. Load nodes are similar, but replace accesses of the form x.f1.f2 with y.f.f1.f2. Note that this works only because $a$ sets up an edge from y to $n$. Store nodes have to handle aliases, e.g. in `atomic { me.car = you.car ; dave.car.fuel = 100 }` it is clear that me, you, and dave are accessed, but it is not clear which car is accessed. If me was an alias of dave then the accessed car is described by `you.car`, otherwise the assignment has no effect and we must lock `dave.car`. Alias analysis can help here, but in this presentation we assume conservatively that everything can be an alias, hence the function $t$ introduces new edges from y to any node that has the appropriate field edge leading to it. The only alias we can assert is that x is an alias of x; in other words, we can kill `x.f` from the graph. This means killing an edge like $\xrightarrow{f}$, which we can do only if it is not used by any other paths, which we require with the two negated existential predicates. Array loads and stores are similar to their field counterparts.

It is possible to improve the accuracy of the analysis using type information, e.g. if $x : A[]$ and $z : B[]$ in `atomic { x[1] = y ; z[1].f = 10; }` then there is no need to infer the path y. Since the two arrays have different types, x cannot be an alias of z and thus the access `z[*]` will suffice. Similarly, we can use type information to distinguish between identically-named fields in different classes. Points-to information could also be used.

## 4   Lock Insertion

In this section we describe in detail our approach for inserting lock acquisition and release code into an atomic section. We describe how we detect deadlock and roll back the locking code, and how the analysis supports readers/writers and early unlocking.

### 4.1   Inferring Locks from a Path Graph

The path graphs analysis outputs a minimised DFA. We first process this graph looking for cycles and widened array access edges (i.e. $\xrightarrow{[*]}$ edges). Nodes reachable from such edges are marked as dirty, and the edges are removed. The graph is now acyclic and we perform a depth first search to pick out paths to lock. In the atomic section on line (53) of Table 1 we dirty the far-right node and remove the two edges pointing to it. We infer the paths {this, this.allClients, this.allClients.buckets}, that can be locked directly (in prefix order); we have to use a multilock to lock the dirty node. We use type information (the element type of the `buckets` array) to get the type of the objects represented by the dirty node (`HashEntry`), and we lock the multilock associated with this type. We associate a multilock with each class that guards all instances of the class. This lock allows subordinate instance locks to be acquired only when it is not held. Because classes are subsumed by subtyping, we also lock any subtypes of the class, of which there are none in our example. We also have multilocks for array types, e.g. for `Object[x][y]` accesses.

We wanted to use read/write locks, i.e. locks that allow multiple threads to have the read lock so long as no thread has the write lock. We were surprised to discover that the path graph representation already encodes this information. Because each node in the graph is a specific CFG node, and the CFG node determines the access type (load/store = read/write), the node index can be used to determine read/write locking. The only caveat is that we have to make sure that we preserve this information when collapsing the NFA to a minimised DFA.

Consider `atomic { y = x.f ; y.g = 10 }`, for which we would lock x, !x.f. If x was null, then this block would throw a `NullPointerException` (NPE). More importantly, so would our locking code. In general, throwing an exception from the locking code would not preserve the semantics of the atomic section, as there may be side-effects from before the NPE that now never occur. We need to either check for `null` before locking, or catch the NPE. If x is `null` we do not lock it, or x.f. There is a similar problem with `ClassCastException`, e.g. `atomic { y = ((A)x).f ; y.g = 10 }`, for which we also infer x,x.f. If the type of x does not have a field f, then we must cast it to A. We must therefore either check that that this is possible, or catch the exception. Null pointer analysis and points-to information can minimise the number of checks required.

## 4.2   Deadlock

Existing approaches guarantee the absence of deadlock at compile-time by always acquiring locks in the same order, and if such an ordering cannot be found they typically coarsen the granularity. Our type multilocks are static, thus can be statically ordered, e.g. alphabetically. Our instance locks cannot be statically ordered, but rather than coarsen the granularity, we detect deadlock and roll back the lock acquisition phase at run-time. Although this sounds like a transaction, there are no side effects to roll back, so no transaction log is required. This means that we have to take all locks at the beginning of the atomic section. We expect deadlock to be rarer than transaction collision, because the lock acquisition phase is much shorter than a whole atomic section, so we do not anticipate live locking to result. It also offers the possibility of high-priority threads forcing low-priority threads to give up their locks if they are stalled in a lock-acquisition phase.

Deadlock is typically detected at run-time by looking for cycles in a waits-for graph. Many systems check for deadlock, such as the Java Hotspot VM. This information is available at runtime, as it is needed by the lock implementation, but checking for cycles at each failed lock acquisition still incurs a performance penalty. This is a trade-off however, as we have better granularity as a result of keeping instance locking. If there are more CPUs than awake threads, this computation will be performed on a CPU which would otherwise be idle, eliminating the runtime penalty.

## 4.3   Parole

If an atomic section has finished accessing an object, but still has a lot of computation left to complete, it can release the lock early to gain finer granularity. We can also demote write locks to read locks, and multilocks to instance locks.

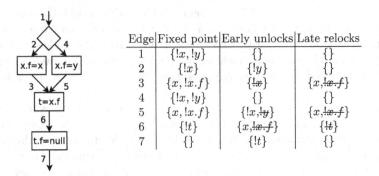

| Edge | Fixed point | Early unlocks | Late relocks |
|------|-------------|---------------|--------------|
| 1 | $\{!x,!y\}$ | $\{\}$ | $\{\}$ |
| 2 | $\{!x\}$ | $\{!y\}$ | $\{\}$ |
| 3 | $\{x,!x.f\}$ | $\{\cancel{!x}\}$ | $\{x,\cancel{!x.f}\}$ |
| 4 | $\{!x,!y\}$ | $\{\}$ | $\{\}$ |
| 5 | $\{x,!x.f\}$ | $\{!x,\cancel{!y}\}$ | $\{x,\cancel{!x.f}\}$ |
| 6 | $\{!t\}$ | $\{x,\cancel{!x.f}\}$ | $\{\cancel{!t}\}$ |
| 7 | $\{\}$ | $\{!t\}$ | $\{\}$ |

**Fig. 3.** Result of path graph analysis applied to early release

This is particularly important in the context of conservative analysis. Figure 3 is a simple example that demonstrates much of the power of early unlocking. We provide, at each edge, the path graph at the fixed point of the analysis, after it has been converted to a DFA, minimised, and reduced to locks. An exclamation mark represents a write lock. All of the locks in this example are paths.

At the entry of the atomic section (edge 1), we take the locks $\{!x,!y\}$ using the deadlock detection/rollback strategy described above. Once this is successful, execution will follow one of the branches. One branch (4,5) will cause us to eventually access both objects, and the other (2,3), only $!x$, as reflected by the edges 2 and 4 in the table. The analysis records that at edge 2, only the lock $!x$ is required, so by subtracting the two sets we can calculate locks to release, i.e. the *Early unlocks* column. If the set of locks increases, e.g. from edge 2 to edge 3, we have to acquire the extra lock in order for a later release to be well-balanced, we list this in the *Late relocks* column. Such locks have already been acquired by the thread, reacquiring them just increases the re-entrant counter. There is no risk of deadlock. We always acquire before release, to make sure we do not let the re-entrant counter reach zero. Thus locking remains two-phase.

At an assignment, where locks are translated from one variable to another, there will usually be a pair of redundant acquire/release actions. We used a simple alias analysis to remove redundant locking, denoted with strike-through. This also allows us to avoid redundant locking on known-to-be null or newly constructed objects. The remaining acquires and releases serve useful purposes: Unlocking $!y$ at edge 2 allows other threads to proceed in parallel, as this thread is now certain it will not write to (or read) $y$. Releasing $x$ and $!t$ at edges 6 and 7 respectively allows the atomic section to terminate with all locks released. Acquiring $x$ and releasing $!x$ at edge 5 allows other threads to read in parallel, as this thread no longer needs to write to $x$. The analysis similarly demotes a multilock to an instance lock, e.g. when a list is searched for an object which is then accessed. In the case of array indexing using a computed index, even if the analysis was equipped with more powerful array access edges and transfer functions, we would have to take a multilock as we would not statically know what element will be accessed. However, once the array index has been computed, the analysis would demote the multilock to an instance lock and similarly allow other threads to proceed.

The spurious lock of $x$ at edge 3 is necessary because at this time $x$ and $x.f$ are aliases, and the releases at edges 6 and 7 will serve to release the same lock twice. Therefore, in the branch we must acquire $x$ once more to balance the forthcoming releases. Aside from using the alias analysis to remove redundant locking, we were surprised that we needed no extra mechanism to set up early lock release. Our path graph analysis turned out to be powerful enough to encode read/write information and early release information in its basic form.

Sowing unlocking code throughout the invoked functions of an atomic section causes problems when one of the functions is called from more than one context. A number of solutions present themselves: Aggressively in-lining functions is simple and minimises contention, but will increase the size of the program and may cause performance problems such as cache misses. It should be possible to release locks after the call has returned, but a reference would have to be kept to the objects in question in case re-assignment renders them inaccessible. Alternatively, we could acquire a given lock once for each access, and release it after each access, but this would introduce more overhead. We chose to use the first technique, duplicating methods to ensure they are only called from more than one context in the case of recursion.

## 4.4   Splitting the Atom

Sometimes, it is desirable to turn off the atomicity of an atomic section for a period, perhaps to do some lengthy thread-local computation, or to communicate with other threads. It is possible to refactor the code into two separate atomic sections, but challenging because atomic sections are lexically scoped. To allow easy expression, we use a **preempt** section which when placed inside an atomic section, releases/reacquires locks to break the atomic section into two distinct parts. We have used this construct to implement wait/notify semantics.

The implementation of preempt sections uses the same program analysis as the implementation of atomic sections. A preempt section is represented in an atomic section's CFG by a *black hole* node that blocks the propagation of the path graph. This induces lock releases before the preempt, and acquisitions after it. We have to detect deadlock and backtrack when re-acquiring the locks after the preempt section. Figure 4 is the CFG of an atomic section that called wait() between a pair of object accesses. We have annotated the edges with the fixed point locks, acquires, and releases, as in Fig. 3. The grey circular node is the black hole node. The code for the wait/notify implementation is in Fig. 5.

## 5   Experiment

We have attempted to evaluate our approach on an existing application. We have implemented a subset of Java, with primitive types, classes, reference types, arrays, inheritance, overloading, dynamic binding, branches, loops, and early returns. All the examples in the paper were written in this language.

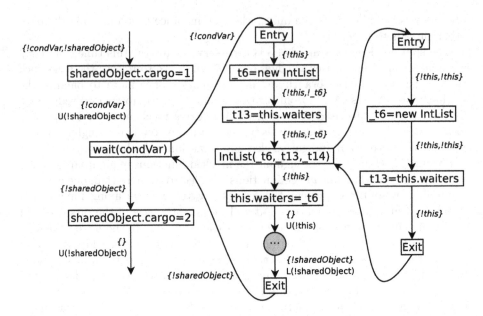

**Fig. 4.** CFG of an atomic section that calls `wait()`. The fixed point of the analysis is in italics, early lock release is in roman, e.g. U(!this). We have omitted redundant lock acquires and releases. The two `this` locks in the *far right* function correspond to the `this` variables in the `wait()` function and the converter, which are distinct. Our `sharedObject` is an instance of `IntList`, given in Fig. 5.

```
class IntList {
        IntList next; int cargo;
        IntList (IntList next, int cargo) {
                this.next = next;
                this.cargo = cargo;
}        }

class ConditionVariable {
        IntList waiters;
        void wait() {
                atomic {
                        waiters = new IntList(waiters,threadid);
                        preempt { park; }
        }        }
        void notify() {
                atomic {
                        unpark waiters.cargo;
                        waiters = waiters.next;
        }        }
        void notifyAll() {
                atomic {
                        while (waiters!=null) { notify(); }
}        }        }
```

**Fig. 5.** The code for the wait/notify implementation referenced above. The `IntList` records a queue of waiting threads, so that `notify` can wake them up. The keyword `threadid` gets the id of the current thread. The `unpark` and `park` keywords allow suspending and resuming of threads, by thread id.

Previous work [19,4] has used the AOLserver [1] source code (which is publicly available) as a case study. AOLserver is a high performance http server, written in C, which uses Tcl as a scripting language to drive dynamic content. Although multiple Tcl interpreters can be running simultaneously, e.g. for simultaneous client connections, they are essentially orthogonal. The actual concurrency is handled with C code where a shared store is provided for communication between Tcl interpreters. The source code was annotated with atomic sections and a form of guard annotation (which we do not need) by the authors of [19], who kindly made the source code available to us. The authors of [4] have a lock inference algorithm which they also benchmarked with the annotated AOLserver. Their approach was very different to ours, and we were interested in comparing their results with ours.

Since our analysis has not been implemented for C, we would have to translate AOLserver in order to process it. AOLserver is a large piece of software, so we chose one particular compilation unit, `tclvar.c` which the previous work seemed to find most demanding. We tried to reproduce the original code as closely as possible. Although it was written in C, the code slipped quite easily into an object-oriented design. Because our analysis is at this stage a whole-program analysis, we also had to implement a small part of the Tcl API. Some of the Tcl functions we left as stubs or only partially implemented, but we were careful to reproduce any accesses the real Tcl API would perform. As such, we are actually analysing more code than the previous work.

Although our implementation was naive, using Java data structures to store the analysis state, we hoped to get reasonable times for the AOLserver code. For each atomic section, we recorded how many nodes were present in the CFG, and how long it took to solve on a P4 3.2GHz CPU with 1GB of RAM, running the Java Hotspot VM v1.6.0. We also give the number of read/write multilocks (RM,WM), and how many read/write instance locks (RI,WI) taken at the top each atomic section. These results are presented in Fig. 6. The solve time includes the time spent minimising the path graph and inferring a set of locks at each edge. Our analysis is much faster than [4], as it works directly on the CFG without a costly setup phase, and the solving phase is faster too. Since each atomic section is treated separately, the time is linear in the number of atomic sections. Most of the time is spent cloning and garbage collecting.

# 6   Related Work

A number of techniques exist to verify programmer implementations of atomicity, such as: type checking [3], type inference [8], model checking [13], theorem proving [9] and run-time analysis [26]. Some of this work has used variants of ownership types, to specify the guarding relationship between objects. Consequently, they can support more powerful guarding disciplines, where static locks can be avoided altogether, but at the cost of additional annotations.

As discussed in Sect. 2, transactional memory is an optimistic implementation of atomicity, but relies on detecting interference from other threads and the

| Atomic section | CFG Node count | Solve time (seconds) | RI | WI | RM | WM |
|---|---|---|---|---|---|---|
| 1 | 219 | 0.566 | 2 | 4 | 4 | 0 |
| 2 | 242 | 0.489 | 2 | 4 | 4 | 0 |
| 3 | 284 | 0.728 | 1 | 4 | 3 | 1 |
| 4 | 203 | 0.345 | 3 | 3 | 3 | 0 |
| 5 | 319 | 0.946 | 1 | 4 | 3 | 1 |
| 6 | 277 | 0.694 | 2 | 4 | 5 | 0 |
| 7 | 101 | 0.119 | 1 | 0 | 4 | 1 |
| 8 | 286 | 0.897 | 2 | 4 | 4 | 0 |
| 9 | 360 | 2.385 | 2 | 4 | 7 | 0 |
| 10 | 169 | 0.164 | 3 | 3 | 4 | 0 |
| 11 | 272 | 0.759 | 1 | 4 | 5 | 0 |

The results in [4] state 2399 seconds for this file. Our total time was approximately 8 seconds.

**Fig. 6.** Results of applying our analysis to the AOLserver `tclvar.c` fragment

ability to roll back. It can allow more parallelism but at the cost of IO, and the risk of livelock. Software transactional memory has significant runtime overhead.

More recently, there have been several proposals for lock inference. Initially, [7] was an extension of the authors' type checking techniques, where incomplete synchronisation could be statically corrected. The authors admit that the added locks could introduce deadlock, whereas the following proposals all guarantee absence of deadlock through establishing a static order on lock allocations. A from-scratch proposal [19] required guard annotations, which although allowed the expression of instance locks as well as static locks, seemed not to be as powerful as the object-object relationships in e.g. [8]. Additionally, programs were rejected if the assignments interfered with the guarding discipline (they did not translate paths as we do).

The approaches in [25,15] did not require guard annotations, using just points-to information to indicate static locks. They handle assignment by increasing the granularity so that the lock guarding the lvalue and rvalue are the same. While [25] did have annotations, they were for the orthogonal purpose of partitioning an object's fields into separately-locked groups, as opposed to the typical approach (which we follow) where all an objects fields are guarded by the same lock. Allowing more parallelism, recent work [4,10] has allowed instance locks without needing annotations, but only in special aliasing circumstances.

## 7  Conclusion and Future Work

By solving the deadlock problem with a runtime technique, we were able to take instance locks rather than static locks. Instance locking is an opportunity for finer granularity and more parallelism. We embrace this opportunity by statically inferring accesses (in the form of paths), without having to reject assignments to variables containing accessed objects. Unlike previous work, we do not merge the locks of different objects if they once resided in the same variable.

In order to improve the speed of the analysis, it would be useful to analyse a method in isolation. Then this method summary (consisting of new accesses and translations) could instantiated in the various places the method is called.

It may be necessary, when dealing with e.g. native code that can't be analysed, to provide such a summary manually, to act as a realistic stub.

Using thread-local-object and may-happen-in-parallel analyses such as those in [10], it would be possible to omit some of the lock acquisitions. This would reduce the overhead, and less time spent acquiring locks would mean fewer deadlocks resolved at runtime. Also, if a group of locks are always acquired together, or not at all, it makes sense to join them into a single lock, also reducing the overhead of lock acquisition.

If it were possible to infer some form of ownership annotations [3], we might be able to use instance locks instead of static locks to handle iterations over objects, and non-trivial array indexes. We would like to try using points-to information, both as a foundation for multilocks (instead of using type information as we currently do), to see if this results in better granularity. Points-to information could also be used by the path graph analysis, to avoid adding so many edges at store CFG nodes.

Our aim was to create a finer-grained locking discipline than that used by previous lock inference techniques. This paper describes our approach which produced promising results. We are now moving our analysis to full Java, using the Soot [24] framework.

**Acknowledgements.** We are grateful to EPSRC and Microsoft for supporting this work. We also thank Tim Harris and the SLURP research group at Imperial College for interesting discussions, Tristan Allwood for proofreading, and Dossy Shiobara and the AOLserver project for helpful correspondence.

# References

1. AOLserver, a highly scalable, multi-threaded application server, http://aolserver.com/
2. Ananian, C.S., Asanovic, K., Kuszmaul, B.C., Leiserson, C.E., Lie, S.: Unbounded transactional memory. In: High-Performance Computer Architecture, 2005. HPCA-11. 11th International Symposium, pp. 316–327 (2005)
3. Cunningham, D., Drossopoulou, S., Eisenbach, S.: Universe Types for Race Safety. In: VAMP 2007, pp. 20–51 (September 2007), http://pubs.doc.ic.ac.uk/universes-races/
4. Emmi, M., Fischer, J.S., Jhala, R., Majumdar, R.: Lock allocation. In: POPL 2007: Proceedings of the 34th annual ACM SIGPLAN-SIGACT symposium on Principles of programming languages, pp. 291–296. ACM Press, New York (2007)
5. Eswaran, K.P., Gray, J.N., Lorie, R.A., Traiger, I.L.: The notions of consistency and predicate locks in a database system. Commun. ACM 19(11), 624–633 (1976)
6. Flanagan, C., Abadi, M.: Types for safe locking, 91–108 (1999)
7. Flanagan, C., Freund, S.N.: Automatic Synchronization Correction. In: Synchronization and Concurrency in Object-Oriented Languages (SCOOL) (2005)
8. Flanagan, C., Freund, S.N., Lifshin, M.: Type inference for atomicity. In: TLDI 2005: Proceedings of the 2005 ACM SIGPLAN international workshop on Types in languages design and implementation, pp. 47–58. ACM Press, New York (2005)

9. Freund, S., Qadeer, S.: Checking concise specifications for multithreaded software. In: Workshop on Formal Techniques for Java-like Programs (2003)

10. Halpert, R.L., Pickett, C.J.F., Verbrugge, C.: Component-based lock allocation. In: Malyshkin, V.E. (ed.) PaCT 2007. LNCS, vol. 4671, Springer, Heidelberg (2007)

11. Harris, T., Fraser, K.: Language support for lightweight transactions. ACM SIG-PLAN Notices 38(11), 388–402 (2003)

12. Harris, T., Marlow, S., Peyton-Jones, S., Herlihy, M.: Composable memory transactions. In: Proceedings of the tenth ACM SIGPLAN symposium on Principles and practice of parallel programming, pp. 48–60 (2005)

13. Hatcliff, J., Robby, D.M.B.: Verifying atomicity specifications for concurrent object-oriented software using model-checking. In: Steffen, B., Levi, G. (eds.) VMCAI 2004. LNCS, vol. 2937, pp. 175–190. Springer, Heidelberg (2004)

14. Herlihy, M., Eliot, J., Moss, B.: Transactional Memory: Architectural Support For Lock-free Data Structures. In: Proceedings of the 20th Annual International Symposium on Computer Architecture, pp. 289–300 (1993)

15. Hicks, M., Foster, J.S., Pratikakis, P.: Lock inference for atomic sections. In: Proceedings of the First ACM SIGPLAN Workshop on Languages Compilers, and Hardware Support for Transactional Computing (TRANSACT) (June 2006)

16. Hopcroft, J.E., Ullman, J.D.: Introduction to Automata Theory, Languages and Computation. Addison-Wesley, Reading (1979)

17. Kumar, S., Chu, M., Hughes, C.J., Kundu, P., Nguyen, A.: Hybrid transactional memory. In: Proceedings of the eleventh ACM SIGPLAN symposium on Principles and practice of parallel programming, pp. 209–220 (2006)

18. Lomet, D.: Process structuring, synchronization, and recovery using atomic actions. ACM SIGOPS Operating Systems Review 11(2), 128–137 (1977)

19. McCloskey, B., Zhou, F., Gay, D., Brewer, E.: Autolocker: synchronization inference for atomic sections. ACM SIGPLAN Notices 41(1), 346–358 (2006)

20. Moore, K.E., Hill, M.D., Wood, D.A.: Thread-level transactional memory. TR1524, Comp. Science Dept. UW Madison (March 31, 2005)

21. Rajwar, R., Herlihy, M., Lai, K.: Virtualizing transactional memory. In: Proceedings of the 32nd International Symposium on Computer Architecture, pp. 494–505 (2005)

22. Scherer III, W.N., Scott, M.L.: Advanced contention management for dynamic software transactional memory. In: Proceedings of the twenty-fourth annual ACM SIGACT-SIGOPS symposium on Principles of distributed computing, pp. 240–248 (2005)

23. Shavit, N., Touitou, D.: Software transactional memory. In: Proceedings of the fourteenth annual ACM symposium on Principles of distributed computing, pp. 204–213 (1995)

24. Vallée-Rai, R., Co, P., Gagnon, E., Hendren, L., Lam, P., Sundaresan, V.: Soot - a java bytecode optimization framework. In: CASCON 1999: Proceedings of the 1999 conference of the Centre for Advanced Studies on Collaborative research, p. 13. IBM Press (1999)

25. Vaziri, M., Tip, F., Dolby, J.: Associating synchronization constraints with data in an object-oriented language. SIGPLAN Not. 41(1), 334–345 (2006)

26. Wang, L., Stoller, S.D.: Runtime analysis of atomicity for multithreaded programs. IEEE Trans. Softw. Eng. 32(2), 93–110 (2006)

# Supporting Legacy Binary Code in a Software Transaction Compiler with Dynamic Binary Translation and Optimization

Cheng Wang, Victor Ying, and Youfeng Wu

Programming System Lab
Microprocess Technology Labs
Intel Corporation
2200 Mission College Blvd.
Santa Clara, CA 95052, USA
{cheng.c.wang,victor.ying,youfeng.wu}@intel.com

**Abstract.** Transactional memory (TM) has been shown to be a promising programming model for multi-core systems. We developed a Software-based Transactional Memory (STM) compiler that generates efficient transactional code for transactions to run on a STM runtime without the need of transactional hardware support. Since real-world applications often invoke third party libraries available only in binary form, it is imperative for our STM compiler to support legacy binary functions and provide an efficient solution to convert those invoked inside transactions to the corresponding transactional code. Our STM compiler employs a Lightweight Dynamic Binary Translation and Optimization Module (LDBTOM) to automatically convert legacy binary functions to transactional code. In this paper, we describe our LDBTOM system, which 1) seamlessly integrates the translated code with the STM compiler generated code to run on the STM runtime, and 2) optimizes the translated code taking advantage of dynamic optimization opportunities and STM runtime information. Although the binary code is inherently harder to optimize than high-level source code, our experiment shows that it can be translated and optimized into efficient transactional code by LDBTOM.

## 1 Introduction

Transactional memory [3][11][12][15][16] provides a powerful programming model to design concurrent programs. This model guarantees a large region of code, i.e. a transaction, to be executed atomically, and thus enables ordinary programmers to write correct and efficient concurrent applications without using locks. Many difficult issues associated with lock-based programs, such as deadlock, non-scalable composition, priority inversion, can thus be alleviated or eliminated.

To support Software Transactional Memory (STM [1][7][11][19]) or hardware assisted software transactional memory (HASTM [2]), memory operations inside a transaction need to be augmented with STM runtime API calls to check for

L. Hendren (Ed.): CC 2008, LNCS 4959, pp. 291–306, 2008.
© Springer-Verlag Berlin Heidelberg 2008

concurrency conflicts and log for transaction rollback. Existing STM compiler [7] for C/C++ programs can automatically insert the API calls to STM runtime (called barriers) for memory operations inside the transactions, if the program source code is available. Unfortunately, real-world applications often invoke third party libraries available only in binary form not compiled by a STM compiler. It is imperative for STM compilers to allow legacy binary functions to be called inside transactions. Otherwise, the usability of STM would be greatly limited. For example, a transaction may need to call a "*qsort*" library function. If library functions are not allowed to be called inside a transaction, the user would have to re-implement it in source code and compile it with the STM compiler.

We will refer to non-transactional library code the "legacy code". There are a number of approaches to support legacy code in STM compiler. One way is for the library supplier to provide a separate transactional version of the library. This not only places a significant burden on the library development and validations, but also poses engineering issues with managing multiple versions of the same library. There are also old libraries that cannot be recompiled. Another way is to statically translate library routines called in a transaction to transactional version. However, dynamically linked library routines may not be available at compiler time. Even if the library code is available at compile-time, static translation is known to be limited and may not be able to translate certain routines when indirect branches or calls are present. It is also possible to use special hardware to trap memory load and store operations so that the barrier operations can be executed for these operations. That approach, however, increases hardware costs on die area and power consumption. Our STM compiler [7] employs a Lightweight Dynamic Binary Translation and Optimization Module (LDBTOM) [8] to automatically convert the legacy binary functions to transactional code if they are called inside transactions at runtime.

There are many existing works on STM runtime systems [12][13][19], STM compilers [1][7][11] and Dynamic Binary Translation techniques [4][8][8][9][17]. However, to seamlessly integrate these techniques together for legacy binary code support in software transactional memory brings challenges. For example, a normal dynamic binary translator translates all the binary code in the whole application. But in our case, LDBTOM must only translate the legacy code, and must not translate the transactional code generated by STM compiler. Translation of the transactional code generated by the STM compiler not only slows down the program, but may also cause severe problems, such as livelocks [5], in the STM runtime. Therefore, we need close collaborations between the dynamic binary translation and STM compiler to distinguish the legacy binary code from the transactional code generated by STM compiler. Sophisticated program analysis may help identify legacy function calls inside transactions, but it is capable of completely solving the problem, especially in the present of indirect function calls and indirect branches. As another example, while the compiler generated code may be shared among different threads, most dynamic binary translation systems (including our DBT system) implement thread-private code cache for its simplicity of implementation. The efficient linking between thread-shared compiler-generated code and the thread-private DBT-generated code is a challenging issue. Furthermore, most of stack memory are private to the thread and thus do not need memory conflict checking. However, there are situations where a stack location may be shared among multiple threads and to generate efficient and correct code for stack references inside transactions poses challenges for dynamic binary translation.

On the other hand, LDBTOM can optimize the translated code taking advantage of dynamic optimization opportunities. For example, the dynamic optimization allows us to generate efficient STM code based on the assumption that stack variables are not shared among different threads. In case the program execution makes it possible for stack variables in one thread accessible to other threads, we can flush and regenerate new STM code conservatively before the stack variable sharing actually happens.

Overall, this paper makes the following major contributions.

- We develop a seamless framework to support legacy library code in a STM compilation system.
- We provide a complete solution to make sure that no legacy code will be executed without translation and no compiler generated transactional code are translated, even when the static type checking fails to detect user's programming error. We also provide efficient solutions for linking between the thread-shared compiler-generated code and the thread-private DBT-generated code.
- We developed a number of dynamic optimization techniques, such as stack variable filtering, dead register and conditional code (%eflags) saving elimination, redundant barrier elimination, inlining, etc, to dramatically reduce the overhead of translated code for transactional execution.
- We provide experimental result comparing translated code vs. STM compiler generated code using SPLASH-2 benchmark and a set of concurrent data structure benchmarks. Even though legacy binary code usually has very little high-level information available for sophisticated analysis and optimizations, our experimental results on SPLASH-2 benchmark shows that LDBTOM only causes about 1% overhead over compiler optimized STM code. Even for the data structures benchmarks which spend almost all their execution time inside legacy functions called inside transactions (to stress test the LDBTOM overhead), the LDBTOM optimized code runs only about 80% slower than the hand-optimized STM code. In contrast, straightforward translation would perform more than 8 times slower than the hand-optimized code.

The rest of the paper is organized as follows. Section 0 discusses the related work. Section 0 overviews the STM compiler. Section 0 describes LDBTOM infrastructure and transformations. Section 0 discusses optimization strategies. Section 0 provides experimental results. Section 0 concludes the paper and points out future research directions.

## 2   Related Work and Issues

Different kinds of hardware transactional memory mechanisms are described in [3][16][18]. Software transactional memory was introduced in [12][19]. Efficient implementations of STM in managed environment were provided in [1][11]. An efficient implementation of STM in unmanaged environment was developed in [7]. Hybrid transactional memory [14] proposes to combine HW and SW transactional memory implementations.

Dynamic binary translation has been an active research topic in recent years. It has be used to support backward compatibility [4], enhance reliability [8] and security [9], reduce power consumption [17], as well as improve programmability, as reported in this paper, to support transactional memory.

JudoSTM [14] annotates the program source code to specify transactions, and implements a transactional memory system through dynamic binary rewriting. With program source code available, dynamic binary rewriting for the whole transactions seems less efficient.   Our LDBTOM takes advantages of sophisticated static compilation and only dynamicaly translates and optimizes the legacy code in transactions.

There are a number of open issues remaining to support legacy binary code in STM. Transactions need to support rollback in case a conflict is detected. The users must ensure that the codes insides transactions do not perform operations that cannot be rolled back, such as the system calls and input/output operations.  System call and I/O issues are being actively addressed in research community with open nested transaction [13] and restricted transaction [6]. These are general issues for transactional memory and are not unique to legacy code so we consider them beyond the scope of this paper.

There is also the issue with software implemented synchronization operations (e.g. lock, barrier) in legacy code.  Lock based programs can use different locks for different critical sections, so that critical sections controlled by different locks do not necessarily synchronize with each other, even when there are conflict memory accesses among them.  But transactions are required to synchronize with each other whenever there are conflict memory accesses among them, just as if all of them are controlled by a single lock.  Thus the single-lock semantics for transactions is different from the semantics of the individually locked sections, and straightforwardly converting locked sections to transactions may result in deadlock [5].  Lock-based programs may also implement barriers to join multiple threads together, while transaction can not accomplish the barrier synchronizations easily. These are general issues with converting lock-based program to transactions, no matter the locks are used in source code or legacy binary code. We conducted a preliminary study to address this issue in a separate paper [20].

In this paper, we assume that the user will decide that a library routine does not invoke system calls, I/O operations, and locked-sections, and can be called inside a transaction.  There are significant portions of legacy code, e.g. majority of routines provided in LIBC and LIBM, etc, that can be safely called inside transactions as long as they are translated to check for conflict and log operations for rollback. This paper targets this portion of libraries.  LDBTOM currently report runtime errors when I/O and system calls in legacy code are translated.

# 3  STM Compiler

Our STM compiler [7] targets C/C++ programs. The compiler provides programming language constructs to write programs with transactions.   An example code illustrating the transaction constructs is shown in Fig. 1. The *tm_atomic* pragma specifies that the statement (usually a block statement) following it is a transaction (an atomic operation). If a conflict is detected during the execution of a transaction, the state of the transaction will be rolled back to the same as before the transaction execution and the transaction is re-executed. Transactions can also be nested. We support closed nested transactions [13]. In our implementation, when a conflict is detected in a nested transaction, the outmost transaction is aborted. If a *tm_abort()* intrinsic operation is executed inside a nested transaction, the innermost transaction is rolled back. When an inner transaction completes, its memory updates are not actually committed until the out-most transaction commits. The *tm_commit()* intrinsic operation explicitly commits a transaction before it reaches the end.

The *tm_function* pragma specifies a transactional function (e.g. *foo()*) that may be called inside a transaction. For each transactional function, the STM compiler creates a transactional clone and calls it inside transactions while calls the original function outside transactions. For a function called inside a transaction that is not specified as *tm_function*, the compiler will treat it as a legacy function and generate code to convert the function to transactional at runtime. For the example in Fig. 1, the function *qsort()* is not declared as a *tm_function* and is converted to a transactional routine at runtime.

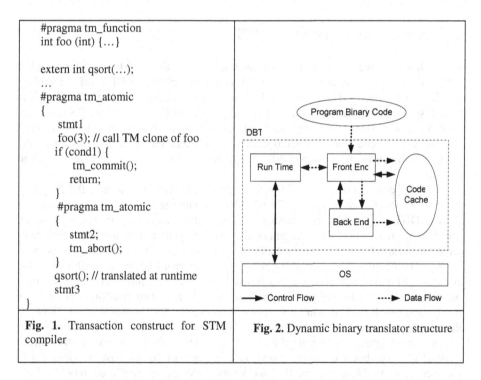

```
#pragma tm_function
int foo (int) {...}

extern int qsort(...);
...
#pragma tm_atomic
{
    stmt1
    foo(3); // call TM clone of foo
    if (cond1) {
        tm_commit();
        return;
    }
    #pragma tm_atomic
    {
        stmt2;
        tm_abort();
    }
    qsort(); // translated at runtime
    stmt3
}
```

**Fig. 1.** Transaction construct for STM compiler

**Fig. 2.** Dynamic binary translator structure

In order to execute a transaction atomically, the STM compiler needs to insert calls to STM runtime routines (called barriers) for memory read and write operations inside the transaction to detect conflict with the memory accesses in other transactions. The read and write barriers first make sure no other transaction currently owns the data being accessed. The write barrier then acquires ownership for the data being updated, updates the data in place, and keeps the old value in an undo-log in case the transaction has to rollback. The read barrier logs the data version so it can be checked at transaction commit time to make sure that the set of data read in the current transaction is consistent with respect to the committed transactions. In addition to the barriers, the STM compiler also generates code to checkpoint the live-in values at the beginning of the transaction, rollback transaction to the initial state when a conflict is detected or when a *tm_abort()* intrinsic is invoked, and commit the transaction results at the end of the transaction.

The primary overhead for STM compiler generated code is the barrier operations. To reduce the overhead, the STM compiler generates inlined barrier code to reduce function call overheads. It also uses compiler analysis to determine thread-private references that can never conflict with accesses in other transactions so as to omit their barriers. Furthermore, the STM compiler eliminates redundant barriers for data accesses with the same addresses. With these optimizations, the STM compiler generated code performs comparative to hand-optimized code and is competitive to fine-grain lock-based code, and much better than coarse-grain locking version when running on multiple processors [7].

## 4   Compiler Integration with DBT

For a library function called inside a transaction, the STM compiler invokes LDBTOM to convert it to a transactional function at runtime. LDBTOM is based on our Dynamic Binary Translation (DBT) research framework: StarDBT [8]. The overall structure of StarDBT is shown in Fig. 2. The DBT runs on top of OS as a user-level run-time system. The program binary code is dynamically translated and stored into the code cache. The translated code can be executed under the control of the DBT, which allows us to apply different dynamic binary translation techniques to the code.

The DBT consists of three individual modules: the *Runtime* module, the *Frontend* module and the *Backend* module. The *Runtime* module provides the system supports for the DBT. The *Frontend* module manages the execution for dynamic binary translation. It dynamically recognizes the original program instructions, translates them into instructions in the code cache, and controls the code execution in the code cache. The *Frontend* module also collects program profiling information during the code execution and selects hot traces based on the profiling information for run-time optimization by the *Backend*. The *Backend* module performs run-time optimization for the dynamic binary translations. It builds an intermediate representation (IR) from the hot traces selected by the *Frontend* module. It then performs optimizations on the IR, and finally generates optimized code into the code cache to improve performance.

StarDBT has been used for many research works to improve reliability [9], enhance security [10], etc. In this work, we leverage a simplified module from StarDBT called LDBTOM, to support legacy binary code in STM. The compiler invokes LDBTOM directly in the generated code with the address of the library function passed as a argument for translation. LDBTOM starts to translate the code at this address and runs the translated code from the translation code cache.

When a translated library function returns to a transaction or calls back to an STM compiler generated function, the execution should continue to the compiler generated transactional code without translation. For this purpose, the STM compiler adds all the entry points in the compiler generated code to LDBTOM's runtime dispatch table, including returning points for library functions called in transactions. If LDBTOM finds the branch/call target in the dispatch table, the branch/call will directly connect to the targeted code. Otherwise the code at the target will be translated before execution. Therefore, the added entry points in the dispatch table will naturally cause LDBTOM to go back to the compiler generated STM code for execution.

Once a library function is translated, subsequent calls to the same function should not invoke LDBTOM again. To accomplish this, STM compiler builds a table, called Translation Linkage Table (TLT), similar to the Procedure Linkage Table for shared libraries, with one entry per static call site that may call a legacy library function in STM compiler generated code. Each call to a library function is generated as an indirect call through the corresponding entry in the TLT. The first time a library function is called, its TLT entry contains LDBTOM's entry point to translate the legacy function. After that, the TLT entry contains the starting address of the translated function, and late call to the function is mostly an indirect call through the TLT without translation. This scheme works well for direct calls to library functions. For an indirect call, however, the library function pointed to by the function pointer may change at runtime. Consequently, we cannot simply place the starting address of the translated function in the TLT entry. Instead, we place a dispatch table lookup routine in that entry. The lookup routine searches the dispatch table to determine if the current function pointer is to an already-translated function. If so, the translated function is directly called. Otherwise, LDBTOM is invoked to translate the indirectly called function. The TLT entry for an indirect call may also be expanded to include a few conditional branches for those frequently called targets.

LDBTOM uses a thread-private code cache for each user thread. For a parallel loop body, the same static code is executed by multiple threads, and the code needs to be compiled to work with code in multiple code caches in different threads. Our STM compiler creates a thread-private TLT for each thread and uses a thread-private descriptor to direct the static call to use the thread-private TLT to transfer control to the thread-private code cache.

Specifically, the STM runtime provides a runtime library *stmGetTxnDesc()* to get a thread-private transaction descriptor. All the thread-private memory accesses go through the thread-private transaction descriptor. We add one field in the transaction descriptor, which points to the thread-private TLT. To access the thread-private TLT, STM compiler generates a global index variable storing an index to the thread-private TLT, for each call site to a legacy function. For program with separately compiled modules, our compiler puts all the index variables into a special segment *.tlt* in the object file and the program linker will combine them together into a global index table (GIT). At the program initialization for STM, we initialize each entry in the GIT with the TLT table offset. When a thread is initialized, we allocate and initialize a thread-private TLT for the thread with the same size as the GIT. Then we can save the thread-private TLT pointer in the transaction descriptor and use the global index variable to access the entry in the thread-private TLT for a particular function call. Fig. 3 shows the code for program initialization and thread initialization. *GIT_head* is the first index variable in GIT and *GIT_tail* is the last index variable in GIT. The

| // program initialization<br>prog_init() {<br><br>   ...<br>   Index = 0;<br>   for(p = &GIT_head;<br>     p != &GIT_tail; p++) {<br>     *p = index++;<br>   }<br>   GIT_size = index;<br>} | // thread initialization<br>thread_init() {<br>   ... // allocate transaction descriptor<br>   desc = stmGetTxnDesc();<br>   desc->TLT = malloc(GIT_size * ENTRY_SIZE);<br>   For(index = 0; index < GIT_size; Index++) {<br>     if (the call site is a direct call)<br>        desc->TLT[index].proc = LDBTOM;<br>     else<br>        desc->TLT[index].proc = dispatch_lookup;<br>   }<br>} |
|:---:|:---:|
| **(a) program initialization** | **(b) thread initialization** |

**Fig. 3.** Initialization for thread-private TLT

STM runtime defines these two index variables and makes sure they are the first entry and last entry in the GIT. *GIT_size* is the GIT table size.

Fig. 4 shows the code for a function call to legacy function in transaction. index_L is the index variable for function call at L. We use the thread-private descriptor and index_L to access the thread-private TLT entry and make an indirect function call to LDBTOM. LDBTOM can easily patch the thread-private TLT entry with the translated code in the thread-private code cache so that future function calls go directly to the translated code.

| ```
int foo (void);

main (…){
    #pragma tm_atomic
    {
        …
        L: foo();
    }
}
``` | ```
int   index_L; // in segment .tlt

main (…) {
    #pragma tm_atomic
    {
        …
        desc = stmGetTxnDesc();
        …
        call            (*desc-
>TLT[index_L].proc)(…);
    }
}
``` |
|:---:|:---:|
| **(a) source code** | **(b) STM code** |

**Fig. 4.** Thread-private TLT for legacy function call

Another issue is determining the target of a function pointer and generating correct code when the function pointer is called inside a transaction. A function pointer always points to the normal version of a function if it is compiled by the STM compiler, or a legacy binary function. If it points to an STM compiler generated function, the transactional version must be called instead. If it points to a legacy binary function, however, the LDBTOM must be invoked to translate the function to transactional version.

In the source code, a function pointer can be declared as transactional with a tm_function pragma, such as fp in Fig. 5(a). The tm_function information can be maintained by the compiler as part of the type of the function declaration. However, for an unmanaged language like C, the compiler seldom performs strict type checking, especially when the program modules are compiled separately. For example, if the code in Fig. 5 (a) and (b) are separately compiled and then linked together, the program will compile fine without any error or warning, although the call through fp() actually goes to a binary function (bar), even though it is declared as a transactional function pointer.

| | |
|---|---|
| ```#pragma tm_function``` <br> ```int foo (void);``` <br><br> ```#pragma tm_function``` <br> ```int (fp *) (void);``` <br><br> ```main (…) {``` <br>   ```func2 ();``` <br>   ```#pragma tm_atomic``` <br>   ```{``` <br>     ```…``` <br>     ```foo ();``` <br>     ```fp ();``` <br>   ```}``` <br> ```}``` | ```extern    int    (fp    *)``` <br> ```(void);``` <br> ```int bar(void) { … }``` <br><br> ```func2 () {``` <br>   ```…``` <br>   ```fp = bar;``` <br>   ```…``` <br> ```}``` |
| **(a) function call** | **(b) function declaration** |

**Fig. 5.** Transactional function pointers

| // declared to be atomic <br> #pragma tm_function <br> int foo(int) <br> ... <br> fp1 = foo; <br> fp2 = qsort; // lib <br><br> #pragma tm_atomic <br> { <br>   (*fp1)(3); <br>   (*fp2)(...) <br> } | #pragma tm_atomic <br> { <br> if(*fp1== "no-op marker") <br>   call **( fp1 – 4) <br> else <br>   Invoke_LDBTOM (fp1); <br> if(*fp2== "no-op marker") <br>   call **( fp2 – 4) <br> else <br>   Invoke_LDBTOM (fp2); <br> } | <foo-4>: <br> # address of <br> # transactional clone <br> foo_tm <br> <foo>: <br> # no-op marker <br>   cmpl %eax, 0xmagic <br> # actual function here <br> <foo_1>: <br>   push %ebp; <br>   ... |
|---|---|---|
| (a) source code | (b) runtime checking code | (c) assembly code supporting runtime check |

**Fig. 6.** Handling function pointers inside transactions

Our STM compiler inserts a special "no-op marker" in the beginning of the normal version of the function it generated. It also places the address of the transactional clone at a fixed offset, e.g. 4 bytes, away from the normal function entry. The "no-op marker" is a special no-op unique to the user application being compiled, such as an instruction that loads a special STM reserved memory to an unused register. Since a legacy library function does not have this special marker, this allows a quick runtime check to determine whether a function is an STM compiler generated function or a legacy library function. For a call through a function pointer invoked inside a transaction, if the pointer points to a STM compiler generated normal function, the pointer is adjusted and the transactional clone is called. If the pointer points to a legacy library function, LDBTOM is invoked to translate the code in legacy library.

Fig. 6 shows the indirect calls with function pointers. The transaction first calls the function *foo()* through the function pointer *fp1*. The code generated for the call to *foo()* inside the transaction first checks that the first instruction at the function entry is the no-op marker, and then calls the transactional clone of *foo()* pointed to by *(fp1 – 4)*. The transaction next calls the function *qsort* through the function pointer *fp2*. Since *qsort* is a legacy function whose first instruction is not the no-op marker, LDBTOM is invoked to translate the *qsort* function to a transactional clone. Outside the transaction, the call to *foo()* is simply generated as a call to *foo_1()*, a function that is equivalent to *foo()* except it skips the first no-op marker instruction.

## 5  Dynamic Optimizations

For each memory reference in a legacy function called in a transaction, LDBTOM inserts code to save the machine context (e.g. registers), pass the memory address to the STM runtime, call an STM runtime routine (*stmReadBarrier* for load and *stmWriteBarrier* for write) to check for conflict, and then restore the machine context. Fig. 7 shows the basic instrumentation for one memory reference. The basic instrumentation incurs noticeable overhead if not optimized.

| movl   %eax, DWORD PTR [%ebp+08h] | save | %eflags |
|---|---|---|
| | save | caller saved regs |
| | pass | PTR [%ebp+08h] to STM runtime |
| | call | stmReadBarrier |
| | addl | %esp, 0x4h |
| | restore | caller saved regs |
| | restore | %eflags |
| | movl | %eax, DWORD PTR [%ebp+08h] |
| **(a) before translation** | **(b) after translation** | |

**Fig. 7.** Basic Instrumentation for Legacy code

LDBTOM performs the following optimizations to reduce the barrier overhead.

- Analyze the binary code to identify thread-private memory references, such as push and pop operations, which do not need barriers.
- Use liveness information to eliminate unnecessary register save/restore. For example, if a register or the *%eflags* is dead at a reference, it does not need to be saved and restored for that reference. For another example, if a register is not used in a block/trace, it does not need to be saved or restored for each instrumentation site in the block/trace, and saving/restoring the register at the block/trace boundary is sufficient.
- Inline the STM runtime call to eliminate the call and return overhead. Since aggressive inlining increases code size dramatically, we inline only the hot paths in the STM runtime routines.

## 5.1 Filtering Local References

IA32 program frequently uses stack memory to store local data due to the limited number of general purpose registers. One benefit of stack data is that it is often private to a thread, and we may not need to track them for conflict detection. However, there are cases where the address of a stack data is passed to another thread and thus the stack data become shared among threads, although this situation happens very rarely. To filter barriers for stack references safely and aggressively, we need to solve the following two problems.

1. Decide whether any local data on stack is shared among different threads.
2. Decide which memory operation is a stack local data access.

Neither of the above problems can be easily solved by statically scanning the binary code. We solve the problems by taking the advantage of the dynamic binary translation opportunity. To check that no stack data are shared among threads, we leverage the paging memory protection mechanism provided in IA32 ISA. Each thread maintains its own paging table and protects the stack area as accessible only by the owner thread. In case that a thread accesses the stack of other threads, a memory fault triggers LDBTOM to flush all the translated code in the code cache and retranslates them without further filtering optimization of the barriers for stack references.

Stack references often are indexed by the stack pointer register *%esp* and the stack frame register *%ebp*. To check that *%esp* register points to the thread stack, LDBTOM examines all instructions that update *%esp* register with a large constant or a variable (With this update, the program may switch stack to memory space unprotected by our memory protection mechanism). If such an update is detected, LDBTOM flushes the code cache and retranslates the program without further filtering optimization.

The *%ebp* registers may be temporarily used as scratch register in leaf functions. We use the dynamic control flow graph information to track the *%ebp* status. An assignment that moves *%esp* to *%ebp* will cause *%ebp* pointing to the stack. If all the predecessors of a block being translated have *%ebp* pointing to the stack, the current block can performs the filtering optimization. If an instructions updates *%ebp* register with a large constant or a variable, the stack filtering optimization will not be performed. In case LDBTOM finds out that *%ebp* does not point to the stack at the end of a newly translated block, but a successor block has already been optimized based on the assumption that *%ebp* points to the stack, LDBTOM will create a new version of the successor block to run without filtering optimization. LDBTOM also dynamically checks *%ebp* after a function call returns. If *%ebp* no longer points to stack after the function call returns, code cache will be flushed and retranslated.

## 5.2 Dead Saving/Restore Elimination

In the base implementation LDBTOM saves/restores all caller-saved registers (*%eax*, *%ecx* and *%edx*) and *%eflags* register at each barrier. This is not always necessary as some registers may be dead at the barrier site. We use a simple analysis to detect the liveness of registers, and remove those unnecessary register saves/restores.

To eliminate dead saving/restores, each unfiltered load/store instruction maintains a local status word for %eax, %ecx, %edx, and %eflags. A global status word is initially set with "unknown" for all the registers. During a reverse traversal of the instructions, when a register is defined as a destination register, it is set as "dead" in the global status word. If a register is used as source register, it is set as "live". After an unfiltered load/store instruction is processed, the global status is assigned to the local status word of the load/store instruction. After all instructions in the block are scanned, if a register is never used in the block (with an "unknown" status), we save the register at the beginning and restore it at end of the block. For the other registers, we don't need to save/restore them at an unfiltered load/store if the register is dead in the local status word.

### 5.3  Barrier Inlining

Inlining the barrier routines can reduce function call and return overhead. But inlining the entire barrier increases code size significantly, so we only inline hot paths, and switch to slow path when conflict detected or READ/WRITE set buffer is full. The hot paths are identified the same as in the STM compiler [7].

## 6  Experimental Results

We use a suite of SPLASH-2 benchmark and three concurrent data structure benchmarks, *avltree*, *btree* and *hashtable*, to demonstrate LDBTOM support in the STM compiler. We run our experiment on a Unisys ES7000 Linux system, with 16 processors. Each processor is an Intel Xeon MP CPU 3.0G Hz, with 8KB L1 Data cache, 512K L2 Cache, 4M L3 Cache, and 32M on-board L4 Cache. The system has a 400MHz system bus, 3.2GB/s front side bus bandwidth, 8G main memory, and a dual channel DDR 400. Each data point in the result is obtained from the average of 10 runs.

In real-world applications like SPLASH-2, only a small portion of code (on average 4%) runs in transactions. Among them, three benchmarks, *barnes*, *radiosity* and *cholesky*, have function calls within transactions, but none of them are external library calls. To measure the overhead of LDBTOM, we compile the program in two different ways: 1) declare all the functions called insides transactions as *tm_function* so that the compiler will generate transactional code for these functions (denoted as *Compiler* in the figures), and 2) do not declare any function called inside transaction as *tm_function* so that the compiler will invoke LDBTOM to dynamically translate them into transactional code (denoted as *LDBTOM* in the figures). Fig. 8 (a) shows the performance results running in a single thread. On average, the overhead of LDBTOM is only about 1%.

Fig. 8 (b) shows the scalability for the benchmark *Cholesky*. Since the LDBTOM overhead is very small, the scalability is similar for both versions. The other benchmarks also show similar scalability between Compiler version and LDBTOM version.

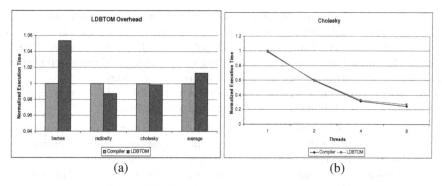

(a) (b)

**Fig. 8.** LDBTOM for SPLASH2

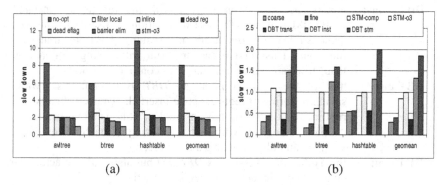

(a) (b)

**Fig. 9.** Optimization benefits and translation overhead

Since the SPLASH-2 has only a small portion of code running in transactions, we also use a set of concurrent data structures benchmarks, which spend almost all their execution time inside transactions to stress the LDBTOM overhead. For the concurrent data structures, each benchmark has hand-coded version optimized for STM execution, together with a fine-grain locking version and a coarse-grain transaction version. For the transaction version of the benchmarks, each coarse-grain locked section is coded as a transaction. Most of the transactions in the programs consist of a number of function calls. To stress LDBTOM overhead, we treat all the functions called inside the transactions as library functions translated by LDBTOM. We measure the performance of LDBTOM, using the hand-optimized version (**stm-o3**) as the baseline, with no optimization (**no-opt**) and with the following optimizations, running on a single processor.

| | |
|---|---|
| **filtering local:** | Filter local variables indexed by esp/ebp |
| **inlining:** | Inlining fast path + Filtering local |
| **dead reg:** | Eliminate dead register saving/restore+ Inlining |
| **dead eflag:** | Eliminate dead %eflags and reg saving /restore |
| **barrier elim:** | Redundant barrier eliminations+dead %eflags |

Fig. 9 (a) shows the optimization benefits. On the average, without optimization LDBTOM translated code is about 8x slower than hand-coded version. After optimizations, LDBTOM translated code is only about 80% slower than hand-coded version. The most beneficial optimizations are local filtering. All other optimizations contribute to the performance improvement, but not as significantly.

We also classify the overhead in LDBTOM translated code. We compare the performance for the following cases running with a single thread.

**fine:**       this is the original fine-grain locking version of the benchmarks.

**coarse:**     this is the original coarse-grain locking version of the benchmarks.

**STM-o3:**     this is the hand-coded STM version.

**STM-comp:**   this is the version generated by our STM compiler. This version is highly optimized and achieves performance similar to or better than the hand-optimized versions.

**DBT trans:**  this is the transaction version with the functions translated by LDBTOM, but no STM instrumentation is inserted. This version demonstrates the overhead of invoking DBT to translate the function. This version can only run with a single thread, as the load/stores are not instrumented for conflict detection

**DBT inst:**   this is the same version as *DBT trans* but also with the saving/restoring of registers code inserted. The actual calls to STM runtime routines are not inserted. This version measures the overhead associated with saving/restoring of machine context. This version can only run with a single thread.

**DBT stm:**    this is the same version as *DBT inst* but also with the actual barrier code for conflict detection being inserted.

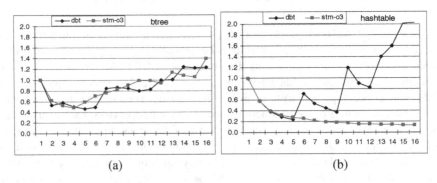

**Fig. 10.** Scalability of benchmark

Fig. 9 (b) shows that LDBTOM translation overhead is small (compare bars marked with **DBT trans** and **fine**). This overhead can be even smaller for larger applications than the data structures, since these benchmarks run only for a short time and the DBT startup time is more noticeable. The overhead to save/restore machine context is relatively high, and **DBT inst** has about 3X higher overhead than **DBT trans**. When the STM barriers are inserted, the DBT translated version (**DBT stm**) is about 80% slower than the hand-optimized STM code (**STM-o3**).

We also compare the scalability of the code translated by LDBTOM with the hand-coded version. Fig. 10 (a) shows that LDBTOM generated *btree* scales similar to the hand-optimized STM code. For *hashtable*, however, Fig. 10 (b) shows that the LDBTOM generated code scales only to five processors. With 6 or more processors, the LDBTOM generated code for *hashtable* actually runs slower with more cores. This is because that currently LDBTOM uses thread-private code cache to store translated code. Consequently, for a parallel program running with multiple, say 16, threads, the legacy code in the parallel regions will be translated 16 times, one for each thread. Since translation for different threads cannot fully be performed in parallel yet, the translation overhead will increase when running with more threads. There is also potential issue with the increased pressure on the instruction cache. We plan to address this issue in two directions in the future: 1) make the LDBTOM translation and optimization for different threads fully parallel, and 2) implement a shared code cache so the translated code can be reused by multiple threads. The zigzag in Fig. 10 (b) also suggests that there are load imbalance issues.

## 7  Summary and Future Work

In this paper, we develop novel techniques for integrating a dynamic binary translation module into a STM compilation environment to support transactional memory for legacy binary code, and evaluate a number of optimization techniques to reduce the overhead of the translated code. We measure the effectiveness of these techniques on a suite of SPLASH-2 benchmarks and a set of concurrent data structures benchmark. For the SPLASH-2 benchmarks, on the average, the LDBTOM generated code is only about 1% slower than STM compiler generated code. For the concurrent data structure benchmarks which have almost all the code inside transactions, LDBTOM generated code is about 80% slower than the hand-optimized STM code on a single thread, even though binary code is inherently harder to optimize than high-level source code and a straightforward translation would be more than 8 times slower than the hand-optimized code.

There are a number of open issues that we want to address in future work. We currently don't support I/O or system calls inside transactions. We also don't consider signal handling inside a transaction. Software implemented synchronizations using shared variables pose a challenge to the dynamic binary translator to convert them to transactional code. The scalability issue with thread-private cache is also an interesting future research topic.

## References

1. Adl-Tabatabai, A., Lewis, B.T., Menon, V.S., Murphy, B.M., Saha, B.: T. Compiler and runtime support for efficient software transactional memory. In: PLDI 2006 (2006)
2. Adl-Tabatabai, et al.: Hw Acceleration For a Software Transactional Memory System. In: Micro 2006 (2006)
3. Ananian, C.S., Asanovic, K., Kuszmaul, B.C., Leiserson, C.E., Lie, S.: Unbounded transactional memory. In: 11th International Symposium on High-Performance Computer Architecture, 2005. HPCA-11, February 12-16, 2005, pp. 316–327 (2005)

4. Baraz, L., Devor, T., Etzion, O., Goldenberg, S., Skaletsky, A., Wang, Y., Zemach, Y.: IA-32 Execution Layer: a two-phase dynamic translator designed to support IA-32 applications on Itanium®-based systems. In: Micro-36 2003 (2003)
5. Blundell, C., Lewis, E.C., Martin, M.M.K.: Deconstructing Transactional Semantics: The Subtleties of Atomicity. In: Annual Workshop on Duplicating, Deconstructing, and Debunking (WDDD) (June 2005)
6. Blundell, C., Lewis, E.C., Martin, M.M.K.: Unrestricted Transactional Memory: Supporting I/O and System Calls within Transactions. Technical Report CIS-06-09, Department of Computer and Information Science, University of Pennsylvania, Philadelphia, PA (April 2006)
7. Wang, C., Chen, W., Wu, Y., Saha, B., Adl-babatabai, A.: Code Generation and Optimization for Transactional Memory Constructs in an Unmanaged Language. In: CGO 2007 (2007)
8. Wang, C., Hu, S., Kim, H.-s., Nair, S., Breternitz Jr., M., Ying, Z., Wu, Y.: StarDBT: An Efficient Multi-platform Dynamic Binary Translation System. In: Choi, L., Paek, Y., Cho, S. (eds.) ACSAC 2007. LNCS, vol. 4697, pp. 4–15. Springer, Heidelberg (2007)
9. Borin, E., Wang, C., Wu, Y., Araujo, G.: Software-Based Transparent and Comprehensive Control-Flow Error Detection. In: CGO 2006 (2006)
10. Qin, F., Wang, C., Li, Z., Kim, H.-s., Zhou, Y., Wu, Y.: LIFT: A Low-Overhead Practical Information Flow Tracking System for Detecting Security Attacks. In: Micro-39 2006 (2006)
11. Harris, T., Plesko, M., Shinnar, A., Tarditi, D.: Optimizing Memory Transactions. In: PLDI 2006 (2006)
12. Herlihy, M., Luchango, V., Moir, M., Scherer, W.N.: Software Transactional Memory for Dynamic Sized Data Structures. In: PODC 2003 (2003)
13. Hosking, A., Moss, J.E.B.: Nested transactional memory: Model and preliminary Sketches SCOOL (2005)
14. Olszewski, M., Cutler, J., Steffan, J.G.: JudoSTM: A Dynamic Binary-Rewriting Approach to Software Transactional Memory. In: PACT 2007 (2007)
15. Moir, M.: Hybrid Transactional Memory. Sun Microsystems Technical Report
16. Moore, K.E., Bobba, J., Moravan, M.J., Hill, M.D., Wood, D.A.: LogTM: Log-based Transactional Memory. In: HPCA 2006 (2006)
17. Wu, Q., Reddi, V.J., Wu, Y., Lee, J., Connors, D., Brooks, D., Martonosi, M., Clark, D.W.: Dynamic Compilation Framework for Controlling Microprocessor Energy and Performance. In: Micro-38 2005(2005)
18. Rajwar, R., Herlihy, M., Lai, K.: Virtualizing Transactional Memory. In: Proc. of the 32nd Annual Intl. Symp. On Computer Architecture (June 2005)
19. Shavit, N., Tuitou, D.: Software Transactional Memory. In: PODC 1995(1995)
20. Correct and Consistent Transactional Memory System (submitted for publication)

# Author Index

# Lecture Notes in Computer Science

Sublibrary 1: Theoretical Computer Science and General Issues

For information about Vols. 1– 4639
please contact your bookseller or Springer